GEORGE ~~ANNAS~~ is Associate Professor of Law and Medicine, Boston University School of Medicine, and Chief of the Health Law Section, Boston University School of Public Health. Professor Annas holds degrees in law, public health and economics from Harvard University, and is the author of ACLU handbook *The Rights of Hospital Patients.*

LEONARD H. GLANTZ is Assistant Professor of Health Law at Boston University Medical School, and the Associate Director of Boston University's School of Public Health. A psychologist and lawyer, he is co-author of *Informed Consent to Human Experimentation: The Subject's Dilemma.*

BARBARA F. KATZ is Associate Counsel to the University of Massachusetts Medical Center. An author and lecturer, she has served on national task forces dealing with critical health issues.

Also in this Series

THE RIGHTS OF ALIENS	44925	$1.95
THE RIGHTS OF CANDIDATES AND VOTERS	49940	$2.75
THE RIGHTS OF EX-OFFENDERS	44701	$1.95
THE RIGHTS OF GOVERNMENT EMPLOYEES	38505	$1.75
THE RIGHTS OF HOSPITAL PATIENTS	53694	$2.50
THE RIGHTS OF LAWYERS & CLIENTS	42382	$1.95
THE RIGHTS OF MENTAL PATIENTS	77024	$2.50
THE RIGHTS OF MENTALLY RETARDED PERSONS	54064	$2.50
THE RIGHTS OF MILITARY PERSONNEL	33365	$1.50
THE RIGHTS OF OLDER PERSONS	44362	$2.50
THE RIGHTS OF PARENTS	76729	$2.50
THE RIGHTS OF THE POOR	28001	$1.25
THE RIGHTS OF PHYSICALLY HANDICAPPED PEOPLE	47274	$2.25
THE RIGHTS OF RACIAL MINORITIES	75077	$1.95
THE RIGHTS OF REPORTERS	38836	$1.75
THE RIGHTS OF SUSPECTS	28043	$1.25
THE RIGHTS OF TEACHERS	25049	$1.50
THE RIGHTS OF UNION MEMBERS	46193	$2.25
THE RIGHTS OF YOUNG PEOPLE	77032	$2.50
YOUR RIGHTS TO PRIVACY	75895	$2.50

Where better paperbacks are sold, or directly from the publisher. Include 50¢ per copy for mailing; allow 6-8 weeks for delivery.
Avon Books, Mail Order Dept., 224 W. 57th St.
New York, N.Y. 10019

AN AMERICAN
CIVIL LIBERTIES
UNION HANDBOOK

THE RIGHTS OF DOCTORS, NURSES AND ALLIED HEALTH PROFESSIONALS:
A Health Law Primer

**George J. Annas,
Leonard H. Glantz,
and Barbara F. Katz**

General Editor of this series:
Norman Dorsen, *President, ACLU*

 A DISCUS BOOK/PUBLISHED BY AVON BOOKS

THE RIGHTS OF DOCTORS, NURSES, AND ALLIED HEALTH PROFESSIONALS: A Health Law Primer is an original publication of Avon Books. This work has never before appeared in book form.

AVON BOOKS
A division of
The Hearst Corporation
959 Eighth Avenue
New York, New York 10019

Copyright © 1981 by The American Civil Liberties Union (ACLU) Incorporated
Published by arrangement with
The American Civil Liberties Union Incorporated
Library of Congress Catalog Card Number: 80-69898
ISBN: 0-380-77859-9

All rights reserved, which includes the right to reproduce this book or portions thereof in any form whatsoever except as provided by the U.S. Copyright Law. For information address
The American Civil Liberties Union, Inc.,
132 West 43rd Street, New York, New York 10016

First Discus Printing, June, 1981

DISCUS TRADEMARK REG. U.S. PAT. OFF. AND IN OTHER COUNTRIES, MARCA REGISTRADA, HECHO EN U.S.A.

Printed in the U.S.A.

10 9 8 7 6 5 4 3 2 1

Acknowledgments

Many individuals contributed to the ideas, content, and format of this book. Especially important were the law, medical, nursing, health management, and undergraduate students we have taught over the past decade. Their enthusiasm and concern for the issues discussed in this book provided us with the inspiration we needed to keep this project alive. All of our colleagues in the health law field have been helpful. Special thanks, however, are due to Professor John Robertson of the University of Texas School of Law at Austin whose insightful comments on the manuscript did much to shape the final product. Professor Joseph Healey of the University of Connecticut School of Medicine and Professor Frances Miller of Boston University Law School each provided valuable and appreciated commentary. Many students, some of whom are now practicing health law, contributed their time and energy. These include Steve Postema, Jane Greenlaw, Judy Miller, Judy Shriberg, Betty Krikorian, Thomas Lewis, Suzanne Weakley, Janet Jackim, Richard Wayne, Patricia Callahan, Sherry Liebowitz, and Susan Silbersweig. Mary Annas again produced a remarkably complete and accessible index. Special thanks are due to Elizabeth Ollen who reviewed and edited the entire manuscript, and to Margaret Scott for her careful typing.

DEDICATION

To Katie and David
and to the patients and health care providers
of their generation

Table of Contents

Preface

This guide sets forth your rights under present law and offers suggestions on how you can protect your rights. It is one of a continuing series of handbooks published in cooperation with the American Civil Liberties Union.

The hope surrounding these publications is that Americans informed of their rights will be encouraged to exercise them. Through their exercise, rights are given life. If they are rarely used, they may be forgotten and violations may become routine.

This guide offers no assurances that your rights will be respected. The laws may change and, in some of the subjects covered in these pages, they change quite rapidly. An effort has been made to note those parts of the law where movement is taking place, but it is not always possible to predict accurately when the law *will* change.

Even if the laws remain the same, interpretations of them by courts and administrative officials often vary. In a federal system such as ours, there is a built-in problem of the differences between state and federal law, not to speak of the confusion of the differences from state to state. In addition, there are wide variations in the ways in which particular courts and administrative officials will interpret the same law at any given moment.

If you encounter what you consider to be a specific abuse of your rights you should seek legal assistance. There are a number of agencies that may help you, among them ACLU affiliate offices, but bear in mind that the ACLU is a limited-purpose organization. In many communities, there are federally funded legal service offices which provide assistance to poor persons who cannot afford the costs of legal representation. In general, the rights that the ACLU defends are freedom of inquiry and expression; due process of law; equal protection of the laws; and privacy. The authors in this series have discussed other rights in these books (even though they sometimes fall outside the ACLU's usual concern) in order to provide as much guidance as possible.

Thee books have been planned as guides for the people directly affected: therefore the question and answer format. (In some areas there are more detailed works available for "experts.") These guides seeks to raise the largest issues and inform the non-specialist of the basic law on the subject. The authors of the books are themselves specialists who understand the need for information at "street level."

No attorney can be an expert in every part of the law. If you encounter a specific legal problem in an area discussed in one of these handbooks, show the book to your attorney. Of course, he or she will not be able to rely *exclusively* on the handbook to provide you with adequate representation. But if your attorney hasn't had a great deal of experience in the specific area, the handbook can provide helpful suggestions on how to proceed.

Norman Dorsen, President
American Civil Liberties Union

The principal purpose of this handbook, and others in this series, is to inform individuals of their legal rights. The authors from time to time suggest what the law should be, but the author's personal views are not necessarily those of the ACLU. For the ACLU's position on the issues discussed in this handbook, the reader should write to Librarian, ACLU, 132 West 43rd Street, New York, N.Y. 10036.

Introduction

Shortly after one of the authors, George J. Annas, wrote *The Rights of Hospital Patients* in 1975,[1] a physician attending a seminar on medical ethics at the Hastings Center in New York asked, "Why don't you write a book about the rights of doctors?" The response was that doctors, unlike patients, are usually able to look out for their own rights, and to hire professional representation when they cannot. That excuse sufficed for more than a year. However, when we were approached in 1976 by the editors of this series to do a "doctors' book," we decided that the task had much to commend it.

First, we decided to include all health care providers, especially nurses and allied health professionals, because they are increasingly responsible for most direct patient care. Second, we saw a danger that someone might write a handbook on how doctors could use the law to dominate their patients, a primer on how the law can help bully the reluctant patient into submission. We do not believe such a volume would serve any useful purpose. While this book will undoubtedly aid health care providers to avoid being sued for medical malpractice, this is neither its purpose nor its main consideration. Third, we believe that ignorance of the law on the part of providers is extremely costly to patients and providers alike, and that a volume that accurately presents basic legal knowledge for health care providers can be of tremendous help to their patients as well.

We have written this book on the premise that, almost all the time, the interests of the health care provider and the patient are the same. For example, they probably agree in wanting the patient to have a specific operation or treatment, in wanting to have the cost covered by insurance, in wanting to terminate extraordinary treatment of a hopeless patient, in wanting unrestricted visiting, in wanting to have the father-to-be in the delivery room, etc. It is therefore in the interest of both patients and their providers to know how things they both want can be accomplished, and when and why they cannot.

These issues can no longer be resolved entirely within the provider-patient relationship. Providers not only have formal relationships with their patients, but also have relationships with other providers, health care institutions, and numerous government agencies. A provider's relationship with these institutions and individuals is often a very complex one, and providers often find themselves confused and therefore submissive in cases where they do not understand their rights. As health care has become the major service industry in the United States, and as the government—federal, state, and local—has become the major source of funding for the industry, the decisions of public regulatory agencies are increasingly significant. Whether an operation is covered by insurance may depend on an interpretation of the policy by a bureaucrat, or on the review of its "necessity" by another health care professional or committee; whether medical research may be done may depend on a determination of the hospital's institutional review board and the Food and Drug Administration; whether a medical student or foreign medical graduate may practice in a certain setting may depend on state statutes and licensing regulations; whether husbands are permitted in the delivery room may depend on hospital policy; and whether life-sustaining treatment of a terminally ill patient may be terminated may depend both on state law and hospital policy.

In all of these cases, both the health care provider *and* the patient will be better off if the law regarding provider rights is understood, and the means of change or challenge is well articulated. We would go even further. An understanding of the law can be as important to the proper care of patients as an understanding of emergency medical procedures or proper drug dosages. This statement may appear outrageous or ironic to the typical provider, but a few examples will help explain what we mean.

The cost of ignorance or fear of the law can be high,

both in money and in human suffering. Monetarily, the cost of malpractice insurance premiums, which is passed on to the general public, has risen from some $250 million in 1970 to over $2 billion in 1980. This has resulted not only in higher costs, but in some doctors deciding to "go bare" and practice medicine without insurance—a risk both to their own and to their injured patient's financial future. Much more important than premiums in measuring the cost of misunderstanding of the law are the costs of defensive medicine—both positive (performing an unnecessary procedure) and negative (failing to perform a necessary procedure). Such unnecessary testing, most widely exemplified by unnecessary X-rays in the emergency room, annually costs an estimated $2 to $10 billion. While this range is so wide as to open the statistics to considerable question, there is no doubt that the cost of misunderstanding is high.[2]

Negative defensive medicine, such as doctors refusing to operate on "high risk" patients, or refusing to practice in certain high risk specialties, will decrease when providers learn their rights. One pervasive example is the physician who fails to stop to help the victims of an accident. This is said to be the result of doctors' fear of lawsuits; they believe that, if they try to help, they are opening themselves to malpractice suits. Since there is not one reported case in which a health care professional in this country has had to pay any money damages to anyone suing him for stopping and rendering aid and allegedly aggravating the patient's condition, it is probably fair to say that a misunderstanding of the law has led to a number of unnecessary deaths and much unnecessary suffering.

Ignorance of the providers' rights to treat minors in emergencies led to a seventeen-year-old rape victim being left for four hours in the middle of the night without any professional help in a major hospital. And misunderstanding of the law in 1978 led to the following instances in Massachusetts: a terminally ill patient was defibrillated seventy times within a twenty-four hour period; a baby whose brain had been completely destroyed was kept alive by artificial ventilation, surgery, and antibiotics even though all agreed the case was "hopeless" and the parents had asked that heroic measures be discontinued; a terminally ill heart attack victim with almost no brain activity was continually resuscitated for more than thirty days after the doctors and nurses agreed the case was hopeless and the relatives asked that extraordinary measures be discontinued; and incurable babies with Tay-Sachs or Wernig-Hoffman's disease were continually resuscitated against the wishes of their parents. In all of these cases the health care providers were "forced" to inflict such inhumane torture on their patients because they believed that directions to do so from hospital administrators had the force of law and they were powerless to refuse.[3]

This list could be greatly expanded, but we trust the point has been made: ignorance of the law and of their own rights can cause providers to inflict great suffering on patients both by omission and commission.

Rights can be thought of as moral claims, political statements, metaphysical musings, and legal declarations. This is not a treatise on "rights" as a concept. Where the term is used in this book it denotes a claim against another (person, institution, governmental unit, etc.) that the law will recognize and support. In this regard it will generally be seen as wrong to violate a right, and the legal system will recognize that the person whose rights have been violated should be given an avenue of redress for the consequences of the violation.[4]

This book is written for all health care providers. Most of the material, however, focuses on physicians. This is simply because most of the law to date—the statutes, regulations, and judicial decisions—concerns the activities of physicians, usually in the hospital context. There is some indication that this is changing. More laws and regulations are being written about nurses in general and the nurse-practitioner specifically. It is also likely that regulation of other allied health care professionals will follow a similar course as their responsibilities grow.

The importance of nonphysicians in health care can be partially understood in terms of numbers. In 1976 (the last year for which complete statistics are available), there were 112,000 dentists in the United States and 200,000 dental assistants, hygienists, and laboratory technicians; there were 375,000 physicians, almost a million registered nurses, another million nursing aides and orderlies, and 460,000 licensed practical nurses. There were 120,000 pharmacists, 18,000 chiropractors, 20,000 optometrists,

38,000 speech pathologists and audiologists. There were a quarter of a million emergency medical technicians and about the same number of medical laboratory workers. There were 12,000 electrocardiographic technicians, 12,000 medical record administrators, 30,000 operating room technicians, 36,000 respiratory therapists and technicians, 25,000 physical therapists, and 45,000 dieticians, to name only groups with very large memberships. All of these professionals should find this book of value to them in their dealings with patients, other providers, and state and private regulators.

All of the material on physicians is relevant to *every* health care provider for at least two additional reasons. First, a provider must know what the rights of physicians are before he or she can decide if it is appropriate to challenge the physician's decision about a patient whom they are both caring for. Second, the principles enunciated in judicial decisions regarding physicians are likely to be used also in deciding similar cases brought against other health professionals—dentists, optometrists, nurses, physician assistants, nutritionists, social workers, occupational therapists, or any others. Pronouns designating sex of health care providers are used randomly.

The question-and-answer format of this ACLU handbook series has presented the authors with the opportunity to voice the concerns of those working in the field. During most of the past decade we have participated in and given seminars, courses, lectures, and conferences on health law for physicians, nurses, respiratory therapists, birth attendants, medical and laboratory technicians, medical record administrators, and others across the United States and Canada. In preparing the lists of questions to be answered in each chapter we have tried to include those most frequently asked by health professionals in a variety of geographic locations and health care settings. We know that most of them cannot be answered in any but a general way, but it is our goal to present an outline of the major issues involved, and to suggest, in the footnotes, places you can go for further reading. There are also times, of course, when it will be prudent to consult a lawyer—either your own or one representing the health care agency for which you work—since most health law varies somewhat from state to state.

None of this is in any way meant to conceal our biases. We believe in patients' rights and believe that the health care system's only justification for public support is its service to society. These beliefs have sometimes interfered with our work on this book, and may account for the fact that it took three years longer to complete than we planned. Although the ability to use it or abuse it varies depending on one's status and income, the law is the same for everyone. We have attempted to present the law of health care clearly and concisely. Where there are controversies we have identified them. And where our own views might color our analysis, we have stated those views.

It is our hope that this volume will help doctors, nurses, and allied health professionals to work *with* patients to obtain goals they and their patients believe are important. While this won't change the world, it should make the lives of both patients and their providers somewhat easier.

NOTES

1. G. ANNAS, THE RIGHTS OF HOSPITAL PATIENTS (New York: Avon Books, 1975).
2. *See generally* Annas, Katz, & Trakimas, *Medical Malpractice Litigation under National Health Insurance: Essential or Expendable?* 1975 DUKE L.J. 1335 (Jan. 1976), and sources cited therein.
3. Annas, *Reconciling Quinlan and Saikewicz: Decision Making for the Terminally Ill Incompetent,* 4 AM. J. LAW & MED. 367, 387 (1979).
4. *See, e.g.,* C. FRIED, RIGHT AND WRONG (Cambridge: Harvard U. Press, 1978); J. RAWLS, A THEORY OF JUSTICE (Cambridge: Harvard U. Press, 1971); and R. DWORKIN, TAKING RIGHTS SERIOUSLY (Cambridge: Harvard U. Press, 1977).

PART ONE

Rights to Practice
Health Care

I

Licensure and Staff Privileges

Physicians, nurses, and a number of allied health professionals must be licensed to practice their profession. Governmental licensing should protect the public and foster professionalism. However, the fact that licensing is a matter of state law means that there is no uniform system. In the words of Robert Derbyshire, a physician who is the country's leading expert on licensure: "There are so many variable laws and regulations concerning both initial licensure and discipline of physicians that for all practical purposes the United States is composed of a group of tightly organized kingdoms." [1] A similar statement can be made regarding the granting of hospital privileges to doctors, and the licensing and disciplining of nurses and other allied health professionals. Nevertheless, there are a number of generally applicable legal considerations. It is the purpose of this chapter to identify and examine these and to apply them to the governmental and hospital setting.

Is there a right to be licensed as a health professional?

The answer to this question, like the answer to so many legal questions, depends upon the answer to another: "Why do you want to know?" If you mean "Can anyone become a physician, or nurse?" the answer is clearly no. Even legislation designed to improve opportunities for disabled applicants does not require that professional schools admit candidates for the health professions who cannot meet certain physical requirements. For example, a nursing school need not accept an applicant who is partially deaf. [2] On the other hand, a person who has met the educational requirements for a state license cannot be discriminated against

3

on the basis of race, color, sex, or creed by the licensing authority.

There is no general "right" to be licensed. It is the limitations on governmental and private activity that relate to an individual's license, rather than the labels of "right" and "privilege," that are important. Nevertheless, the idea persists that health care practice is a "right." In response, one leading medical commentator has argued that "the single most salutary change that could occur in state licensing laws would be the clear embodiment in the laws of the concept of the medical license as a privilege, under the ultimate control of the people, who grant the privilege." [3]

The right/privilege distinction may have a psychological importance that interferes at times with the accountability of health professionals to the public. However, changing the terms would in no way alter existing legal rights that licensees have, regardless of whether their freedom to practice is termed a privilege or a right. It has been suggested, for example, that words like *privilege, property,* and *liberty* be "put to one side" and that the real question is how actions taken by the government against a licensee can be reconciled with the dictates of justice. [4] It strikes us that this is the proper question. Regardless of the label, courts will strive to treat professionals fairly, and will go to great lengths to provide them due process of law, because their licenses are viewed, at the very least, as something of "tremendous value to the individual."

A similar situation exists in the area of hospital privileges, at least in public hospitals. As one court has put it, while a physician has no "right" to use any particular hospital for her patients, this is a "valuable privilege" that is entitled to be protected by due process of law. [5]

What is the history of health care licensing?

The U.S. Constitution mentions neither medicine nor health. The power to promote and protect the public's health accordingly rests with the governments of the individual states. The federal government is involved in health care regulation only indirectly: primarily through the powers to raise and spend money and to regulate interstate commerce. Examples of the former type of regulation are the Medicare and Medicaid insurance programs, and Veterans Administration Medical Centers. Interstate commerce regulations include such things as drug regulations under the U.S. Food and Drug Administration.

The states have much broader inherent authority in the area of health, safety, and welfare. They had this authority before the founding of the United States and maintained it thereafter. Little effort, however, was taken to exercise it in the area of health care with any effectiveness until this century. In 1757, for example, historian William Smith wrote: "Few physicians among us are eminent for their skill. Quacks abound like locusts in Egypt . . . the profession is under no kind of regulation. Any man at his pleasure sets up as physician, apothecary and surgeon." [6]

While sporadic attempts were made at regulation by states, medical schools, and medical societies during the next century and a half, little progress was evident as late as 1900. The late nineteenth century was the heyday of quacks, charlatans, and snake-oil salesmen, but the average physician of that time probably did little better with most of his patients. [7]

After 1850, the medical profession began concerted attempts to improve both its public image and economic status. One way to accomplish these goals was to erect legal barriers to entry into the profession. Properly constructed, these laws could simultaneously enhance the public's view of the profession (because practitioners had to meet certain qualifications) and create an economic monopoly (because nonphysicians would be legally prohibited from "practicing medicine"). The rationale proposed to the state legislatures was that such licensing would protect the public from charlatans and quacks who preyed on the sick.

Physician education was reformed, licensing was made mandatory in all states, and by the 1930s the profession had attained very high status. Richard Shryock describes the dramatic change in his survey of licensure: "In view of their low status as late as the 1880s, this position of doctors a half century later revealed them in a Cinderella role unique in the history of American professions." [8]

Other health care professions followed suit for the same reasons. The first nurse licensing statute was enacted in 1903, and two decades later all states were licensing nurses. As with physicians, licensing of nurses was initially permissive (a grant of a professional title and prestige), and only later became mandatory (a requirement of practice that created a legal monopoly).[9]

What are the purposes of licensing?

There are two primary rationales for licensing: to protect the public, and to protect the licensed profession. As to the first interest, the idea is that the public must seek certain services in time of need, and that many members of the public will, of necessity, have to rely on those with qualifications which they cannot personally verify. Thus, by requiring certain minimum qualifications for holding oneself out as a physician or nurse, for example, the legislature insures that some degree of quality will be assured and that the public's interest will be served.[10]

Licensing is at least as favorable to the profession. This is because the license creates an economic monopoly that limits competition and increases prices, and also gives the holders of the license prestige that they might not otherwise enjoy. The primary arguments against governmental regulation of industry are analogous: critics assert that the regulated industry is almost always able to "capture" the regulator and use it to its own economic advantage.

Is there any uniformity in state licensing requirements?

There is some, and the trend is toward uniform standardized testing. In medicine, for example, a uniform examination, the Federation Licensing Examination (FLEX) was introduced in 1968. By 1979, *every* state had adopted this examination as its own state examination. Applicants who have not passed the uniform National Board examination sequence (used by all U.S. medical schools) are required to take and pass the FLEX. But the problem of foreign medical graduates entering the United States to practice persists, and there is some concern over the growth and quality of off-shore medical schools. One response has been a proposal for a more vigorous FLEX examination, one that would be given in two parts. FLEX I would be administered after graduation, but before internship or residency, and would be designed to assess the knowledge, problem-solving ability, and clinical judgment of the applicant. FLEX II would be a clinically oriented examination designed to test the applicant's ability to practice medicine independently, and would be the prerequisite for full licensure.[11]

Even though testing is becoming standardized, licensing in one state does not automatically qualify one to practice in another. Reciprocity may be granted, but the state has the option of requiring the applicant to retake its qualifying examination, or reviewing the applicant's professional record, character, and past conduct.

When may a licensing board discipline a licensee?

A licensing board generally needs express statutory authority to discipline a licensee for a particular reason. Statutory grounds for discipline in almost all states include insanity, mental or physical incapacity, and conviction of certain crimes. Because of the need for specificity, the trend has been for states to expand the statutory definitions of conduct warranting disciplinary action,[12] and the majority of states have included medical malpractice or professional incompetence as a cause for disciplinary action.[13] Other examples include fee-splitting,[14] certain advertising,[15] overcharging or overtreating of patients, overutilization of facilities,[16] unprofessional prescribing of drugs,[17] conviction of a state or federal drug offense,[18] and hospital peer-review suspension of a physician's privileges.[19] In states whose statutes do not specify particular types of unprofessional conduct or incompetence, the board will be given broad discretionary power in interpreting and applying its own standards.

What procedures must a board follow in a disciplinary case?

A licensing board is a public administrative agency, and as such its procedures must satisfy the constitutional requirements of due process. The licensing board must also adhere strictly to its own rules and procedures. It may not alter these for some applicants and not for others.

The basic procedures for disciplinary action are nearly identical in all states.[20] Often these procedures are set forth in the state's administrative procedure act and incorporated into the professional practice act. Disciplinary procedures provide that a licensee who is charged with unprofessional behavior be given sufficient notice of the charges and an opportunity for a hearing before any final disciplinary action is taken. The licensee has the right to be represented by counsel, and to present and cross-examine witnesses. Since the licensee has the right to judicial appeal of a final decision, the licensing board is required to keep an accurate and adequate record of the proceedings to serve as the basis for appeal.

A few state statutes provide for investigations to be made by others than those involved in final decision-making,[21] but in most states, boards investigate, prosecute, judge, and sentence. While the constitutionality of this practice has been challenged and upheld,[22] better practice is to separate investigation and prosecution from judging and sentencing whenever possible, since this is likely to be fairer to the licensee.

Although all states provide for notice and hearing, some states have empowered the medical licensing board to temporarily suspend a license to practice without a hearing when it believes that the licensee poses an immediate danger to the public. The board is generally required to hold a hearing within a short time after such a suspension, so that the licensee may contest it. This power is almost never used.

Can licensing boards discipline licensees for any criminal act or any conduct involving "moral turpitude"?

Courts have traditionally given licensing boards broad authority to determine what actions indicate that a physician may be a danger to the public. In an early case, the Supreme Court ruled that a board could revoke a physician's license because he was convicted of a felony, even though the statute permitting revocation on this ground was passed after the doctor's conviction. The Court declined to find this an *ex post facto* law because "The state is not seeking to further punish a criminal, but only to protect its citizens from physicians of bad character." [23]

Chief Justice Rugg of the Massachusetts Supreme Judicial Court set forth the rationale for a "character" requirement in 1921:

Soundness of moral fibre to insure the proper use of medical learning is as essential to the public health as medical learning itself. Mere intellectual power and scientific achievement without uprightness of character may be more harmful than ignorance. Highly trained intelligence combined with disregard of the fundamental virtues is a menace.[24]

The courts, nonetheless, require some connection between the immoral or illegal activity and the practice of medicine itself. In a California case, for example, a physician's license was suspended and he was placed on probation for five years on condition he be treated and supervised by a psychiatrist until "cured." The physician had been found by the board to have engaged in an act of moral turpitude by making sexual advances to an undercover policeman in a public men's room.

The physician argued that even if it was an act of moral turpitude, it was done outside of his professional activities and not related to them. The court, however, concluded that the connection was close enough:

As an internist he is in intimate physical contact with his patients, and while he may be dedicated to treating them in an exemplary manner, the opportunity to falter and his frailty in exercising restraint exist. Unfortunately, appellant's problem apparently stays with him most, if not all of the time; and in light of his present conduct, there is little assurance that it will be relegated to isolated places and occasions away from his patients.[25]

The majority emphasized that the licensing board's primary purpose "is not to punish the doctor, but rather to protect the public." The 2–1 decision drew a strong dissent in which it was argued that there was no evidence that this physician's "private" conduct ever interfered with his practice of medicine, and that therefore discipline in the case was not warranted.

A 1979 case from Massachusetts indicates that courts are prepared to go even further.[26] Dr. David A. Levy was a highly successful practitioner who owned and operated eleven nursing homes. He pleaded guilty to thirty-one counts of grand larceny from the Massachusetts Department of Public Health and sixteen indictments charging the submission of false data to the Massachusetts Rate Setting Commission. He was given a two-year suspended sentence, fined $32,500, and ordered to pay restitution of $313,854 and to divest himself of all his nursing homes. The Board of Medicine revoked his license on the basis that "crimes to which the defendant pleaded guilty are serious offenses against statutes *closely related to the practice of medicine*" (emphasis supplied).

The physician appealed. He argued in court that the crimes of which he had been convicted were not closely related to the practice of medicine, but involved his actions as a nursing home administrator. The court had no sympathy for this argument.

Noting that in excess of 90 percent of the population is now covered by some form of private or governmental health insurance, the court found "the modern practice of medicine involves *financial management,* as well as the care and treatment of patients" (emphasis supplied). Therefore, "an intentional misdeed relating to third-party payors reflects adversely on a physician's fitness to practice medicine. It is irrelevant that it is a third party, and not a patient, who is being defrauded."

These opinions illustrate the problem that boards and courts have in attempting to separate the private lives of licensees from their professional activities. It is not the law that you are a health care professional twenty-four hours a day; but it is the law that you can lose your license for any illegal or immoral activity that indicates to the licensing board (and a reviewing court) that you pose a danger to patients, or that your conduct is related to the practice of your profession.

What can legally be done about the impaired or disabled health practitioner?

The problem of the alcoholic, drug-dependent, or physically or mentally ill practitioner is one that affects all professions. It is estimated, for example, that 5 to 10 percent of physicians are disabled. Three general views on the problem seem to predominate:

1. Disabled physicians are a danger to the public, and the public has a right to see that such physicians are disciplined to stop them and discourage others from practicing.
2. Disabled physicians are sick, and the medical profes-

sion should see that they are treated in a nonpunitive and noncoercive setting.

3. Disabled physicians are both sick and a danger to patients, and their practice should be suspended and they should be treated and permitted to return to practice only in a carefully controlled setting until recovery is complete.[27]

The first position is probably the one held by most non-physicians. It is based on the premise that the disabled physician can do serious damage to patients and that the public has a right to be protected against such harm. Recent stories—Dr. John Nork's string of unnecessary and disabling back operations in California, performed while he was under the influence of drugs; the drug-addicted Marcus brothers, twin obstetricians from New York; and Dr. William E. Miofsky, the anesthesiologist accused of unnatural sexual acts on anesthesized patients [28]—have dramatized to the public how little the medical profession has done to police itself and protect patients from the impaired physician.

Instances like this have led to a number of legislative initiatives. In California, for example, hospitals are required to report all denials, removals, or restrictions of hospital privileges to the state's Medical Quality Assurance Board. In New York, legislation (termed the "tattletale act" by some physicians) requires physicians to report incompetent and disabled physicians to the licensing agency. This makes the long-standing ethical obligation of the AMA's Principles of Medical Ethics a legal one as well: physicians should "strive to expose those physicians deficient in character or competence, or who engage in fraud or deception."

The first position, that impaired physicians should be disciplined, is articulated in a report by three physicians with the State Medical Board of Virginia:

It is vital that the deviant, incompetent, "sick" doctor be reported and disciplined. If such a physician is allowed to continue to practice, he himself, his patients, and the entire medical profession are all losers. The doctor's torment is prolonged, his patients' lives are endangered, and the profession's standards are lowered. The need for medical discipline is great. The public demands it, the government demands it, and the medical profession *must* demand it.[29]

It is probably fair to say that the second position, that the disabled physician is sick and should be treated non-punitively, is one held by the majority of practicing physicians.[30] The argument is that "peer review" mechanisms in hospitals are the most appropriate ways to identify such physicians. Disabled physicians should be "taken aside" by their fellow physicians and convinced in a friendly, non-threatening manner to accept treatment.

The third position argues that these two functions are not necessarily incompatible, and that ways should be developed to use discipline to encourage treatment and rehabilitation. The California statute, for example, requires the board to "take such action as possible to aid in the rehabilitation of physicians." And the position of the AMA, which encourages both state medical society programs and reporting to the licensing authority, falls into this category. Their Model Bill on Disabled Physicians, often called the sick doctor bill, has been enacted in one form or another in more than thirty states. This bill provides that the licensing board can require a complete physical and mental examination of any physician believed unable to "practice medicine with reasonable skill and safety to patients due to physical or mental illness, including deterioration through the aging process or loss of motor skill, or abuse of drugs, including alcohol." After the examination, usually conducted by a special committee of the state medical society, a report is sent to the licensing board. The physician may voluntarily request a restriction on her license, the board may take no action, or the board may begin formal proceedings against her license. The purpose of the law is to make it somewhat easier and swifter to take action against a disabled physician than it would be to take action for other reasons. The thrust is to encourage physicians to seek help voluntarily and to have restrictions placed on their licenses consistent with the degree of disability.

Nevertheless, while the boards may want to both discipline and rehabilitate, they have neither resources nor expertise in treating alcoholism or drug dependency. We suggest that the following steps would be of benefit to both the public and health professionals:

1. State and county medical societies should develop programs to deal with disabled physicians with an aim of identifying them and getting them into treatment or behavior modification programs *before* they become a danger to their patients. These programs can be entirely confidential and run independent of the licensing authority.

2. Hospitals should conduct similar programs with the same degree of confidentiality.

3. Once the physician is actually a danger to patients, however, her conduct legitimately becomes a public matter. While rehabilitation and treatment should still be encouraged, it is now secondary to patient protection. Therefore, all physicians and hospitals should be required by law, under penalty of losing their own licenses, to report such physicians to the licensing authority. As a corollary, hospitals should be required to report all denials, removals, or resignations of privileges, and all restrictions on privileges, to the state licensing authority; and malpractice insurance companies should be required to report all malpractice settlements or payments, together with the facts, in cases where final payment is more than a certain amount, perhaps $5,000.

4. Licensing boards that do not have it should be given the legal authority to order physical and mental examinations on short notice.

Do physicians have the right to challenge their denial of appointment to a hospital staff, failure to renew appointment, or termination of appointment?

Yes, and the trend is to provide physicians with more rather than fewer due process rights. It must be emphasized at the outset, that hospitals have a legal obligation to monitor the quality of care rendered in their institutions, and to curtail or revoke staff privileges of physicians who present a danger to patients. Nevertheless, hospitals cannot arbitrarily deny privileges, and must afford some measure of due process in removing or curtailing privileges. The degree of due process protection afforded to the physician often depends on whether the hospital is *public* or *private,* or whether it is engaged in *"state action."*

If the hospital is a *public or governmental institution,* courts have usually held that the Constitution requires that physicians be afforded the same type of substantive and procedural due process applicable to actions by state licensing boards. Therefore, the physician must have at least written notice of the charge, a chance to be heard with counsel by an impartial panel, an opportunity to confront his accusers and present his own witnesses, and a record of the proceedings for use on appeal. In addition, the rules the hospital adopts relative to staff privileges (usually set forth in the hospital's by-laws) must be reasonable, nonarbitrary rules that are related to clinical standards of patient care and can be applied objectively.[31]

While the right/privilege distinction is not one we favor, some courts have characterized a staff position at a public hospital as a "right," and at a private hospital as a "privilege":

A duly licensed physician or surgeon has a right to practice his profession in the public hospitals of the state so long as he stays within the laws and conforms to all reasonable rules and regulations or actions of the hospital's governing authorities that are not unreasonable, arbitrary, capricious or discriminatory.[32]

In this case the term "right" has an operational meaning: it affords the physician Constitutional due process. It should not be surprising, therefore, that many physicians whose privileges have been threatened or revoked have attempted to get courts to find that the private hospital involved is engaged in state action. Receipt of Hill-Burton funds, tax exemptions, Medicare and Medicaid funding, etc., have all been used to try to get courts to find state action. While the results of such litigation have been mixed, the most consistent view is that for a court to find state action on the basis of public funding in a privileges case, the court must conclude that the public funding (1) is significant, (2) has a relationship to the conduct complained of, and (3) furthers an unconstitutional activity.[33] An example is a rule that excludes nonwhite physicians from a hospital staff.[34]

Finally, for *private hospitals,* not engaged in state action, a majority of states have continued to adopt a hands-off policy.[35] The general rule is that "private hospitals have the right to exclude licensed physicians and surgeons from the use of the hospital for any cause deemed sufficient by its managing authorities." [36] Even though this is still the majority rule, two important points should be stressed.

The first is that even private hospitals must follow their own internal by-laws, and if these provide for such things as notice and hearing, the physician must be afforded these if he so desires. Second, a growing minority of courts have found that even private hospitals must afford staff physicians some *minimal due process,* such as the "opportunity to answer the charges upon which his exclusion rests." [37] A New Jersey court, for example, has determined that a private hospital "has a duty to the public" and is operated for the public good, for a public purpose, and while they are "private in the sense that they are non-governmental, are hardly private in other senses." Accordingly, the power to select and retain members of the medical staff is "rightly viewed as a fiduciary power to be exercised reasonably for the public good." [38]

A California court, using similar language about public interest and fiduciary duty, has required the following elements of "minimal due process" in regard to staff appointments and renewals:

Minimal due process includes at least an opportunity for a hearing, preceded by appropriate notice, a written statement of charges or reasons for the denial of appointment or reappointment, a right of the physician to call witnesses on his behalf, a right to cross-examine the hospital witnesses, and a right to have a written decision of the hearing body along with the basis of the decision.[39]

We suggest that the California and New Jersey approaches are the modern trend, and that private hospitals should adopt by-laws that supply their staff physicians at least "minimal due process" as defined by these courts. Those that do not will come under increasing challenge from both their staff members and the courts.

Do nurses and other allied health professionals have any of the same due process rights physicians have?

Not unless these terms are set forth in an employment contract. The nurse or allied health professional, unlike the physician, is almost always a full-time employee. Accordingly, their rights as employees are set forth in an employment contract. If no such contract exists, the nurse or allied health professional is, in general, subject to discharge by the employer "for good cause, bad cause, or no cause at all." [40] The type of employment in which nurses are generally employed is termed employment "at will," and as such can be terminated at the will of either the employee or the employer.

Employees at public hospitals may have some recourse under civil service regulations or state and federal statutes that protect them from unjust dismissal.[41] In addition, if the hospital is a state hospital or is engaged in state action, it probably cannot fire a nurse or allied health professional for exercising his constitutional rights, such as the right to free speech.[42] There is some hope that courts or legislatures will recognize that nurses and allied health professionals should be protected from arbitrary firing if the activities that prompted the dismissal were for the protection of patients from negligent or illegal activities.[43] It must be recognized, however, that this is not yet the rule, and a nurse's employment contract or union contract is currently his only real protection against arbitrary action against him.[44]

Can health care professionals challenge hospital rules?

Challenges to hospital rules are almost universally unsuccessful in the courts. This is because the courts have found that hospitals have a duty to provide high quality patient care and will uphold almost any hospital rule that arguably has as its purpose the protection of the health and safety of patients, or the improvement of patient care.[45] As one court put it, hospital boards are "responsible for upgrading the standards of health care to be maintained in the hospital . . . and the court is charged with the narrow responsibility of assuring that the qualifications imposed by the Board [on staff members] are *reasonably related* to the operation of the hospital and *fairly administered.*" [46]

Examples of requirements that have been upheld are a requirement that all members of the staff obtain medical malpractice insurance [47] and a requirement that any surgeon who is not a member of the department of obstetrics and gynecology be required to request a consultation with one of its members before performing any major gynecologic operation in the hospital.[48] On the other hand, vague and overly broad by-laws, such as those providing that a reduction of privileges can be made whenever it is in the best interest of the hospital and its patients, have been struck down.[49]

In the past, osteopathic physicians were often denied privileges, but the current trend is to recognize them as equal to MDs in both legislation and court decisions.[50] Podiatrists and chiropractors have been afforded hearings on their request for privileges when the hospital had a flat rule that prohibited their membership on the staff as against the public interest, although in the absence of express legislation they generally have no right to membership on the staff of either private or public hospitals.[51]

NOTES

1. R. Derbyshire, Medical Licensure and Discipline in the United States xiii (Baltimore: Johns Hopkins Press, 1969). On licensure laws in general, see F. Grad & N. Marti, Physicians' Licensure and Discipline (Dobbs Ferry, N.Y.: Oceana Publications, 1980).

2. Southeastern Comm. College v. Davis, 442 U.S. 397 (1979); Hull, Should Handicapped People Be Allowed to Attend Nursing School? 1(3) Nursing Law & Ethics 1 (March, 1980).

3. S. Jonas, Medical Mystery 173 (N.Y.: W. W. Norton, 1978).

4. W. Gellhorn, C. Byse & P. Strauss, Administrative Law 424 (7th ed., Mineola, N.Y.: Foundation Press, 1979).

5. Alpert v. Board of Governors, 286 App. Div. 542, 145 N.Y.S.2d 534 (4th Dept. 1955).

6. R. Shryock, Medical Licensing in America, 1650–1965, 5 (Baltimore: Johns Hopkins Press, 1967). And see Cohen, Professional Licensure, Organizational Behavior, and the

Public Interest, 51 MMFQ/HEALTH AND SOCIETY 73 (1973).

7. *See, e.g.,* S. LEWIS, ARROWSMITH 157 (N.Y.: New American Library, 1961) (first published in 1925).

8. *See generally* SHRYOCK, *supra* note 6.

9. N. Weisfeld, Licensure of Primary Care Practitioners (staff paper of National Academy of Sciences, Institute of Medicine, Div. of Health Manpower & Resources Development, Washington, D.C., January 11, 1977) at 7. Not all states require nurses to be licensed to practice nursing.

10. Annas, *The Case for Licensing,* 8(5) MEDICOLEGAL NEWS 12 (Oct. 1980).

11. Galusha, *Uniform Licensure: An Attainable Goal, or a Myth?* 66(10) FED. BULL. 291 (Oct. 1979); Morton, *The Flex I-Flex II Concept,* 67(11) FED. BULL. 329 (Nov. 1980), *and see* Sounding Boards or Medical License, 303 (23) New Eng. J. Med. 1356 (Dec. 4, 1980).

12. *See, e.g.,* State *ex rel* Inscho v. Missouri Dental Board, 339 Mo. 547, 98 S.W.2d 606 (1936) (five separate findings of inefficient and unsatisfactory dental work were insufficient to revoke a dentist's license absent a statutory provision expressly stating incompetence as a ground); State Board of Medical Examiners v. Weiner, 68 N.J. Super. 468, 172 A.2d 661 (1961) (the court refused to uphold revocation of an osteopath's license on the grounds of medical malpractice since the legislature had not included it as a statutory ground, but did allow revocation for another reason). In some instances this has resulted in highly specific definitions, such as the definition of actionable "unprofessional conduct" in California, which includes failure of a physician to arrange for the transfer of a terminally ill patient to another physician in order that a "living will" may be carried out.

13. States that do not provide for medical malpractice or professional incompetence as a ground for disciplinary action include: Alabama, Alaska, Connecticut, Georgia, Kentucky, Kansas, Maryland, Mississippi, New Mexico, Oklahoma, Pennsylvania, South Carolina, South Dakota, Utah, Vermont, Wisconsin, and Wyoming.

14. In Arizona, Colorado, Georgia, Idaho, Illinois, Kentucky, Maryland, Michigan, Minnesota, Nevada, New Mexico, Ohio, Rhode Island, South Dakota, Tennessee, West Virginia, and Wisconsin.

15. Advertising prohibitions vary and include absolute prohibi-

tion, which is probably unconstitutional. See discussion in Chapter XIV.

16. In Arkansas, Hawaii, Illinois, Louisiana, Maryland, Oregon, Rhode Island, and Washington.

17. In Alaska, California, Delaware, Idaho, Illinois, Indiana, Maine, Michigan, Mississippi, Montana, Nevada, New Jersey, Ohio, South Dakota, Tennessee, Texas, Utah, Virginia, and Washington.

18. In Arkansas, California, Colorado, Mississippi, Montana, Nevada, Tennessee, and Virginia.

19. In Florida, Mississippi, Rhode Island, and Texas.

20. AMA State Legislative Report (Sept. 1977).

21. *E.g.,* Colorado, New York, and North Dakota.

22. Withrow v. Larkin, 421 U.S. 35 (1975).

23. Hawker v. New York, 170 U.S. 189, 196 (1898). *Accord,* Furnish v. Board of Medical Examiners, 149 Cal. App. 2d 326, 308 P.2d 924, 927 (1957). The proceedings are civil, rather than criminal, in nature. Arthurs v. Stern, 560 F.2d 477, 478 (1st Cir. 1977).

24. Lawrence v. Board of Registration in Medicine, 239 Mass. 424, 429 (1921).

25. McLaughlin v. Board of Medical Examiners, 35 Cal. App. 3d 1010, 111 Cal. Rptr. 353 (Ct. App. 2d Dist. 1973).

26. Levy v. Board of Registration and Discipline in Medicine, 392 N.E.2d 1036 (Mass. 1979). *Accord,* Windham v. Board of Medical Quality Assurance, 163 Cal. Rptr. 566 (Ct. App. 2d Dist. 1980). *See* Annas, *When Criminal Conduct Can Be the Basis for License Revocation,* 67 FED. BULL. 72 (March 1980).

27. *See generally* G.J. Annas, *Who to Call When the Doctor Is Sick,* 8(6) HASTINGS CENTER RPT. (Dec. 1978) 18.

28. On Nork, *see* Gonzalez v. Nork, lower court opinion excerpted in S. LAW & S. POLAN, PAIN AND PROFIT 215–45 (New York: Harper & Row, 1978). The story of the Marcus brothers is fictionalized in B. WOOD & J. GEASLANT, TWINS (New York: Putnam, 1977). On Miofsky, *see* Stammer, *Coverup Hinted in Case of Alleged Doctor-Molester, Los Angeles Times,* March 26, 1979, at 3.

29. R. GREEN, G. CARROLL, & W. BUXTON, THE CARE AND MANAGEMENT OF THE SICK AND INCOMPETENT PHYSICIAN (Springfield, Ill.: Charles C. Thomas, 1978). *And see generally* Rensberger, *Unfit Doctors Create Worry in Profession, N.Y. Times,* January 26, 1976, at 1.

30. *See* Annas, *supra* note 27, reporting on a September 1978

AMA Conference on the Impaired Physician held in Minneapolis, Minnesota.

31. *See* A. Southwick, *The Physician's Right to Due Process and Equal Protection,* HOSPITAL AND MEDICAL STAFF (May 1978) 30, 32.

32. Nashville Mem. Hosp. v. Binkley, 534 S.W.2d 318 (Tenn. 1976).

33. Barrett v. United Hosp., 376 F. Supp. 791 (S.D.N.Y. 1974). And *see* Sokol v. University Hosp., 402 F. Supp. 1029 (D. Mass. 1975) (no relationships between state funds and hospital activity); Mulvihill v. Julia L. Butterfield Mem. Hosp., 329 F. Supp. 1020 (S.D.N.Y. 1971) (state regulation of hospitals does not make their activity state action); Ward v. St. Anthony Hosp., 476 F.2d 671 (10th Cir. 1973) (tax exemptions and receipt of Medicare and Medicaid funds do not transform hospital into arm of the state).

34. Simkins v. Moses H. Cone Mem. Hosp., 323 F.2d 956 (4th Cir. 1963). *And see generally* Shields, *Guidelines for Reviewing Applications for Privileges,* Hospital Medical Staff (Sept. 1980) 11.

35. A 1978 survey of the cases in 32 states indicated that courts in 22 of them favored continued adherence to the traditional hands-off doctrine with regard to staff decisions at private hospitals. Blum, *Medical Discipline and Procedural Due Process: Evaluation of Hospital Staff Proceedings,* Report to the National Center for Health Services Research (Grant No. R01 HS 02044–01A1) (Boston University Health Policy Center, 53 Bay State Rd., Boston, Massachusetts, 1978) at 49.

36. Nashville Mem. Hosp. v. Binkley, 534 S.W.2d 318 (Tenn. 1976).

37. Westlake Comm. Hosp. v. Superior Court of Los Angeles County, 551 P.2d 410 (Cal. 1976).

38. Greisman v. Newcomb Hosp., 40 N.J. 389, 192 A.2d 817 (1963); *and see* Davidson v. Youngstown Hospital Assoc., 19 Ohio App. 2d 246, 250 N.E.2d 892 (1969).

39. Ascherman v. San Francisco Medical Soc'y, 39 Cal. App. 3d 623, 114 Cal. Rptr. 681 (1974). New Hampshire, Ohio, and Vermont have similar court decisions.

40. Shapiro & Tune, *Implied Contract Rights to Job Security,* 26 STANFORD L. REV. 335 (1974). *And see* Hyatt, *Employment at Will and the Law of Contracts,* 23 BUFFALO L. REV. 211 (1973).

41. Summers, *Individual Protection Against Unjust Dismissal: Time for a Statute,* 62 VIRGINIA L. REV. 481, 497 (1976).

42. *See, e.g.,* Bach v. Mt. Clemens Gen. Hosp., 448 F. Supp. 686 (E.D. Mich. 1978) (dismissal of nurse for derogatory remarks about a hospital physician at a meeting of County Government Sub-Committee on Emergency Medical Services upheld because hospital was found not to be engaged in state action).

43. *See* Summers, *supra* note 41.

44. *See* Chap. XV, The Union Movement in Health Care Institutions.

45. *See, e.g.,* D. WARREN, PROBLEMS IN HOSPITAL LAW 31–36 (3rd ed., Germantown), (Md.: Aspen, 1978).

46. Kahn v. Suburban Community Hosp. 45 Ohio St. 2d 39, 340 N.E.2d 398 (1976), *citing* Sosa v. Board of Managers of Val Verde Mem. Hosp., 437 F.2d 173 (5th Cir. 1971) (emphasis supplied).

47. Pollock v. Methodist Hosp., 392 F. Supp. 393 (E.D. I.a. 1975), *and* Holmes v. Hoemako Hosp., 117 Ariz. 403, 573 P.2d 477 (1977).

48. *See, e.g.,* Annas, *Validity of a Private Hospital's Rule Requiring Consultation Prior to Surgery,* 5 ORTHOPAEDIC REV. 83 (May, 1976) *discussing* Fahey v. Holy Family Hosp., 336 N.E.2d 309 (Ill. 1975).

49. *E.g.,* Milford v. People's Community Hosp. Auth., 4 Mich. App. 142, 144 N.W.2d 687 (1966), *and* WARREN, *supra* note 45, at 59.

50. WARREN, *supra* note 45, at 65.

51. *Id. and, e.g.,* Aasum v. Good Samaritan Hosp., 542 F.2d 792 (9th Cir. 1976) (chiropractor required to be afforded minimum due process when his application was considered); *and* Shaw v. Hospital Authority of Cobb County, 507 F.2d 625 (5th Cir. 1975) (podiatrist entitled to due process hearing on application rejection).

II

Nursing and the Law

Nursing as a profession has made rapid advances since its first textbook was published in 1879 and its first national association was organized in 1896. Much of this progress reflects achievements of society in general and the health care system in particular. But most of the credit lies in the persistent efforts of the practitioners of the science of nursing to obtain professional status for their work. The result has been an increasing expansion of the nurse's role into areas of health not previously sanctioned by either law or medicine. Not only has nursing experienced an expansion of duties, but it has also seen a correlative increase in legal obligations and responsibilities of which the modern nurse must be aware.

What educational requirements must be met to enter the field of nursing?

In general, registered nurses, as distinct from practical nurses, enter their field after having graduated from one of three preparatory nursing programs, and after having met other state statutory requirements. Historically, the largest number of nursing students received their nurses' training in what is commonly referred to as a diploma school, generally a hospital-based program where nurses are trained and engage in patient care.[1] This entails an intensive two- or three-year program that stresses bedside experience and direct care of patients as well as classroom work.

Recently, however, the two other major nurses' training programs have become more popular and may surpass the popularity of the diploma schools. Nurses may be graduated from universities or colleges under a bachelor's degree program or from a junior college associate degree program. The college or university provides the educational base, rather than the hospital. The four-year baccalaureate program stresses the importance of general nursing education, rather than hospital-based experience; the associate degree condenses practical instruction and some general education into a two-year program.[2] About 25 percent of all practicing nurses currently hold bachelor's degrees in nursing.

Nursing students may also enter the profession as practical nurses. A practical nurse has a high school education and has completed a one-year vocational education course at a community agency, a public vocational school, or a junior or senior college. The substance of this program is limited to the elementary nursing practices and introductory educational courses.

What is the practice of nursing?

Attempts to define nursing, through state statutes, as well as suggestions propounded by the American Nurses' Association (ANA), have not always been successful. State nurse practice acts may be classified as either traditional or modern.[3] Traditional statutes draw upon the model definitions of "professional nurse" (i.e., registered nurse) and "practical nurse," as advocated by the ANA in 1973.[4] The registered nurse, as traditionally understood, is educated in the biological, physical, and social sciences and in nursing skills; functions to observe patients and carry out treatments authorized by physicians; and, as a result, cares for the sick, aids in the prevention of disease, and conserves health. The education, function, and activities of practical nurses are defined as similar, but more elementary.[5] More modern nurse practice acts and the recently amended ANA definitions, on the other hand, define nursing very broadly, so as to allow for the advancement and expansion of the practice into other areas of health care.[6] Finally, some state laws specifically prohibit nurses from practicing medicine.[7]

Definitions and explanations of the practice of nursing are general and vague, and frequently do not provide concrete evidence or guidance in analyzing particular situations. For example, an issue that is receiving attention is the controversy over whether seemingly diagnostic acts of a nurse are outside of the practice of nursing and, therefore, amount to the illegal practice of medicine.

What is diagnosis and when may a nurse make a diagnosis?

Diagnosis is a "mental process whereby one or more persons appraise a situation and make a decision based on their judgment, that may or may not lead to action." [8] Diagnosis is the act of making a judgment, and would thus appear to rest solely within the scope of medical, and not nursing, practice. The traditional nurse practice acts very clearly state that diagnosis is not within the nurse's practice. The modern statutes do not condemn or reject the practice of diagnosing as a nursing duty, but do not specifically condone it.[9]

Yet, as Murchison and Nichols have written, studies show that diagnosis is well within the boundaries of the actual practice of nursing, and has always been a duty of professional nursing. But a proper term to describe the modern, expanded nursing role, which certainly includes diagnostic functions, has never been selected.[10] While nurses do perform acts of diagnosis, those acts are probably not *medical* diagnoses, but, rather, are *nursing* diagnoses. Several state courts have determined that to diagnose, in the medical sense, is to determine the existence of a disease from its symptoms and not simply to judge the gravity of those symptoms presently being manifested.[11]

The question of a nurse providing care and making judgments that infringe upon the practice of medicine arises most dramatically in the emergency room or special care units. A nurse practicing in these settings must consider several legal and ethical points. For example, a nurse practicing in an emergency room has a duty to make a triage decision about whether an emergency exists. It is the nurse's obligation to make a determination within the reasonable limits of judgment of a nurse with his training and experience. If the nurse makes an honest decision that there is no unmistakable indication of an emergency, and that decision is not unreasonable for a nurse of his training, then neither the nurse nor the hospital can be held liable for malpractice.[12] Thus, within a certain range, the nurse is obligated to make an initial nursing diagnosis to determine whether there is an emergency requiring immediate care, a doctor's supervision, or admission to the hospital.

A nurse who makes a "medical" rather than a "nursing" diagnosis may risk being prosecuted for practicing medicine without a license. The nurse may also be sued for malpractice if a patient is injured as a result of his actions. Some states even allow a trial jury to *infer* that the nurse acting outside the scope of nursing was negligent in causing the alleged harm to the patient.[13] On the other hand, a nurse must consider the facts peculiar to the situation, such as the need for emergency room treatment, the absence of a supervising physician, and his own competence and obligation to care for the patient.

A nurse who carries out protocols is not practicing medicine, even though nursing judgment may also come into play. In other words, if the nurse follows well-established medical guidelines for specific situations, he is working for or with a physician under a protocol, and is not practicing medicine. Further, it seems likely that a court will not discredit a nurse's judgment if it is based on his education and experience and does not intrude into the physician's domain. It also appears that an exception permits nurses to make medical diagnoses in emergency situations. This allows the nurse to do all that is necessary and proper, including medical diagnosis. There are, unfortunately, few guidelines in determining whether or not a nurse has made a judgment or performed outside the scope of nursing practice.

As the nurse's role continues to expand, nurses will more frequently need to make a diagnosis or other judgment. Professional organizations are gathering legal and medical opinions in order to revise state nurse practice acts to give the health professions guidance in their day-to-day activities. Future nurse practice acts will give greater flexibility in responsibilities, by emphasizing the individual nurse's background, competence, and skills.[14]

What is a nurse practitioner?

A nurse practitioner is a registered professional nurse who has acquired nursing skills and education beyond those required for a licensed nurse. Generally, this means graduation from an accredited school of nursing, licensing by a state board of nursing, at least two years of professional work, and nurse practitioner training lasting from four months to more than a year.[15] This added education can lead to a master's degree or other certificate of achievement. Many nurse practitioners fill expanded nursing roles in maternal and child care, adult and family care, or in psychiatric health care. They are most frequently employed in organized health care programs, such as clinics or hospitals, and in rural practices. The ANA has defined the responsibilities of a nurse practitioner.[16] Most of these include the traditional nursing skills. But other responsibilities of the nurse practitioner were formerly the sole province of medicine, such as medical diagnosis and the selection of therapy. A nurse practitioner may see a patient, determine that the patient suffers from an upper respiratory infection, and then institute a specific course of treatment.

The nurse practitioner's activities are based upon protocols developed jointly by a physician and a nurse practitioner. Nevertheless, it may be argued that the nurse is making what has traditionally been considered a medical diagnosis. This is why the nurse practitioner is often in the center of the controversy surrounding nursing practice and diagnosis. The registered nurse may make diagnoses in only limited situations. The nurse practitioner regularly makes independent decisions, in collaboration with a physician, and is authorized to do so by the relevant sections of the nurse practice acts. These are of two types. Some statutes provide for the regulation of the nurse practitioner by state licensing boards, which promulgate rules and regulations pertinent to the newly expanded role. Others allow traditionally medical functions to be delegated to the nurse practitioner on the ground that the delegation was approved by the nursing and medical boards.[17] Federal guidelines on reimbursement for certain activities by the nurse practitioner are similar to the latter type.[18]

Nurse practitioners may specialize and be certified, for example, as emergency room nurse practitioners, pediatric nurse practitioners, or geriatric nurse practitioners. One of the best known of the specialties is the nurse-midwife, who is a registered professional with additional knowledge and skills gained through an organized program of study and clinical experience, and who expands the role of the nurse to include the management of mothers and babies. In practice, the nurse-midwife will follow the pregnancy's progress and deliver the baby alone unless a deviation from normal progress makes it necessary to call in a physician.[19]

A nurse practitioner is not the same as a physician assistant, although a nurse practitioner may aid or assist a physician in treating patients. Physician assistants are not licensed to practice independently, as are nurse practitioners, but practice under the supervision and license of the physician who employs them. Because of this, a recent case in the State of Washington upheld, against a challenge by the state nurses' association, a regulation that authorized physician assistants to issue prescriptions for medication and write medical orders for patient care.[20] The court held that physician assistants are *agents* of the physician, and therefore nurses executing orders issued by physician assistants would not be exposed to any liability, since the order was legally the order of the physician.

The nurse practitioner role arose as a result of efforts to expand nurses' responsibilities. The nurse practitioner's roots date back to the 1930s and to nurse-midwives, who were then being trained to carry out selected routine tasks of obstetricians and other physicians. There evolved an increasing interest in providing maximum health care for the public at a minimal cost. The nurse practitioner was seen as the focal point for meeting this objective.[21]

Just how well these expectations have been met is illustrated in several studies of the nurse practitioner in action.[22] One involving pediatric nurse practitioners found that parents of patients seemed to accept the practitioner and, in return, the practitioner was satisfied with the role; that more patients were seen by the practitioner than by a physician alone, resulting in more efficient use of the physician's time; and that the quality of care was maintained.[23] Nurse practitioners are gradually being accepted as professionals whose role is that of provider of primary health care.

What is nursing malpractice?

Malpractice may be broadly defined as professional negligence. Whether a professional is negligent is determined by analyzing the person's performance, or nonperformance, in a given situation against the appropriate "standard of care." [24] Since the nurse is granted a privilege, through licensure, of providing health care, the actions, or omissions, of a nurse are not measured against the standard of what the reasonably prudent *person* would do in a given situation, but are judged against what the reasonably prudent *nurse* would do.

The problem, however, is in determining the exact standard of care against which the nurse's act or omission is measured. During a suit against a nurse, the testimony of an expert witness, one who is trained in nursing or medicine, is often offered in court as evidence of the standard of care. In other cases, evidence of a standard may be presented by referring to definitions of standards of care by various professional associations. For example, the American Nurses' Association has promulgated general standards and assessment factors for five nursing specialty areas: community health, geriatrics, maternal and child health, medical-surgical, and psychiatric-mental health. It has also been suggested that professional standards of care should vary according to the differing education and practical experiences of nurses.[25]

But whatever legal standard of care is applied, if it is determined that the nurse's action or failure to act was below the standard and caused the patient injury, the nurse may be liable in a malpractice suit.

Is the professional standard of care the same for all types of nurses?

As a rule, each type of nurse must comply with the standard of care recognized for the professional level at which the nurse practices. Therefore, registered nurses are held to the standard of care of a reasonably prudent and competent registered nurse. Registered nurses who have specialized in an area of practice, or who have continued their education to a master's or doctor's degree, are held to a higher standard of care than a registered nurse without such additional training.

What is the standard of care for a student nurse?

The rule is that a student nurse is held to the standard of a reasonably competent and prudent professional nurse.[26] Courts have indicated that patients have a right to expect the competent performance of nursing services, so that anyone who acts as a nurse, performing those functions customarily considered to be the practice of nursing, is held to the standard of a professional. Thus, in the performance of nursing duties, students are held not to the standard of a reasonable nursing student, but to that of a reasonable professional. While at first glance this may seem harsh, we believe that it is an equitable allocation of risk for the substandard performance of nursing functions, and encourages the careful delegation and supervision of nursing student activities.

Who is responsible for a nurse's malpractice?

The nurse is always legally responsible for his own acts. However, a hospital or physician may also be held liable for his negligence.

Under the doctrine of *respondeat superior,* a hospital that employs a nurse is liable for his wrongful acts or omissions even though the hospital itself was not negligent. A physician may also be liable for the negligence of her employees in the same manner as the hospital is liable. This doctrine applies when there is a "master-servant" or employer-employee relationship, and is predicated upon the employer's ability and responsibility to control and direct the performance and duties of the employee. Therefore, when the nurse as employee performs a negligent act *within the scope of employment,* or does what he was hired to do in a negligent manner, the hospital or physician is responsible, as is the nurse.[27]

Does a private duty nurse have the right to practice in a particular hospital?

No. Any rights of a private duty nurse to practice in a particular hospital are provided in the terms of the contract, if any, between the nurse and the facility.[28] Refusal to grant visiting privileges, or termination of such privileges (so long as no provisions of any existing contract are violated) does not give the nurse a basis for suing the hospital.

Can a nurse ever be held legally liable for the negligence of another person?

Not directly. Nursing supervisors are entrusted with directing and controlling subordinate personnel, but they are not legally responsible for the negligent acts or omissions of those they supervise. Rather, the hospital or physician who hired the employees remains legally responsible for them. However, a supervisor nurse can be negligent by failing to carry out the supervisory duties of his position. For example, if he has reason to believe that a subordinate will perform a certain task negligently, assigning that task to that employee may constitute negligence for which the supervisor must answer. The acts or omissions of nurses who are also supervisors are measured againt the standard of care of a competent supervisor.

The same theory applies to the situation of instructors and students. An instructor will not be held liable for the negligence of her students in performing activities which she has taught them. However, if the instructor has the student perform a task the student is not yet capable of performing in a manner consistent with the applicable standard of care, the instructor can be found independently negligent, and thus liable for the harm.

Is the nurse obligated to report irregular conduct or orders of another health care provider?

Yes. Not only does a nurse have the legal obligation to perform the practice of nursing within a certain standard of care, he also has a responsibility to bring appropriate matters of health care to the attention of a physician, the hospital administrator, or both. In such a position, the nurse is a "watchdog" for ensuring that the patient has the proper care. Indeed, the ANA's Code for Nurses likens the nurse's role to that of an advocate for the patient.[29] If a nurse recognizes that a patient is receiving substandard or improper medical care, he has a responsibility to alert the attending physician. If she fails to make appropriate changes, it is incumbent upon the nurse to advise either the appropriate department head or other administrative personnel so that appropriate remedial actions may be taken. This can relieve the nurse of further legal responsibility for the patient. But if the nurse fails to act, and harm results to a patient, he may be liable for negligence.

Perhaps the leading court case in this area of health law involved a young man who broke his leg while playing football and was taken to the community hospital.[30] The emergency room doctor applied traction and a plaster cast. Soon afterward, the man complained of great pain in his toes. The toes turned dark and swollen and later became cold and insensitive. Within three days following admission, the physician split the cast, thereby cutting the leg. Nurses observed blood, seepage, and a foul stench coming from the wounds. After two weeks, the patient was transferred to another hospital, where the gangrenous leg was amputated below the knee. If the nurses had made proper observations and reported them to the physician or the hospital administration, it is likely that a consultant would have been called in time to save the leg. In the court's words, a verdict for the patient was supported by the evidence because

> . . . the jury could reasonably have concluded that the nurses did not test for circulation in the leg as frequently as necessary, that skilled nurses would have promptly recognized the conditions that signalled a dangerous impairment of circulation . . . and would have known that the condition would become irreversible in a matter of hours. . . . At that point it became the nurses' duty to inform the attending physician and, if he failed to act, to advise the hospital authorities so that appropriate action might be taken.[31]

A more recent case relies on similar reasoning. The hospital's policy permitted a nurse to question the propriety of a physician's order or the physician's failure to act by first advising the doctor and then, if he took no action, advising the department head. While the nurse here did contact the physician, she failed to report all of the patient's symptoms, and, following the physician's continued inaction, she failed to report the questionable practice to higher authorities. The patient's claim against the negligent nurse was upheld.[32] The ANA's Code for Nurses prescribes the course a nurse should take when questioning the quality of patient care. It provides in part as follows:

> When the nurse is aware of inappropriate or questionable conduct in the provision of health care, concern should be expressed to the person carrying out

the questionable practice and attention called to the possible detrimental effect upon the client's welfare. . . . If indicated, the practice should then be reported to the appropriate authority within the institution, agency, or large system. There should be an established mechanism for the reporting and handling of incompetent, unethical, or illegal practice within the employment setting so that such reporting can go through official channels and be done without fear of reprisal.[33]

The duty to advise and report applies not only in a situation when improper or substandard care is being given by a physician, but also when a nurse encounters an illegible or incomplete order, or an order which he feels is beyond his competence. If the order cannot be read or is incomplete, the nurse's duty is to contact the physician who wrote the order and obtain clarification. To administer the order without such clarification might result in injury to the patient and, possibly, in legal liability to the nurse. If the order appears erroneous, a reasonably prudent and competent nurse would inquire further by confirming it with the physician. A nurse cannot sit back in this case and believe that the physician would bear all responsibility for the mistake; the nurse, too, could be liable. Finally, when ordered to perform a task beyond his competence, or beyond the scope of employment, the nurse has a duty to so advise the physician or hospital authorities and must refrain from performing that act.[34] The nurse may properly refuse to carry out the order to protect the patient from anticipated harm. The nurse's obligation to report also extends to incompetence he sees among nursing colleagues.

Nurses often encounter hostility from physicians or colleagues when they attempt to raise legitimate questions concerning the quality of patient care.[35] However, the nurse must remember that to bow to such pressure not only may result in his negligence and legal liability, but would also be a shirking of his responsibility to the patient. To foster effective physician-nurse communications and thereby improve patient care, the hospital should develop a means whereby nurses can, without fear of retaliation, report questionable nursing or medical practices.

First, written procedures or guidelines should be adopted and made available to nurses. These guidelines should tell nurses who is to receive any reports of poor care. Nurses should be encouraged by the administration to freely contact this person, and those who do so should receive the full support of the administration. It needs to be underlined to nurses, as well as to medical personnel, that reporting substandard care is a legitimate nursing function. Second, nurses who make these reports should be kept informed of any investigations or administrative decisions regarding the questionable conduct. In that way, the nurses will receive feedback as to the correctness of their judgments.[36] While there is an inherent danger of overzealous reports from nurses, this risk is well outweighed by the risk of harm to patients and the possibility of malpractice suits if there is no reporting system.

Does a nurse have the right to answer a patient's questions?

Yes. A recent case of significance involves a nurse whose license was suspended for six months by the Idaho Board of Nursing. According to the testimony of the nurse, a physician had told his patient that she was dying of myelogenous leukemia, and had offered chemotherapy as a last resort. Upon approaching the patient with the drug and discussing its side effects, the nurse was told by the patient that she was apprehensive about it, and related her belief that she'd already controlled her leukemia for twelve years with natural foods and that God would perform a miracle on her behalf. The nurse discussed alternative forms of cancer treatment, specifically the "natural approach," including such things as nutrition, herbs, and laetrile, although she said that these were not sanctioned by the medical profession. The family informed the physician about this, and charges were brought against the nurse for interfering with the patient's treatment and with the doctor-patient relationship. The nursing board found her guilty of "unprofessional conduct," and its decision was supported by the Idaho State Nurses' Association.[37]

On appeal to the Idaho Supreme Court, the decision was reversed, but not specifically on the substantive issues in the case. Rather, the court found that the nurse's due process rights had been violated in that neither the licensing statute nor the Board of Nursing regulations specifically defined the term "unprofessional conduct" so as to indicate what acts undertaken by the nurse are forbidden.

This case is unusual in that the court did not defer to the expert decision of an administrative agency, as is customary. This would seem to reflect the court's concern for the fact that a nurse was being disciplined "for the act of talking to the patient." [38] As so phrased, it would be difficult to perceive how this action could be unprofessional conduct. While such an act on the part of a nurse may not be legally protected from possible adverse action by her employer if considered contrary to the physician's or hospital's policies, it seems likely that, under most circumstances, it would not justify suspension or revocation of a nurse's license.

Of course, as with all actions, there are some limits to what a nurse can do in this area. For example, discussions of alternative treatments that have been medically established as ineffectual, outmoded, or dangerous to the patient would seem to fall within this category. The nurse's conduct would be judged by the standard of the nursing profession, *i.e.*, what a reasonable nurse would do. Answering a patient's inquiries concerning his condition or possible treatment alternatives is part of nursing practice and responsibility, and therefore in conformity with what a reasonable nurse would do.

Does a nurse have a right to refuse an order she thinks is contrary to good nursing practice?

Yes. Sometimes a nurse is placed in a situation in which she is given a false sense of security about possible liability. For example, if a physician orders a surgical nurse not to make a sponge count, she may feel relieved of her responsibility for any malpractice suit which might arise from a sponge remaining in the patient's body. Yet the nurse, as an independent professional, may not be relieved of responsibility merely be relying on the physician's assertion that he will take full responsibility. She has an obligation to take further action, including questioning the physician on his decision, and even taking the sponge count on her own initiative and informing the physician of its outcome. If the count shows that a sponge is missing and the physician, upon being so informed, does not take any additional steps on the matter, such as ordering an X-ray, the nurse again has an obligation, not only to question the physician on this, but also to go beyond the doctor and report the matter to people in higher authority, such as the nursing supervisor, the director of nursing, and the hospital administrator.

Under such circumstances, the nurse should always note the details of these transactions in the patient's record, including not only her own observations, but also the responses of all people contacted by her. Not only does this provide a complete and accurate record for the patient's benefit, but it also protects the nurse, who, without such documentation, runs the risk of being found negligent for not adequately performing her duty toward the patient. It will also record the position taken by the different parties, in case their memories should conflict in the future.

What legal obligations does a nurse have in administering medications?

In the administration of medications, nurses will not be protected from liability simply because they are following a physician's orders. A nurse must make an independent judgment of the validiy of the medication order. If it is clearly wrong, the nurse must contact the physician and question him about the order. This is part of the nurse's obligation to safeguard the patient. When a medication is ordinarily administered by a nurse without the direct supervision or detailed instruction of a physician, liability for negligent performance of the nurse will rest not with the physician, but with the nurse and the hospital.[39] Before a nurse administers any medication, she should insist that instructions for administration be outlined. She should in each case be sure of the "five rights": the right drug for the right patient in the right dosage at the right time and via the right route.[40] The nurse should always keep abreast of new drug developments and should know just what the drug is, why it is given, and what contraindications and incompatibilities it may have. Similarly, if it appears that a medicine's label was tampered with or that it was improperly stored, the nurse should seek a replacement and promptly notify the nurse-supervisor. Each of these suggestions encourages the nurse to be a reasonably prudent and competent professional.[41]

Should a nurse keep detailed notes in the patient's record?

Yes. Good charting, in the form of accurate and complete nurse's notes, is a critical element of the nurse's duty to the patient. It provides an ongoing record of an important aspect of the patient's health care history. Thus it details information necessary for continued health care by future providers, enables review of the quality of the care provided, and allows for meaningful patient knowledge of and participation in his own health care. In this way the patient is the ultimate beneficiary of a nurse's good record-keeping.

Beyond that, it is often the key evidence in determining guilt or innocence of a defendant health practitioner sued for malpractice. Accurate, complete, and legible charts are the best evidence a nurse may present. Formerly, many courts did not allow nurses' notes or other clinical records to be used as evidence, but now they are admissible in most courts, though some still exclude this type of evidence entirely. Others exclude only those medical or nursing notes that contain opinions or conclusions, and admit those containing only observations into evidence. Still others admit the total record if it is made in the regular course of the business of the hospital or clinic and if it is made at or about the time of the act being recorded.[42] The nurse should take care in writing or annotating a chart. Erasures may make the chart suspect and, therefore, not good and reliable evidence. For the nurse's own protection he should chart even routine procedures, because even these acts may be scrutinized in court. Further, notes on the chart as to the patient's actions or refusal to follow physician's orders may show the patient's own negligence, known as contributory negligence, and may disprove the patient's allegations that health care personnel are responsible for his injury.

Should nurses carry their own malpractice insurance?

Generally, it is the hospital, as a corporation, that makes the contract with the insurance company for its professional liability coverage. Although the insurance contract is technically made between the insurer and the named insured, coverage may also extend to other insured persons under what is called an omnibus clause. If an omnibus clause is included in that hospital's policy, physicians, nurses, and other health personnel, as employees of the hospital, may also be covered.[43]

Therefore, it was formerly thought that nurses, at least hospital nurses, had no need for their own professional liability coverage. It was argued that nurses were covered under the hospital's policy as its employees and therefore were amply protected. Another argument was that nurses were rarely sued, in part because the law formerly did not hold them liable, and in part because nurses generally lacked personal resources sufficient to pay a judgment rendered against them.[44]

The recent trend, however, is to encourage nurses to obtain their own professional liability insurance. Many justifications for this stance may be offered. As has been emphasized, nurses are legally responsible for their own professional acts and may not substitute their employer as the culpable party. Second, nurses employed by hospitals may find that the hospital insurance coverage does not extend to cover nurses. Many hospital plans can be extended to cover the nurse as an employee at the option of the employee via what is known as an endorsement to the basic coverage. However, even when this optional coverage is accepted by the employee, its actual coverage may be available only when the nurse performs as an employee acting within the scope of employment. Should the nurse act outside of this scope, there might be no coverage for professional liability. In another situation, the nurse employed by a physician might find, to his dismay, that the physician's policy does not cover his liability as an individual. The policy may cover only the physician's own liability for the malpractice of her employees. Finally, for those nurse practitioners who practice independently, there is no other party who is liable for the nurse's negligence, and so no one else who would purchase insurance to cover it.

Administrative or supervisory nurses, like other nurses, should also obtain their own professional liability insurance policies. These nurses may be personally responsible for the alleged injury, or, as a result of their supervisory position, may have acted negligently in their supervision of other employees. Current legal procedures allow an injured patient to sue even those remotely connected with the situation.[45] The benefits payable or advantages gained by having coverage outweigh the cost of coverage. The typical professional liability insurance coverage will pay the amount of the judgment, or the settlement if the case does not go to trial, but only up to the amount of the policy; the costs of legal defense and representation; and court costs.

Nurses who work for a physician, clinic, hospital, or other organized health care unit should carefully examine the existing professional liability insurance policy to determine if nurses as individuals are covered. Even if it appears that the nurse as an individual employee may be covered under the employer's policy, the safest measure is for the nurse to obtain a personal insurance policy.

What does the future hold for the nursing profession?

Consistent with the already expanding role of the nurse in the provision of nursing care and the rising costs of medical care, it seems that, in the future, nurses will have a greater range of tasks and responsibilities than they presently perform. The key to this expansion is an acceptance by the public, by other health care providers, and by nurses themselves of the professional status of nursing. The nursing profession has been dynamic and will continue to be responsive to the changing needs of society. As a result, the education of nurses will undergo modification.

But what will most likely be the greatest advance is the further extension of nursing practice into areas that formerly were the sole province of doctors. Gradually, collaborating rather than competing with physicians, nurses will provide primary care to more patients than physicians will.

NOTES

1. *Statement on Nursing Education: Status or Service Oriented?* 53 BULL. N.Y. ACAD. MED. 491–92 (June 1977).
2. *Id.* at 496–97.
3. V. HALL, STATUTORY REGULATION OF THE SCOPE OF NURSING PRACTICE—A CRITICAL SURVEY 7 (The National Joint Practice Commission, Chicago, 1975).
4. The ANA defines the "practice of professional nursing" to be:

   . . . the performance, for compensation, of any acts in the observation, care, and counsel of the ill, injured, or infirm or in the maintenance of health or prevention of illness of others, or in the supervision and teaching of other personnel or, the administration of medications and treatments as prescribed by a licensed physician or dentist requiring substantial specialized judgment and skill and based on knowledge and application of the principles of biological, physical, and social science. The foregoing shall not be deemed to include acts of diagnosis or prescription of therapeutic or corrective measures.

   It defines "practical nursing" as:

   . . . the performance, for compensation, of selected acts in the care of the ill, injured, or infirm under the direction of a licensed professional nurse or a licensed physician or a licensed dentist; and not requiring the substantial specialized skill, judgment, and knowledge required in professional nursing.
5. NURSING AND THE LAW 59 (C. Streiff, ed., 2d ed.; Rockville, Md.: 1975).
6. Andreoli, *Ambulatory Health Care and the Nurse Practitioner,* 14 ALA. J. MED. SCI. 57, 59 (1977).
7. HALL, *supra* note 3, at 30.
8. I. MURCHISON & T. NICHOLS, LEGAL FOUNDATIONS OF NURSING PRACTICE 91 (New York: 1970).
9. HALL, *supra* note 3, at 8.
10. MURCHISON & NICHOLS, supra note 8, at 89–91.
11. Note, *Acts of Diagnosis by Nurses and the Colorado Professional Nursing Practice Act,* 45 DENVER L.J. 467, 471 (1968).

12. Wilmington General Hosp. v. Manlove, 54 Del. 15, 174 A.2d 135 (1961).
13. NURSING AND THE LAW, *supra* note 5, at 61.
14. Regan, *Nursing and the law,* 39 R.N. 1, 25 (January 1976); Note, *Acts of Diagnosis, supra* note 11, at 470–81.
15. Andreoli, *supra* note 6, at 59, 60 J. Gimble, *Identifying the Nurse Practitioner,* 70 J. AM. DIETETIC ASS'N 283 (1977).
16. American Nurses' Association, Nurses in the Extended Role Are Not Physician's Assistants (Interim Executive Committee of Counsel for Pediatric Nurse Practitioners, Kansas City, Mo., July 5, 1973).
17. Kissam, *Physicians' Assistants and Nurse Practitioner Laws: A Study of Health Law Reform,* 24 KAN. L. REV. 1, 25–27 (1975).
18. 42 Fed. Reg. 60, 880 (1977).
19. American College of Nurse Midwives, Statement of Functions, Standards and Qualifications for Practice of Nurse-Midwife 1 (New York: 1973).
20. Washington State Nurses' Ass'n v. Board of Med. Examiners, 605 P.2d 1270 (Wash. 1980).
21. Gimble, *supra* note 15, at 282; *Functions and Reimbursement of Nurse Practitioners, Report of the American Medical Association Council on Medical Service to the House of Delegates (1977),* 42 COM. MED. 3, 184 (Mar. 1978).
22. Andreoli, *supra* note 6, at 60–61.
23. Andrews & Yankauer, *The Pediatric Nurse Practitioner: I. Growth of the Concept,* 71 AM. J. NURS. 504, 506 (1971).
24. For a more detailed discussion of malpractice and its elements, *see* Chapter XII.
25. Note, *A Revolution in White—New Approaches in Treating Nurses as Professionals,* 30 VAND. L. REV. 846–49 (1977). *And see* Wilmington Gen. Hosp. v. Manlove, 54 Del. 15, 174 A.2d 135 (1961).
26. PROBLEMS IN HEALTH LAW 80 (D. Warren, ed., 3d ed.; Germantown, Md.: Aspen, 1978).
27. For a further discussion of the *respondeat superior* doctrine, *see* Chapter XII.
28. Ashley v. Nyack Hosp., 412 N.Y.S.2d 388 (N.Y. App. Div. 1979).
29. American Nurses' Association, Code for Nurses with Interpretive Statements (1976). Section 3: "The Nurse Acts to Safeguard the Client and the Public When Health Care and

Safety Are Affected by Incompetent, Unethical, or Illegal Practice of Any Person." Subsection 3.1, "The Role of Advocate," provides as follows:

> The nurse's primary commitment is to the client's care and safety. Hence, in the role of client advocate, the nurse must be alert to and take appropriate action regarding any instances of incompetent, unethical, or illegal practice(s) by any member of the health care team or . . . system. . . .

And see Greenlaw, *Reporting Incompetent Colleagues*, 1(2) NURSING LAW AND ETHICS 4 (Feb. 1980).

30. Darling v. Charleston Community Mem. Hosp., 33 Ill. 2d 326, 211 N.E.2d 253 (1965).

31. 211 N.E.2d at 258.

32. Utter v. United Hosp. Center, 236 S.E.2d 213 (1977). *See* Malone v. Longo, 463 F. Supp. 139 (E.D.N.Y. 1979) for a case discussing the responsibility of a nurse to report the incompetence or negligence of another nurse.

33. ANA Code, *supra* note 29, Section 3.2. Section 3.3, "Follow-up Action," provides additional guidance:

> When incompetent, unethical, or illegal practice . . . is not corrected within the employment setting and continues to jeopardize clients' care and safety, additional steps need to be taken. The problem should be reported to other appropriate professional organizations or the legally constituted bodies concerned with licensing of specific categories of health workers or professional practitioners.

34. *See Id.*, Section 6.5, "Accepting Responsibility":

> If the nurse does not feel personally competent or adequately prepared to carry out a specific function, the nurse has the right and responsibility to refuse. . . .

35. Hershey, *Physician Reaction to Quality of Care Assessments by Nurses*, HOSP. MED. STAFF, July 1976, at 9.

36. Other suggestions as to procedures that might be implemented to facilitate such nurse input are made by Hershey, *supra* note 35, at 10–11. On the issue of defamation see Greenlaw, *Reporting Incompetent Colleagues II: "Will I Be Sued for Defamation?"* 1(5) NURSING LAW & ETHICS 5 (1980), discussing Malone v. Longo, 463 F. Supp. 139 (E.D.N.Y. 1979).

37. Tuma v. Idaho Board of Nursing, 593 P.2d 711 (Utah 1979).

38. *Id.* at 717. *And see* Greenlaw, *Responding to Patients' Re-*

quests for Information, 1(4) NURSING LAW & ETHICS 6 (April 1980). *See also* Misericordia Hosp. Med. Center v. NLRB 623 F.2d 808 GdCtr. 1980), discussed in Greenlaw, *Employer Retaliation: The Myth and the Reality*, 2(1) Nursing Law & Ethics 7 (Jan. 1981) (employee reinstated who had been terminated for providing information to JCAH survey team).

39. *See* Su v. Perkins, 211 S.E.2d 421 (1974) (discussion of nurse's negligent administration of medication).

40. St. Paul Insurance Company, Preventive Practices to Avoid Nurses' Negligence Claims (1978). See *How to Avoid Liability in Administering Drugs*, MALPRACTICE DIGEST, July–Aug. 1978, at 1.5, *and* Rollins, *What Nurses Should Know about Administering "New Drugs,"* 1(6) NURSING LAW & ETHICS 1 (June–July 1980).

41. For further discussion of legal issues regarding drugs, *see* Chapter VI.

42. Pavalon & Robin, *Damage Suits Based on Nursing Malpractice*, 57 ILL. BAR J. 286 (1968).

43. For a general discussion of malpractice insurance, *see* Chapter XII.

44. *See* E. HOYT, LAW OF HOSPITAL AND NURSE (1958).

45. Gouge, *Cause for Concern—The Nurse's Potential for Legal Liability*, MALPRACTICE DIGEST, July-Aug. 1978, at 3.

III

Allied Health Professionals
and the Law

The rise of the hospital in the nineteenth century brought about specialization and a division of labor. A system of care based on the team approach, which required an ever-increasing number of trained and experienced hospital workers, was developed.

For example, at the Presbyterian Hospital in New York, a special diet kitchen opened in 1892. In 1901 an X-ray and photographic department was opened, and expanded in 1907 to include its first nonphysician X-ray technician. The hospital hired its first laboratory assistant in 1910. In 1912, a New York Hospital opened a surgical pathological laboratory and a medical records room.[1] A change took place in the duties of hospital workers, with dieticians, social workers, and laboratory, X-ray, and physical therapy technicians taking their place alongside physicians in the provision of health care, with some providing their services outside of the hospital setting.

This chapter will discuss the still developing and changing category of allied health care providers, and analyze the legal rights and responsibilities of its member groups.

Who is an "allied health care provider"?

The term "allied health care provider" includes all professional, technical, and supportive workers in the fields of patient care, community health, public health, environmental health, and related health research. Their activities support, complement, or supplement the professional functions of practitioners and administrators.[2] They range from the technician with six weeks of on-the-job training to the person with a doctoral degree or beyond.[3] Estimates of the number of specialties in the allied health field range from one hundred to over two hundred.[4] Workers in this field can be divided into those who act autonomously—including optometrists, physical therapists, and speech pathologists/audiologists—and those who work under supervision, such as X-ray technologists, medical technologists, dental hygienists, respiratory therapists, occupational therapists, dieticians, physicians' assistants, medical assistants, and operating room technicians.

How are allied health care providers regulated?

There are various mandatory and voluntary means for regulating these workers. Regulation can take the form of licensure by a state, certification by professional or technical societies, recognition of graduates of approved programs of education or training, or simple registration.

Registration is the most limited use of the state's regulatory powers, whereby the state gives a list of providers to potential users. There are differing views as to the appropriate format for a system of registration. One method requires individuals to list their names in the official register if they engage in certain activities, although there is no power to deny individuals the right to engage in those activities if they are not willing to be listed.[5] Others make registration contingent upon meeting certain requirements, such as level of education, payment of fee, etc., but do not give the state the power to punish unregistered workers unless they claim to be registered.[6]

In *certification,* the appropriate organization warrants that the person certified has attained a certain level of knowledge and skill. Certification provides the public with an *a priori* judgment of competence, but does not prohibit practice by those who have not been certified.[7]

Certification is the major form of regulation. The Department of Health and Human Services (HHS) has listed twenty-eight nongovernmental academies, associations, boards, and registries that certify allied health personnel.[8] Some of these are of quite long standing; the American Occupational Therapy Association, for instance, was founded in 1917.[9] Professional organizations, especially those of technologists and technicians, regulate their professions by specifying minimum educational standards, surveying and accrediting educational programs, publishing lists of accredited programs, and certifying personnel who meet certain requirements of education and competency.[10]

Licensure is by far the strongest form of regulation. If an occupation is subject to licensing, an individual must obtain a license from a recognized authority in order to engage in that occupation. Regulations governing licensing will generally specify the knowledge and skills required, as well as how this knowledge is to be obtained and demonstrated. [11] Members of several allied health professions are required by all states to have licenses—e.g., dental hygienists, physical therapists, pharmacists, optometrists.[12]

Who is liable for the negligence of an allied health care provider?

Each allied health care provider is legally responsible for his own acts of negligence.[13] However, his employer, whether hospital or individual physician, may also be liable for his negligent acts under the doctrine of *respondeat superior*. Accordingly, employers are liable for the torts of an employee as long as the employee is acting within the scope of employment.[14]

Thus, in a recent Oregon case, a hospital was found liable for injuries suffered by a patient when he collapsed during physical therapy and dislocated his recently rebuilt hip.[15] The physical therapist had allowed the plaintiff to become exhausted and fall from a table. In a Louisiana case, the hospital was held liable for its X-ray technician's negligence in failing to determine if a patient was capable of standing unaided.[16] The patient was not; she fell while X-rays were being taken, and broke her ankle.

Similarly, a physician was found liable for the negligent acts of his X-ray technician in a case where a woman, who had accompanied her son to the physician's office, was requested to hold another child's feet when an X-ray was being taken. When the technician turned on the electric current, a spark flashed from the mechanism to the woman's head, resulting in injury.

The court said that the technician was acting within the scope of her employment:

> Acts may be said to be within the scope of the serv-ant's [employee's] employment where specifically di-rected, or where they are clearly incidental to the master's [employer's] business. It is not essential that the act be specially authorized by the master. An act is within the scope of the servant's employment, where necessary to accomplish the purpose of his employ-ment, and intended for that purpose, although in ex-cess of the powers actually conferred on the servant by the master.[17]

The court went on to say that, when injury occurs while the actor is employed in the usual course and for the benefit of the employer, there is a presumption that the servant (employee) is acting within the scope of his authority. When the employee is engaged in furthering the employer's business, the latter is liable even though the former is disobeying orders.

The taking of the X-ray was found to be within the scope of the technician-servant's employment, and her implied authority included control of the patient. The technician's act of inducing another to assist in holding a patient, while not actually authorized, was nevertheless incidental to a furtherance of the physician's business, and the physician was liable for the result.

In addition to liability under *respondeat superior,* an employer may also be held responsible for allowing an employee to engage in activities for which he has inade-quate training or experience. This liability is based on the employer's independent negligence in permitting the em-ployee to undertake acts which thereafter, due to the employee's negligence, injure the patient. For example, in one case, the court decided that a jury would be warranted in finding that a physician was negligent when he allowed his assistant, who had graduated from high school and worked for two years as a nurse's aide in a hospital, to do such things as remove stitches, inject penicillin, and re-move and reapply bandages.[18] Similarly, a dentist was found responsible for allowing his dental assistant to ad-minister anesthetics, remove teeth, and suture oral tissue, procedures that only a licensed dentist could lawfully perform.[19]

May a physician ever be liable for the negligence of a hospital employee?

Yes. The "borrowed-servant" rule says that an employer is not liable for injury negligently caused by an employee or "servant" if the latter is, at the time, in the special service of another. A supervising physician, rather than the hospital, may be held liable for the employee's negligence if the employee is found to be the physician's borrowed servant or agent because, for example, she has given the employee specific instructions or otherwise exercised supervision or control. However, giving instructions to a hospital employee will not, by itself, render the physician liable for the employee's negligence in carrying out those instructions. The determining factor is the right to control and direct the means and methods of the servant's work.

Although the doctrine is being subjected to increasing judicial review, resulting in its modification or abolition in many states, it may still be applied in some cases involving allied health providers. For example, the Minnesota Supreme Court decided that it was possible for a hospital-employed X-ray technician to be the borrowed servant of a physician in a suit by a patient who was burned by the guidelight.[20]

Must an allied health care provider always follow a physician's orders?

Other than independent practitioners, hospital staff members will generally be held to have discharged their duty of reasonable care as long as they comply with orders left by the attending physician. However, circumstances arise in which no orders have been provided, or where there is good reason to question the propriety of the orders which have been given. In such cases, the staff is obligated to question these orders and, in an emergency situation, to act in contravention of them.

While most of the cases on the subject of the hospital staff's duty to follow physicians' orders involve nurses, it would seem that they would apply to any member of the hospital staff.[21] The duty to question any suspect orders is greatest for those occupations that require the greatest amount of training and involve the greatest exercise of independent judgment.

May an allied health care provider ever be held to the same standard of care as a physician?

A series of cases have held that whenever an individual performs a *medical* service, that individual will be held to the same standard of care as a doctor performing the same task. No real guidance is provided by the decisions as to what constitutes a medical service, but it appears that any task traditionally performed by physicians is medical. This makes it difficult for physicians to delegate tasks to allied health workers without having them held to the physician's standard.

One case involved a patient who was injured after fainting while on an X-ray table. The court held that the same rules concerning negligence should apply to "technicians, attendants and practitioners engaged in all kindred and related branches and fields of the medical profession." [22] The technician's duty was held to be identical to that of the radiologist.

Another case involved a non-MD medical assistant who cut a patient while removing a cast from his arm. Although the court at times seemed to confuse medical assistants with nurses, the assistant was found negligent when measured against the rules governing a physician's duty in performing this service. The court found it necessary to "consider the degree of care which would have been demanded of the doctor had he removed the cast himself in order to determine whether or not [the medical assistant] was negligent." [23]

The results of these two cases were used in an analogous case to find a university biology professor negilgent in his supervision of an experiment that required a senior student to withdraw blood from volunteers. The court said:

> The law is well settled that nurses and medical technicians who undertake to perform medical services are subject to the same rules relating to the duty of care and to liability as are physicians in the performance of professional services. . . . We believe that the same rule applies to a professor of biology in a uni-

versity who approves and undertakes to supervise a project which included the performance of a medical function.[24]

Do hospital workers have the right to a healthy workplace?

Although there are statutes that require employers to maintain a safe workplace, the hospital may argue that the employee assumed the risk of the conditions of employment. One feature in considering a hospital's liability for injuries to its employees is the fact that some of the dangers involved in hospital work may not be readily apparent. If the risks are encountered unknowingly, the hospital cannot defend itself with the assumption-of-risk defense. The Georgia Appeals Court dealt with this type of risk in a case in which a nurse's aide contracted hemolytic staphylococcus due to the hospital's negligence.[25] Although the hospital knew the danger of infection, it failed to take any precautionary measures, and the plaintiff had no knowledge of the risk of infection.

Although the hospital is not an insurer of the safety of its employees, the court said that it does have the duty to use reasonable care to protect them against the dangers of employment that might reasonably be expected to produce disease. The court recognized that the employee assumes the ordinary risks of employment. But, using the "assumption-of-skill" doctrine, the court concluded that if the employer's technical and scientific knowledge of the business involved is sufficiently superior to that of the employee, the employer has the duty to warn the employee of the dangers involved.[26]

Does the allied health provider have an independent obligation to the patient beyond his obligation to his employer?

The answer depends on the type of practitioner. It depends on the autonomy of the provider, his field of expertise, the extent of his skill, and the licensure requirements involved, among other factors.

While there is no case law specifically addressing this issue, the relationship between the allied health care provider and the patient is analogous to other types of relationships. The physician-patient relationship is thought to be based on the physician's skill, learning, and experience, and on the patient's reliance, faith, and confidence in the physician. It is a consensual relationship that requires the patient and the physician knowingly to accept each other.

The essential elements of this relationship will often be missing when dealing with an allied health care provider. Physicians themselves often have no authority to decide which member of the hospital's staff will be assigned to them. Accordingly, it could not really be said that the patient is entrusted to the care of the staff member, unless some notion of implied consent is used. Likewise, the hospital staff will generally not have any choice in accepting or refusing to care for a particular patient. Moreover, since the patient will usually pay a bill submitted by the hospital, rather than by individual staff members, another element of the relationship is missing.

The situation will presumably be different for autonomous workers, who are actually chosen by their patients and who submit bills to them, since these practitioners have the capacity to enter into a relationship with a patient independent of any physician.

Allied health care providers expose themselves to added potential liability by becoming more directly involved with the patient than required by their position. Although some providers are placed under a duty to refer patients for care to other health care providers under appropriate circumstances, this duty does not seem applicable to all occupations. Optometrists and opticians have an affirmative duty to refer patients in whom they discover pathological conditions.[27] Social workers also have a duty to refer patients whose problems are outside of their area of expertise.[28] However, less highly trained workers would not be expected to recognize unusual conditions. Of course, the less training a worker has, the more closely she should be supervised by someone expected to recognize a condition requiring additional treatment.

Some obligations to patients, however, are common to all health care providers. These include the necessity to obtain informed consent from the patient before performing an invasive procedure, the obligation to answer patient questions truthfully, and the responsibility to keep confidential information obtained from the patient during the course of the relationship.

What is a physician assistant?

The job category of the physician assistant (PA), sometimes referred to as a physician's extender, is created on the premise that many tasks previously performed only by physicians can be performed equally well by specially-trained professionals. Reports of the AMA, AHA (American Hospital Association), and HHS recommended that the states amend their medical practice acts to codify the physician's right to delegate medical tasks to various types of health personnel who work under his "supervision and control." [29] PAs perform such tasks as interviewing patients, taking medical histories, and doing routine physical examinations. They perform or assist in routine laboratory studies, such as drawing blood, doing urinalysis, or recording electrocardiograms. Changing dressings, treating burns or common ailments, suturing and caring for cuts and wounds, making patient rounds in the hospital, and administering intravenous fluids are other aspects of their work. They may specialize in orthopedics, surgery, urology, pathology, or child health, or may master life support systems and medical emergency technology.[30]

There are no nationwide uniform provisions governing physician assistants. Forty-four states have varying requirements applicable to PAs. PAs are usually totally under the control of the medical licensure board. The state laws providing for the use of PAs have been of two types: general delegatory statutes and regulatory authority statutes.

The general delegatory statutes amend the state medical practice act and permit a PA to perform medical acts under the supervision of a physician. The definition of required training and qualifications for a PA is left to the individual physician who employs him, as is the definition of a PA function. This type of PA statute has been passed in a number of states, including Colorado and Connecticut.[31]

Regulatory authority statutes authorize a specific organizational entity, usually the state board of medical examiners, to regulate the activities of PAs and permit them to work under the direct supervision of physicians. These statutes may be passed as amendments to the medical practice acts, and the regulated activities may be defined by law or by the board through regulations. This type of PA legislation has been adopted by most of the states that have dealt with the issue, including California and New York.[32]

The regulatory authority statutes specify the qualifications and scope of functions for PAs, including procedures for certifying both the physician assistant and the supervising physician. Most of the laws specify minimum ages and the length and type of training, and provide for equivalency and proficiency testing to substitute experience for educational requirements.

Physicians are limited by most state laws to supervising no more than one or two PAs.[33] The apparent purpose is to ensure effective supervision of their performance. All the statutes call for some degree of "supervision and control" of the PA by the physician, although their terminology is subject to varying interpretations. This supervision can occur on at least three levels: over-the-shoulder, on-the-premises, or remote with regular monitoring and review. Typically, the statutes do not define supervision and control, leaving this question to be resolved by the courts on a case-by-case basis.[34]

Should a physician assistant inform the patient that he is a PA?

Yes. The patient must be aware that he is being treated or examined by a PA rather than by a physician. A patient who consents to treatment by a PA without notice of the PA's status may be deemed not to have consented and, therefore, may be entitled to sue for lack of informed consent.

The type of consent necessary is uncertain. PAs might wear distinctive badges signifying their status, as is required by regulation in California and Massachusetts, or require patients to sign consent forms. The notice obligation could also be satisfied by communicating it orally to the patient as part of the informed consent process.[35] Generally the obligation to obtain informed consent rests with the physician. However, in situations in which a PA functions relatively independently of a physician, the duty to obtain informed consent would be his.

What is the standard of care a physician assistant must meet?

One approach to this question is to hold the PA to the standard of care of the average PA under the same or similar circumstances. Courts may, however, hold the PA to the same standard of care as the physician. There is no general agreement as to which standard of care is most feasible.

One side argues that the PA is not licensed, as are other health care professionals, such as nurses. Although nurses have a standard of care separate from that of a physician, they do not perform the same functions as physicians. The PA is viewed as an extension of the physician, thus making it reasonable to hold her to the same standard of care. This theory has recently been recognized by the Supreme Court of the State of Washington, which held that PAs could issue prescriptions for medications since, unlike nurses, they act as agents of physicians rather than independent practitioners.[36]

Does a physician assistant have a duty to refer patients to the supervising physician or other practitioners?

Since the PA will often see the patient first, she has the responsibility of deciding when to refer the patient to the physician. Proper referral is important in achieving quality health care, and failure of the PA to refer a patient may, under certain circumstances, result in liability for negligence. It is unclear whether the standard for determining the duty to refer will be that of the average physician or of the average PA.

Who is responsible for the negligence of a physician assistant?

The PA is, of course, liable for his own negligent acts. The physician may also occur liability for the PA's negligent acts. This liability is based on the doctrine of *respondeat superior,* which holds the physician liable for the wrongful acts of her employee, even if the physician's conduct is without fault.[37] Before there can be any liability, an employer-employee relationship must exist between the physician and her assistant, and the negligent act of the employee must have occurred within the scope of his employment. The physician may also be liable for her own

independent negligence if she does not use due care in the
selection of a PA, or if she delegates a task to the PA
which she knew or should have known was beyond his
ability. Overall, however, the emergence of the PA does
not pose unique legal problems for the physician, but
merely parallels the issues raised by the use of nurses and
other allied health care personnel.

What is the standard of care to which a physicial therapist will be held?

Physical therapists plan and administer physical treatment for patients referred by a physician in order to re-
store bodily functions, relieve pain, and prevent disability
following disease, injury, or loss of a body part. In addition to manipulatory exercises prescribed for rehabilitation, physical therapy involves the use of physical agents
such as sound, heat, and light in the treatment of injury
and disease.[38]

Registered physical therapists have generally received
formal training and have passed examinations given by
either state or national accreditation boards.[39] All states require therapists to be licensed, and therapists must comply
with the legal requirements where they practice. Both the
AMA's Committee on Allied Health Education and Accreditation, and the American Physical Therapy Association accredit educational programs in physical therapy.

There are currently about 25,000 physical therapists in
the United States. They work in varied settings, including
hospitals, rehabilitation centers, nursing homes, home-
health agencies, and private practice. In 1973, one-fourth
of all physical therapists were in private practice and
worked on a contract basis with various institutions and
agencies.[40]

The appropriate standard of care requires that the therapist, whether practicing in a hospital or independently,
work under a physician's orders and guidance. This allows
the therapist more independence than would at first appear: the fact is that the prescribing physician often does
not know the technicalities of the necessary treatment, and
may only specify the desired result. Thus the therapist is
effectively independent in determining the proper methods
of treatment and is responsible for their correct application.[41]

In determining liability for injuries sustained by a patient while undergoing physical therapy, the rules are the ones generally applicable in medical malpractice cases; the standard is that of a reasonably prudent physical therapist.

The Kentucky Court of Appeals dealt with a case involving injuries received during the administration of physical therapy, in which a patient had gone to the rehabilitation center for treatment to permit her to use an artificial leg.[42] She was given an initial examination by a physician. In the course of treatment by a therapist, her hip was fractured.

The court found that, although the physical therapist involved had completed the formal training required, she was not licensed at the time of the injury. However, this fact was determined to have no bearing on the therapist's negligence. In addition, it was not known whether or not the physician fully explained the required procedure to the therapist. The court indicated that, if he had failed to do so, the jury could find him liable, but this would not eliminate the independent liability of the therapist.

Does a social worker need a license to practice?

Social work has been defined as "service and action to affect changes in human behavior, a person or person's emotional responses, and the social conditions of individuals, families, groups, organizations, and communities, which are influenced by the interaction of social, cultural, political, and economic systems."[43] Social workers in the health field, whether they work in a hospital, nursing home, out-patient clinic, or other health setting, are responsible for helping patients and families to cope with problems resulting from illness, recovery, and rehabilitation. There are no standard work activities for social workers, since their duties vary with the places they work. Three areas of specialization within the profession are medical social work, psychiatric social work, and clinical social work.

Training for social work has existed on all levels, from on-the-job training for community-oriented paraprofessionals to graduate studies in accredited social work schools. At present, there are twenty-one states with requirements for either licensing or registration of social workers. Regulation takes one of three forms. The first type is a multilevel licensing act that classifies social workers according to their professional training and competence.[44] In general, such legislation requires a minimum of a bachelor's degree for licensure, but higher levels have greater educational and practice requirements. A second type of regulatory act licenses only private practitioners, exempting everyone else from its provisions.[45] A third method of regulating is to certify or register social workers rather than to license them.[46] The effect of a certification or registration statute is to register social workers who wish state recognition of their position, but such a statute does not prohibit those who don't from practicing.

Is a medical social worker an independent practitioner?

Much has been written about how ill-defined the role of a social worker is in a health care setting. Only since the formation of the National Association of Social Workers in 1955 has social work come into clear focus as a profession.[47] Attempts at providing a definition stress that medical social work is greatly influenced by the development of the hospital as the major vehicle for the delivery of health care. Yet recent statistics indicate that only half of the general hospitals in the United States employ social workers.[48] The Joint Commission on Accreditation of Hospitals did not require hospitals to have social service departments until 1971. Unfortunately, hospital-based social workers are still not regarded as full-fledged members of the "medical team." [49]

It appears that the objectives and methods of the social worker often lead to conflict with other professionals in the hospital. Many physicians resent what they view as interference by social workers with the management of their patients. It has been noted that, as a secondary professional service within the hospital, social work must always be related to the primary requirements of medical treatment, so the physician must have dominant authority. "The social worker must function within an authority system that places his profession in a subordinate position and forces it to carve out for itself whatever professional responsibilities it assumes. And when it does assume certain responsibilities, it often lacks the recognized authority to carry out those activities adequately." [50]

The traditional assumption is that the social worker is an "assistant" to the physician, who is in charge of the patient. Although many social workers accept this situation, changes are taking place. The changes can in part be attributed to the increasing sophistication of social workers, in terms of both their knowledge and their politics, making them less willing to take orders from physicians. Partly responsible, too, is the growing disillusionment with the medical establishment and its increasing costs.[51] In line with these changes, the Internal Revenue Service now allows the cost of psychotherapy performed by social workers to be deducted on tax returns as a medical expense.

The trend is to consider social workers as independent professionals. Because of this, insurance companies are urging social workers to purchase their own professional liability coverage, even though there are no reported cases of malpractice actions against social workers.[52] Areas of potential liability for social workers include treatment without informed consent, failure to treat according to the standards of the profession, and failure to consult with or refer to a specialist if necessary.

When are pharmacists liable for malpractice?

In one sense, pharmacists are not truly autonomous in that they generally carry out the instructions of physicians or other health care providers, rather than perform their own diagnoses and formulate their own treatment plans. However, they are autonomous in the sense that they do not work under direct supervision. An emerging field is that of the self-employed consultant pharmacist. This is a broadening of the traditional professional role, as the pharmacist helps to prescribe medication, rather than merely dispense it.[53]

There are currently about 120,000 pharmacists in the United States. The actual duties of pharmacists depend largely on the type of establishment in which they are employed. The great majority of pharmacists work in different types of community pharmacies, and a growing number are employed by hospitals.

There are two professional degrees awarded in pharmacy, the bachelor of science and the doctor of pharmacy. All states, except one, require graduation from an accredited school of pharmacy, which involves about five years of study beyond high school. Almost all states additionally require an internship. All states have laws on the licensing and registration of pharmacists.

As with all other health care providers, pharmacists have always been subject to lawsuits for malpractice.[54] A pharmacist who does not act with "due care" and who, as a result, injures a patient, would be liable for money damages. Pharmacists should not dispense a drug different from the one prescribed, should dispense the dosage prescribed, in the form prescribed, and place the proper directions for use on the container. It should come as no surprise that a pharmacist was successfully sued when he dispensed a tranquilizer instead of the prescribed birth-control pills, which resulted in an unwanted pregnancy,[55] or another, when he compounded a prescription with excessive quantities of caustic drugs that resulted in severe facial burns for the user.[56]

What are the major legal issues faced by optometry?

The practice of optometry is as old as the existence of eyeglasses, but has only become a licensed specialty in the United States during this century. The Doctor of Optometry (OD) degree generally requires two years of pre-optometric courses in basic sciences, and four years in a school of optometry. The practice of optometry, like that of many other nonphysician health care providers, has never been wholly satisfactory, and their role in the examination of eye conditions continues to increase.

The major source of controversy is that as primary sources of eye care, both optometrists and ophthalmologists perform similar basic outpatient services for many patients—even though their methods vary. This has led to significant friction between these two groups, with ophthalmologists—who are physicians with additional specialty training—often arguing that the role of optometrists should be limited instead of expanded. For example, approximately half of the states now have statutes that permit optometrists to use drugs for *diagnostic* purposes. Even though these statutes usually require optometrists to pass courses in general and ocular pharmacology as a prerequisite for using such drugs, many opthalmological organizations have opposed such laws on the basis that optometrists are not qualified to use these drugs or to treat potential adverse reactions they might produce.[57]

Optometrists make a determined effort to recognize disease and to refer the patient for medical attention.[58] This is perfectly appropriate, and it is the area of referral that probably presents the optometrists with most of his potential malpractice liability. In one case from Alaska, for example, an optometrist examined a four-year-old child whose mother had noticed his eyes crossing. The optometrist noted what he described as an "inactive vitreous hemorrhage" at the examination, and prescribed eyeglasses. The child's condition did not improve, and even though he was finally referred to an ophthalmologist six months later, his eye had to be removed. In the trial, the dean of the optometrist's school testified that the optometrist had acted properly. Nevertheless, the court found that he was negligent in failing to make an immediate referral because diagnosis was a medical, not an optometric act. In the court's words, "the important consideration is that the optometrist be able to see and identify the hemorrhage. It then becomes his responsibility to refer the patient to a medical doctor for diagnosis and treatment." [59] The court states that referral should be "immediate." While this case can be criticized, it indicates that when allied health care professionals take on increased responsibilities, or attempt to function in roles traditionally reserved for physicians, courts will either require them to refer problem cases immediately, or hold them to the standard of a physician in their care and management of patients.

What is the legal liability of respiratory therapists and technicians?

These fields are paradigmatic of technological advances in medicine. There was no real function for these allied health personnel until the invention and widespread use of mechanical respirators. Since the late 1950s, however, these groups have expanded rapidly and are seen in almost all hospitals. Four levels are generally recognized:

1. Respiratory Therapist: a graduate of a program designed to prepare him for the examination of the American Registry of Respiratory Therapists, a college and hospital affiliation including a BS or an AS degree.

2. Registered Respiratory Therapist: one who has passed the examination.
3. Respiratory Therapy Technician: a graduate of a one- or two-year hospital-based program, often in association with a community college, that is designed to prepare him for the examination of the Technician Certification Board.
4. Certified Respiratory Therapy Technician: a person who has passed the examination.

The duties of a respiratory therapist vary greatly from rural hospitals to large urban teaching hospitals. At one time women were excluded from the job category because (in the words of one chief therapist of a large active department), "girls aren't strong enough to push tanks."

For the most part, departments have responsibility for:

1. Emergency resuscitation (CPR)
2. Continuous mechanical ventilation and the weaning of patients from ventilators
3. Supervision of the care of respiratory and cardiac patients in ICU's and CCU's
4. Emergency Room coverage
5. Postoperative care
6. Chest PT, ambulation therapy, and cardiac and respiratory rehabilitation
7. Monitoring of oxygen and humidity therapy
8. Maintenance of equipment with the responsibility for quality control and the enforcement of safety regulations involved with its use
9. Teaching of non-respiratory personnel as to the most efficient use of respiratory care and consultation
10. Inservice education within the RT department
11. Clinical rounds to review and reassess the care received by patients on the service

Duties may also include intubating patients, drawing of arterial blood gases, laboratory analysis, and bedside and pulmonary/function laboratory testing.

The future of RT will probably include more in the area of patient teaching, outpatient department and home care, and the expansion of respiratory and cardiac rehabilitation programs.

Their liability will be based on the same standards as that of other allied health care professionals. In areas within their training and job descriptions, they will be held to the standard of a qualified respiratory therapist (or whatever their title is) under the same or similar conditions. In areas where they are arguably practicing medicine, they may be held to the standard of a physician.[60]

Who is responsible for the actions of an X-ray technician?

X-ray technicians, or radiologic technologists, follow the instruction of a physician in taking X-ray films of parts of the human body for use in diagnosis of medical problems. They are responsible for the care and safety of patients who are having X-rays taken. There are presently about 80,000 X-ray technicians working in hospitals, clinics, physicians' offices, private medical laboratories, and clinics, among other locations. A high-school diploma is required for entry into a formal educational program in X-ray technology. Professional education takes two years and may be provided by certificate programs in hospitals or associate and bachelor's degree programs in colleges and universities. Certification for X-ray technicians is voluntary. New York, New Jersey, and California have state certification programs, and a number of other states are also establishing requirements.

In general, X-ray technicians exercise little independent judgment or control. Hospitals that employ X-ray technicians are open to liability for the technician's negligence under the doctrine of *respondeat superior*. For example, in one case a patient was given Dramamine before she was taken to the X-ray room. While the technician was taking the X-rays, the patient fell from the table. The hospital was found liable for injuries sustained in her fall.[61]

However, it is possible that, under certain circumstances, the X-ray technician could be found to be the "borrowed servant" of the physician in charge of the patient's care, so that he, as opposed to the hospital, would be responsible for the technician's negligence. For example, in a case discussed earlier, a patient was burned upon contact with a guidelight.[62] The X-ray machine to which it was attached was operated by an X-ray technician in the employ of the hospital. The court decided that sufficient evidence of direction and control by the physician had been presented to make it possible to decide that the X-ray technician was a borrowed servant. The following evidence on this point was presented: the physician told the technician when and where to take X-rays, actually assisting in aligning the machine; the technician would not leave the operating room until dismissed by the physician; and the technician considered the physician to be her "boss" while she was in the operating room.

An interesting case involved a suit for breach of an employment contract by a discharged X-ray technician. The technician claimed that the termination was in retaliation for her refusal to perform catheterizations, stating that she was not properly trained to perform such procedures and that only a licensed physician or nurse could legally do so. The court held that "the public policy of the State of New Jersey may require that this State adopt the rule . . . that an employment at will may not be terminated by an employer in retaliation for an employee's refusal to perform an illegal act." [63]

Do allied health professionals need their own malpractice insurance?

Autonomous health care providers have a more serious malpractice problem than do supervised health care workers, as evidenced by the difference in insurance rates.[64] In 1972, it was found that, except for psychologists and speech pathologists, insurance rates were higher for self-employed autonomous practitioners than for providers employed by others.[65] Pharmacists practicing only in hospitals were considered to be slightly better insurance risks than those who practiced in the community.

In spite of the low frequency of claims against supervised health care personnel, their professional associations are concerned about malpractice insurance. Many have sponsored or endorsed malpractice insurance programs for their members. Most supervised health care personnel are employees rather than self-employed practitioners. Generally, they work in hospitals, clinics, or offices of autonomous health care providers. Malpractice actions arising out of their alleged negligence often involve their employees under the doctrine of *respondeat superior*. Thus, most employers insure themselves for liability for negligence committed by their employees. Of course, this does not abolish the individual liability of the supervised employee.[66] Such employees may also be sued by an employer for reimbursement of any financial loss suffered by the employer on the employee's account.

The insurance industry makes malpractice coverage available to both physician assistants and their physician employers. Although existing case law indicates that the normal physician's malpractice insurance policy does not protect the physician against vicarious liability for his PA's acts, an endorsement is available, providing increased coverage at a cost approximating that of another office nurse. The PA is generally charged half the premium charged the employer, with the exact amount depending on the specialty involved. The premiums paid by PAs are somewhat higher than those for other allied health personnel, perhaps because the PA performs more tasks with less supervision than other workers. The newness of the PA in the work force is also a factor.

NOTES

1. *Working in Hospitals: Then and Now,* 1199 NEWS, Sept. 1976, at 25.
2. Yerby, *Regulation of Health Manpower,* in INSTITUTE OF MEDICINE, CONTROLS ON HEALTH CARE 96 (1974).
3. *See* R. PURTILO, THE ALLIED HEALTH PROFESSIONAL AND THE PATIENT (Philadelphia: Saunders, 1973).
4. Yerby, *supra* note 2.
5. Carlson, *Health Manpower Licensing,* 35 LAW & CONT. PROB. 849, 867 (1970).
6. Hardcastle, *Public Regulation of Social Work,* 22 SOCIAL WORK 14, 15 (Jan. 1977).
7. Carlson, *supra* note 5; Hardcastle, *supra* note 6, at 16.
8. Yerby, *supra* note 2, at 98.
9. *Id.*
10. Roemer, *Licensing and Regulation of Medical and Medical-Related Practitioners in Health Service Teams,* 9 MED. CARE 42 (1971).
11. Hardcastle, *supra* note 6, at 16.
12. Analysis of 1973 State Health Manpower Licensure, Legislation Appendix B (Health Law Center, Aug. 1974).

13. The same general principles of negligence apply to allied health care providers as apply to all other individuals. For a discussion of these general principles, *see* Chapter XII.

14. D. WARREN, PROBLEMS IN HOSPITAL LAW 106 (3d ed.; Germantown, Md.: Aspen, 1978). For a general discussion of *respondeat superior,* see Chapter II.

15. Forsyth v. Sisters of Charity of Providence, 39 Or. App. 851, 593 P.2d 1270 (1979).

16. Albritton v. Bossier City Hosp. Comm'n, 271 So.2d 353 (La. App. 1972).

17. Kelley v. Yount, 12 A.2d 579 (1940). *See* Gray v. McLaughlin, 179 S.W.2d 686 (1944).

18. Delaney v. Rosenthall, 196 N.E.2d 878 (1964).

19. State Dental Council and Examining Board v. Pollock, 318 A.2d 910 (Pa. Sup. Ct., 1974). *See also* Board of Gov. of the Reg. Dentists of Okla. v. Burk, 551 P.2d 1122 (Okla. 1976); Illinois State Dental Soc'y v. Iole, 312 N.E.2d 328 (Ill. App. Ct. 1974).

20. Synnott v. Midway Hosp., 178 N.W.2d 211 (Minn. 1970); *see* Miller v. Hood, 536 S.E.2d 278 (1976); Benardi v. Community Hosp. Ass'n, 443 P.2d 708 (1968); Monk v. Doctors Hosp., 403 F.2d 588 (1968); Schwarz, *The Allied Health Professions and Malpractice Liability,* in NEW DEVELOPMENTS IN LAW/MEDICINE 15–17 (Ann Arbor, Mich.: Institute of Continuing Legal Education, 1974).

21. *E.g.,* Toth v. Community Hosp. at Glen Cove, 22 N.Y.2d 255, 239 N.E.2d 368 (1968).

22. Favalora v. Aetna Cas. & Sur. Co., 144 So.2d 544 (La. App. 1962).

23. Thompson v. Brent, 245 So.2d 751 (La. App. 1971).

24. Butler v. Louisiana State Board of Educ. 331 So.2d 192 (La. App. 1976).

25. Thigpen v. Executive Comm. of the Baptist Convention, 114 Ga. App. 839, 152 S.E.2d 920 (1966).

26. For a discussion of the impact of the Occupational Safety and Act in this area, *see* Chapter XV.

27. Liability of Optometrist or Optician for Malpractice, 51 A.L.R.3d 1273, §2(a).

28. Green & Cox, *Social Work and Malpractice,* 23 SOC. WORK 102 (1978).

29. Licensure of Health Occupations (Dec. 1970) (Report of the AMA Council on Health Manpower adopted by the House of Delegates); American Hospital Association, Statement on Licensure of Health Care Personnel (Nov. 1970)

(adopted by Board of Governors); HEW Report: Report of the National Advisory Commission on Health Manpower (1967).

30. *See* Scanlon, *The Malpractice Aspects of Emergency Care by Non-Physicians,* 12 GONZ. L. REV. 676 (1977).

31. COLO. REV. STAT. ANN. §12–36–106(3)(1); CONN. GEN. STAT. ANN. §20–9.

32. CAL. BUS. & PROF. CODE §2510–22; N.Y. EDUC. LAW §6530–36 (McKinney) and N.Y. PUB. HEALTH LAW §3700–02 (McKinney).

33. Kissam, *Physician's Assistant and Nurse Practitioner Laws: A Study of Health Law Reform,* 24 U. KAN. L. REV. 57 (1975).

34. *See* Sadler & Sadler, *Recent Developments in the Law Relating to the Physician's Assistant,* 24 VAND. L. REV. 1193, 1200 (1971).

35. *See* Note, *Physicians and Surgeons—The Expanding Role of the Physician's Assistant,* 76 W. VA. L. REV. 162, 171.

36. Washington State Nurses' Ass'n v. Board of Med. Examiners, 605 P.2d 1269 (Wash. 1980). For a fuller discussion of this case, *see* Chapter II.

37. For a more detailed discussion of the *respondeat superior* doctrine, *see* Chapter II.

38. Malpractice: Physical Therapy, 53 A.L.R.3d 1250, §2(b).

39. Health Careers Guidebook, U.S. Dept. of Labor & Dept. of HEW, No. 0–275–583 (1979) at 182. *See* Attorney General Opinion, No. 80–079, Ohio, Nov. 26, 1980.

40. Shear, *The Malpractice Problem for Non-Physician Health-Care Professionals,* Report of the Secretary's Commission on Medical Malpractice, Appendix DHEW No. OS 73–89, Dept. of HEW (1973) at 646.

41. Note, *Regulation of Health Personnel in Iowa,* 57 IOWA L. REV. 1004, 1131 (1972).

42. Meiman v. Rehabilitation Center, Inc., 444 S.W.2d 78 (Ken. Ct. App. 1969). *See* Leidy v. Deseret Enterprises, 381 A.2d 164 (Penn. Sup. Ct. 1977).

43. Model Bill, National Association of Social Workers, *cited in* Kern, *State Regulation of Social Work,* 10 VALPARAISO U.L. REV. 261, 264 (1976).

44. *E.g.,* MICH. STAT. ANN. §§18.365(1) *et seq.* (1980 Supp.).

45. *E.g.,* LA. REV. STAT. ANN. §37:2718.

46. *E.g.,* CAL. BUS. & PROF. CODE §9020–21.

47. Green & Cox, *Social Work and Malpractice,* 23 SOC. WORK 101 (Mar. 1978).

48. *Hospital Social Work: Consumers' Critiques,* HEALTH PER-SPECTIVES, Nov./Dec. 1976, at 2.

49. Rudolph, *New Approaches to Educating Social Work Professionals for Administrative Roles in a National Health System,* 3 SOC. WORK IN HEALTH CARE 431, 434 (1978).

50. Olsen & Olsen, *Role Expectations for Social Workers in Medical Settings,* 12 SOC. WORK 70, 70–71 (July, 1967).

51. Falck, *Social Work in Health Settings,* 3 SOC. WORK IN HEALTH CARE 395, 396 (1978).

52. Green & Cox, *supra* note 47, at 100–101. For a general discussion of the elements of malpractice, *see* Chapter XII.

53. Shear, *supra* note 40, at 649.

54. The standards set out in Chapter XII on malpractice also pertain to pharmacists. *See also* Chapter VI for further discussion of the legal issues involving drugs.

55. Troppi v. Scarf, 31 Minn. App. 240, 187 N.W.2d 511 (1971).

56. Adams v. American Druggist Ins. Co., 245 So.2d 808.

57. The fight over whether or not optometrists should be allowed to use drugs for treatment is even more bitter—only two states (West Virginia and North Carolina) currently permit it, and three (Alabama, Connecticut, and Washington) specifically prohibit it. *And see* Mansberg, *The Case of the 1,600 Eyes,* OPTOMETRIC MANAGEMENT 33 (June, 1977).

58. M. HIRSCH & R. WICK, THE OPTOMETRIC PROFESSION (New York: Chilton Book Co., 1968) at 299.

59. Steele v. United States, 463 F. Supp. 321, 325 (D. Alaska 1978). Most other cases involving optometrists have been on the issues of advertising and using trade names (*e.g.,* Friedman v. Rogers, 440 U.S. 1 [1979]); getting reimbursed under Medicare for their services (*e.g.,* Pushkin v. Califano, 600 F.2d 486 [5th Cir. 1979]); and revocation of license (Dixon v. State Board of Optometric Examiners, 565 P.2d 960 [Colo. 1977]) (license properly revoked for unlawfully permitting unlicensed employees to practice optometry). As optometrists extend their practice into other areas, their liability will, of course, increase. *See, e.g.,* Pierce & Kleinstein, *Screening for Hypertension by Optometrists,* 67 AJPH 977 (Oct. 1977).

60. *See* B.A. Shapiro, R.A. Harrison, & C.A. Trout, Clinical Applications of Respiratory Care, (Chicago: Year Book Medical Publishers, Inc., 1975) and S. McPherson, R.R.T.,

Respiratory Therapy Equipment. (St. Louis: C.V. Mosby Co. 1977).

61. McNight v. St. Francis Hosp. & School of Nursing, 585 P.2d 984 (Kan. 1978).

62. Synnott v. Midway Hosp., 178 N.W.2d 211 (Minn. 1970).

63. O'Sullivan v. Mallon, 390 A.2d 149 (Sup. Ct. N.J. 1978).

64. For a general discussion of malpractice insurance, *see* Chapter XIII.

65. Shear, *supra* note 40, at 645.

66. The question of whether such employees should purchase their own malpractice insurance is analogous to the discussion of this issue in regard to nurses in Chapter II.

PART TWO

Rights in the
Provider-Patient Relationship

IV

Informed Consent and
Refusing Treatment

One of the most critical and controversial issues in the
provider-patient relationship involves consent. Recent court
actions have caused many providers to fear that the legal
system has set up burdensome and arbitrary standards for
obtaining a patient's consent to undergo medical procedures. However, the issue of consent is not a new one.
It is based in the common law enforcement of the concept
of personal autonomy and self-determination. In 1905 an
Illinois court wrote:

> Under a free government at least, the free citizen's
> first and greatest right which underlies all others—the
> right to the inviolability of his person, in other words,
> his right to himself, is the subject of universal ac-
> quiescence, and this right necessarily forbids a physi-
> cian . . . to violate without permission the bodily
> integrity of his patient by a major or capital opera-
> tion.[1]

In this chapter we explore the role of consent in the
provider-patient relationship, the uses of proxy consent,
and the right of the patient to refuse to consent to medical
procedures.

**Must a provider obtain consent before rendering medical
care?**

Yes. The requirement that patients must consent prior
to obtaining medical care historically comes from the law

71

of civil battery. Battery is an intentional, unconsented-to, touching of a person. In establishing a battery there is no requirement that the plaintiff show that the defendant intended to do harm—it need only be proven that there was intent to touch. Likewise, when a person consents to physical contact, there is no battery.[2] The modern trend, as discussed later in this chapter, is to view informed consent as a duty of health providers, the breach of which is negligence.

How is consent obtained?

Consent can be obtained orally, in writing, or can be implied by actions of the patient. In the hospital setting, consent has traditionally been obtained through the use of blanket consent forms. A typical form might read as follows:

I hereby authorize the performance of any medical or surgical procedure, either major or minor, including the administration of local or general anethesia, which may be deemed necessary by the attending physician or surgeon during my stay at this hospital.

Such a form technically meets the consent requirement. However, it is so vague and broadly worded as to give the patient almost no information about what it is he is consenting to. For this reason such forms should not be used, and indeed, are generally found legally ineffectual by the courts.[3] Because of the use of such forms, and lack of communication of more detailed information about treatment to patients, the courts have created the doctrine of informed consent.

What is the doctrine of informed consent?

The doctrine of informed consent is that prior to consenting to undergo a procedure, a patient must be told about the procedure, the risks of death and serious bodily harm inherent in it, its benefits, the alternatives to the procedure, and major problems of recuperation. The reason for this is that before one can decide to consent to a touching, one should know the implications of that touching. As one court has pointed out, the doctrine of informed consent is based on four postulates:

1. Patients are unlearned in the medical sciences.
2. A person of adult years and sound mind has the right to determine whether or not to submit to medical treatment.
3. The patient's consent, to be effective, must be an informed consent.
4. The patient has an abject dependence upon his physician for the information upon which he relies in reaching his decision.[4]

The concept of informed consent can be seen as a special form of communication between a physician and patient. The physician has the knowledge that a patient needs to make a reasoned decision to undergo a medical procedure. Only the patient can weigh the facts the physician is aware of against the patient's own subjective needs and desires. Informed consent requires communication of these facts to the patient to promote patient self-determination.

What is the scope of the duty to disclose?

In 1960, the Kansas Supreme Court decided a case involving a woman who had undergone a mastectomy for breast cancer, which was followed by a course of cobalt radiation therapy. As a result of this therapy the patient suffered injury to the skin, bone, and cartilage in her chest. Although the therapy was performed properly and without negligence, the radiologist did not inform the patient of these potential risks inherent in the procedure. The court held that the radiologist was

obligated to make a reasonable disclosure to the patient of the nature and probable consequences of the suggested or recommended cobalt irradiation treatment, and he was also obligated to make a reasonable disclosure of the dangers within his knowledge which were incident to, or possible in, the treatment he proposed to administer.[5]

The court requires the disclosure of risks that might occur when the procedure is properly performed. Neither this decision, nor more recent decisions, requires the disclosure of the risk that the procedure might be negligently performed.

A majority of jurisdictions measure the physician's duty to disclose by "good medical practice," by what a reasonable practitioner would have disclosed under similar circumstances, or by the medical custom in the community. A number of courts, however, have adopted a more patient-centered rule. In one case the U.S. Court of Appeals for the District of Columbia stated,

> The duty to disclose . . . arises from phenomena apart from medical custom and practice. The latter, we think, should no more establish the scope of duty than its existence. Any definition of scope in terms purely of a professional standard is at odds with the patient's prerogative to decide on projected therapy himself. . . . The scope of the physician communication to the patient, then, must be measured by the patient's needs, and that need is the information material to the decision. Thus the test for determining whether a particular point must be divulged is its materiality to the patient's decision: all risks potentially affecting the decision must be unmasked.[6]

Similar language has been adopted by other courts, such as this from the supreme court of Rhode Island:

> The decision as to what is or is not material is a human judgment, in our opinion, which does not necessarily require the assistance of the medical profession. The patient's right to make up his mind should not be delegated to a local medical group—many of whom have no idea as to his informational needs. The doctor-patient relationship is a one-on-one affair. What is a reasonable disclosure in one instance may not be reasonable in another. This variability negates the need of the plaintiff showing what other doctors may tell other patients.[7]

What kinds of risks must be disclosed?

Although courts talk about "material" risks, the term is rather vague. A pair of commentators have clarified the term:

The ideal rule would require that a risk be disclosed when the patient would attach importance to it, alone or in combination with others, in making his decision whether or not to consent to the treatment in question. . . . A risk is thus material when a reasonable person, in what the physician knows or should know to be the patient's position, would likely attach significance to the risk or cluster of risks in deciding whether or not to undergo the proposed therapy.[8]

Risk of death or serious bodily harm must, of course, be disclosed.[9] However, in each case the physician must consider the seriousness of the harm along with the probability that it will occur. Thus, a one-in-a-thousand risk of paralysis is obviously a greater risk than a one-in-a-hundred risk of a runny nose.

A potential disability that dramatically outweighs the potential benefits of the therapy should be disclosed. When one looks at the informed consent decisions, one sees that the cases do not deal with trivial side effects. They involve risks of paralysis, sterilization, death, deafness, disfigurement, and other serious complications.

Must a patient's consent be given in writing?

With the exception of consent to experimental procedures covered by federal regulations (see Chapter VII), consent need not be written. Some states have recently required women to sign consent forms prior to abortions. It is a common mistake to confuse the consent process with written consent forms. Consent involves a patient being informed and then giving permission to the physician to perform the recommended procedure. A consent form, on the other hand, is a document that records the consent transaction, so that if a dispute arises in the future, it can be established what the patient did, in fact, consent to. For this reason it is a good idea for the consent form to summarize what the patient has been told about the risks, benefits, and alternatives to the procedure, rather than merely stating that the patient has been informed of these aspects of his care. Consent is a process; the consent form is evidence that the process took place. In situations in which a patient gives oral consent but does not sign a consent form, the provider can acquire some protection by writing a detailed note in the patient's record describing what the patient has been told, and the patient's understanding of and consent to the procedure.

Should consent be obtained for the administration of drugs or the use of nonsurgical procedures?

The theory behind informed consent does not apply only to surgical procedures. Any time a patient is subjected to a risk that would be deemed "material," informed consent should be obtained. For example, the American Heart Association in one of its publications includes a proposed consent form for exercise testing.[10]

If a drug puts a patient at risk, the patient should be so informed. An obvious example would be telling a long-distance truck driver that a particular medication might make him drowsy. In one case, a court has recently ruled that it was a question for the jury to decide whether or not the manufacturer of Anacin had satisfactorily warned the public of the dangers of prolonged use of the drug by stating that if pain persisted for more than ten days, the user should consult a physician.[11]

A corollary to this rule requires drug companies to fully inform physicians of adverse side effects of their products.[12]

Should patients be informed of limitations of a health-care facility?

Yes, if those limitations would be material to a patient. In one case a pregnant woman contracted with a fourteen-bed clinic for obstetrical care during her pregnancy and delivery. While in labor her physician determined that a caesarian section was necessary, but the clinic did not have the facilities necessary to perform the procedure. The patient was transferred to a local hospital, where it was determined that the unborn child was dead. A federal appeals court ruled that a facility may limit the scope of services it provides as long as it informs its patients of the limitations.[13]

Are there times when a procedure may be performed without obtaining a patient's informed consent?

Yes. The patient may be treated without consent in an emergency if the patient is unable to consent.[14] If a procedure is simple and the danger remote, and commonly understood to be remote, disclosure need not be made.[15] No disclosure needs to be made when the patient asks that risks not be disclosed. However, in this situation the physician should document the request in the patient's record, and might wish to have the patient sign a document waiving his right to be informed. It is also important that the patient understand that there *are* risks to the procedure, even if he doesn't want to know just what they are; otherwise his waiver of this information might itself be uninformed. Risks that are likely to be known to the average patient, or are in fact known to the patient because of past experience with the procedure, need not be disclosed.[16] The case of incompetent patients is discussed later in this chapter.

There are also times when a disclosure need not be made because it would "unduly agitate or undermine an *unstable* patient" (emphasis added).[17] However, this "therapeutic exception" to the rule is just that—an exception. Where a doctor relies upon this exception he should document why the particular patient in question was not given certain information. This documentation should be sufficient to prove by a preponderance of the evidence that the doctor "relied upon facts which would demonstrate to a reasonable man the disclosure would have so seriously upset the patient that the patient would not have been able to dispassionately weigh the risks of refusing to undergo the recommended treatment." [18]

Is it possible for a patient to give implied consent to a procedure?

Yes. A good deal of medical practice is based on implied consent, which means that the patient gives consent through his acts and behavior. Thus, if someone stands in a line of people waiting to be vaccinated and then holds up his arm in order to be vaccinated, he has given his consent to the vaccination.[19] Because no information is communicated by the physician to the patient, a physician should rely on the implied consent doctrine only for procedures that are routine and relatively free of risk and when it can be expected that the patient understood the nature of the procedure and the risks involved. Routine physical examination and the drawing of blood samples are examples of procedures in which implied consent is sufficient.

If a surgeon discovers an unforeseeen condition during an operation, may she treat that condition if the patient has not consented to it?

When a surgeon discovers that a condition exists that requires immediate attention, an additional procedure may be performed without consent if it constitutes an emergency. Thus, when a surgeon operated on a woman he thought was suffering from a tubal pregnancy, but discovered that she was suffering from acute appendicitis, a court held that the removal of the appendix was permissible.[20]

Even when no emergency exists, a procedure may be extended when the extension is considered minor and is reasonably within the scope of the procedure originally consented to. In one case a physician performing an appendectomy discovered enlarged cysts on the patient's ovaries and punctured them. The court, holding this extension to be proper, stated: "the surgeon may extend the operation to remedy any abnormal condition in the area of the original incision whenever he, in the exercise of his sound judgment, determines that correct surgical procedure dictates and requires such an extension of the operation originally contemplated." [21]

However, if there is no emergency, no extension is permissible that would result in the loss of some organ or normal function. A surgeon who performed an ovarectomy, which he claimed was necessary due to the condition of the patient's ovaries and fallopian tubes discovered during an appendectomy, was found liable for such an extension of the operation.[22] The scope of the operation should not be extended beyond the operative field originally consented to, either. Where a patient consented to an operation on her right ear, and the surgeon decided that the left ear needed surgery also, and operated on that ear, the court held that such a procedure constituted a battery.[23]

The general theory behind the cases permitting extension of operations is that a patient consents both to having a condition treated, and to undertaking certain risks. As long as the procedure is extended in order to treat the general problem the patient sought to have treated and does not increase the risk, or cause disabilities the patient did not agree to incur, the extension will be deemed proper.

Of course, if a patient expressly forbids any extension of the operation, it should not be undertaken. If it is possible to foresee that an extension of a procedure may be necessary before the procedure is performed, it is prudent to obtain the patient's explicit consent to such an extension.

Is the consent of a family member necessary when the patient is a competent adult?

No. This is so even when the family member has a direct interest in the procedure. This question most often arises when the family member is the spouse. In one case a physician performed a successful hysterectomy on his patient. The patient's husband sued the physician, alleging that he interfered with his "marital rights." Prior to the surgery, the husband had notified the physician that he "strenuously objected" to the performance of the surgery. The court held that the consent of the husband was unnecessary and that he has no right to a "childbearing wife." [24]

Is the consent of a family member sufficient when the patient is incompetent?

There is some authority for the proposition that a spouse may consent for an incompetent patient. In one case where a psychiatric patient required electroshock treatments, and his physician believed it could be harmful to the patient to disclose the possible hazards involved in the treatment, a court held that the wife's consent would be sufficient. [25] However, recent advances in the rights of mental patients make reliance on this type of case inadvisable.

As a general proposition, no one can make a legally binding decision on behalf of an incompetent adult until appointed that person's legal guardian, after a judicial determination of incompetency. Once a guardian is appointed, only the guardian can make treatment decisions. However, it is a general custom in the medical community to ask for the consent of the next of kin, and some judicial decisions imply that there is some authority vested in the next of kin. For example, in one case a court hints that adult sons may consent to medical procedures required by their incompetent mother, even though they are not her guardians, and the court refuses to appoint them as guardians.[26] Even if the next of kin may not give a binding consent for an incompetent person as it applies to that patient, by signing a consent form they may be waiving *their* own rights to any future legal action. Their consent also demonstrates that the physician consulted with those persons most concerned about the patient's well-being. This being the case, patients may be discouraged from suing a physician for performing a procedure with only the consent of a relative, but would not be foreclosed from bringing such a suit.

Where the procedure to be performed constitutes emergency treatment, no consent is required, as discussed above. Nevertheless, informing the next of kin would be advisable. Where the procedure is elective, the safest route is to have a guardian appointed.

What does it mean to be incompetent?

In the context of medical care, a person is deemed competent if he can understand the nature and consequences of an illness or condition, and the nature and consequences of the proposed medical procedure. This is a factual question requiring discussion with the patient to answer. An unconscious patient is obviously incompetent. With this exception, no easy categorization of incompetence exists.

A patient can be rendered incompetent by mental illness, mental retardation, senility, drugs, alcohol, pain, and other conditions. However, the fact that someone is mentally ill or mentally retarded, or committed to a mental hospital, does not automatically render him incompetent. For example, in one case a sixty-year-old woman who had been involuntarily committed to a mental hospital with a diagnosis of schizophrenia was discovered to have a lump in her breast. She refused to consent to a biopsy, which would be followed by removal of her breast should cancer be found. She refused because her aunt had died after a similar procedure and she was afraid of the operation. At the court hearing the woman testified that she did not want to undergo the procedure because "it could interfere with her genital system, affecting her ability to have babies, and would prohibit a movie career." The court found that, although she was getting more delusional, she had consistently opposed the surgery in her lucid periods, and therefore found her competent to refuse the surgery.[27] The court specifically found that the patient's refusal to undergo the procedure was not due to her delusions, and found further that she knew that she might die as a result of her refusal.

Another case involved a seventy-seven-year-old woman who suffered from gangrene of the foot, and who refused to undergo a recommended amputation. Although the court found that the patient was combative and defensive at times, that she was sometimes confused, that her train of thought wandered, and that her conception of time was distorted, it also found that she demonstrated a high degree of awareness and acuity. The patient made clear that she did not wish to have the operation, even though she knew that decision would probably lead shortly to her death. The testimony clearly indicated that she made her choice "with full appreciation of the consequences." As a result of this, she was found to be competent.[28]

This case also addresses another issue of competence. A patient's competence is often not questioned as long as the patient agrees to undergo the proposed medical procedure. As this court pointed out,

> Until she changed her original decision and withdrew her consent to the amputation, her competence was not questioned. But the irrationality of her decision does not justify a conclusion that Mrs. Candura is incompetent in the legal sense. The law protects her right to make her own decision to accept or reject treatment, whether that decision is wise or unwise.[29]

Thus, if physicians determine a patient competent to consent to an operation, the court will use that to find the patient competent to refuse consent. In fact, in the case under discussion, the physicians were willing to perform the procedure on the basis of the patient's consent alone even during the time of the trial.

Since all people are presumed to be competent until proven otherwise, anyone who wishes to treat a person without his consent on the basis of that person's incompetency should be prepared to prove that because of some mental or physical disease or disability, the patient cannot understand the nature and consequences of the proposed procedure and the consequences of refusing to undergo the procedure. The refusal to undergo the procedure, however "irrational" that decision may be, is not itself enough to prove incompetency.

Can a doctor determine that a patient is incompetent?

The *facts* that indicate that a patient is or is not competent are available to physicians, and physicians are capable of making determinations that a patient is confused or appears not to comprehend what is being said to him. Only a court, however, may adjudge a person to be *legally* incompetent, and may authorize another person to consent to the treatment of the incompetent patient.[30]

Can a competent patient always refuse to consent to a procedure?

Yes. There is no doubt that a competent person may refuse to undergo a procedure not required to save that person's life. In certain circumstances this right may not be accorded mental patients or prisoners, and courts are presently struggling to define the rights of those populations.[31]

The complicated and controversial issue arises when the discussion turns to individuals who refuse life-saving treatment. The clear trend is to recognize a patient's right to refuse life-saving treatment, although there is legal authority to the contrary. But this authority is relatively weak. Almost all the cases discussing this issue involve Jehovah's Witnesses who refuse to consent to blood transfusions, but who do not refuse medical care. Therefore, when courts order the administration of blood to this group of patients, they authorize an invasion of the person's body that is relatively unobtrusive compared to the procedures the patient has consented to.

In many of these cases the patient does not truly oppose the transfusion, but instead refuses to *consent* to the transfusion. Perhaps the most widely cited "compulsory" transfusion case is known as the Georgetown College Case.[32] It involved a twenty-five-year-old mother of a seven-month-old child. Both the patient and her husband expressed to the judge their belief that if the transfusion was ordered by the court the responsibility for the transfusion would be the court's and not theirs. Although they did not consent, they also did not oppose it.

In another case, a thirty-nine-year-old father of four refused to consent to a transfusion. He signed a release form and was coherent and rational. The first thing this patient said when the judge entered the hospital room—before the judge asked any question—was that while he would not consent to the transfusion, he in no way would resist if the court ordered it. The judge explained that he could not force the transfusion and that the patient could resist by simply putting his hand over the site where the needle would be inserted. The patient replied that once the court order was signed, he would in no way resist the transfusion.[33]

These cases obviously do not support the statement that these courts forced treatment on unwilling patients. We can compare them to a 1972 case involving a thirty-four-year-old father of two who was seriously injured and required a transfusion. When queried by the judge, the patient expressed the belief that he would be deprived of everlasting life if the judge ordered the transfusion. The patient said, "It's between me and Jehovah, not the courts. . . . I'm willing to take my chances. My faith is that strong. I wish to live, but with no blood transfusions. Now get that straight." [34] In this case no transfusion was ordered.

Since 1973, when the U.S. Supreme Court explicated the concept of the constitutional right to privacy, a number of courts have determined that the right to privacy is broad enough to include the right to decide to refuse treatment.[35] Recent cases, including those discussed above, involving refusal to submit to foot amputation or breast biopsy, demonstrate the willingness of courts to enforce this right. However, no court has said that the right to refuse treatment is absolute.

What are the limits on the right of competent persons to refuse treatment?

Courts have said that the individual's right to refuse treatment must be balanced against a variety of state interests. These state interests include: (1) the preservation of life, (2) the protection of innocent third parties, (3) the prevention of suicide, and (4) the maintenance of the ethical interests of the medical profession.

1. *The preservation of life:* Courts agree that the interest in the preservation of human life must be balanced against the traumatic cost of saving that life. The New Jersey Supreme Court has stated that the state's interest in preserving life declines as the level of bodily invasion increases and the prognosis dims.[36] More recently, courts in both New Jersey and Massachusetts have focused on the nature of the invasion on the patient, since "prognosis" can be a subjective and personal matter. Courts in both states refused to order amputations of legs of patients whose lives could have been saved by the procedures.[37] Both the patients believed that their prognosis, lives in wheelchairs and beds, was not good.

The state's interest in preserving the life of a competent adult who is willing to die rather than undergo a painful and debilitating procedure is probably never compelling enough to force treatment.

2. *The protection of innocent third parties:* This is probably the strongest state interest that has been expressed. Usually this means that the state should be able to require treatment of a parent because the parent's death would have an adverse psychological and financial impact on his children. Although this argument has enormous emotional appeal, it also has enormous conceptual problems. First, it sets up two classes of persons, parents and nonparents, and penalizes parents by depriving them of a right because they are parents. It would also mean that courts would have to make determinations on a case-by-case basis of the impact of the death of a parent on his children. Would an impoverished child abuser have more of a right to refuse treatment than a wage-earning model parent? Finally, this concept would require a competent adult to undergo a medical procedure for the benefit of a specific third party. This could raise untold problems in the future if permitted by the courts.

3. *Prevention of suicide:* Although once seen as a problem, courts have begun to relegate this concern to footnotes. Like murder, suicide (or self-murder) requires a specific intent to cause death, and an action putting the death-producing agent in motion. In cases of refusing treat-

ment the patient does not want to die, but rather does not wish to undergo a certain treatment, and is willing to accept death as a consequence of that decision. Additionally, an individual patient does not set in motion the death-producing agent, since patients do not cause their illnesses or conditions.

4. *The maintenance of the ethical integrity of the medical profession:* Medical ethics do not require the forcible treatment of unconsenting competent patients, therefore courts should not order treatment on this basis.

What can be said with certainty is that courts have not ordered competent individuals to undergo any treatment more invasive than a blood transfusion, and they are unlikely to do so in the future. The specter of a competent patient being strapped down, chemically restrained, or even arrested so that he could be forced to undergo a medical procedure he does not want is so abhorrent to a free society that all medical professionals (and lawyers and judges) should work to make sure it does not occur. As one judge has already pointed out, "The notion that an individual exists for the good of the state is, of course, quite antithetical to our fundamental thesis that the role of the state is to ensure a maximum of individual freedom of choice and conduct." [38]

Who has a right to refuse life-saving treatment for an incompetent patient?

The answer to this question involves us in one of the most controversial and undefined areas of medical jurisprudence. Courts have begun to realize that neither good medical practice nor the law requires that incompetent patients be treated with all the resources that medical science and technology have to offer. They have found that since competent individuals have the right to refuse treatment, a way must be found to enable incompetents to have a similar right exercised on their behalf.

The most famous case, *Matter of Quinlan*,[39] was decided in 1976 by the New Jersey Supreme Court. At the time the case was brought, Ms. Quinlan was twenty-two years old and in a "chronic vegetative state." She required constant medical attention and it was thought that she would die if removed from the respirator. All the physicians who examined her concluded that she suffered from incurable brain damage and would never emerge from her comatose condition. Her parents wanted her taken off the respirator, but the physicians refused to do so. Since she was an adult, her father petitioned the court to be appointed her guardian with the explicit power to order the removal of the respirator. The trial court refused to do this.[40] On appeal the New Jersey Supreme Court found that the right to privacy was broad enough to include the right to refuse treatment in such a dire situation, and that this right could be exercised by a guardian. The court also found that physicians were leery of terminating treatment in such cases because of fear of possible civil and criminal action being taken against them. As a result of this, the court found that if the patient's physician concluded that there was "no reasonable possibility" of the patient's returning to a "cognitive, sapient state," and if the "guardian and family" of the patient concurred, and if a hospital "ethics committee" made up of physicians, lawyers, social workers, and theologians agreed with this conclusion, then the patient could be removed from the respirator and all participants in the decision would be immune from civil and criminal liability.

A second case was decided by the Massachusetts Supreme Judicial Court in 1977.[41] The *Saikewicz* case involved a sixty-seven-year-old profoundly retarded resident of a state institution who was suffering from acute myeloblastic monocytic leukemia. Expert medical testimony indicated that with chemotherapy only 30 to 50 percent of patients achieve remission (usually for two to thirteen months), that persons over sixty have more difficulty tolerating the treatment than younger people, that success rates are lower in older people, that the side effects would make this patient feel uncomfortable and sicker, and that this patient would probably have to be restrained in order to administer the treatment properly. Without the treatment the patient would die without discomfort and would live from a few weeks to several months. As a result of these factors the *guardian ad litem*, i.e., a guardian for the lawsuit only, and physicians recommended that chemotherapy not be administered. Both the trial court and Supreme Court agreed with this recommendation. In almost every area the *Saikewicz* court agreed with the *Quin-*

lan court. They disagreed in one respect, however. Unlike the New Jersey court, the *Saikewicz* court held that if the parties wanted immunity from civil and criminal liability, they would have to apply to a court and not merely go to a hospital ethics committee.

It should be pointed out that neither court requires recourse to either courts or ethics committees.[42] One needs to consult these bodies only when one wants immunity from suit. Since no health care provider has ever been prosecuted for terminating treatment of such seriously ill individuals, the need for such immunity is highly questionable. This point can be underscored—the facts are that the highest courts of the two states that have had the opportunity to decide the issue have decided that it is *not* always in the best interests of the seriously ill incompetent patient to receive treatment, that physicians and families or guardians working together can make decisions to suspend treatment based on certain criteria, and that mechanisms exist, when desirable, to have the legality of these decisions reviewed.

What criteria have courts established to determine when treatment of an incompetent can be stopped or withheld?

Both the *Quinlan* and *Saikewicz* courts have adopted the "substituted judgment" doctrine in one form or another. The *Saikewicz* court stated that the primary test is "to determine with as much accuracy as possible the wants and needs of the individual involved." [43] The *Quinlan* court stated that "The only practical way to prevent destruction of the right [to refuse treatment] is to permit the guardian and family of Karen to render their best judgment, subject to the qualification hereinafter stated, as to whether she would exercise it in the circumstances." [44]

The goal is to treat the incompetent as he would choose to be treated if he were competent. In a case such as *Quinlan* this would be possible, since Quinlan was competent for many years and it is likely that her family, with whom she had a long and loving relationship, could determine what she would want. However, in *Saikewicz,* or the case of a seriously ill newborn, this would be impossible to apply since there is no way of determining what the patient would want. In such a case it would be necessary to determine what is in the patient's best interest in judging the pros and cons of treatment.

May the incompetent's "quality of life" be taken into account?

The answer to this question depends to a large extent on what is meant by the ambiguous term "quality of life."

A lower court case in Maine involved a newborn who was blind, had no left ear, some abnormal vertebrae, and "some brain damage." The child also had a tracheal-esophogeal fistula, and the parents and physicians decided that this defect should not be corrected because the child would have a life "not worth preserving." The court found that "The doctor's qualitative evaluation of the value of life to be preserved is not legally within the scope of his expertise." [45] The court found that since the repair of the fistula was in no sense "heroic," and that the treatment did not involve serious risk, the procedure must be performed.

In *Saikewicz* the probate court listed six factors weighing against the ordering of treatment. One of those factors was the quality of life possible after treatment. The Massachusetts Supreme Judicial Court in reviewing this segment of the probate court opinion stated, "To the extent that this formulation equates the value of life" of *Saikewicz* as a retarded person "with any measure of the quality of life, we firmly reject it." [46] However, the *Saikewicz* court did say that "quality of life" could be used as a criterion as long as it refers to the continuing pain and disorientation precipitated by the treatment.

It seems clear that courts will not permit nontreatment decisions to be made on the basis of the incompetent's future mental or physical handicap, but may allow such decisions to be made based on pain or suffering the individual will experience in the future.

It can, however, be argued that the *Quinlan* court's decision is based on a quality-of-life determination, since they decided that lack of cognition and sapience is grounds for terminating treatment. Interestingly, the term "quality of life" appears nowhere in that decision.

Is it legal to write "do not resuscitate" (DNR) orders?

Since there was great concern in Massachusetts that physicians always had to go to court before terminating treatment after *Saikewicz* was decided, a case was brought to determine the answer to the question. The case involved a sixty-seven-year-old woman afflicted with Alzheimer's disease, an incurable, degenerative brain disease.[47] At the time of trial she was essentially vegetative, immobile, speechless, unable to swallow without choking, fed through a nasogastric tube, and catheterized. Her life expectancy was no more than a year, and it was expected that within this time she would suffer a cardiac or respiratory arrest. Her attending physician and her family all wanted a DNR order issued. The question for the court was whether such an order was legal. The court found that the issuance of a DNR order in such a situation was legal:

> This case does not offer a life-saving or life-prolonging treatment alternative within the meaning of the *Saikewicz* case. It presents a question peculiarly within the competence of the medical profession of what measures are appropriate to ease the imminent passing of an irremediably, terminally ill patient in light of the patient's history and condition and the wishes of her family. That question is not one for judicial decision, but one for the attending physician in keeping with the highest traditions of his profession, and subject to court review only to the extent that he has failed to exercise "that degree of care and skill of the average qualified practitioner, taking into account the advances of the profession." [48]

The court states the obvious—where there is nothing to be done, nothing need be done.

In its footnote 10, the appeals court quotes approvingly and extensively from the National Conference on Standards for Cardiopulmonary Resuscitation (CPR) and Emergency Cardiac Care (ECC) as follows:

> The purpose of cardiopulmonary resuscitation is the prevention of sudden, unexpected death. Cardiopulmonary resuscitation is not indicated in certain situations, such as in cases of terminal irreversible illness where death is not unexpected or where prolonged cardiac arrest dictates the futility of resuscitation efforts. Resuscitation in these circumstances may repre-

sent a positive violation of an individual's right to die with dignity. When CPR is considered to be contra-indicated for hospital patients, it is appropriate to indicate this in the patient's progress notes. It also is appropriate to indicate this on the physician's order sheet for the benefit of nurses and other personnel who may be called upon to initiate or participate in cardiopulmonary resuscitation.

"Do not resuscitate" orders are legal in cases of hope-lessly terminally ill patients. Such orders should be put in writing. Surreptitious DNR orders can do more harm than good by making it look as if the physician and nursing staff are committing a forbidden act. Of course, DNR orders should not be entered for competent patients un-less they have consented.

Do any statutes address the problem of making non-treatment decisions for incompetent patients?
Besides the general guardianship statutes, one state, Arkansas, has a statute that specifically permits relatives to execute a "living will" on behalf of a minor or men-tally incompetent person. It reads as follows:

If any person is a minor or an adult who is physi-cally or mentally unable to execute or is otherwise incapacitated from executing [a living will] document, it may be executed in the same form on his behalf:
  (a) by either parent of the minor;
  (b) by his spouse;
  (c) if his spouse is unwilling or unable to act, by his child aged eighteen or over;
  (d) if he has more than one child aged eighteen or over, by a majority of such children;
  (e) if he has no spouse or child aged eighteen or over, by either of his parents;
  (f) if he has no parent living, by his nearest rela-tive; or
  (g) if he is mentally incompetent, by his legally appointed guardian.
     Provided, that a form executed in compli-ance with this Section must contain a signed

statement by two physicians that extraordinary means would have to be utilized to prolong life.[49]

This appears to give the nearest of kin an almost unlimited right to refuse treatment on behalf of a relative. It lists no criteria or standards limiting such actions, and would appear to give a dangerous and uncontrollable amount of power to relatives. Fortunately, this statute authorizes physicians to rely on this document but does not *require* them to do so. Therefore, the physicians' medical judgment on the appropriateness of withholding treatment can act as a safeguard.

Who is authorized to consent to the treatment of minors?
Ordinarily, the consent of one parent is required before a medical procedure can be performed on a minor. The reason for this is that historically the law has attempted to protect minors from their own improvident acts. One way the law has done this is by creating the presumption that minors are incompetent to consent to their own medical care. Any person who treats a minor without the parent's consent is guilty of battery, since minors are not legally capable of consenting to being touched. As a result of this, the parent, who is the natural guardian of the child, is required to consent to the child's care.

Although this rule has great force as it pertains to young children, there are so many exceptions governing older minors that, in many cases, the rule has been swallowed by the exceptions. These exceptions will be discussed below.

In the vast majority of states, a person is deemed an adult upon reaching the eighteenth birthday. Three states retain age twenty-one, and four age nineteen.

Must a physician obtain a parent's consent before giving a minor emergency medical care?
If the medical situation provides a physician with time to contact a child's parents, it is good practice to do so. However, as discussed earlier, if the situation is so urgent that there is no time to seek parental consent, or if the parent cannot be contacted, the child, regardless of age, may be treated.

It is important when taking advantage of this rule to

make sure the medical situation is such that an emergency truly exists. In one relatively old case, the defendant doctor amputated the foot of a fourteen-year-old boy who was injured in an automobile accident. The doctor was sued on the grounds that there was no consent; the doctor defended by contending that emergency treatment was required. The jury, presented with conflicting testimony, decided there was no emergency and set damages at $8,000.[50]

May a physician treat an emancipated minor without parental consent?

Yes. An emancipated minor is one who is no longer under the care, custody, and control of his parents. Thus a married minor or one who is in the armed forces is always considered to be emancipated from his parents. It can be generally said that a minor who is living apart from his parents and is self-supporting is emancipated for the purpose of consenting to medical care. Some states have codified the emancipated minor rule. In Massachusetts a minor who is living apart from his parents or guardian and is "managing" his own financial affairs may consent to medical treatment by statute, with certain exceptions.[51] A similar provision exists in California for minors fifteen years of age or older.[52] Similar provisions exist in the statutes of several other states.

May "mature minors" consent to medical care?

No court in recent history has found any health care provider liable for treating a minor over fifteen years old without parental consent, where the minor has consented to his own care. Courts have found that a nineteen-year-old (when the age of majority was twenty-one) could consent to the use of a local anesthetic even though his mother had specifically stated she wished that a general anesthetic be administered,[53] that a seventeen-year-old could consent to a vaccination required by his employer,[54] and that a seventeen-year-old could consent to the minor surgical care necessary to treat an injury incurred when her finger was caught in a door.[55] In essence, the mature minor rule means that when the minor is capable of appreciating the nature, extent, and consequences of the medical treatment, the minor is able to consent to his own care.

Cases utilizing the mature minor rule generally involve older minors, treatments that are rendered for the benefit of the minor (not organ transplant donors or blood donors), and treatments that are necessary when some reason exists for not asking permission of a parent, including the refusal of the minor to do so. Additionally, the treatment at issue usually involves standard and relatively low-risk procedures. One is best advised not to rely on the mature minor rule for performing cardiac surgery, for example. Some states have adopted the mature minor rule by statute.[56]

Who is liable for the medical bills of a minor?

When a minor receives care with parental consent, the parent is liable. However, when care is rendered on the basis of the minor's consent and no effort is made to contact the parents, it would appear that the parents are not liable for the care, although the minor is. This is equally true of emancipated minors. However, parents are responsible for medical bills incurred as the result of treating an emergency, even though they have not been contacted. See Chapter XIV for further discussion of this point.

Are there other situations in which minors may consent to their own treatment?

Yes. More than half the states have laws permitting minors to be treated for several diseases or conditions without parental consent. A significant number of states permit children to consent to treatment of drug dependency. A large number of states also permit pregnant minors to consent to medical care associated with the pregnancy, although many states exclude consent to abortion from these statutes.[57] The issue of abortion is discussed in Chapter X.

As a practical matter, no case can be found in which a physician who has treated any minor for one of the above-mentioned conditions has been sued for rendering such care, even where no statute exists permitting such treatment without parental consent. It is extremely unlikely that any health care provider who renders standard medical treatment for venereal disease, any other communicable disease, pregnancy, or drug dependency, in a situation where the minor refuses to consult his parents, would be held liable merely for rendering such care.

May minors be given contraceptive information and devices without their parents' consent?

Although health care providers are rightly concerned about how to handle such a controversial issue, there are no cases that we could find that punish anyone for providing contraceptive counseling or devices to adolescents.

It seems clear that the First Amendment would prohibit any interference with the dissemination of factual *information* regarding contraception.

In terms of contraceptive *devices,* the Supreme Court has held that a state may not prohibit the distribution or use of contraceptives by married or unmarried adults.[58] In a 1977 case the Court extended this rule by striking down a New York law that prohibited the sale of nonprescription contraceptives to persons under the age of sixteen. As with the abortion case, the Court found that the constitutional right to privacy applies to minors, and since the state cannot outlaw abortions for minors, or even require parental consent for a minor to obtain an abortion, it would make no sense to permit the state to outlaw the sale of contraceptives to minors. Although the case dealt specifically with nonprescription contraceptives, its reasoning would be equally applicable to prescription contraceptives.[59]

May parents commit a minor to a mental institution without the minor's consent?

The Supreme Court has recently ruled that parents may commit a minor to a mental institution without the child's consent, and without undergoing any type of court procedure, as long as the commitment statute requires that a mental health professional first evaluate the child and decide that such care is necessary and appropriate.[60] Such a parentally enforced commitment is considered a "voluntary" commitment of the child. The full import of this case, however is not yet certain, since the children involved were all quite young, and none could be considered mature minors. A case involved the rights of mature minors will have to be brought before any definite answer can be given.

The rights of parents to commit children, and the rights of children to commit themselves, or to obtain release from mental hospitals, is a matter of state law. For example, in Hawaii a parent may only commit a child younger than fifteen years of age.[61] In Pennsylvania the child must be younger than fourteen,[62] in Washington a child over thirteen must also consent to his voluntary commitment,[63] and in West Virginia a child over twelve must give his consent.[64] Thus, even if the Supreme Court gives states great latitude in their laws that enable parents to commit their children, state legislatures have adopted, and will continue to adopt, a variety of statutory schemes that protect the rights of children who face "voluntary" commitment by their parents or the state.

NOTES

1. Pratt v. Davis, 118 Ill. App. 161, 166 (1905); aff'd, 224 Ill. 30, 79 N.E. 562 (1906).
2. PROSSER, LAW OF TORTS, 34, 101 (St. Paul, Minn.: West, 1971).
3. Rogers v. Lumbermen's Mut. Cas. Co., 119 So.2d 649 (La. 1960).
4. Cobbs v. Grant, 8 Cal.3d 229, 502 P.2d 1 (1972).
5. Natanson v. Kline, 186 Kan 393, 350 P.2d 1093, (1960); rehearing denied, 187 Kan 186, 354 P.2d 670 (1960).
6. Canterbury v. Spence, 464 F.2d 772 (D.C. Cir. 1972).
7. Wilkenson v. Vesey 295 A.2d 676, 688 (R.I. 1972).
8. WALTZ & INBAU, MEDICAL JURISPRUDENCE 161–2 (New York: Macmillan, 1971).
9. Canterbury v. Spence, supra note 6, at 244.
10. American Heart Association, Exercise Testing and Training of Individuals with Heart Disease or at High Risk for Its Development: A Handbook for Physicians.
11. Torsiello v. Whitehall Laboratories, 398 A.2d 132, (N.J. Sup. Ct. App. Div. 1979).
12. See, e.g., Salmon v. Parke Davis & Co., 520 F.2d 1309 (4th Cir. 1975).
13. Hernandez v. Smith, 552 F.2d 142 (5th Cir. 1977).
14. PROSSER, supra note 2, at 103.
15. Cobbs v. Grant, supra note 4, at 245.
16. Wilkinson v. Vesey, supra note 7, at 689.

17. *Id.* at 689.
18. Cobbs v. Grant, *supra* note 4, at 246.
19. O'Brien v. Cunard, 157 Mass. 272, 28 N.E. 266 (1891).
20. Barnett v. Bachrach, 34 A.2d 626 (Mun. Ct. App. D.C. 1943).
21. Kennedy v. Parrott, 243 N.C. 355, 362 90 S.E.2d 754, 759 (1956).
22. Wells v. Van Nort, 100 Ohio St. 101, 125 N.E. 910 (1919).
23. Mohr v. Williams, 95 Minn. 261, 104 N.W. 12 (1905).
24. Murray v. VanDevander, 522 P.2d 302 (Okla., 1974); *and see* Karp v. Cooley, 493 F.2d 408 (5th Cir. 1974).
25. Lester v. Aetna Cas. & Surety Co., 240 F.2d 676 (5th Cir. 1957); *see also* Steele v. Woods, 327 S.W.2d 187, 198 (Mo. 1959).
26. Petition of Nemser, 51 Misc.2d 616, 273 N.Y.S.2d 624 (Sup. Ct. 1966).
27. *In re* Yetter, 62 Pa. D. & C. 2d 619 (1973).
28. Lane v. Candura, 376 N.E.2d 1232 (Mass. App. 1978).
29. *Id.* at 1235–6.
30. *Id. See also In re* Quackenbush, 383 A.2d 785 (Morris Cty., N.J., Probate Ct. 1978).
31. *See, e.g.,* Comm. of Corrections v. Myers, 399 N.E.2d 452 (Mass. 1979) (Prisoner forced to undergo hemodialysis treatments); Rogers v. Okin, 478 F. Supp. 134 (D.Mass. 1979) (Competent mental patients may refuse psychotropic medications in nonemergency situations); Rennie v. Klein, 476 F. Supp. 1294 (N.J. 1979) (Competent mental patients can refuse psychotropic drugs, but refusal may be overturned by an "independent psychiatrist" after an informal hearing).
32. 331 F.2d 1000 (D.C. Cir. 1967).
33. U.S. v. George, 239 F. Supp. 752 (Conn. 1965).
34. *In re* Osborne, 294 A.2d 372, 374 (D.C. Ct. of App. 1972).
35. *See, e.g., In re* Quinlan, 355 A.2d 647 (N.J. 1976); Superintendent of Belchertown v. Saikewicz, 370 N.E.2d 417 (Mass. 1977). For a more detailed discussion of these cases *see* Annas, *Reconciling Quinlan and Saikewicz: Decision-making for the Terminally Ill Incompetent,* 4 AM. J. LAW & MED. 367 (1979).
36. *In re* Quinlan, *supra* note 35, at 669.
37. Lane v. Candura, *supra* note 28; *In re* Quackenbush, *supra* note 30.

38. *In re* Osborne, *supra* note 34, at 372, 375 n.5.
39. *See* note 35.
40. *In re* Quinlan, 137 N.J. Super. 227, 348 A.2d 801 (Ch. Div. 1975).
41. Superintendent of Belchertown, *supra* note 35.
42. *See In re* Earle Spring.
43. Superintendent of Belchertown, *supra* note 35, at 430.
44. *In re* Quinlan, *supra* note 35, at 664.
45. Maine Medical Center v. Houle, Maine Super. Ct. Civ. Action No. 74–149 (1974).
46. *Supra* note 35, at 432; *and see* Buchanan, *Medical Paternalism or Legal Imperialism*, 5 AM J. LAW & MED. 97, 104 (1979).
47. *In re* Shirley Dinnerstein, 380 N.E.2d 134 (Mass. App. Ct. 1978).
48. *Id.* at 139.
49. ARK. STAT. ANN. §82–3801.
50. Rogers v. Sells, 61 P.2d 1019 (Okla. 1936).
51. MASS. GEN. LAWS ch. 112, §12F.
52. CAL. CIV. CODE §34.6.
53. Bishop v. Shurly, 237 Mich. 76, 211 N.W. 75 (1926).
54. Gulf & S.I.R. Co. v. Sullivan, 155 Miss. 1, 119 So. 501 (1928).
55. Younts v. St. Francis Hosp., 205 Kan. 292, 469 P.2d 330 (1970).
56. *See, e.g.,* MISS. CODE ANN. §41–41–3(h).
57. *See* A. SUSSMAN, THE RIGHTS OF YOUNG PEOPLE 224–28 (New York: Avon Books, 1977) for a table of state statutes authorizing the treatment of minors.
58. Griswold v. Connecticut, 381 U.S. 479 (1965); Eisenstadt v. Baird, 405 U.S. 438 (1972).
59. Carey v. Population Services, 431 U.S. 678 (1977); *see also* Comment, *Parental Consent Requirements and Privacy Rights of Minors: The Contraceptive Controversy*, 88 HARV. L. R. 1001 (1975).
60. Parham v. J.R. 442 U.S. 584; Secretary of Public Welfare v. Institutionalized Juveniles, 442 U.S. 640 (1979).
61. HAW. REV. STAT. §334–60(a)(2).
62. PA. STAT. ANN. tit. 50 §7201.
63. WASH. REV. CODE §72.23.070(2).
64. W. VA. CODE §27–4–1(b).

V

Emergency Care

The lesson of this chapter is: In an emergency, treat first and ask legal questions later. This is both good medicine and good law.

How does the law define an emergency?

There is no universally recognized definition of an emergency, and the law will generally accept the determination of health care professionals, if consistent with accepted practice, in defining an emergency condition or situation. The most common definition is that an emergency is any injury or acute medical condition liable to cause death, disability, or serious illness if not immediately attended to.

Obvious examples of emergency conditions that require the *immediate* attention of a physician or properly trained health professional *to prevent loss of life* include:

Massive hemorrhage from major vessels
Cardiac arrest
Cessation or acute embarrassment of respiration
Profound shock from any cause
Rapidly acting poison
Anaphylactic reactions
Acute epidural hemorrhage
Acute overwhelming bacteremia and toxemia
Severe head injuries
Penetrating wound of the pleura or pericardium
Rupture of an abdominal viscus
Acute psychotic state.[1]

An emergency condition need not be this serious, however, and could include serious lacerations, broken bones, or high fever.

The leading case dealing explicitly with the right to receive emergency treatment, for example, involved a four-month-old baby with diarrhea and fever.[2] The family physician prescribed medication by phone on the second day of the illness and saw the child during office hours the third day. The child did not sleep at all the third night, and on the morning of the fourth day the parents, knowing their doctor was not in that day, took him to an emergency room. The nurse on duty refused to examine the child, saying hospital policy forbade treating anyone already under a doctor's care without first contacting the doctor (a dangerous and anachronistic policy), which she was unable to do. The parents took the child home and made an appointment to see their family doctor that night. The child died of bronchial pneumonia during the afternoon.

The court ruled that the parents could recover from the hospital for refusal to treat in an "unmistakable emergency," if they could demonstrate that a similarly trained health professional would have recognized it as such. Its reasoning was that people should be able to rely on the "established custom" of the hospitals to render aid in such cases in its emergency room. A person who requires emergency aid but is refused is worse off for having been delayed in obtaining treatment.

Does a provider have an obligation to render treatment in an emergency room to a patient who is suffering from an emergency medical condition?

Yes. Providers must render treatment in this situation. While courts that have examined this question have all come to the same conclusion, some have used different reasoning to arrive at it. Almost every court faced with a patient needing emergency care has repudiated the old doctrine that a hospital has to accept only those whom it chooses.[3] This in fact may be the only *legal* right to medical care (in the absence of a specific statute, like those concerning Medicaid, veterans' assistance, etc.) that citizens currently have in the United States. Most courts follow the principle of reasonable reliance as discussed in the previous question.

Those that follow the reasonable reliance rule include a case in which a patient, who was suffering from frostbite, was being treated by a doctor who attempted to gain admission for his patient. The hospital refused unless he paid a $25 admission fee, and not until much later did the patient gain admission to another hospital. The patient eventually had to have his feet amputated.[4] In a second case the plaintiff attempted to receive treatment for an obviously broken arm, which the hospital refused.[5]

An example where the court refused to follow the reasonable reliance doctrine involved two young children who were burned when a stove in their home in Sonora, Mexico, exploded. They were rushed across the United States border to a private hospital in Bisbee, Arizona. The personnel in the emergency ward of that hospital, owned by the Phelps Dodge Corporation, refused to treat them, and their injuries were worsened because of the refusal.[6] The Supreme Court of Arizona declined to adopt the reasonable reliance rule, but found that the hospital had a duty to admit emergency patients and provide emergency care based on the statutes and regulations of the State of Arizona. The regulations required all general hospitals to maintain an emergency room, and from this policy the court concluded that "such a hospital may not deny emergency care to any patient without cause."

Other courts have arrived at the same conclusion on the basis of public policy,[7] and on the basis that hospitals that have tax-exempt status, and maintain emergency wards, cannot turn away patients with emergency medical conditions.[8]

Who has the right to decide if the patient is actually experiencing an emergency?

Courts have not wanted to interfere in any way with the functioning of the modern emergency room, and have so far been willing to hold whomever the hospital designates as the triage officer responsible for making this decision in accordance with good and accepted practice for a person of similar training. Therefore, when the designated triage officer or person in charge of admission to the emergency room is a registered nurse, he will be held as the person responsible for making decisions consistent with those that would be made by a reasonable prudent nurse with his training and experience.[9]

On the other hand, hospitals must comply with their own rules, and will be liable if they do not. In one case, for example, an intern, on July 4, his second day in the emergency room, improperly diagnosed a man as having a sore throat without making use of any of the indicated tests.[10] He prescribed antibiotics, the man returned to his hotel room with his family, and when they awoke the next morning he was dead. Autopsy revealed that death was caused by asphyxia, resulting when the larynx, tonsils, and epiglottis swelled, blocking the trachea. An appeals court found that the hospital had a rule that the intern could not release emergency room patients until he had contacted the "on-call" physician. The intern was unable to contact this physician, although he tried for three and a half hours before releasing the patient. The court found that the hospital's breach of its own emergency ward standards—by failing to actually have a physician who was available to back up the intern—created a jury issue as to whether or not this failure was negligence on the hospital's part that led to the patient's death.

In another case, in which a patient who was sent home died of a heart attack, the court found that it was up to the jury to decide if the emergency room nurse adequately fulfilled her duty toward the patient.[11]

Of course, patients who are not actually experiencing emergency conditions cannot sue the hospital for failure to treat them as emergency patients.[12] The judgment of whether or not an emergency actually exists must be made from the symptoms presented at the time of admission or refusal—and not by hindsight, after the emergency condition has actually caused the patient harm.[13]

How quickly must the emergency patient be seen and treated?

The answer varies with the emergency condition, but the patient requiring immediate care should receive it, and the hospital emergency room should have a policy that makes this possible. When a patient enters an emergency room bleeding from a shotgun wound in his arm, is not seen for two hours, is then transferred to another hospital, and dies shortly after arrival, the first hospital is likely to be found responsible for the death because of its delay in treatment.[14]

Does a patient have a right to be seen by a physician?

The patient with an emergency condition should be seen and examined by a physician. Both the federal government, in the Medicare Conditions of Participation, and the American College of Surgeons, in their Standards for Emergeny Departments in Hospitals, specify that "every applicant for treatment should be seen by a physician." [15]

What case law there is also indicates that if there is reasonable basis for suspecting that an emergency exists, a patient has a right to be examined and treated by a physician. In an Alabama case, for example, an automobile accident victim was brought in with back pain. A nurse examined him and found no injury. She refused to either call a doctor or admit the patient. The following day, in another hospital, he was found to have a broken back. The first hospital was held liable.[16]

Similarly, in a New York case, a patient was taken to an emergency ward with chest pain and shortness of breath. He told the nurse on duty he thought he was having a heart attack. Because he did not have the proper type of health insurance, however, she refused to admit him or call his physician to the hospital. The patient returned home and died, and the court decided that the hospital could be found liable for the death.[17] Of course, hospital personnel have a duty to monitor emergency room patients and take steps to prevent any foreseeable further injuries.[18]

After an emergency patient begins receiving treatment, must treatment be continued?

Generally, treatment must be continued until a patient can be transferred or discharged without harm. In one case, a woman with a stab wound was examined and had her wound cleansed and dressed by an intern. She was then transferred to another hospital where she died a short while later during exploratory surgery. The court found that the hospital had not supplied adequate emergency treatment prior to ordering a transfer, and this contributed to the patient's death.[19]

Another case involved a victim of an auto accident. After pulse and blood-pressure checks and a brief abdominal exam, the intern in charge left the patient unattended. After about forty-five minutes he was transferred to another hospital where he died thirty minutes later from internal injuries. The court found that the hospital had failed to provide adequate emergency treatment.[20]

In implementing its provisions for reimbursement to hospitals that do not participate in Medicare, HHS has also promulgated standards for establishing when an emergency ends. The regulation provides: "An emergency no longer exists when it becomes safe from a medical standpoint to move the individual to a participating hospital or other institution, or to discharge him." [21] Under this standard, one court ordered Medicare benefits to a woman for her entire eighty-six-day hospitalization.[22] The court was persuaded by her doctor's statement that he would not have taken responsibility for her discharge if it had occurred any earlier.

Does a doctor or nurse have an obligation to treat a patient with an emergency condition even if hospital policy requires a down payment or prepayment prior to treatment and the patient is unable to pay?

Yes. In one case, an eleven-year-old boy was taken to a hospital for an emergency appendectomy. Two hours later, after having been placed in bed and given medication, the hospital discharged him because his mother could not immediately pay $200.[23] Although the court properly treated the case as an issue of negligent discharge rather than as one of refusal to administer emergency aid, the case is an example of a court finding that essential hospital treatment must be administered without regard to cost or ability to pay.

Several states have addressed the issue of cost in their statutes obligating hospitals to extend emergency aid. In one state the law requires that the hospital must "not before admission question the patient or any member of his or her family concerning insurance, credit or payment of charges, provided however, that the patient or a member of his or her family shall agree to supply such information promptly after the patient's admission." [24]

In the process of adopting a broad obligation on the

part of hospitals to render emergency aid, the Wisconsin Supreme Court said: "It would shock the public conscience if a person in need of medical emergency aid would be turned down at the door of a hospital having emergency service because that person could not at that moment assure payment for the service." [25] In this case the court was not directly concerned with a refusal to aid for lack of the patient's ability to pay but was construing a state law requiring counties to pay hospital costs for the medically indigent. Nonetheless, the implication is that the duty to render emergency aid when the hospital has the facilities cannot be obviated by the patient's poverty.

The same rationale would seem to apply to patients with conditions necessitating emergency treatment who have outstanding unpaid bills at the hospital. The hospital could not refuse to treat their emergency conditions simply because their past bills were not paid up. And the hospital may not transfer indigent patients to other facilities if the transfer endangers the life or health of the patients.[26]

Some states enforce their emergency policy with *criminal* sanctions. In 1979 a hospital administrator in Texas was indicted on misdemeanor charges for refusing to admit a seriously ill infant for emergency treatment allegedly because the parents did not have a $400 deposit for services. The eleven-month-old son of migrant farmworkers died several hours later. The charges were filed under a Texas law requiring hospitals to render emergency services regardless of the patient's ability to pay. The administrator denied the charges and attributed the incident to a language barrier.[27]

Can a hospital, by contract, make emergency ward physicians solely responsible for all negligent acts committed in the emergency room?

While there are some Georgia cases to the contrary,[28] the modern rule is that no matter how such a contract is worded, both the physicians *and* the hospital will be responsible for the negligent acts of the physicians *if* the hospital maintains control over the actions of the physicians or if the public is led to believe that the services being rendered by the physicians are hospital services. Courts have consistently held that even if a contract specifies that physicians will be considered independent contractors only, and not employees, the hospital is responsible for their actions if they can exercise control over them.

Control can be found in hospital regulations and policies which cover the emergency room, staff privileges, and compensation agreements.[29] In addition, even if emergency room physicians are characterized as independent contractors, the hospital will still be held legally responsible for their negligence because, in the absence of some clear indication to the contrary, the public has a right to rely on the common assumption that emergency ward personnel work for and on behalf of the hospital.[30] "Patients are not bound by secret limitations contained in a private contract between the hospital and the doctor."[31]

Do health professionals have a right to refuse to render emergency care outside the emergency ward?

Usually. It has generally been held that health professionals, like other private citizens, have no legal obligation to come to the aid of their fellow citizens in distress—even life-threatening distress. The real reasons some professionals do not render aid probably has little to do with lawsuits (since no successful lawsuits have ever been filed against a Good Samaritan physician or nurse), but involves either not being able to render emergency care, or not wanting to get involved.[32]

In early 1977 a Massachusetts ophthalmologist was accused of refusing to see a week-old infant with a serious eye infection because the mother was a Medicaid recipient. The mother and child had to be driven into Boston from Cape Cod for treatment, a distance of some sixty miles. While the accusation could not be proved at a hearing, it did cause the Massachusetts Board of Registration in Medicine to consider how it could require physicians in the state to render "essential" services to those in need of them.

As part of this debate, the Massachusetts Medical Society proposed that the physician's "ethical obligation" of treating all emergency patients be made a legal one. Subsequently, on October 20, 1977, the Massachusetts Board became the first licensing board in the country legally to require all physicians under its jurisdiction to render emergency services to the best of their ability. The regulation reads in part:

A licensee shall render medical services to a person experiencing a medical emergency. A medical emergency is a set of circumstances which immediately threatens a person's life or is likely to cause serious injury absent the provision of immediate professional assistance. A licensee shall presume that a person who is referred to him by another licensee for the purpose of securing medical services of an emergency nature is experiencing a medical emergency.[33]

Likewise, the 1980 version of the AMA's Ethical Principle on acceptance for treatment reads, "A physician shall . . . *except in emergencies* be free to choose whom to serve . . ." (emphasis supplied).

What are Good Samaritan statutes?

Good Samaritan statutes have been enacted in all fifty states to encourage physicians and other health care providers to stop and render emergency aid to anyone who requires it without undue fear of being sued for negligence. While statutes vary, most protect those health care providers covered by statute from liability for injury resulting from care rendered in "good faith" or without "gross negligence."[34]

Although the statutes claim to provide protection, the language is often ambiguous and has created problems of interpretation. For example, only twenty-two statutes define emergency care, and most of these do it poorly.[35] Thirty-five statutes require that the care rendered be rendered gratuitously, but eleven fail to define this term adequately.[36] The location for coverage and the extent of it is also often the subject of litigation. In general, however, it is fair to say that the thrust of the legislation is to protect persons offering assistance other than that which they have a legal duty to render. Thus, care by hospital personnel in the hospital should properly be excluded from coverage by these statutes.[37]

Are health care providers likely to be used for treating emergency cases in the absence of a clearly-worded Good Samaritan statute?

No. In an emergency, treat first and ask legal questions later. A good-faith attempt to save a life is your best defense to any potential charge of negligence; and in fact there are no reported cases of any physician or health care provider ever being successfully sued for rendering emergency care.

The *Report of the Secretary's Commission on Medical Malpractice* concluded that "the legal risks in rendering emergency medical care to accident victims in non-health-care settings are minimal, if not infinitesimal." [38] The Commission adopted as one of its official findings the conclusion that "there is no factual basis for the commonly asserted belief that malpractice suits are likely to stem from rendering emergency care at the scene of accidents." The Commission recommended "widespread publicity be given to this fact in order to allay the fears of physicians, nurses, and other health-care providers in this regard and to encourage the rendering of aid in non-hospital emergency situations." [39]

Given this, it may make good sense to abolish existing Good Samaritan statutes rather than try to amend them to remove their defects. The reason is that they apparently do not act as an incentive for health care providers to render emergency assistance. A survey was conducted in 1963, at the height of the lobbying effort for Good Samaritan statutes, by the legal department of the AMA. Physicians were asked whether they were willing to stop to render aid to the victims of roadside accidents. Almost 50 percent responded that they would not render such care, whether or not a Good Samaritan statute was in effect. [40] Also, while we know of no studies on this, it is likely that most competent practitioners feel little need to be protected from a negligence charge, and these statutes may only serve to bolster the confidence of the marginal or poorly trained practitioner. A poorly worded statute will discourage emergency care, and a well-worded statute may have little or no effect. [41]

NOTES

1. FLINT, EMERGENCY TREATMENT AND MANAGEMENT, 88 (3rd ed.; Philadelphia: Saunders, 1964).
2. Wilmington Gen. Hosp. v. Manlove, 54 Del. 15, 174 A.2d 135 (1961).

3. *See* Powers, *Hospital Emergency Service and the Open Door*, 66 MICH. L. REV. 1455 (1968).
4. Stanturf v. Sipes, 447 S.W.2d 558 (Mo. 1969). *And see* Fabian v. Macyko, 344 A.2d 569 (Pa. Super. 1975) (phone call to emergency room alone insufficient to create reliance).
5. Williams v. Hospital Auth. of Hall County, 119 Ga. App. 626, 168 S.E.2d 336 (1969).
6. Guerrero v. Copper Queen Hosp., 112 Ariz. 104, 537 P.2d 1329 (1975).
7. Mercy Medical Center of Oshkosh v. Winnebago County, 206 N.W.2d 198 (Wis. 1973).
8. East. Ky. Welfare Rights Org. v. Simon, 506 F.2d 1278 (D.C. Cir. 1974), *vacated on other grounds*, 426 U.S. 26 (1976). *Compare* Newsom v. Vanderbilt U., 453 F. Supp. 401 (M.D. Tenn. 1978) (Indigents must be afforded due process in distribution of free care required by Hill-Burton).
9. Wilmington Gen. Hosp. v. Manlove, 54 Del. 15, 174 A.2d 135 (1961). On the effectiveness of nurses in this role *see* Albin *et al.*, *Evaluation of Emergency Room Triage Performed by Nurses*, 65 AM. J. PUB. HEALTH 1063 (1975).
10. Fjerstad v. Knutson and Sioux Valley Hosp., 271 N.W.2d 8 (S.D. 1978); 291 N.W.2d 786 (S.D. 1980).
11. O'Neil v. Montefiore Hosp., 202 N.Y.S.2d 436, 11 A.D.2d 132 (App. Div. 1960); *and see* Carr v. St. Paul Fire & Marine Ins. Co., 384 F. Supp. 821 (W.D. Ark. 1974) (involving the negligent actions of an LPN and two orderlies) *and* Dumer v. St. Michael's Hosp. 69 Wis.2d 766 233 N.W.2d 372, (1975) (emergency room nurses and attendants do not make medical diagnoses). *And see* Hicks v. United States, 368 F.2d 626 (4th Cir. 1966).
12. *See, e.g.*, Campbell v. Mincey, 413 F. Supp. 16 (N.D. Miss. 1975), *aff'd mem.*, 542 F.2d 572 (5th Cir. 1976). (The authors cite this case, but note that it involves childbirth, seldom considered by the court an emergency condition *per se,* and that the case may well have been decided against the plaintiff because she was black.)
13. Wilmington Gen. Hosp. v. Manlove, 54 Del. 15, 174 A.2d 135 (1961).
14. New Biloxi Hosp. v. Frazier, 245 Miss. 185, 146 So.2d 882 (1962).

15. Letourneau, *Legal Aspects of the Hospital Emergency Room,* 16 CLEV.-MAR. L. REV. 50, 60 (1967).
16. Citizens Hospital Assoc. v. Schoulin, 48 Ala. 101, 262 So.2d 303 (Ala. App. 1972). *See also* Thomas v. Corso, 265 Md. 84, 288 A.2d 379 (1972).
17. O'Neill v. Montefiore Hosp., 202 N.Y.S.2d 436 (1960).
18. McEachern v. Glenview Hosp., 505 S.W.2d 386 (Tex. Civ. App. 1974); *and see* Modave v. Long Isl. Jewish Medical Center, 501 F.2d 1065 (2d Cir. 1974), *and* Olson, *Be Ready for Out-of-Control EW Patient,* HOSPITAL MED. STAFF (Nov. 1978) at 20.
19. Jones v. City of New York, 134 N.Y.S.2d 779 (Sup. Ct. 1954), *modified,* 143 N.Y.S.2d 628 (App. Div. 1955).
20. Methodist Hosp. v. Ball, 50 Tenn. App. 460, 362 S.W.2d 475 (1961). *See also* Mulligan v. Wetchler, 332 N.Y.S.2d 68 (Sup. Ct. 1972).
21. 42 C.F.R. §405.191(b)(2) (1973).
22. Brewerton v. Finch, 320 F. Supp. 68 (N.D. Miss. 1970).
23. LeJeune Rd. Hosp. v. Watson, 171 So.2d 202 (Dist. Ct. App. Fla. 1965).
24. N.Y. PUB. HEALTH LAW, §2805–b(1) (1973).
25. Mercy Medical Center of Oshkosh v. Winnebago County, 206 N.W.2d 198, 201 (Wis. 1973).
26. Harper v. Baptist Medical Center, 341 So.2d 133 (Ala. 1976). *And see* Nance v. James Archer Smith Hosp., 329 So.2d 377 (Fla. App. 1976).
27. *Reported in* American Medical News, Jan. 19, 1979, at 11. *See also* Medical World News May 15, 1978, at 39–40, discussing refusal of entry case involving a $500 deposit. Woman died of meningitis complications a few days later. A verdict of $950,000 was returned against the physician who turned the patient away. *Cf.* Kucera, *Narrow Definition of Emergency Can Spell Litigation,* HOSPITAL MED. STAFF (Sept. 1978) at 21, 22–23.
28. Pogue v. Hospital Auth. of DeKalb County, 120 Ga. App. 230, 170 S.E.2d 53 (1969); Overstreet v. Doctors Hosp., 142 Ga. App. 895, 237 S.E.2d 213 (Ga. 1977) (neither case, however, considered the issue of reasonable reliance by the public or the appearance of an emergency ward run and controlled by the hospital).
29. Mduba v. Benedictine Hosp., 52 A.D.2d 450, 384 N.Y.S.2d 527 (App. Div. 1976); Scott v. Brookdale Hosp. Center, 60 A.D.2d 647, 400 N.Y.S.2d 552 (App. Div. 1977).

30. *Id. But see* Badeaux v. East Jefferson Gen. Hosp., 364 So.2d 348 (La. Ct. App. 1978) (which utilized the same control tests, but affirmed a summary judgment for the hospital in the absence of any countervailing affidavits by the plaintiffs on that issue).

31. Mduba, *supra* note 29, at 529.

32. Annas, *Law & Medicine: Myths and Realities in the Medical School Classroom*, 1 AM. J. LAW & MED. 195 (1975).

33. Regulations of the Massachusetts Board of Registration in Medicine, 243 CMR 2.06(10)(a).

34. *See generally* Zaremski, *Good Samaritan Statutes: Do They Protect the Emergency Care Provider?* 7(1) MEDICOLEGAL NEWS 5 (Spring 1979); *and see* Scanlon, *The Malpractice Aspects of Emergency Care by Non-Physicians*, 12 GONZ. L. REV. 676 (1977).

35. Zaremski, *supra* note 34, at 6.

36. *Id.*

37. Guerrero v. Copper Queen Hosp., 112 Ariz. 104, 527 P.2d 1329 (1975); Hamburger v. Henry Ford Hosp., 91 Mich. App. 580, 284 N.W.2d 155 (1979). *Contra*, McKenna v. Cedars of Lebanon Hosp., 155 Cal. Rptr.3d 631 (Ct. App. 1979).

38. Report of the Secretary's Commission on Medical Malpractice (DHEW Pub. No. [OS] 73–88, 1973) at 16.

39. *Id.*

40. *Id.*

41. *See* Annas, Editorial, *Negligent Samaritans Are No Good*, 7(1) MEDICOLEGAL NEWS 4 (Spring 1979); Annas, *Beyond the Good Samaritan*, 8(2) HASTINGS CENTER RPT. 16 (April 1978), *and* Segal, Editorial, *In Emergencies Is Consent Necessary?* J. LEGAL MED. (Oct. 1975) at 4.

VI

Drugs and Controlled Substances

The use and distribution of drugs in the United States are governed by a complex set of state and federal laws and regulations, designed to accomplish a variety of purposes. First, the federal government hopes to exclude from interstate commerce drugs that are not both "safe and effective." This function is performed by the United States Food and Drug Administration (FDA), exercising its authority under the Food, Drug, and Cosmetic Act [1] and involves, for the most part, regulating the manufacturers of drugs. This chapter will only touch upon this topic. Second, both state and federal laws and regulation exist for the purpose of keeping "controlled substances" out of the hands of individuals who would use (or abuse) such substances for recreational as opposed to therapeutic purposes. The use of such substances is regulated primarily by the federal Controlled Substances Act (CSA) and similar laws at the state level.[2] The CSA will be discussed in some detail, as it has direct impact on providers of health care. Third, certain drugs, which have toxic or habit-forming qualities, are prohibited from public consumption without the guidance of a health care professional. Unlike over-the-counter drugs, which may be purchased by anyone, these drugs may be purchased only by a consumer who presents a valid prescription to a pharmacist. Laws regulating these drugs will also be discussed in some detail.

Since the drug laws are so complex, and various jurisdictions impose specific requirements, any reader who is involved in the prescription or administration of drugs is encouraged to consult local laws and regulations pertaining to such practices.

111

DRUGS

What is a drug?
Federal law defines the term "drug" as

1. any article that appears in the United States Pharmacopeia, official Homeopathic Pharmacopeia, or official National Formulary
2. any article intended for use in the diagnosis, cure, mitigation, treatment, or prevention of disease in humans or other animals
3. any article other than food intended to affect the structure or any function of the body of men or other animals
4. any article used as a component of any articles listed above.[3]

Although this definition appears to be quite detailed, in reality it is not at all clear where the dividing lines fall between drugs, devices, foods, and cosmetics, although the Secretary of Health, Education, and Welfare has authority to make such determinations by regulations.

What is a prescription drug?
A drug becomes a prescription drug when the FDA finds that a drug is habit forming because it contains certain narcotic or hypnotic substances, or when the drug's toxicity or potentially harmful effects, or the measures necessary to its use, make it unsafe except when used under the supervision of a practitioner.[4] Prescription drugs are sometimes called "legend drugs," because their original labels must contain the legend "Caution: Federal law prohibits dispensing without prescription." [5]

The FDA has broad discretion in determining which drugs are to be classified as prescription drugs. In one case the FDA classified as prescription drugs all preparations of Vitamin A containing more than 10,000 IU (International Units) per dosage form and of Vitamin D containing more than 400 IU per dosage form.[6] Although these vitamins were available over the counter in lower dosages, the

FDA found that prolonged use of these vitamins at those dosages could have serious toxic effects. This classification was challenged by industry and the court upheld the classification of the FDA. The court held that the FDA's determinations that a drug be deemed a prescription drug will be overturned only if such a finding is "arbitrary, capricious or contrary to law." [7]

Do states have any role in classifying prescription drugs?

Once the FDA deems a drug a prescription drug it may be sold only by prescription. Most state laws merely require a prescription for any drug for "which a prescription is required by the Federal Food, Drug, and Cosmetic Act." [8] However, some states, such as California, may require prescriptions for drugs that are not prescription drugs under federal law. [9] States may have more stringent prescription drug laws than the federal law, but they may not have less stringent laws.

How are prescription drugs ordered and dispensed?

Under federal law a prescription drug may be dispensed only by written prescription, by oral prescription that is promptly reduced to writing and filed by the pharmacist, [10] or by refilling a written or oral prescription if authorized in the original prescription, or oral order. [11] In institutions, drug orders are used instead of prescriptions.

Who has the right to prescribe drugs?

Federal law leaves this entirely up to state law, referring to a "practitioner licensed by law to administer such drugs." In most states this means physicians, dentists, podiatrists, and veterinarians. [12] Prescribing involves choosing a drug and ordering it in suitable dosages with proper instructions. State law and regulations dictate the nature of prescriptions. In California, for example, the statute requires all prescriptions to contain the name and address of the patient, the name and quantity of the drug prescribed, direction for use, date of issue, the name, address, and telephone number of the prescriber, his license classification, and his signature. [13] If the drug is a controlled substance the prescriber's Drug Enforcement Administration number must be given. In some states, instructions as to substitution of generic drugs must be included. If the prescription is refillable this must be stated.

What information must the pharmacist include on the label of a prescription drug she dispenses?

Although federal law requires prescription drugs to carry extensive labeling when sold to pharmacists and to those authorized to prescribe them, it requires relatively little labeling for consumers of prescription drugs.[14] The label must have the name and address of the dispenser, the serial number and date of the prescription or its filling, the name of the prescriber, the name of the patient if contained in the prescription, the directions for use, and cautionary statements if contained in the prescription.[15] Over-the-counter drugs require much more extensive labeling.

CONTROLLED SUBSTANCES

What is a controlled substance?

Controlled substances are drugs that may be abused, such as narcotics, stimulants, and depressants. Although these substances were regulated through a number of federal laws for over half a century, in 1970 congress passed the Comprehensive Drug Abuse Prevention and Control Act.[16] Title II of this act is the Controlled Substances Act (CSA), which directly affects the prescriber, dispenser, and consumer of controlled substances.

How are controlled substances classified?

All controlled substances are divided into five schedules, as follows:

Schedule I drugs have a high potential for abuse, have no currently accepted medical use in the United States, and are not accepted as safe for use. Drugs found in this schedule are outlawed (with a minor exception discussed below). Substances such as heroin, marijuana, LSD, and a variety of opiates are found in this schedule.

Schedule II drugs have a high potential for abuse; they have a currently accepted medical use in the United States; and abuse of them may lead to severe psychological or physical dependence. Schedule II drugs include morphine, codeine, cocaine, and amphetamines.

Schedule III drugs have a currently accepted medical use in the United States, have smaller potential for abuse than drugs in Schedules I and II, and, if abused, may lead to moderate or low physical dependence or high psychological dependence. Drugs that appear in Schedule II also appear in Schedule III, but in lower concentrations per dosage unit.

Schedule IV drugs have a lower potential for abuse than drugs in Schedule III; they have a currently accepted medical use in the United States; and their abuse may lead to limited physical or psychological dependence. Drugs in this schedule consist mainly of depressants such as phenobarbital.

Schedule V drugs have lower potential for abuse than drugs in Schedule IV; they have a currently accepted medical use in the United States; and their abuse may lead to limited physical or psychological dependence. These drugs tend to contain very limited concentrations of narcotic drugs combined with non-narcotic active ingredients such as terpin hydrate elixir with codeine.[17]

Under the CSA, the Attorney General has the authority, in cooperation with the Secretary of Health and Human Services, to add drugs to a specific schedule, remove a drug from all scheduling, or move a drug from one schedule to another.[18]

Who has the right to prescribe controlled substances?

Only practitioners who are registered with the Drug Enforcement Administration (DEA) may prescribe or order scheduled drugs, with the following exception.[19] An intern, resident, foreign-trained physician, or physician on the staff of a Veterans Administration Medical Center may prescribe, administer, or dispense controlled substances under the institution's registration as long as: it is done in the usual course of his professional practice; the practitioner is legally authorized to do so in the jurisdiction in which he is practicing; the institution has verified the practitioner's legal authority to so act in the jurisdiction; the practitioner is acting within the scope of his employment at the institution; and the institution authorizes the practitioner to prescribe, dispense, and administer controlled substances under its DEA registration number, and assigns a code to the practitioner, which must be written as a suffix after the institution's registration number on all prescriptions.[20]

When does a practitioner have the right to issue a prescription for a controlled substance?

A prescription for a controlled substance may be issued only for a legitimate medical purpose by a practitioner acting in the usual course of his professional practice.[21] A prescription is an order for medication which is dispensed to or for an ultimate user.[22] Therefore a prescription may not be issued by a practitioner in order for him to obtain controlled substances for the purpose of dispensing these drugs to his patients. A prescription may not be issued for the dispensing of narcotic drugs for detoxification or maintenance treatment.[23] However, a physician may administer (but not prescribe) narcotic drugs to a person for the purpose of relieving acute withdrawal symptoms when necessary while arrangements are being made for referral for treatment. Not more than one day's medication may be administered to the person at one time, and such treatment may not be rendered for more than three days.[24] These rules do not affect a physician who wishes to administer or dispense narcotics to persons with intractable pain, or to maintain or detoxify a person as an incidental adjunct to medical or surgical treatment of conditions other than addiction.[25] One who wishes to administer or dispense narcotics for purposes of detoxification or maintenance treatment must register specially for this activity.[26]

Who may fill a prescription for controlled substances?

Only a pharmacist who is individually registered or employed in a DEA-registered pharmacy or DEA-registered institution may fill such prescriptions.[27]

Who is responsible if a prescription for a controlled substance is filled when it was not issued for legitimate medical purposes?

Both the prescriber and pharmacist can be responsible. Where a physician issues prescriptions to patients without examining them or taking a history to diagnose and treat some condition, the physician can be subject to criminal action for violation of the CSA. A pharmacist who knowingly fills a prescription that was not issued for a legitimate medical purpose is also criminally liable.[28]

Thus, a pharmacy owner who had to buy a million Ritalin tablets in an eleven-month period in order to fill the prescription of a particular clinic ought to have known that something unusual, and probably illegal, was going on.[29] In another case, a pharmacist who dispensed 1,600 Dilaudid tablets to one customer in less than a month was found guilty of willfully and knowingly violating the CSA.[30]

What are the requirements for prescribing Schedule II drugs?

All Schedule II drugs must be prescribed in writing, with one narrow exception. In an emergency a registered practitioner may prescribe a drug orally as long as the quantity prescribed and dispensed is limited to an amount adequate to treat the emergency, the prescription is reduced to writing by the pharmacist, and the pharmacist makes a good-faith effort to confirm the identity of the prescriber (such as calling back the prescriber using her phone number listed in the telephone directory); within seventy-two hours, the prescribing practitioner should deliver a written prescription for the emergency prescription to the pharmacist.[31] If the prescription is mailed it must be postmarked within seventy-two hours of the oral communication. The pharmacist is required to notify the local DEA office if he does not receive a written prescription.[32]

An emergency is defined as a situation in which the prescribing practitioner determines that:

1. Immediate administration of the controlled substance is necessary for proper treatment of the intended ultimate user;
2. No appropriate alternative treatment is available, including administration of a drug which is not a controlled substance under Schedule II of the act; and
3. It is not reasonably possible for the prescribing practitioner to provide a written prescription to be presented to the person dispensing the substance prior to the dispensing.[33]

Schedule II prescriptions may not be refilled.[34] If a pharmacist is unable to supply the full quantity called for in the prescription, he may partially fill the prescription, note this fact on the face of the prescription, and fill the remaining portion of the prescription within seventy-two hours. If the pharmacist cannot fill the remaining portion of the prescription within seventy-two hours he must so notify the prescriber. No further quantity can be supplied after seventy-two hours.[35]

The label must show the date of filling, the pharmacy name and address, the serial number of the prescription, the patient's name, prescriber's name, and directions for use or cautions, if any, contained in the prescription or required by law.[36]

What are the requirements for prescribing drugs listed in Schedules III, IV, and V?

These requirements are less stringent than those for Schedule II drugs. A registered practitioner can prescribe in writing or orally. The pharmacist must reduce verbal prescriptions to writing, but need not obtain a written prescription from the prescriber.[37] If authorized by the prescriber, Schedule III and IV prescriptions may be refilled up to five times, but for not longer than a six-month period, at which time a new prescription is required.[38] Schedule V prescriptions may be refilled in accordance with the prescriber's instructions.[39] All refills must be noted and initialed on the back of the prescription. Prescriptions and refillings for Schedule III, IV, and V drugs may be partially filled as long as it is noted on the prescription, the total quantity dispensed in all partial fillings does not exceed the quantity prescribed, and no dispensing occurs six months after the date the prescription was issued.[40]

May controlled substances ever be dispensed without a prescription?

Yes. Not all controlled substances are prescription drugs, especially some of those found in Schedule V. The pharmacist may dispense such drugs as long as she is authorized under state law to dispense controlled substances (but a nonpharmacist employee may not, even under the pharmacist's supervision); she does not dispense more than 240cc of such a controlled substance containing opium nor more than 120cc of any other controlled substance; and she does not dispense more than forty-eight dosage units of such a substance containing opium, nor more than twenty-four dosage units of any other substance, to the same purchaser in a forty-eight-hour period. The purchaser must be at least eighteen years old, and the pharmacist must require the purchaser to furnish suitable identification. A bound book must be maintained by the pharmacist that contains the name and address of the purchaser, the name and quantity of the controlled substance purchased, the date of purchase, and the name or initials of the pharmacist dispensing the substance.[41]

May states impose additional limitations on the prescribing of controlled substances?

Yes. For example, Massachusetts state law prohibits filling a prescription for a Schedule II or III substance with more than a thirty-day supply, with the exception of two drugs.[42] In New York, Schedule II prescriptions must be written on a special state form that is filled out in triplicate. The physician and pharmacist keep one copy each for five years, and one copy must be filed with the state Department of Public Health.[43] This requirement was upheld as constitutional by the U.S. Supreme Court.[44]

May a Schedule I drug ever be used by a practitioner?

Yes, but only pursuant to the research protocol approved by the FDA and DEA, and only after a separate DEA registration has been obtained.[45]

Is it ever necessary to obtain multiple registrations?

Yes. Registrations have a strong geographical aspect, so that if a physician has two offices where he regularly *administers* or *dispenses* controlled substances as a regular part of his practice, and therefore maintains supplies of such substances, he must have a separate registration for each office. If he has two offices but only *prescribes* controlled substances from one, but administers or dispenses them at the other, he needs only one registration. Likewise, pharmacies with more than one location must have multiple registrations.[46]

Likewise, registrations are issued for particular purposes. Federal regulations list eleven separate categories requiring individual registration, including manufacturing, distribution, dispensing, conducting research with Schedule II–V drugs, conducting narcotic treatment programs with Schedule II–V narcotics, conducting research and instructional activities with Schedule I drugs, as well as other activities.[47]

Registration in one category sometimes carries with it authority to engage in coincidental activities. For example, a person registered to dispense Schedule II–V drugs is also authorized to conduct research and to conduct educational activities with such drugs.[48] And a person authorized to manufacture or import any class of controlled substances is also authorized to distribute substances in that class.[49]

When may a registration be denied, suspended, or revoked?

The CSA compels the DEA to issue a registration for Schedule II–V drugs to a practitioner who is "authorized to dispense or conduct research under the law of the state in which they practice." [50] Pharmacies are also required to be registered if they are authorized to dispense under the law of the state in which they conduct business.[51] Registration may be revoked or suspended if the registrant falsified his application; has been convicted, under the law of the United States or any state, of a felony relating to a controlled substance; or has had his state license or registration suspended, revoked, or denied by a state authority and is no longer authorized under state law to engage in manufacturing, distribution, or dispensing of controlled substances. The revocation or suspension can be limited to a particular substance. Prior to suspension or revocation, a registrant is entitled to notice and hearing. Suspension and revocation of registration is independent of any criminal prosecutions that may be brought.[52]

GENERIC DRUGS

What are antisubstitution laws?

In the 1950s, in an effort to reduce the sale of counterfeit drugs shaped, colored, and labeled like legitimate products, state legislatures passed "antisubstitution laws," which made it a crime for a pharmacist to dispense a drug other than the one specifically prescribed.[53] Some of these statutes were quite specific in outlawing the dispensing of a "different drug or brand of drug" in lieu of the one ordered.[54]

Some statutes were more ambiguous, prohibiting the dispensing of an "imitation of another drug," [55] or "an ingredient or article different in any manner from the ingredient or article prescribed." [56] Even in states with antisubstitution laws, if the physician prescribes generically, rather than by brand, any brand of that drug may be dispensed.

What are generic "drug substitution" laws?

A number of states have recently revoked their antisubstitution laws, and have replaced them with laws that permit brand substitution. Although these laws are sometimes referred to as permitting "drug substitution," [57] none of these laws permits the pharmacist to substitute a different *drug* from the one prescribed. And none of these laws *requires* a physician to prescribe generically. As one commentator has pointed out, "It simply assumes that a physician's source selection (*i.e.*, a prescription naming a brand) is a deliberate selection and not a shorthand for a generic prescription." [58]

What do generic substitution laws require?

These laws are a matter of state legislation, so various states have different provisions. A number of states have positive-formulary provisions, which means that when substitution is permitted, only brands that appear on a formulary prepared by a specific organization may be substituted.[59] Other states use a negative-formulary system whereby brands are listed that are deemed to be nonequivalent.[60] Virtually all state laws require or imply that cost savings should be passed on to the consumer, and some laws directly address the issue by, for example, prohibiting a pharmacist charging a different professional fee for filling generic prescriptions.[61] A number of laws require consumer notification or consent in order for substitution to occur.[62] In some states the pharmacist is *required* to substitute the less expensive generic equivalent unless the practitioner or purchaser indicates otherwise.[63]

There are a variety of other provisions found in generic-substitutions laws, including special labeling provisions, the posting of brand name and approved generic equivalent drugs, and requirements for notifying the physician if a generic is to be substituted.

Do generic substitution laws put the pharmacist at greater risk for malpractice?

Some commentators, many of whom represent or work for drug companies that manufacture brand name drugs, have argued that laws permitting substitution increase the pharmacist's liability.[64] In a very minor way this is true in some jurisdictions. The issue arises when a pharmacist substitutes one brand for another, she is making a professional judgment that these brands are indeed interchangeable. As discussed above, many states have positive formulary laws, in which some agency or board produces a list of interchangeable brands. When a pharmacist dispenses drugs from these lists, she should have no increased liability, since these brands have been formally deemed to be interchangeable, and the pharmacist does not exercise judgment in this regard. In states where there is a negative formulary, the pharmacist should not dispense those brands deemed to be not interchangeable. In states where neither of these systems exist, the pharmacist is in the same position she has always been in when the physician has prescribed generically—that is, she chooses the brand with no formal guidance. In this situation if the pharmacist knows, or should have known in the exercise of reasonable prudence, that the drug she dispenses is inferior to others available, she could be liable. However, as long as the pharmacist acts as a reasonable pharmacist would in similar circumstances, that is to say, that other pharmacists would dispense the same brand of drug, she will not be liable for negligence. It is of course essential for a pharmacist making brand choices to keep up to date with information regarding bio-equivalent drug products.

A number of states have specifically addressed the issue of the pharmacist's liability in regard to generic substitutions. In one form or another these states specify that the pharmacist will not be subjected to greater liability for dispensing in accordance with substitution laws.[65]

Do physicians have a right to prescribe, and pharmacists have a right to dispense, a drug for a use that has not been approved by the FDA?

Although this is a matter of some controversy, it would appear that drugs may be prescribed and dispensed in dosages different than those recognized by the FDA as safe and effective, and for indications other than those recognized by the FDA.[66] Section 505 of the Food, Drug, and Cosmetics Act prohibits the introduction into commerce of a drug unless an Investigational New Drug exemption has been obtained or a New Drug Application has been approved. A drug is approved for such shipment after it has been shown to be safe and effective in specific doses. The role of the FDA focuses on interstate shipment, not on use. The Food, Drug, and Cosmetic Act is not intended to interfere with the practice of medicine. In a notice of proposed rule-making the FDA has stated,

As the law now stands, therefore, the Food and Drug Administration is charged with the responsibility for judging the safety and effectiveness of drugs and the truthfulness of their labeling. The physician is then responsible for making the final judgment as to which, if any, of the available drugs his patient will receive in the light of the information contained in their labeling and other adequate scientific data available to him.[67]

Once a drug is on the market, a physician may exercise his professional judgment as to how it will be used.

Very little is known about how often physicians prescribe drugs for uses not indicated on their labels. What data does exist, however, suggests there is considerable prescribing for nonindicated uses for inpatients, and somewhat less for outpatients. One study of hospitalized patients showed that three particular drugs were used very frequently for unlabeled uses: cephalexin (78 percent of the time), allopurinol (57 percent), and propranolol (66 percent). The authors concluded that physicians are not greatly influenced by the recommendations in the package insert, and, in the case of propranolol, that the package insert was seriously out of date.[68]

In a more recent study of the charts of five hundred outpatients, researchers found that approximately 9 percent of all prescriptions were for unlabeled indications. They also surveyed physicians and found little awareness that the drugs were not being used in a manner consistent with their labeling.[69]

Caution, however, must be exercised for such unapproved uses. Should the patient be injured by the drug, the physician may be sued for malpractice. In such a case the physician must be prepared to demonstrate that he knew of the approved uses and dosages, and prove that he was acting reasonably when he prescribed or used the drug in an unapproved manner.[70]

In a situation in which a pharmacist receives a prescription he knows is for an unapproved use, or in a dosage that substantially deviates from what is approved or recommended by the manufacturer, he should contact the prescribing physician to make sure no error was made. It has been suggested that in really questionable cases, the pharmacist should obtain a written acknowledgment and even have the physician agree to protect the pharmacist from liability.[71]

A more difficult question exists when a physician or pharmacist orders a drug from out of state, intending that it will be used in an unapproved manner. By doing this the physician or pharmacist causes an unapproved drug to be put into interstate commerce.[72] This could constitute violation of the law, although in a given circumstance it would be difficult to prove the requisite intent.

Does a physician have a right to administer drugs that are not approved for any use?

Even though the Food, Drug, and Cosmetic Act does not regulate or interfere with the practice of medicine, if the drug in question has not been approved for any purpose it will not be marketable in interstate commerce. This means it will be virtually inaccessible. This issue has been discussed recently in the context of using Laetrile to treat cancer patients. The FDA has never found Laetrile to be safe and effective, and therefore shipment of the drug has been prohibited. In 1975, terminally ill cancer patients applied to the federal courts in Oklahoma to prevent the FDA from prohibiting the shipment of Laetrile for use by such patients. The lower federal court found, among other things, that by preventing terminal cancer patients from obtaining Laetrile the FDA had violated the patients' constitutionally protected right to privacy,[73] and the federal appeals court found that the FDA's use of safety and effectiveness criteria has no reasonable application to terminally ill cancer patients.[74] The appeals court then went on to order the FDA to permit limited interstate shipment of Laetrile. The U.S. Supreme Court reversed the decisions, finding that the federal law makes no exception for terminally ill patients, and that the FDA had the authority to ban drugs not found to be safe and effective.[75]

Again, it must be emphasized that the issue in this case focuses on shipment and not on use. If a physician could totally manufacture the drug within the borders of one state, the drug could be used without violating federal law. In this context it is interesting to note that every person who operates any establishment engaged in the interstate or intrastate manufacture of drugs must register with the Secretary of HHS and is subject to a variety of regulatory mechanisms.[76] However, practitioners who are licensed by law to prescribe or administer drugs and who "manufacture, propagate, compound or process drugs or devices solely for use in the course of their professional practice" are exempt from this requirement.[77] A similar exemption exists for pharmacists.[78]

A physician risks a malpractice suit if a patient has a bad result from the use of a drug which is approved for no purpose, and use of such a drug may be deemed unprofessional conduct by a licensing board.

NOTES

1. 21 U.S.C. 321 *et. seq.*
2. P. L. 91–513; 21 U.S.C. 801 *et. seq.*
3. 21 U.S.C. 321(g).
4. 21 U.S.C. 353(b)(1).
5. 21 U.S.C. 353(b)(4).
6. National Nutritional Foods Ass'n. v. Weinberger, 512 F.2d 688 (2d Cir. 1975), *cert. den.,* 423 U.S. 827.

7. *Id.* at 704.
8. *See, e.g.,* N.Y. EDUC. LAW §6810.
9. Cal. HEALTH & SAFETY CODE §26663.
10. 21 U.S.C. 353(b)(1)(c).
11. *Id.*
12. *See, e.g.,* Cal. BUS. & PROF. CODE §4036.
13. *Id.*
14. 21 U.S.C. 352.
15. 21 U.S.C. 353(b)(2).
16. P.L. 91–513.
17. P.L. 91–513 §202.
18. P.L. 91–513 §201.
19. P.L. 91–513 §302.
20. 21 C.F.R. 1301.24(c).
21. 21 C.F.R. 1306.04(a).
22. 21 C.F.R. 1306.02(e).
23. 21 C.F.R. 1306.04(c).
24. 21 C.F.R. 1306.07(b).
25. 21 C.F.R. 1306.07(c).
26. 21 C.F.R. 1306.07(a).
27. 21 C.F.R. 1306.06.
28. 21 C.F.R. 1306.04(a); U.S. v. Green, 511 F.2d 1062 (7th Cir. 1975), *cert. den.* 423 U.S. 1031.
29. *Id.*
30. U.S. v. Kershman, 555 F.2d 198 (8th Cir. 1977).
31. 21 C.F.R. 1306.11(d).
32. 21 C.F.R. 1306.11(d)(4).
33. 21 C.F.R. 1.110.
34. 21 C.F.R. 1306.12.
35. 21 C.F.R. 1306.13.
36. 21 C.F.R. 1306.14.
37. 21 C.F.R. 1306.21.
38. 21 C.F.R. 1306.22.
39. 21 C.F.R. 1306.31(a).
40. 21 C.F.R. 1306.23.
41. 21 C.F.R. 1306.32.
42. MASS. GEN. LAWS ch. 94c §23.
43. N.Y. PUB. HEALTH LAW §3331–39.
44. Whalen v. Roe, 429 U.S. 589 (1977).
45. 21 C.F.R. 1301.22(a)(7), 1301.32(a)(6), 1301.33.
46. 21 C.F.R. 1301.23.
47. 21 C.F.R. 1301.22(a).
48. 21 C.F.R. 1301.22(b)(6).

49. 21 C.F.R. 1301.22(b)(1).

50. P.L. 91–513 §303(f).

51. *Id.*

52. P.L. 91–513 §304; 21 C.F.R. 1301.41 *et seq.*

53. SILVERMAN & LEE, PILLS, PROFITS, AND POLITICS 142–43 (Berkeley: University of Cal. Press, 1974).

54. *See, e.g.,* ALA. CODE §34–23–8; ILL. ANN. STAT. ch. 56½ §503.1–4 (Smith-Hurd supp. 1972).

55. CONN. GEN. STAT. ANN. §19–226 (1969).

56. FLA. STAT. ANN. §465.101h (1972).

57. Brennan, *Drug Substitution—Boon to Consumers versus Legal Traps for the Professional,* J. LEGAL MED. 20 (Mar. 1976).

58. Chadwick, *Physician-Controlled Source Selection—A Suggested Approach to Substitution,* J. LEGAL MED. 26, 29 (March 1976).

59. *See, e.g.,* MASS. GEN. LAWS ch. 112 §12D; VA. CODE ANN. §54–524.101.9; KY. REV. STAT. §217.822.

60. *See, e.g.,* DEL. CODE ANN. 24 §2589; FLA. STAT. ANN. §465.025.

61. *See, e.g.,* MONT. REV. CODE ANN. §27–703; OHIO REV. CODE ANN. §4729.38; WIS. STAT. ANN. §450.075.

62. *See, e.g.,* MONT. REV. CODE ANN. §27–703; ALASKA STAT. §08.80.295; DEL. CODE ANN. §2589; OHIO REV. CODE ANN. §4729.38.4.

63. *See, e.g.,* MASS. GEN. LAW ANN. ch. 112 §12D; KEN. STAT. ANN. §65–675.

64. *See* Brennan, *supra* note 57; Sonnenreich, *State Substitution Laws—A Lawyer's View,* 2 U.S. PHARMACIST 1 (Apr. 1977).

65. *See, e.g.,* OR. REV. STAT. §689.845; R.I. GEN. LAWS ANN. §42–18.1–5.

66. GIBSON, MEDICATION, LAW & BEHAVIOR 320–32 (New York: John Wiley and Sons, 1976).

67. 37 Fed. Reg. 16,503, 16,504 (Aug. 14, 1972).

68. Mundy, Flechenstein, & Mazzullo, *Current Medical Practice and the Food and Drug Administration: Some Evidence of the Existing Gap,* 229 JAMA 1744 (Sept. 23, 1974).

69. Erichson, Bergman, Schneeweis, & Cherkin, *The Uses of Drugs for Unlabeled Indications,* 243 JAMA 1543 (Apr. 18, 1980); *And see,* Rollins, *What Nurses Should Know*

about Administering New Drugs, 1(6) NURSING LAW & ETHICS 1 (June–July, 1980).

70. Mulder v. Parke, Davis & Co., 288 Minn. 332, 181 N.W. 2d 882 (1970).

71. DEMARCO, PHARMACY AND THE LAWS 213 (Germantown, Md.: Aspen Systems Corp., 1975).

72. GIBSON, *supra* note 66, at 331–32; *supra* note 67.

73. Rutherford v. United States, 438 F. Supp. 1287, 1298–300 (W.D. Okla. 1977).

74. Rutherford v. United States, 582 F.2d 1234, 1236 (8th Cir. 1977).

75. United States v. Rutherford, 544 U.S. 442 (1979); Rutherford v. United States, 616 F.2d 455 (10th Cir. 1980) (holding that Laetrile could not qualify for any exemptions from the FDA's new-drug requirements, and that it is within the FDA's authority to forbid even terminally ill patients to take Laetrile since drug regulation is "within the area of governmental interest in protecting the public health"). *See* Annas, *Laetrile: Should the Dying Patient Decide?* 1(7) NURSING LAW & ETHICS 1 (Aug.–Sept. 1980).

76. 21 U.S.C. 360.

77. 21 U.S.C. 360(g)(2).

78. 21 U.S.C. 360(g)(1).

VII

Human Experimentation
and Research

The law's attitude toward human experimentation in medicine has changed radically over the past four decades. Before World War II, courts tended to view experimentation as quackery, and often held physicians absolutely liable for injuries suffered by patients. Any major deviation from standard medical practice was considered malpractice: physicians experimented at their own peril.[1]

Courts now generally support the medical profession's research enterprise as both legitimate and necessary for medical progress. Perhaps the case that best illustrates the judiciary's new perception of medical experimentation is one involving the treatment of cancer. A farmer was suffering from cancer of the lip. He told his physician that he did not want surgery, and accordingly was treated with drug injections for nine months. After that time the cancer had spread so much that the physician discharged the patient and sent him home. The farmer sued the physician, alleging both wrongful experimentation and abandonment. The court commented:

> . . . we believe the pivotal question is whether a physician who uses a method other than X-ray, radium and surgery in treating cancer, by that act alone, indulges in malpractice. The appellant concedes that these three methods "have the blessing of the American Medical Association" but he contends that there is no sure cure for the ailment and "no unanimity of opinion as to which of said procedures should be employed on [sic] a particular case."

This Court will take judicial notice of the supreme effort being made by the members of the medical profession and by the citizenry as well to conquer the great human killer, cancer. The fight is unrelenting. . . . The reason, of course, for the intensive campaign is that the disease is out of hand because the *remedy is so far unfound.* . . .

We do not propose to indicate what form the record in this case would appear to be the proper treatment in a given case. . . . But we do have a conviction that the heroic effort being made by members of the medical profession and other scientists only emphasizes that *an enemy is so far being fought in the dark and that one man should not be condemned from the fact alone that he chooses a weapon that another may consider a reed.* . . . [emphasis supplied] [2]

The court concluded, "If there is no certain cure and if the physician did not indulge in quackery by representing he had one," then no malpractice can be found solely because he experimented with possible cures.

This chapter presents the law's view of licit and illicit human experimentation, and reviews the factors that distinguish one from the other. Its theme is the development and application of legal doctrines designed to permit human experimentation to continue while attempting to guarantee that the rights of research subjects are protected.

Why did the law become involved in human experimentation?

As in most areas of medicine, the law has been reactive rather than prospective; reaction has been to atrocities rather than to "standard medical activity." Thus one finds the most comprehensive and authoritative legal statement on human experimentation embodied in the Nuremberg Code, which was articulated in a court opinion concerning the trial of twenty-three Nazi physicians for "war crimes and crimes against humanity" during World War II. The court rejected the defendants' contention that their experiments with both prisoners of war and civilians were consistent with the ethics of the medical profession as evidenced by previously published experiments on venereal diseases, plague, and malaria, among others. Instead the court found that only "certain types of medical experiments on human beings, when *kept within reasonably well-defined bounds*, conform to the ethics of the medical profession generally."

The basis of the code is a type of natural law reasoning. In the court's words: "All agree . . . that certain basic principles must be observed in order to satisfy moral, ethical, and legal concepts." Principle 1 demonstrates the primacy the court placed on the concept of consent:

1. The voluntary consent of the human subject is absolutely essential.

   This means that the person involved should have *legal capacity to give consent;* should be so situated as to be able to exercise *free power of choice*, without the intervention of any element of force, fraud, deceit, duress, over-reaching, or other ulterior form of constraint or coercion; and should have *sufficient knowledge* and *comprehension* of the elements of the subject matter involved as to enable him to make an understanding and enlightened decision. This latter element requires that before the acceptance of an affirmative decision by the experimental subject there should be made known to him the nature, duration and purpose of the experiment; the method and means by which it is to be conducted; all inconveniences and hazards reasonably to be expected; and the effects upon his health or person which may *possibly* come from his participation in the experiment.

   The duty and responsibility for ascertaining the quality of the consent rests upon each individual who initiates, directs, or engages in the experiment. It is a personal duty and responsibility which may not be delegated to another with impunity [emphasis supplied].[3]

The Nuremberg Code thus requires that the consent of the experimental subject have at least four characteristics: it must be competent, voluntary, informed, and comprehending. The code has been adopted by the United Nations and used as the basis for other international documents, such as the Declaration of Helsinki. It is a part of international common law, and can properly be viewed as both a criminal and civil basis for liability in the United States.[4]

The United States has had its own medical experimentation scandals. In a 1963 study, terminally ill patients at the Jewish Chronic Disease Hospital in Brooklyn, New York, were injected with live cancer cells to test their immune response. The patients were not informed of the type of cells injected, only that it was a "skin test."[5] In the "Tuskegee study," treatment was withheld for decades from a group of poor black rural males who had syphilis so that the natural course of the disease could be studied.[6] In the "Willowbrook experiments," retarded children were deliberately infected with hepatitis in order that experimentation on a potential vaccine could continue.[7] In the early 1960s, more than two million thalidomide tablets were distributed to 20,000 patients in the United States by 1,267 physicians as part of a research study. When told of the potentially toxic effects of the drug on fetuses, more than 400 made no effort to contact their patients directly, and many of these were unable to do so because they had kept no records of those to whom they had given the drug.[8] And in 1970, seventy-six Mexican-American women who requested "the pill" at a clinic were given a placebo so that subjective side effects could be monitored; ten became pregnant.[9]

In 1966, Dr. Henry Beecher of Harvard Medical School reported on twenty-two unethical experiments that took place in the United States after the promulgation of the Nuremberg Code.[10] Examples included deliberate withholding of penicillin from sufferers of streptococcal infection, and the transplantation of a cancer tumor from a daughter to her mother to see if it would produce cancer in the mother. It did. And in 1979, HEALTH/PAC published a study of a series of experiments on obstetrical patients from the late 1960s through the mid-1970s in New York, all of which involved the deliberate subjecting of humans to known harm to confirm previously proven theories.[11]

Legal reactions have included amendments to the Food, Drug, and Cosmetic Act relating to drug testing; regulations by the National Institutes of Health on human experimentation and institutional review; and the creation by Congress of a national commission to study human experimentation (1974–78), and a presidential commission which began work in 1980.[12] While some new rules have been viewed as repressive and anti-intellectual, their context and purpose is to insure that medical experimentation is *not* outlawed, but permitted to flourish in a way consistent with the interest of human subjects and society as a whole.

What are the purposes of obtaining the informed consent of research subjects?

Since informed consent is the critical element in the Nuremberg Code and current federal regulations, and since it is often the source of heated controversy, it is important to review the purposes of the doctrine to understand why it occupies this central position. It has been charged, for example, that informed consent is actually a "legal fiction" designed for three purposes: (1) to block research by a pressure group; (2) to permit compensation for injury as a result of experimentation or treatment; and (3) to transform the doctor-patient relationship into one defined by contract rather than status.[13] While the first two are consequences of the doctrine rather than purposes, the third strikes at the heart of the rationale. In reference to human experimentation, that rationale can be summed up in two objectives: (1) to promote individual autonomy, and (2) to encourage rational decision making.

1. *To promote individual autonomy.*

The purpose of autonomy (or self-determination) is to protect the individual's integrity as a person by denying anyone the right to invade his body without his consent. This simple proposition can be restated in a number of ways and approached from a variety of directions—the ultimate conclusion, however, remains the same. For example, one can label this the "right to be left alone," or the "right to privacy" concerning decisions about one's body. Another approach is the view that research on human subjects must always be viewed as a "joint enterprise" between the researcher and subject to prevent the subject from becoming an object or thing to be used, instead of a human being.[14] Viewed from this perspective, informed consent is necessary to prevent grossly taking advantage of subjects to the point where their humanness is in such question that the types of procedures that are performed on them are expanded beyond what society would view as tolerable.[15]

Still another approach notes that the purpose of human experimentation is ultimately to benefit all through medical progress, but that the burdens or risks of such experimentation will of necessity fall on only a few. In this view the subject is giving a "gift" to society—a gift that cannot rightfully be forcibly taken, and one that is devalued (and the giver debased) insofar as the gift is based on a false assumption concerning the risks involved.[16] As with all of the other approaches, the conclusion is that to adequately protect an individual's autonomy and personhood, it is essential to provide him with enough information to permit him to make up his own mind concerning participation in the proposed experiment.

The view that the promotion of individual autonomy comes at the price of sometimes delaying scientific advances is, we think, adequately dealt with by the oft-quoted argument of Hans Jonas:

> Let us not forget that progress is an optional goal, not an unconditional commitment, and that its tempo in particular, compulsive as it may become, has nothing sacred about it. Let us also remember that a slower progress in the conquest of disease would not threaten society, grievous as it is to those who have to deplore that their particular disease be not yet conquered, but that society would indeed be threatened by the erosion of those moral values whose loss, probably caused by too ruthless a pursuit of scientific progress, would make its most dazzling triumphs not worth having.[17]

2. *To encourage rational decision making.*
While this goal is clearly viewed as secondary by the courts, it is an extremely important function of the informed consent doctrine. If this goal is not achieved, the entire concept is called into serious question. Professors Jay Katz and Alexander Capron, for example, note that the requirement that the researcher catalogue and explain the

risks inherent in any research proposal to the subject requires him to review the literature and animal experiments before embarking on human experimentation. They quote Professor Paul Freund: "To analyze an experiment in terms of risks and benefits to particular groups by way of presentation for consent is a salutary procedure for self-scrutiny by the investigator—like the preparation of a registration statement by a corporation issuing securities." [18]

The hope is that this self-scrutiny will prevent a number of research projects from being performed, or at least postpone their initiation until adequate animal testing has been done. Similarly, one would anticipate that after a candid review of extreme risks, subjects would refuse to participate with such regularity as to make experiments that are inherently too dangerous to be ethically performed on humans *de facto* impossible. It is suggested that the ability to refuse to participate is what is really at stake here, rather than the ability of the subject to fully comprehend all of the aspects of the research proposal and make an independent judgment as to its merit. As Katz and Capron point out, "who other than the patient-subjects, can determine whether the benefits of the procedure, conventional or experimental, outweigh the burdens that will be imposed on them?" [19]

One function of informed consent is therefore to help ensure that those who bear the risks of experimentation will have the final decision as to whether or not it is performed. The argument is that this type of voluntary decision will help minimize the costs to the system of scientific advance since rational decisions are more likely if they are made by those who bear the risk of the decision. Others might also have conflicting motives, such as career advancement. [20]

What are the components of informed consent to human experimentation?

Current federal regulations specify that subjects must be presented with all of the following about the proposed experiment:

1. A statement that the study involves research, an explanation of its purposes and expected duration, and

a description of the procedures to be followed, identifying which are experimental;

2. A description of reasonably foreseeable risks or discomforts;

3. A description of any reasonably expected benefits to the subject or others;

4. A disclosure of appropriate alternative procedures or courses of treatment that might be advantageous to the subject;

5. A statement describing the extent to which confidentiality of records identifying the subject will be maintained;

6. For research involving more than minimal risk, an explanation about any compensation or medical treatments available if injury occurs;

7. An explanation of whom to contact for answers to questions or in the event of injury;

8. A statement that participation is voluntary and that refusal to participate will involve no penalty or loss of benefits; and that the subject may discontinue at any time without prejudice.[21]

An institutional review board (IRB) may waive the requirement for a signed consent form if: (1) the only record linking the subject to the research would be the consent form and this would put the subject at risk regarding confidentiality; and (2) the research presents no more than minimal risk of harm and involves no procedures for which written consent is normally required outside the research context. In addition, some categories of research, such as normal educational research, educational testing, most interview procedures, some observational research, and use of public data, need not be reviewed at all by an IRB. And some categories of research, such as collection of hair and nail clippings, collection of external secretions and small blood samples, voice recordings, and moderate exercise, can be given an "expedited review," and do not require written informed consent.[22]

Do researchers have a right to delegate the duty of obtaining informed consent?

Yes, but the Nuremberg Code makes it clear that obtaining the informed consent of the research subject is the obligation of the researcher: "The duty and responsibility for ascertaining the quality of the consent rests upon each individual who initiates, directs, or engages in the experiment. It is a *personal duty and responsibility* which may not be delegated to another with impunity" (emphasis supplied).

While this issue is not specifically addressed in current federal regulations, we believe that the only way to ensure that the goals of promoting autonomy and rational decision-making are met is to insist that those conducting the research are the ones who actually obtain the subjects' informed consent. Accordingly, nurses and other allied health care professionals, who are not directly conducting the experiment in question, and who are not members of the research team, should not be given (nor should they accept) the responsibility of obtaining consent. However, nonphysician members of the team may be better communicators and so may be the appropriate ones to seek consent.

Who should sign an informed consent document as a witness?

In general, there is no legal requirement that consent forms be witnessed at all. However, their value as *evidence* of the informed consent *process* is greatly strengthened if that process itself was witnessed by someone other than the subject and the researcher. Nonetheless, while it has become common to have these forms witnessed, it is not yet common practice to have the entire information exchange process witnessed.

In nonmedical affairs, a witness usually is a witness to the signature only—that is, the witness observes the person signing the document, and is there to attest that the person appears competent and is not signing under any obvious duress. The human experimentation setting is different. Since the critical elements in the transaction are the *comprehension* by the subject of the information received and its completeness, we believe no witness should sign the form unless she has actually been present during the *entire* consent process, *and* believes that full information was given, that the information was understood, and that the consent obtained is voluntary, competent, and an understanding one. Even though this is not legally required, we believe it is a prudent policy.

The adoption of such a rule protects all three participants. It protects the research subject by adding another person who must be convinced of the quality of the consent process. It protects the witness—from being commandeered into signing a form she may feel very uncomfortable about because she had no independent knowledge of the quality of the consent process. If called upon to testify about the process, the witness need not state that she really doesn't know whether the consent was informed at all, since she did not observe the process. Instead of letting the plaintiff's attorney picture her as a "co-conspirator" with the investigator to get the subject's signature without full disclosure, the witness will be able to respond that she did indeed witness the entire procedure and agreed that fully informed consent had been obtained. Finally, a witness to the entire process is an excellent aide to an investigator who is later charged with failure to obtain informed consent. It is no longer his word against the subject's: the investigator has an independent witness who observed the entire transaction and can testify as to its completeness.

Do nurses and other allied health professionals have a right to refuse to witness informed consent forms?

Yes. Acting as a witness to legal documents is not part of the delivery of health care that nurses and other allied health care professionals are legally obligated to render. On the other hand, these health professionals may feel considerable pressure to sign consent forms as witness. In such cases they should observe the entire consent process, and sign only if they agree that fully informed consent has been obtained. If they are unable to do this for any reason, and still feel that they are not free to refuse to sign the form, they should add after their signature a notation such as "witness to the signature only." This will help clarify their role to all concerned.

It is suggested that in hospitals where the nurses or other staff members believe they are being "used" as witnesses without any input into the actual consent process, they develop an internal staff policy regarding witnessing documents. This policy should set forth the conditions, if any, under which members of the staff will sign a document as a witness.[23]

Is the informed consent of the research subject always necessary for lawful experimentation?

Yes. There are two critical lessons to be learned from the material in this chapter: informed consent is a *necessary precondition* to lawful human experimentation; but informed consent is *not alone a sufficient precondition*. Other requirements, such as the reasonableness of the experiment, review by an institutional review board, and provisions for withdrawal and compensation for harm are discussed below.

There may be some limited circumstances under which consent may be obtained from a proxy.

What are the primary objections to informed consent in the research setting?

The traditional argument against the subject-patient having a major role in decision making is twofold: (1) the subject will never be able to comprehend the information; and (2) the information will unduly frighten the subject, who consequently will not participate in research projects that actually entail only a minimal risk. The conclusion drawn by many who make this argument is that ultimately we must rely not on the transaction between the subject and the investigator. Instead, they argue, we must put our faith in the individual ethical integrity of the investigator to insure that the rights of subjects are protected.[24]

Reliance on the beneficence of the investigator is insufficient and sometimes misplaced. It is the investigator's proper duty to inform and educate the subject sufficiently to enable him to make up his own mind. If the physician-investigator argues this is not possible, she may be saying one of two things: she cannot properly explain the risks and alternatives because she does not understand them herself, or she believes if she does properly explain them, the subject will not consent. In either case the answer is that rational decision making will be promoted both by the development of an adequate disclosure statement, and by the requirement that the subject be given final authority concerning use of the experimental method on him. Of course, she may also be a poor communicator, or consider her subject too stupid to understand her.

The argument that the disclosure of possible risks to subjects may in fact "create" these risks by planting the suggestion of harmful side effects in the mind of the subject is a more recent one. This phenomenon, which is termed "the dark side of the placebo effect," leads some to conclude that subjects should be permitted to "waive" their right to full information for their own safety and protection.[25] A similar argument, of course, is made by physicians who do not want to tell women on "the pill" about potential side effects. Such an argument, however, merely takes us back to where we began—with the experimenter instead of the subject deciding what risks are appropriate for the subject to take. Since the knowledge to be gained by the experiment, and not the health of the subject, may be the primary concern of the investigator, we believe the "therapeutic privilege" is *never* applicable to human experimentation, and that it is against public policy to permit subjects to waive their right to full disclosure.

The reason for this rule is again the promotion of autonomy and rational decision making, and its necessity is underlined by a description of the research subject by Dr. Henry Beecher:

> The experienced clinician knows that if he has a good rapport with his patients they will often knowingly submit, for the sake of "science," to inconvenience and even to discomfort, if it doesn't take very long; but excepting the extremely rare individual, the reality is, patients will not knowingly seriously risk their health or their lives for a scientific experiment. It is ridiculous to assume otherwise. They will not do it.[26]

It is both illegal and unethical to withhold information from subjects for the purpose of inducing them to participate in a research study that they would not participate in if they knew the truth. Only full and honest disclosure as a policy can protect subjects. Moreover, only such disclosure can protect the integrity (and thus the future) of the research expertise itself—since if potential subjects lose faith in the truthfulness of investigators, they will cease to volunteer for *any* studies, even the most benign ones.

Does signing a consent form ensure that the subject understands the information contained in it?

Of course not. The signature on the form is primarily to protect the researcher from a later change of experimentation without consent.[27] The signed form can be used as *evidence* of consent (which can, of course, be refuted) in the event the subject is injured and contends that she was experimented on without consent. Nevertheless, the theory of informed consent itself is designed primarily to protect the subject. To make it work one must ensure that the subject actually is given full information in lay language, given an opportunity to ask all questions she has of the investigator, and given an opportunity to think carefully about her response before committing herself to the project.

In this regard current consent forms are not terribly helpful to the subject. A recent survey of institutions using such forms found that only 18 percent contained the components required by federal regulations, fewer than 20 percent described available alternatives, statements of subject's rights were often missing, and fewer than 7 percent were in language as simple as that found in *Time* magazine.[28] Consent forms are generally incomplete and unreadable, and certainly do not in themselves protect subjects.

Studies of subjects also confirm this conclusion. For example, Bradford Gray has demonstrated, in his study of women involved in trials using an experimental method of labor induction, that even though the subjects had signed a consent form which indicated the experimental nature and risks of the study, 40 percent did not realize that they were in an experimental study when their participation began, and 41 percent did not realize any risks were involved.[29] If this is typical, and there is little reason to suppose it is not, new mechanisms must be developed to supplement oral and printed-form disclosures to ensure that the subjects comprehend the information disclosed.

What other mechanisms might help ensure that the subject's consent is informed?

One is a series of true-false questions on the informed

consent form itself. Failure to answer them all correctly (e.g., Does this study entail any risk of death?) would require additional explanations to the subject until he either comprehended the information or was rejected for the study because of inability to comprehend the information. Another is to require a cooling-off period of at least twenty-four hours between the time consent is sought and the time the subject is requested to agree to participate in the research. Subjects should also routinely be given a copy of the consent form they are asked to sign, and retain a copy of it after they sign it. Other mechanisms include the use of a consent-review committee, or a patient-subject advocate, whose task it would be to ensure the subject actually gave an informed and comprehending consent.

Much more important than the actual content of the form is the timing and setting of the oral communication with the subject and the role or status of the person conveying this information. Yet almost no attention has been paid to these variables. It bears repeating that informed consent is a *process,* not a form—a process by which information is conveyed to the potential subject, who makes a decision about participation only after he has understood the information.

What is an institutional review board (IRB)?

Institutional review boards are committees required by federal regulations to review all research projects before they are funded by the federal government. While recently restated in somewhat more restrictive terms, their mandate is to ensure:

1. That the risks to the subject are so outweighed by the sum of the benefit to the subject and the importance of the knowledge to be gained as to warrant a decision to allow the subject to accept these risks.
2. That the rights and welfare of any such subjects will be adequately protected.
3. That legally effective informed consent will be obtained by adequate and appropriate methods.
4. That the conduct of the activity will be reviewed at timely intervals.[30]

IRBs are the classic form of governmental regulation: the use of public incentives to induce self-regulation on the part of powerful institutions.[31] The IRB system is required if institutions desire to receive public funding for research endeavors. More than five hundred institutions currently operate one or more IRBs. The IRB itself is required to be made up of "not less than five" members of varying backgrounds. Not all can be members of the same profession or sex, or associated with the same institution. In addition to professional competence in research, "the committee must be able to ascertain the acceptability of proposals in terms of institutional commitments, and regulations, applicable laws, standards of professional conduct and practice." [32]

These requirements may seem stringent, but they could be minimally met by having four researchers from the institution on the IRB joined by a lawyer from the community. Since a quorum can be defined as a majority of members, the lawyer need never attend any meeting, or she can be outvoted at all of them, and the "peer-review" IRB will still meet these requirements. While this overstates the case, the most recent study of IRBs by the National Commission for the Protection of Human Subjects of Biomedical and Behavioral Research found that researchers themselves compose two-thirds to three-fourths of IRB membership across the United States, and thus can make decisions even if all nonresearchers oppose them.[33] Fewer than 5 percent of members had any special training for the position, and even of the 30 percent who are not researchers, many are affiliated with the institution in which the research is to be carried out. Even the most heterogeneous boards were no more likely to restrict research than the ones made up mainly of researchers.[34]

The commission's 1975–76 survey was consistent with a 1969 study done by Barber. In the Barber study of three hundred IRBs, only 30 percent reported *ever* rejecting or requiring the modification of more than one project, and only 16 percent required revisions of more than 10 percent of the projects reviewed.[35] In the commission's study, modification of research projects remained a rarity. In only 25 percent of the cases were any modifications made, confined almost exclusively to the content of the consent form. Even these modifications usually failed to improve either the readability or content of the form.[36] Finally, monitoring and review of research was generally perfunctory, usually done by reviewing yearly progress reports.

While IRBs where mandated as a reaction to the types of abuses in research outlined elsewhere in this chapter, it is fair to conclude that while they have enhanced the protection of subjects, they have done more to protect researchers from more stringent controls that might otherwise be mandated. In view of this, the general lack of support of IRBs by researchers must be viewed as ironic and shortsighted. An IRB should be viewed as a helpful partner, not as a hurdle, by conscientious investigators. In cases where an IRB seems to be acting arbitrarily, an appeals mechanism should be available to the aggrieved investigator. Investigators who proceed to do research without IRB approval, where required, run the risk of losing not only federal funds, but their license to practice medicine as well.[37]

Are there experiments that shouldn't be done?

Courts may find that extremely dangerous experimentation is improper and against public policy no matter how complete and informed the consent of the subject.

One may not consent to such things as one's own murder, a duel, a brawl in a barroom, a maiming, or to other such activities that are regarded as a "breach of the peace" or a violation of "public policy." [38] No court has specifically applied this rationale to a legitimate medical experimentation case. Nevertheless, one case indicates the possibility exists. It involves a seventy-five-year-old who claimed to be a physician, but who was not licensed in the state.[39] He treated a fifty-year-old woman who had cancer of the nose, using three salves. By the time of her death, ten months later, her nose was almost completely eroded, and the defendant had been indicted. An analysis of the salves showed that they contained zinc chloride, "a strong corrosive chemical that would eat tissue, flesh or even metal." Physicians testified that use of this chemical was "not approved or recognized in the medical profession." The court ruled that consent "is no excuse for recklessness." The case was, however, remanded for a new trial on criminal assault and battery so that the jury could be properly instructed on intent and criminal negligence.

The case illustrates that no one can consent to an experiment that is done in "such reckless, wanton or flagrant nature as to show utter disregard of the safety of other under circumstances likely to cause injury." One who performs such an experiment is subject to criminal charges of mayhem, assault and battery, and manslaughter if the subject dies as a result, and consent will not be a defense.[40] He will also, of course, be subject to the civil charge of malpractice on the basis that such conduct is either negligent or grossly negligent.

Not only is an individual's right to consent to danger circumscribed by existing criminal law, it is also relatively certain that the state could, if it chose, make all forms of dangerous human experimentation illegal. Such a statute would be based on the general proposition that "the interests of the public require such interference, and that the means are reasonably necessary for the accomplishment of the purpose, and not unduly oppressive upon individuals." [41]

What steps should be taken prior to doing biomedical or epidemiological research based on medical records?

The National Commission endorsed the recommendations of the Privacy Study Commission on this subject, and these recommendations should therefore be considered as basic minimum requirements for legal and ethical record research (the IRB would make any determinations required of a "medical care provider"):

That each medical care provider be considered to owe a duty of confidentiality to any individual who is the subject of a medical record it maintains, and that, therefore, no medical care provider should disclose, in individually identifiable form, any information about any such individual without the individual's explicit authorization, unless the disclosures be: . . .

(c) for use in conducting a biomedical or epidemiological research project, provided that the medical-care provider maintaining the medical record:

(i) determines that such use or disclosure does not violate any limitations under which the record or information was collected;

(ii) ascertains that use of disclosure in individually

identifiable form is necessary to accomplish the research or statistical purpose for which use or disclosure is to be made;

(iii) determines that the importance of the research or statistical purpose for which any use or disclosure is to be made is such as to warrant the risk to the individual from additional exposure of the record or information contained therein;

(iv) requires that adequate safeguards to protect the record or information from unauthorized disclosure be established and maintained by the user or recipient, including a program for removal or destruction of identifiers; and

(v) consents in writing before any further use or redisclosure of the record or information in individually identifiable form is permitted.[42]

Is research on "special populations" ethical and legal?

"Special populations" include children, prisoners, and institutionalized mental patients. Some add fetuses to this list, although they are not recognized as "persons" under the Constitution. Many states have statutes covering research on one or more of these groups. The problem with research on special populations, of course, is that they are particularly vulnerable and therefore can easily be abused. In regard to informed consent, for example, we have seen that to be legally effective it must be voluntary, competent, informed, and understanding. Children are generally considered incompetent by the law, and may not understand; prisoners are a captive population, and their consent may not be voluntary; mental patients in institutions raise all three questions: competence, voluntariness, and understanding.[43]

The National Commission for the Protection of Subjects of Biomedical and Behavioral Research was established by Congress primarily to make recommendations about how research could be ethically conducted on these groups. Chiefly its recommendations, most of which have not yet been formulated into final regulations, permit research on all of these groups under circumstances that are designed to protect them. For example, no research that presents more than a minimal risk can be done on any of these special populations unless there is a medical or scientific reason that it cannot be done on any other population, and the research is scientifically important.

Further, in most cases "consent committees" or "subject advocates" must be appointed to oversee the actual consent process, and to make sure the subject is capable of either giving consent, or at least of "assenting" to the experiment. In some cases, court review is mandated before the experiment may be permitted. In almost every instance, however, ultimate decision-making authority as to which, if any, of these safeguards will be used is in the hands of the IRB. Therefore, the rules concerning these populations need not change substantially in practice.[44]

Is there a constitutional right to conduct scientific research?

It depends how you define "research." While the U.S. Supreme Court has never faced this question directly, there are cases in other areas involving receipt of information and news-gathering from willing sources that indicate that the government could probably not pass a law forbidding free expression of research ideas and the flow of research data.[45]

It also seems likely that the right to free expression of ideas, embodied in the First Amendment, is broad enough to include the right to obtain necessary information from a willing source, i.e., a research subject.[46] Nonetheless, even if recognized as a Constitutional right, the state could still circumscribe it if it could demonstrate a "compelling state interest"—such as the protection of human subjects against exploitation or, as noted previously, protection against extremely dangerous experiments—in so doing.[47] In cases where the federal government actually funds the research project itself, it can impose almost any conditions it deems necessary to further an important or substantial governmental interest so long as the regulation itself is not designed to suppress First Amendment rights.[48]

This chapter is about the rights of researchers and subjects. The conclusion is that the researcher has a right to research, which may even be elevated to the status of a constitutional right in most settings. The subject also has a right to be protected and have his right of self-determination—also a constitutional right—preserved. The challenge of regulating human experimentation remains: the encouragement of scientific advance without sacrificing critical human values embodied in the person of the research subject. It is this challenge the law seeks to meet. We still have miles to go.

NOTES

1. This, and much of the other material in this chapter, is derived from G. ANNAS, L. GLANTZ, and B. KATZ, INFORMED CONSENT TO HUMAN EXPERIMENTATION: THE SUBJECT'S DILEMMA (Cambridge, Mass.: Ballinger Press, 1977).

2. Baldor v. Rogers, 81 So.2d 658, 660 (Fla. 1955). *And see* Stammer v. Board of Regents, 262 App. Div. 372, 29 N.Y.S.2d 38 (1941) *aff'd.* 287 N.Y. 359, 39 N.E.2d 913 (1942).

3. United States v. Karl Brandt, No. 1, Trials of War Criminals, vol. 11, at 181. *Reprinted in* J. KATZ, EXPERIMENTATION WITH HUMAN BEINGS 305 (New York: Russell Sage Foundation, 1972). For a description of the specific criminal acts charged regarding human experimentation, *see* A. MITSCHERLICH and F. MIELKE DOCTORS OF INFAMY (translated by Heinz Norden, 1949), and Mant, *The Medical Services in the Concentration Camp of Ravensbruck,* 17 MEDICO-LEGAL J. 99 (1950).

4. *See* ANNAS *et al., supra* note 1, at 7–9 and sources cited therein.

5. Materials on this case are reprinted in KATZ, *supra* note 3, at 10–65.

6. *See* Brandt, *Racism, Research and the Tuskegee Syphilis Study,* 8:6 HASTINGS CENTER RPT. 21 (Dec. 1978). The survivors and their heirs eventually settled a lawsuit against the federal government for $37,500 each minus attorney fees. As of July 1979 only 17 of the approximately 600 participants had not been so compensated. N.Y. Times, July 29, 1979, at 26.

7. *See* ANNAS *et al., supra* note 1, at 179–80 and sources cited therein.

8. INSIGHT TEAM OF THE SUNDAY TIMES OF LONDON, SUFFER THE CHILDREN: THE STORY OF THALIDOMIDE (New York: Viking Press, 1979).

9. Medical World News 18–19 (Apr. 16, 1971). The study involved 398 women and was cosponsored by Syntex Labs and the Agency for International Development. Text of article reprinted in KATZ, *supra* note 3, at 791–92.

10. Beecher, *Ethics and Clinical Research*, 274 NEW ENG. J. MED. 1354 (1966).

11. Rosenberg, *Human Experimentation: Adding Insult to Injury*, HEALTH/PAC BULL. (1979 double issue) at 2, 43–47.

12. Annas, *All the President's Bioethicists* 9(1) HASTINGS CENTER RPT. 14 (Feb. 1979).

13. Stone, *The History and Future of Litigation in Psychopharmacologic Research and Treatment, in* R. GALLANT & R. FORCE, eds., LEGAL AND ETHICAL ISSUES IN HUMAN RESEARCH AND TREATMENT 32–33 (New York: SP Medical & Scientific Books, 1978).

14. *See, e.g.,* P. RAMSEY, THE PATIENT AS PERSON, 5 (New Haven: Yale U. Press, 1970).

15. *See, e.g.,* M. Mead, *Research with Human Beings: A Model Derived from an Anthropological Field Practice,* 98 DAEDALUS 361, 374 (1969).

16. *See, e.g.,* R. TITTMUSS, THE GIFT RELATIONSHIP (New York: Pantheon Books, 1971).

17. Jonas, *Philosophical Reflections on Experimenting with Human Subjects,* 98 DAEDALUS 219, 245 (1969).

18. J. KATZ and A. CAPRON, CATASTROPHIC DISEASE: WHO DECIDES WHAT? 88 (New York: Russell Sage Foundation, 1975).

19. *Id.* at 39. *And see* Freund, *Legal Frameworks for Human Experimentation,* 98 DAEDALUS 314, 323 (1969).

20. *See* D. MECHANIC, THE GROWTH OF BUREAUCRATIC MEDICINE, 261 (New York: John Wiley & Son, 1976).

21. 45 CFR 46.116, promulgated in 46 FED. REG. 8366, 8386 (Jan. 26, 1981) to take effect July 27, 1981. When appropriate, the following additional elements of informed consent must also be provided:
    1. A statement that the research may involve risks to the subject or embryo or fetus which are currently unforeseeable;
    2. Anticipated circumstances in which the research may be terminated without regard to the subject's consent;
    3. Additional costs to the subject that may result from participating in the research;

4. The consequences of a subject's decision to withdraw from the research for orderly termination;

5. A statement that significant new findings developed during the course of the research which may influence the subject's willingness to continue will be provided to the subject;

6. The approximate number of subjects involved in the study. *And see* FDA regulations, 21 CFR. 50.25 (46 Fed. Reg. 8942, 8951, Jan. 27, 1981).

22. 45 CFR §46.117(c); CFR §46.101 and §46.110 (promulgated Jan. 26, 1981).

23. *And see,* Holder & Lewis, *Informed Consent and the Nurse,* 2(2) Nursing Law & Ethics 1 (Feb. 1981).

24. *See, e.g.,* Ingelfinger, *Informed (But Uneducated) Consent,* 287 NEW ENG. J. MED. 465 (1972).

25. Loftus and Fries, *Informed Consent May Be Hazardous to Your Health,* 204 SCIENCE 11 (April 6, 1979).

26. Quoted by MECHANIC, *supra* note 20, at 262.

27. Subjects seem to understand this better than investigators. In a recent study of 200 cancer patients who signed consent forms for chemotherapy, radiation therapy, or surgery, 80% indicated that they believed consent forms were for "protection of physician's rights." Cassileth, Zupkis, Sutton-Smith, & March, *Informed Consent—Why Are Its Goals Imperfectly Realized?* 302 NEW ENG. J. MED. 896, 899 (Apr. 17, 1980). The other portion of this study was seriously flawed. *See* letters to the editor, 303 NEW ENG. J. MED. 459–60 (Aug. 21, 1980).

28. Cooke & Tannenbaum, *A Survey of Institutional Review Boards and Research Involving Human Subjects,* in Appendix to Report and Recommendations on Institutional Review Boards of The National Commission for the Protection of Human Subjects of Biomedical and Behavioral Research, DHEW Pub. No. OS 78–009 (1978) at 1.167. *See also* Grundner, *On the Readability of Surgical Consent Forms,* 302 NEW ENG. J. MED. 900 (Apr. 17, 1980).

29. B. GRAY, HUMAN SUBJECTS IN MEDICAL EXPERIMENTATION 67, 114 (New York: John Wiley & Son, 1975).

30. 45 C.F.R. §46.102(b) and (d) recently replaced by 45 C.F.R. §46.109. *See supra* note 21. For historical background, *see* Curran, *Government Regulation of the Use of Human Subjects in Medical Research: The Approach of Two Agencies,* 98 DAEDALUS 542 (1969). For a com-

plete review of the legal issues surrounding IRBs, *see* Robertson, *The Law of Institutional Review Boards,* 26 UCLA L. REV. 484 (1979).

31. 45 C.F.R. §46.107, *and see* Veatch, *Human Experimentation Committees: Professional or Representative?* HASTINGS CENTER RPT. Oct. 1975 at 31–40.

32. *See* Robertson, *The Law of IRBs, supra* note 30, at 544.

33. National Commission for Protection of Human Subjects of Biomedical and Behavioral Research, Report and Recommendations, Institutional Review Boards (1978) (hereinafter, IRB Report).

34. Cooke & Tannenbaum, *supra* note 24, at 1–61. *See, e.g.,* Fost & Robertson, *Deferring Consent with Incompetent Patients in an Intensive Care Unit,* 2(7) IRB 5 (Aug.– Sept. 1980).

35. B. BARBER, J. LALLEY, J. MAKARUSKA, & D. SULLIVAN, RESEARCH ON HUMAN SUBJECTS (New York: Russell Sage Foundation, 1973).

36. *See* Cooke & Tannenbaum, *supra* note 28, at 1–61 and accompanying tables.

37. *See, e.g.,* In the Matter of David M. Banen, M.D., Massachusetts Board of Registration in Medicine Case #143, decided April 21, 1978. (Physician censured for failure to comply with federal regulations regarding drug experimentation.)

38. *See generally* G. ANNAS *et al., supra* note 1, at 50 and sources cited therein, and Kidd, *Limits of the Rights of a Person to Consent to Experimentation on Himself,* 117 SCIENCE 212 (Feb. 27, 1953).

39. Banovitch v. Commonwealth, 196 Va. 210, 83 S.E.2d 369 (1954). *And see* State v. Bass, 255 N.C. 42, 120 S.E.2d 580 (1961). *And see* discussion in Annas & Glantz, *Psychosurgery: The Law's Response,* 54 B.U.L. REV. 249, 255–56 (1974).

40. *Cf.* State v. Fransua, 85 N.M. 173, 510 P.2d 106 (Ct. App. 1973). (It is no defense to the charge of aggravated battery—shooting the victim in the head—that the victim had declared, "If you want to shoot me, go ahead," and handed the defendant a gun).

41. Lawton v. Steele, 152 U.S. 133, 137 (1894); *and see* Goldblatt v. Hempstead, 369 U.S. 590, 594 (1962). *See also* Fitzsimmons v. New York State Athletic Comm'n, 146 N.Y. Supp. 117 (1914), *aff'd without opinion,* 147

N.Y. Supp. 1111 (1914) (statute regulating boxing does not violate the U.S. Constitution), *and* Tennessee v. Pack, 527 S.W.2d 99 (Tenn. 1975) (state may outlaw the handling of snakes in religious ceremonies since it "has the right to guard against the unnecessary creation of widows and orphans" and "an interest in having a strong, healthy, robust, taxpaying citizenry . . .").

42. Report of the Privacy Protection Study Commission, Personal Privacy in an Information Society 306–7 (Washington, D.C.: U.S. Government Printing Office, 1977). New regulations exempt the following from IRB review and consent requirements: "Research involving the collection or study of existing data, documents, records, pathological specimens, or diagnostic specimens, if these sources are publicly available or if the information is recorded by the investigator in such a manner that subjects cannot be identified, directly or through identifiers linked to the subject." 45 CFR 46.101(b)(5) as amended 46 FED. REG. 8366, 8387 (Jan. 26, 1981).

43. For a complete discussion of the legal issues involved in obtaining informed consent from each of these groups, *see* G. Annas *et al.*, *supra* note 1. *And see* Chapter XI for a discussion of research on the terminally ill. And for a symposium on treating the elderly as a special population, *see* 8(2) IRB 5–9 (Oct. 1980).

44. For details on these proposals, the final reports of the National Commission and the proposed rules of HHS concerning the Protection of Human Services should be consulted. For more on the work of the Commission *See:* Annas, *Report on the National Commission: Good as Gold,* 8(6) Medicolegal NEWS 4 (Dec. 1980) and Jonsen & Yesley, *Rhetoric and Research Ethics: An Answer to Annas,* 8(6) Medicolegal NEWS 8 (Dec. 1980).

45. *See generally,* Robertson, *The Scientist's Right to Research: A Constitutional Analysis,* 51 S. CAL. L. REV. 1203 (1978); *and* Delgado & Millen, *God, Galileo and Government: Toward Constitutional Protection of Scientific Inquiry,* 53 WASH L. REV. 349 (1978).

46. *Id.* and Robertson, *The Law of IRBs, supra* note 30, at 502–6.

47. See *supra* notes 37 to 42 and accompanying text.

48. *See* Robertson, *Scientist's Right to Research, supra* note

45, at 1253–59. The test such conditions would have to meet is articulated in United States v. O'Brien, 391 U.S. 367, 377 (1968):

A government regulation is sufficiently justified if it is within the constitutional power of the Government; if it furthers an important or substantial governmenal interest is unrelated to the suppression of free expression; and if the incidental restriction on alleged First Amendment freedoms is no greater than is essential to the furtherance of that interest.

VIII

Medical Records

There are about a billion visits annually in the United States to doctors' offices and hospitals—each one either generating a new record or adding to an existing one. While at the turn of the century, approximately 90 percent of all medical services were directly delivered by physicians, today fewer than 5 percent of the health care providers are physicians.[1] In the typical hospital, one-third or less of a patient's record will be created by the attending physician.[2]

The variety among medical records is kaleidoscopic. Nevertheless, there is little dispute concerning the primary purposes for which they are kept. In the private physician's office, they are generally maintained to document the patient's history, condition, and treatment; to aid in continuity of care; and to provide a record for billing. In the hospital, Joint Commission Accreditation of Hospitals (JCAH) Accreditation Standards interpret the purposes of the medical record as:

1. A basis for planning patient care and for continuity in the evaluation of the patient's condition and treatment.
2. Documentary evidence of the course of the patient's medical evaluation, treatment, and change in condition.
3. Documentary evidence of communication between the responsible practitioner and any other health professional contributing to the patient's care.
4. Protection of the legal interests of the patient, hospital, and practitioner.

5. A data base for use in continuing education and research.[3]

Of course, all of these rationales can be applied to some extent to records kept in the private office or clinic as well. Nevertheless, there still are physicians who keep almost no records, and it remains fair to state, in both hospital and office practice, that "medical records, as kept for years, have often failed the purposes of lucid communication, education, and rapid retrieval of stored information." [4] With growing governmental involvement in financing and auditing medical care, the purposes of the medical record are likely to continue to expand.

This chapter discusses the major legal issues that surround the making, maintenance, storage, and disposal of medical records. The issue of patient access will also be dealt with, while issues of "privacy" and third-party access to medical records are addressed in Chapter XIII.

What must be included in the patient's record?

A physician's *office records* should conform to "accepted medical practice," and accepted practice is to maintain a record that documents the patient's history, physical findings, treatment, and course of disease.[5] Sufficient information should be included in the record to document the diagnosis and course of treatment. Should a physician or nurse be accused of malpractice or incompetence in the treatment of a particular patient, her record of the case will usually be her best defense. This is because it was made contemporaneous with the events, and is generally viewed as much more reliable than the memory of either the patient or provider. It is thus important for both the patient and provider that complete and accurate records be maintained.

Requirements regarding the maintenance and contents of *hospital records* are usually found in state statutes or regulations which govern hospital licensure. These requirements fall into three groups: (1) those that simply mandate the maintenance of records that are accurate, complete, or adequate; [6] (2) those that set forth broad categories of information to be included; [7] and (3) those that provide specific requirements as to the information that must be included.[8] Provisions for the signing and retention of hospital records are often found in such regulations as well.

While it is unlikely that a hospital would actually lose its license for failure to comply with record requirements, licensing bodies do scrutinize the hospital's procedures for minimizing violations. Moreover, hospitals can and do impose sanctions such as temporary suspension of the operating or admitting privileges of those who fail to meet the record-keeping requirements.[9]

Additional requirements for the content of hospital records have been promulgated by the JCAH. They include:

1. Identification information.
2. Evidence of appropriate informed consent or indication of the reason for its absence.
3. Patient's medical history.
4. Report of patient's physical examination.
5. Diagnostic and therapeutic orders.
6. Observations of patient condition, including progress notes and nursing notes.
7. Report of all procedures, tests, and their results.
8. Conclusions, including the provisional diagnosis, associated diagnoses, clinical resumé, and necropsy reports.[10]

The potential sanction for failure to comply with these requirements is loss of accreditation.

Is there anything that should not be included in a patient's medical record?

The debate on this question is ongoing and unresolved. On one hand are those that argue that literally everything about a patient's condition and background can be relevant to proper diagnosis and treatment. On the other hand there are those who believe that far too much sensitive and nonessential information is finding its way into medical records, to the potential detriment of the patient.

Without attempting to resolve this dispute, it can be noted that, while not illegal, it is inappropriate to include personal criticisms (e.g., this patient is "fat and sloppy"; "shabbily dressed again today"; "I love her perfume") or comments in a patient's record. Such statements can not only unfairly color the attitude of the patient's next medical caretaker who views the record, but also lead to concealment of the record from the patient, not for any legitimate reason, but for fear of embarrassment. A third reason why such comments should not be included in the medical record is that the record may be viewed by many third parties during its lifetime, and even such casual comments may be used against the patient by potential schools, employers, insurers, or governmental agencies.

A suggested rule is to record facts about a patient (e.g., speech is slurred, eyes bloodshot, etc.) rather than conclusions from these observations that may not be true (e.g., patient is an alcoholic).

Who owns medical records?

The general rule is that owner of the paper on which the medical record is written is the "owner" of the record. Some states even have statutes that specify that hospitals "own" the medical records in their custody. Likewise, physicians, even if not covered by statute, can properly be considered the owners of the medical records generated and maintained by them in their private offices.

What rights does the owner of a medical record have?

Ownership of a medical record is a limited, not an absolute, right and should be considered primarily custodial in nature. Possession of the record is governed by many other statutes (e.g., state licensing statutes) and contracts (e.g., Blue Shield contracts) as well as by the interests of the patient himself in the contents of the medical record. While providers have custody of records and strong interests in them, others may have interests strong enough to give them a right of access to the information or a right to a copy of the records themselves.

Does a patient have the legal right to see and copy his medical record?

In the past decade there has been a trend toward increasing patient access to medical records. This trend includes policy changes by physicians and hospitals, judicial decisions, and state statutes and regulations. As access is generally a matter of state law, reference to the situation in your own state will be necessary to determine the precise rights your patients have to access.

In every state, patients can obtain their records by filing a suit against the provider, usually alleging negligence, and subpoena the records for use in developing the case. In at least nine states, the patient is given the statutory right to inspect his hospital record without any resort to litigation.[11] In some the statute applies only after discharge, while in others no such distinction is made. Statutes in some other states also have limitations on psychiatric records. In Colorado, for example, psychiatric records need not be disclosed if, in the opinion of an independent third-party psychiatrist, such disclosure to the patient "would have significant negative psychological impact upon the patient." Other states limit the types of records that are available. For example, in Minnesota access to "laboratory reports, X-rays, prescriptions, and other technical information used in assessing the patient's health condition" is specifically excluded.[12] In still others, such as Tennessee and Mississippi, the patient must show "good cause" before he has a right to view the record, but what is meant by this term is not specified in the statute.[13]

Instead of requiring access to the records themselves, Florida law requires only that "reports" made of physical and mental examinations and treatments be made available to the patient.[14] Many other states have more limited statutes that either provide for access under certain circumstances, or require the patient to obtain access through an attorney, physician, or relative.[15]

Access is guaranteed by judicial decisions in other states, such as Illinois, Nebraska, New York, and Texas. The general theory of the case law is that "the fiducial [trust] qualities of the physician-patient relationship require the disclosure of medical data to a patient or his agent on request,"[16] and that patients have a right to access to their own records based on a "common law right of inspection."[17]

State medical licensing boards are also beginning to recognize the importance of patients having access to their medical records. New York in 1977 and Massachusetts in 1978 have required their licensees to make such records, or a summary of the relevant data in them, available to patients upon request.[18] On the federal level (e.g., Veterans' Administration facilities) the Privacy Act of 1974 requires direct access under most circumstances, and the Privacy Protection Study Commission, established by that act, has recommended, "Upon request, an individual who is the subject of a medical record maintained by a medical care provider, or another responsible person designated by the individual, be allowed access to that medical record including an opportunity to see and copy it." [19]

This recommendation is significantly broader than one made more than five years previously by HEW's Medical Malpractice Commission, which recommended that "states enact legislation enabling patients to obtain access to the information contained in their medical records through their legal representatives, public or private, without having to file a suit." [20]

Psychiatrists and others who wish to do so may keep a "diary" in which they record notes to themselves that will not be available to *anyone* else (even their secretary), if there are things they wish to record for their own use that they do not want the patient (or anyone else) to have access to. If the existence of this diary is known, however, it will be subject to subpoena.

Might access to medical records harm the patient?

The argument that an ignorant patient is a happy patient is unpersuasive—especially when the patient wants specific facts. Patients who *ask* to see their own medical records are not "less anxious" when refused than they would be if access was provided. In fact, every study that has been done supports the conclusion that patient access to medical records is a positive step and poses no threats to their health care.[21]

In one study in Burlington, Vermont, for example, staff physicians in the Rehabilitation Medicine Service at the Medical Center Hospital of Vermont routinely gave patients copies of their records. Of 103 patients surveyed, 88 percent registered moderate to enthusiastic interest in their medical records, 60 percent asked for clarification, and 50 percent made minor corrections in their records.[22]

An Australian study provided open access to records for hospital in-patients. While some believed before the study that the hospital setting "might worsen anxiety," this concern was not borne out and the results indicated positive patient acceptance.[23] The primary problems patients had with the records involved medical abbreviations, vocabulary, and physicians' handwriting. The study also had some therapeutic payoffs. In two cases patients with chronic debilitating diseases expressed their unfounded fear that they had cancer only after reviewing their records. This provided an opportunity for the physician to discuss this belief with them. In another case a pregnant woman found a mistake in her blood type where in fact an Rh incompatibility existed. Similar positive results were reported from a study in a psychiatric unit at a general hospital in the state of Washington, where in-patients were permitted to read their records at will at a central nursing station on the ward.[24] In another study at the Given Health Care Center in Burlington, Vermont, eight thousand patients were given carbon copies of their complete office records. Ninety-three percent felt that the process reduced their anxieties about their health.[25]

Moreover, in places where access is available, no adverse reactions have been reported. In Massachusetts, for example, patient access has been mandated by statute since 1946 without reported incident. And the Privacy Study Commission, hearing from all federal agencies that had adopted access policies under the Privacy Act of 1974, found that "Not one witness was able to identify an instance where access to records has had an untoward effect on a patient's medical condition." [26] Finally, a two-year study at the out-patient department of Boston's Beth Israel Hospital concluded that not only were physicians' fears about liberal patient access to records unwarranted, but also the access policy made the relationship between patients and professionals "more collaborative." [27]

Some physicians have suggested giving all patients carbon copies of their records as soon as they are made. The advantages of this system would include:

1. Increased patient information and education.
2. Continuity of records as patients move or change physicians.
3. An added criterion on which patients may base selection of physicians.
4. Improvement in the doctor-patient relationship by making it more open.

5. An added way for physicians to monitor quality of care.
6. Increased responsiveness to consumer needs.[28]

Such proposals deserve serious consideration, as the burden of proof is now on those who would deny patients access to their records to demonstrate other than self-serving reasons for this policy.

Might disclosure of medical records be harmful to the physician?

This possibility is considered likely by some medical commentators, but we believe the general policy of open access is likely to create far fewer potential problems than a general policy of denying patients access to their records. The late physician-commentator Michael J. Halberstam, a highly respected writer, unequivocally advised against patient access, arguing "the chart is none of the patient's business." He further advised concealing mistakes from patients (at least those that do not seem to have caused any serious damage), and suggested this is not a conspiracy of silence, but "merely the instinctive tact and acumen of people who work together toward the same goal." A final note of paranoia was sounded by Halberstam's description of the medical record as "a time bomb lying in wait to give you trouble two or three years in the future." [29]

Such policies not only tend to perpetuate the public's view that health care providers are trying to hide something from them, but also lead to cynicism about the potential for peer review, and increase the likelihood that a lawsuit will be filed primarily for the purposes of gaining access to medical records.[30] While there is some evidence that a policy of open records does change the content of the records themselves, the evidence is that such changes are usually improvements in records, such as the deletion of personal opinions and the replacement of them with objective data and observations. Health care providers should work toward the development of an atmosphere of openness and trust—not of paranoia and secrecy.

When can the physician or hospital refuse to allow a patient access to his medical record?

If the patient has a statutory right to the record, there is nothing that can legally prevent the patient's access as provided in the statute. However, inherent in the law is the notion of reasonableness. It may be reasonable for a hospital to suggest that the patient's physician be present while the patient inspects the record. On the other hand, it is unreasonable for the hospital to require this in most circumstances. For instance, it is unreasonable for a hospital to deny the patient access to records if the patient must make a treatment decision and needs the information to do so. Any delay in allowing the patient access would be judicially evaluated in light of all of the surrounding circumstances. A hospital or physician may also not make it difficult or impossible for the patient to exercise the right by imposing an exorbitant charge for copying.[31]

Some of the statutes provide, and common sense dictates, that if the physician has good reason to believe that access to the record will be harmful to the patient, the access may be denied. But this is not to be treated casually —the physician must be reasonable in her belief, and should be able to document her belief on the basis of objective evidence. The patient should also be given the opportunity to challenge this decision, or to designate another person to receive the information for the patient.

How should mistakes in medical records be corrected?

One of the legal lessons most health professionals have learned is: *never alter a medical record*. This is excellent advice, since a jury will often consider an altered medical record as the equivalent of admitting negligence. Nevertheless, like almost every rule, this one has some obvious exceptions: the most obvious is when the record is incorrect. There have been many suggestions concerning record alteration. Perhaps the most widely recommended is to cross out the incorrect information in such a way that it is still legible, write in the correct information, and add a dated note that explains why the information was changed (e.g., changed because it was later discovered to be inaccurate).[32] Such a procedure would both maintain the integrity of the medical record and permit the correction of false data. Each physician and hospital should have a procedure for making record corrections. In the event that a patient asks that his record be corrected, and the health care provider determines that no correction is warranted, the patient should at least be permitted to have his own version of the facts added to the record.

How long should medical records be retained?

More than two-thirds of the states have statutes or regulations that provide a specific length of time for the retention of hospital records. These vary from two years (Delaware) to twenty-five (Connecticut, Indiana, Montana, Nebraska, Nevada, South Carolina, Utah, and Wyoming), even thirty (Massachusetts).[33] Where there are no regulations, the length of time for which the office or hospital record should be retained is determined by the reason for its retention: it should be retained for whatever time is necessary to accomplish the purpose for retention.

Retaining medical records as an aid to medical science or to facilitate later treatment of an individual patient will be best accomplished by retaining the records for as long as possible. The length of time will depend upon the size and character of the hospital or physician's facilities, as well as the medical judgments about the scientific value of the particular records.

Retention of records as an aid to either patient enforcement or physician defense of a legal claim will be determined by the particular statute of limitations for the type of legal action. Suits filed after the statutory period are barred, although in most states the bar is not automatic—the plaintiff's suit is allowed unless the defendant pleads the statute as a defense. Most states have a two-year statute of limitations for malpractice and personal-injury tort actions, although states vary from one to three years. In most states the statutory period for contract actions is six years. Certain circumstances such as minority, insanity or the "discovery rule," may cause the statute of limitations to be postponed, interrupted, or suspended from running, thus extending the length of time during which a plaintiff may bring legal action.

Retaining medical records to assist in the collection of accounts will, in most states, require retention for six years from the time at which the debt was incurred, unless such time has been extended by the action, usually in writing, of the person owing the debt.

We recommend these general guidelines regarding the retention of medical records:

1. In the interests of medical science and good patient care, medical records should be retained for as long as possible.
2. At a minimum records should be retained:
   a. if the patient is a competent adult—for the longest statute of limitations which may apply, usually six years
   b. if the patient is an incompetent adult, or becomes such before the six years have expired—until the patient recovers plus the remaining statutory time, or another time prescribed by statute for this specific circumstance
   c. if the patient is a minor—until the patient reaches the age of majority plus the statutory period for malpractice actions, or another period specified by statute for this circumstance.
3. If the physician finds that her facilities preclude the retention of records for any longer than the recommended minimum periods, it is recommended that she notify the patient that his records will no longer be retained, and give the patient or the patient's designee the copy of the record upon payment of a reasonable fee for postage and handling.
4. Microfilm reproductions are as fully admissible in most courts as the original. However, it is advisable to retain the original records for the recommended minimum periods, since the original is more convenient to read and handle, and presence of the original minimizes the possibility of assertions that it has been altered or is incomplete.

What should be done with office records when the physician retires or dies?

Retirement or death of the physician does not alter the confidential nature of his medical records, nor does it relieve the physician or his estate of any professional liability for which he would otherwise be accountable. Thus, the physician, or his estate, should continue to safeguard the confidentiality of his medical records.

The records, as long as they exist, are confidential and the patient continues to have an interest in the information contained therein. They cannot be sold without the patient's permission.

The office of the General Counsel of the American Medical Association has published a position paper entitled "Sale or Disposition of a Medical Practice," which advises that a physician who acquires the practice of a retiring or deceased physician "may not acquire the medical records of the patients without the express written consent and direction of the patient." [34] The general counsel further states that the patient's consent and direction may not be solicited, and that the retiring physician (or the deceased physician's estate) should notify the patient of the termination of the practice and should inform the patient that his records will be forwarded to whichever physician the patient names in writing.

NOTES

1. A. Freedman, *Protection of Sensitive Medical Data*, in M. JENKIN, ed. PATIENT CENTERED HEALTH SYSTEMS 3 (Minneapolis: Society for Computer Medicine, 1975).

2. PRIVACY PROTECTION STUDY COMMISSION, PERSONAL PRIVACY IN AN INFORMATION SOCIETY 278 (Washington, D.C.: U.S. Govt. Printing Office, 1977).

3. JOINT COMMISSION ON ACCREDITATION OF HOSPITALS, ACCREDITATION MANUAL FOR HOSPITALS, 1981 Ed. (Chicago: 1980) at 83.

4. Goldfinger & Dineen, *Problem-Oriented Medical Record*, in HARRISON'S PRINCIPLES OF INTERNAL MEDICINE 9 (Thorn, *et al.*, eds., 8th ed.; New York: McGraw-Hill, 1977).

5. *See, e.g., Approach to Disease*, in HARRISON'S, *supra* note 4, at 3–6.

6. Arizona, Connecticut, Hawaii, Indiana, Iowa, Kentucky, Maine, Ohio, and Virginia.

7. Alabama, Alaska, Florida, Illinois, Kansas, Louisiana, Minnesota, Mississippi, Missouri, Montana, Nebraska, New Hampshire, New Jersey, Oregon, Rhode Island, South Dakota, and Vermont.

8. Arkansas, California, Colorado, Georgia, Idaho, Maryland, Massachusetts, Michigan, Nevada, New Mexico, New York, North Carolina, North Dakota, Oklahoma, Pennsylvania, South Carolina, Tennessee, Utah, Wash-

ington, West Virginia, Wisconsin, Wyoming, and Puerto Rico.

9. *See, e.g.,* Board of Trustees of Mem. Hosp. v. Pratt, 72 Wyo. 120, 262 P.2d 682 (1953), upholding the right of a hospital to suspend the privileges of a physician who did not comply with the requirement to keep records up to date. *And see* Grayson, M.A., *Incomplete Medical Records: Three Case Solutions,* 8 HOSPITAL MEDICAL STAFF (March 1979).

10. JOINT COMMISSION ON ACCREDITATION OF HOSPITALS, ACCREDITATION MANUAL FOR HOSPITALS 1981 Ed. (Chicago: 1980) at 84–88.

11. Colorado (COL. REV. STAT. §25–1–801), Oklahoma (OKLA. STAT. ANN. tit. 76 §19, Connecticut (CONN. GEN. STAT. ANN. §4.104), Illinois (ILL. STAT. ch. 51 §71). Indiana (IND. CODE 34–3–15.5–4), Nevada (NEV. REV. STAT. 629.061), Massachusetts (MASS. GEN. LAWS ch. 111, §70), New York (N.Y. PUB. HEALTH LAW ch. 44, §17), Pennsylvania (PA. STAT. tit. 51 §71).

12. Minn. 144.335(2) (amended, 1976).

13. Tenn. 53–1322 (1974); Miss. §41–9–65 (1962).

14. FLA. STAT. ANN. §458.16.

15. *E.g.,* Hawaii, California, Maine, Missouri, Montana, New Jersey, New Mexico, North Dakota, Utah, Wisconsin. For a state-by-state breakdown and description of specific statutory provisions see M. Auerback & T. Bogue, Getting Yours: A Consumer Guide to Obtaining Your Medical Record (Health Research Group, 2000 P. St., Washington, D.C.: 20036, 1978; $2).

16. Cannell v. Medical and Surg. Clinic, 21 Ill. App. 383, 315 N.E.2d 278, 280 (Ill. App. Ct. 3d Dist. 1974).

17. Hutchins v. Texas Rehab. Comm., 544 S.W.2d 802, 804 (Tex. Ct. Civ. App. 1976). *See also* O'Donnell v. Sherman. Sup. Ct., Middlesex No. 77–4622 (Mass., May 22, 1978, Doerfer, J.). *Contra,* Gotkin v. Miller, 379 F. Supp. 859 (N.Y. 1974), *aff'd,* 514 F.2d 125 (2d Cir. 1975) (former mental patient does not have a constitutional right to a copy of her records under New York law). *See generally* Kaiser, *Patients' Right of Access to Their Own Medical Records: The Need for New Law,* 24 BUFFALO L. REV. 317 (1974).

18. The full Massachusetts regulation [243 CMR 2.06 (13)], which was adopted on Oct. 10, 1978, reads:

REQUIREMENT TO MAKE AVAILABLE CERTAIN RECORDS

a. A licensee shall maintain a medical record for each patient which is adequate to enable the licensee to provide proper diagnosis and treatment. A licensee must maintain a patient's medical record for a minimum period of three years from the date of the last patient encounter and in a manner which permits the former patient or a successor physician access to them in conformity with this section.

b. A licensee shall provide a patient or, upon a patient's request, another licensee or another specifically authorized person, with the following:

    i. A summary, which includes all relevant data of that portion of the patient's medical record which is in the licensee's possession, or a copy of that portion of the patient's entire medical record which is in the licensee's possession. It is within the licensee's discretion to determine whether to make available a summary or a copy of the entire medical record.

    ii. A copy of any previously completed report required for third party reimbursement.

c. A licensee may charge a reasonable fee for the expense of providing the material enumerated in section b.; however, a licensee may not require prior payment of the charges for the medical services to which such material relates as a condition for making it available.

d. Section b. does not apply if, in the reasonable exercise of her professional judgment, a licensee believes the provision of such material would adversely affect the patient's health. However, in such a case, the licensee must make the material available to another responsible person designated by the patient.

19. PERSONAL PRIVACY, *supra* note 2, at 298.
20. Secretary's Report on Medical Malpractice (HEW, DHEW Pub. No. OS 73–88, 1973) at 77.
21. The one "study" that concluded that "record reading did not necessarily lead patients toward a more desirable self-reliance," is seriously defective in both method and

design. The authors interviewed 11 out of 2500 patients at the Peter Bent Brigham Hospital in Boston who had the courage to buck the system and ask to see their medical records. They seemed surprised to find that such patients tended to be the most distrustful, and labeled their record-seeking activity as deviant. But, as Dr. Don R. Lipsitt noted in an accompanying editorial, their analysis smacked of victim-blaming in that it attempted to examine the doctor-patient relationship "simply in terms of the patient's side of the equation." Lipsitt, *The Patient and the Record,* 302 NEW ENG. J. MED. 167, 168 (Jan. 17, 1980). The study was published as a "Sounding Board": Altman, Reich, Kelly, & Rogers, *Patients Who Read Their Hospital Charts,* 302 NEW ENG. J. MED. 169 (Jan. 17, 1980). *And see* letters to the editor on this Sounding Board, 302 NEW ENG. J. MED. 1483–84 (June 26, 1980); and Roth, Woldord, & Meisel, *Patient Access to Records: Tonic or Toxin?* 137 AM. J. PSYCHIATRY 592 (May 1980).

22. Golodetz, Ruess & Milhous, *The Right to Know: Giving the Patient His Medical Record,* 57 ARCH. PHYS. MED. REHAB. 78 (1976).

23. Stevens, Stagg & MacKay, *What Happens When Hospitalized Patients See Their Own Records,* 86 ANNALS INTERNAL MED. 474 (1977).

24. Stein *et al., Patient Access to Medical Records on a Psychiatric Inpatient Unit,* 136 AM. J. PSYCHIATRY 3 (1979).

25. Bouchard *et al.,* reported in *How to Reduce Patients' Anxiety: Show Them Their Hospital Records,* Medical World News, Jan. 13, 1975, at 48.

26. PERSONAL PRIVACY, *supra* note 2, at 297.

27. Knox, *Medical Board Told Patients Should Get Access to Records,* Boston Globe, March 2, 1978 at 15.

28. Shenkin & Warner, *Giving the Patient His Medical Record: A Proposal to Improve the System,* 289 NEW ENG. J. MED. 688 (1973). *See also* Letters to the Editor in response to the proposal, 290 NEW ENG. J. MED. 287–88 (1974).

29. Halberstam, *The Patient's Chart Is None of the Patient's Business,* Modern Medicine, Nov. 1, 1976, at 85–86.

30. *See supra* note 20, at 76–77.

31. Rabens v. Jackson Park Hosp. Foundation, 351 N.E.2d 276 (Ill. 1976).
32. *See, e.g.,* Babin, *Changing Notes in Medical Records: A Proposal,* 6(1) MEDICOLEGAL NEWS 4 (Spring, 1978).
33. A complete state-by-state listing of these provisions is available from Comm. on Health Law & Regulation, I.C.E.A., Box 22, Hillside, N.J. 07205.
34. Sale and Disposition of a Medical Practice, (prepared by General Counsel, American Medical Association), at 14–15.

IX

Privacy and Confidentiality

The more dependent society becomes upon the maintenance of a galaxy of information systems, the more defined two conflicting trends become. The first, exemplified by state and federal "freedom of information" or "sunshine" acts, aims at providing the public access to all information held by governmental agencies. The premise is that public knowledge of the most intimate details of how government works is likely to make government more responsive to the will of the people and to prevent official wrongdoing. The second is exemplified by state and federal laws (e.g., the Privacy Act of 1974) aimed at protecting information about individual citizens from public disclosure. While details remain to be worked out in many areas, the consensus is that with all forms of personal data-keeping systems— credit, insurance, education, taxation, criminal, and medical, to name some of the most important—individuals have or should have a right of privacy broad enough to enable them to examine and correct the information, and to prevent the release of this information without their express consent.

Medical records have been the last to come under public scrutiny, perhaps because medicine has a tradition of "keeping confidences." Nevertheless, as the solo practitioner becomes an endangered species, record keeping in medicine comes to resemble other massive record keeping systems. Accordingly, the rules applied to these systems are likely to become applicable to medical records as well. As to medical records specifically, only a couple of dozen cases have reached the appellate courts. The case law in this area must therefore be considered to be in its infancy, and resort must often be made to public policy and arguments by analogy.

This chapter will continue the discussion begun in the previous chapter by focusing on the legal concepts of privacy and confidentiality, the exceptions to these doctrines, and the considerations that should go into a decision about releasing confidential medical information to anyone but the patient.

What is meant by the terms "confidentiality," "privilege," and "privacy"?

Almost all of the existing law concerning third-party access to medical records can be placed under the headings of confidentiality, privilege, and privacy. As commonly used, to tell someone something in confidence means that the person will not repeat what you said to anyone else. Confidentiality thus presupposes that something "secret" will be told by someone to a second party who will not repeat it to a third party. Relationships like attorney-client, priest-penitent, and doctor-patient are confidential relationships. In the doctor-patient context, confidentiality is descriptive of an express or implied agreement that the doctor will not disclose the information received from the patient to anyone not directly involved in the patient's care and treatment.

A communication is said to be privileged if the person to whom the information is given is forbidden by law from disclosing it in a court proceeding without the consent of the person who provided it. Privilege is a legal rule of evidence, applying only in the judicial context. Moreover, the privilege belongs to the client, not to the professional. Unlike the attorney-client privilege, the doctor-patient privilege is not recognized at common law, and therefore exists only in those states that have passed a statute establishing it. Fewer than a dozen states have no such statute regarding physicians, and most of these do have psychotherapist-patient privilege statutes.

There are at least two senses in which the term privacy is generally used. The first describes a Constitutional right of privacy. This right, while not directly enunciated in the Constitution, was the basis for decisions by the U.S. Supreme Court limiting state interference with birth control and abortion. This right is said to be one of personal privacy and involves the ability of an individual to make important, intimate decisions.

In the more traditional sense the term has been defined as "the right to be let alone, to be free of prying, peeping, and snooping," and as "the right of someone to keep information about himself or his personality inaccessible to others." [1]

Is the maintenance of confidentiality a legal or an ethical obligation of health care providers?

It is both. Historically the doctrine was an ethical duty applicable only to physicians. Currently it is also a legal duty of physicians (as enunciated in case law, and some state licensing statutes), and it is becoming a legal duty of other health care practitioners as well.

The Hippocratic Oath first set out the duty of confidentiality in the following words:

Whatsoever things I see or hear concerning the life of man, in any attendance on the sick or even apart therefrom, which ought not to be noised about, I will keep silent thereon, counting such things to be professional secrets.

This oath has been reinterpreted in Section 4 of the current formulation of the American Medical Association's Principles of Ethics:

A physician shall respect the rights of patients, of colleagues, and of other health professionals, and shall safeguard patient confidences within the constraints of the law.

Similarly, Section 2 of the American Nurses' Association Code provides, "The nurse safeguards the client's right to privacy by judiciously protecting information of a confidential nature." The interpretive statements elaborates:

When knowledge gained in confidence is relevant or essential to others involved in planning or implementing the client's care, professional judgment is used in sharing it. Only information pertinent to a client's treatment and welfare is disclosed and only to those directly concerned with the client's care. . . . The nurse-client relationship is built on trust. This relationship could be destroyed and the client's welfare and reputation jeopardized by injudicious disclosure of information provided in confidence.

The reason for all of these rules, of course, is that health care providers need to know the most personal and possibly embarrassing details of the patient's life to help the patient, and patients are not likely to disclose these details freely unless they are certain that no one else, not directly involved in their care, will learn of them. As one court described the patient's dilemma:

> Since a layman is unfamiliar with the road to recovery, he cannot sift the circumstances of his life and habits to determine what is information pertinent to his health. As a consequence, he must disclose all information in his consultations with his doctor—even that which is embarrassing, disgraceful, or incriminating. To promote full disclosure, the medical profession extends the promise of secrecy. The candor which this promise elicits is necessary to the effective pursuit of health; there can be no reticence, no reservation, no reluctance when patients discuss their problems with their doctors.[2]

What kinds of incidents involving confidentiality get to court?

There are very few reported cases involving breaches of confidentiality. This can mean that such violations are rare, that patients never learn of violations when they do occur, that patients don't think it is appropriate to sue for such violations (because of the cost, uncertain damages, and possible further publicity of the confidential information), or that almost all such cases are settled before they reach an appellate court.

Those cases that have been appealed have most often alleged violation of confidences by physicians in one of the following situations: disclosure to a spouse (involving either a disease related to the marriage or a condition relevant in a divorce, alimony, or custody action); disclosure to an insurance company; or disclosure to an employer.[3]

What function does the privilege doctrine serve?

There are two competing values in this doctrine. The first is that certain types of relationships are potentially so beneficial to individuals and society that they should be fostered by forbidding in-court disclosure of the informational content of the relationship. A privilege is therefore granted to encourage the employment of professionals by individuals who need their services and to promote absolute freedom of communication. The contrary principle is that the courtroom is a place for the discovery of truth, and no reliable source of truth should be beyond the reach of the court. At common law the court's interest in the truth routinely won out, and physicians were forced to testify to the matters disclosed to them by their patients.

The great majority of courts currently agree that the principal reason for the privilege is to encourage a patient to freely and frankly reveal to his physician all the facts and symptoms concerning his condition so that the physician will be in the best possible position to correctly diagnose and successfully treat the patient, and most states have adopted the privilege by statute. Nevertheless, the statutory adoption of the privilege was strongly criticized by John Henry Wigmore, late dean of Northwestern University Law School and perhaps the ultimate authority on the law of evidence. He argued that in most cases it only serves to frustrate the ends of justice by denying truthful information to courts. He contended, for example, that most information communicated to a physician is not intended to be held strictly confidential since most of one's ailments are both immediately apparent and openly discussed, that even when information is intended to be maintained as confidential it would be disclosed to the physician even if no privilege existed. On the other hand, there are so many exceptions to the rule that it probably frustrates justice in very few instances.[4]

What are the sources of the "right of privacy"?

In his book *Privacy and Freedom,* Alan Westin defines privacy as "the claim of individuals, groups, or institutions to determine for themselves when, how, and to what ex-

tent information about them is communicated to others." [5]
He goes on to argue that, as thus defined, the concept has
its roots in the territorial behavior of animals, and its importance can be seen to some extent throughout the history
of civilization. Specific protections of privacy were built
into the Constitution by the framers in terms that were
important to their era. With the subsequent inventions of
the telephone, radio, television, and computer systems,
more sophisticated legal doctrines were developed in an
attempt to protect the informational privacy of the individual.

One such approach, directed toward private rather than
public or governmental invasions, was suggested by Warren and Brandeis in the *Harvard Law Review* in 1890.
They suggested that a legal remedy be developed for individuals whose privacy was invaded by the press or others
for commercial gain. As a result of this and other arguments, a number of states passed statutes making such
invasions actionable at law. While many diverse acts come
under the heading of privacy violations, most involving
medical records would fall in the area generally described
as the "publication [disclosing to one or more unauthorized
person] of private matters violating ordinary decencies."

A court can find the unauthorized disclosure of medical
records an actionable invasion of privacy even without a
state statute that specifically forbids it. As an Alabama
court put it in a case involving disclosure of medical information to a patient's employer: "Unauthorized disclosure of intimate details of a patient's health may amount
to unwarranted publication of one's private affairs with
which the public has no legitimate concern, such as to
cause outrage, mental suffering, shame, or humiliation to
a person of ordinary sensibilities." [6]

The policy underlying the right is that certain information about individuals should not be repeated without their
permission. In the words of one legal commentator: "The
basic attribute of an effective right to privacy is the individual's ability to control the flow of information concerning or describing him." [7] Most of the cases in the
doctor-patient context alleging violation of the right to
privacy have involved actions in which personal medical
information has been published in a newspaper or maga-

zine, and often the suit is against the publisher rather than the physician.[8]

Under what circumstances *must* a health care provider report confidential information about her patient?

While the doctrines of confidentiality and privacy are, on the surface, very powerful legal tools, their effect in the day-to-day practice of medicine is diluted by the exceptions and defenses physicians and other health care providers can raise to a charge of unauthorized disclosure. Indeed, there are times when health care professionals *must* disclose confidential information, even though they may not want to:

1. *Public Reporting Statutes*

Almost all states have listed certain conditions and diseases that must be reported to the public authorities when discovered by the physician. These fall into four major categories: vital statistics, contagious and dangerous diseases, child neglect and abuse, and criminally inflicted injuries. All relevant statutes decree a public policy that takes precedence over the health care professional's obligation to maintain a patient's confidences:

a. In the first category are birth and death certificates. In the case of birth certificates, information about the parents is generally required. If death is sudden or from an accidental cause, or if foul play is suspected, the medical examiner or coroner is usually required by law to do an autopsy and file a complete report of his findings with the district attorney. These reporting statutes are almost universally complied with; failure to do so is generally a misdemeanor punishable by both fine and imprisonment.

b. Typical infectious, contagious, or communicable diseases that must be reported as listed in the California statute for instance, are cholera, plague, yellow fever, malaria, leprosy, diphtheria, scarlet fever, smallpox, typhus fever, typhoid fever, paratyphoid fever, anthrax, glanders, epidemic cerebrospinal meningitis, tuberculosis, pneumonia, dysentery, erysipelas, hookworm, trachoma, dengue, tetanus, measles, German measles, chickenpox, whooping cough, mumps, pellagra, beriberi, Rocky Mountain spotted fever, syphilis, gonorrhea, rabies, and poliomyelitis.[9] Most public health officials agree that only a fraction of many of these diseases are reported by physicians, and this is a major problem.

c. Reporting of child abuse cases is most common in the emergency rooms of large city hospitals. A recent California case, however, concluded that a physician could be held liable to pay damages suffered by a child whose parents seriously abused her after the physician had treated her for a previous injury resulting from abuse that he did not report.[10] Failure to report can also subject a health professional to criminal penalties (most statutes require nurses, social workers, teachers, and others to report), and this obligation should be taken extremely seriously, so that children can be protected from abusive custodians.

d. The final category includes things like "a bullet wound, gunshot wound, powder burn or any other injury arising from or caused by the discharge of a gun or firearm, and every case of a wound which is likely to or may result in death and is actually or apparently inflicted by a knife, icepick or other sharp instrument." [11]

2. Judicial Process

When someone makes his own physical condition an issue in a lawsuit—e.g., a personal injury claim—most courts will permit examination of his physician under oath either before or during the trial. Even in states that have privilege statutes, there are generally many exceptions that would permit bringing medical information into court. For example, medical information is often available in criminal cases, and almost always in malpractice cases. When a judge requires a health care provider to disclose confidential information in a judicial proceeding, the provider must comply or face a penalty (usually imprisonment) for contempt of court.

3. Federal and State Statutes Concerning Cost and Quality Control

There are a variety of state and federal statutes that permit certain monitoring agencies to have access to patient charts for such purposes as peer review, utilization review, studies to protect against provider-reimbursement fraud, and licensing and accreditation surveys. The most pervasive of these is the federal statute and regulations on Professional Standards Review Organizations. Current regulations require that the information collected under this program not be made public in any way in which individual practitioners or patients can be identified.[12]

4. Patient Poses a Danger to Known Third Party

Until very recently, physicians have been held responsible for injuries inflicted on others by their patients only when they were directly negligent in their treatment of the patient. For example, physicians have been held responsible for negligently failing to diagnose TB, thereby placing family members at risk;[13] for wrongly informing a patient's neighbor that smallpox was not contagious;[14] and for wrongly informing the members of a family that typhoid fever[15] and scarlet fever[16] of a sibling would not infect other members of the family.

The California Supreme Court has gone somewhat further than this, and ruled that "When a doctor or a psychotherapist, in the exercise of his professional skill and knowledge, determines, or *should determine,* that a warning is essential to avert danger arising from the medical or psychological condition of his patient, he incurs a *legal obligation* to give that warning" (emphasis supplied).[17] The case involved a patient who had threatened to kill his former girlfriend. The therapist believed him, took some initial steps to have him confined, and then, allegedly on orders from his superior, dropped the case. The patient in fact killed the young woman, and her family sued the therapist. The California Supreme Court declared, in the above-quoted language, that the therapist could be found liable if he had failed to warn the intended victim or failed to take other steps, like confining the patient, to prevent the murder. The case was eventually settled out of court.

The psychiatric profession argued vehemently against this ruling, saying it would curtail the ability of psychiatrists to treat patients, who would not come to them because they feared being reported to the authorities, and would encourage psychiatrists to have potentially dangerous patients committed to mental institutions rather than take a chance of continuing to treat them on an out-patient basis.[18] However one comes out on this question of the individual practitioner's rights versus the rights of society, it must be recognized that the broader we as a society make the health care professional's mandate to report his patient's condition to others, the more like a policeman the professional becomes. Nevertheless, we agree with the California Supreme Court that health care providers have an obligation to society as well as to their patients. When the life of another can be saved by breaching a confidence, and there is no reasonable alternative for accomplishing the same objective, courts (and society in general) will have little difficulty in mandating disclosure.[19]

When do health care providers, at their own option, have a right to disclose confidential information?

The following "optional" disclosure situations are extremely broad, and indicate the vast discretion courts are likely to afford health care professionals acting in good faith:

1. *Implied Consent*

This is probably the major cause of leakage from the current medical-records system. When a patient is in a hospital, for example, she impliedly consents to the viewing of her medical record by all those directly concerned with her care. This may include the nurses on all three shifts, the ward secretary, all medical students, interns, and residents in the hospital, the attending physician and any consultants called in, and perhaps social, psychological, medical, or psychiatric researchers. All of this may take place without the patient being made aware of it, and is a matter of custom. This practice can also be viewed as based on a privilege health providers have to view the records of those they are caring for.

2. *General Release Forms (Consent)*

Upon entering a hospital a patient may be asked to sign a wide variety of forms. One of these is likely to be an authorization which says essentially that the hospital may release medical information concerning the patient to any-one it thinks should have it or to certain named agencies or organizations. This will include such persons as insurance companies and the welfare department (if they are paying all or part of the bill), and other agencies or individuals monitoring cost. No restriction is generally placed on the amount of material that may be released or the use to which many of these third parties may put the information so received. Arguably, however, receivers would be liable for an invasion-of-privacy action if they used the medical information for other than the specific purpose for which the hospital released it.

While we are not aware of the argument ever having been made, it would seem that most of these general-release forms could be attacked as unduly broad and so vague that the patient could not reasonably and knowingly have signed them. The cases regarding the invalidity of blanket surgical consent forms, which give the doctor and hospital authority to perform whatever procedures they think necessary, would support this line of reasoning. Another argument that could be made is that the patient's lack of bargaining power made the form ineffective (e.g., a sick patient may need admission and cannot afford to forego it by refusing to sign a required form).[20]

3. Private Interests of the Patient

Courts afford physicians generous latitude in making disclosures that they believe in good faith are in the best interests of their patients. This rule, for example, is used to justify many disclosures to spouses and near relatives without the patient's consent. This practice has been criticized on the grounds that when only the patient's individual welfare is involved, only the patient should have the right to decide when confidential information should be released.[21] Nevertheless, courts will probably continue to give physicians and hospitals much discretion in this area, so long as they can make a reasonable argument that there were no alternatives available and that the patient's health required the disclosure.

Even though there has been little judicial explication of the content of this exception, one can deduce that such cases as telling a spouse of a patient's heart condition or impending death, or telling an employer of a roofer that the roofer is subject to blackouts would probably qualify (since the patient would be endangering his own life by continuing in this trade).

Are patients really concerned about possible dissemination of their medical information?

While most of the evidence on this question is anecdotal, there seems to be little doubt that patients would prefer to see confidential medical information shared with as few people as possible. A study which tends to confirm this was conducted in Georgia in 1974–75.[22] In July, 1974, the mental health clinics and centers in the state of Georgia were required to send personal information on individual clients to the state capital. Patients were asked to sign the following release form:

> The undersigned patient hereby authorizes the Northeast Georgia Community Mental Health Center to furnish the Division of Mental Health of the Georgia Department of Human Resources a record or records including the following information: patient's name, social security number, and nature of patient's primary disability.

A final clause provided that the information would not be made publicly available. Of 962 clients at the Center's four clinics, no one refused to sign.

From March to September of 1975 Dr. Catherine E. Rosen used two alternative procedures. The same form was used, but in two of the four clinics after reading it the clients were informed orally that if they signed, this information would be placed in the Mental Health computer file. In the other two clinics, this statement was followed by another: "If you do not sign this paper, this identifying information will not be sent into the state offices in the capital and will be kept only locally. In other words, if you don't sign you will get the same services from us as if you did sign."

In the two clinics where only the first "no option" statement was made orally, compliance was again 100 percent as every one of the 109 clients asked signed the form. However, in one of the two clinics where both statements were read, compliance among 259 clients dropped to 41 percent, and in the other clinic compliance among 104 clients dropped to 20 percent. The other variable that probably accounts for the difference between the two clinics is that in the 41 percent clinic the statement was read by a clerk, whereas in the other it was presented by a clinician. It is likely that the personal assurance of the individual who will actually be delivering the services, that refusal to sign will not affect them, is more credible than this same statement from a nonclinician. The concerns expressed by the clients who did not sign included the possible effect that forwarding the information would have on future employment, loss of custody of their children, and fears of the information being used against them some time in the future for some governmental purpose.

Professor Alan Westin concluded from this study that

millions of persons who are clients of government health services *do* care about the circulation of their personal data, and that their consent would *not* be freely obtained for many inadequately protected government data systems if clients really had adequate notice of what was to be done and felt they had a real choice of whether to consent or not.[23]

What type of release form should be used in authorizations for release of medical information by patients?

The Privacy Commission found that in many instances, when an individual applies for a job, for life or health insurance, for credit, or for financial assistance or services from the government, he is asked to relinquish certain medical information. While believing that this is necessary in many cases, the Commission also found that individuals are generally asked to sign open-ended or blanket authorizations with wording such as requiring the recipient to "furnish any and all information on request." [24]

The American Psychiatric Association takes the position that such blanket consents are unacceptable since they do not afford the patient generally accepted informed consent protections.[25] We agree with the APA. However, the Commission thought the APA impractical because patients do not know precisely what information will be disclosed nor what use will likely be made of it. Recognizing these limits, the Commission made the following recommendations:

[w]henever an individual's authorization is required before a medical care provider may disclose informa-

tion it collects or maintains about him, the medical care provider should not accept as valid any authorization which is not:

(a) in writing;

(b) signed by the individual on a date specified or by someone authorized in fact to act in his behalf;

(c) clear as to the fact that the medical care provider is among those either specifically named or generally designated by the individual as being authorized to disclose information about him;

(d) specific as to the nature of the information the individual is authorizing to be disclosed;

(e) specific as to the institutions or other persons to whom the individual is authorizing information to be disclosed;

(f) specific as to the purpose(s) for which the information may be used by any of the parties named in (e) both at the time of the disclosure and at any time in the future;

(g) specific as to its expiration date, which should be for a reasonable time not to exceed one year. . . .

Health care providers have the right to refuse to honor requests that are not specific on the grounds that the patient probably did not understand what he was consenting to. Health care providers should contact the patient directly if they are suspicious of the quality of the consent and thus the legality of the release form.

The Commission also takes the position that when a minor is permitted to consent to treatment for specific conditions, confidentiality must be protected and only the minor should be allowed to consent to release of medical information.[26]

Under what circumstances do health professionals have the right to discuss the patient or his case with other professionals?

Health professionals who are directly involved in the patient's care may discuss the patient's case among themselves without breaching confidentiality. However, they may not discuss the patient or her case with other professionals who are not directly involved in her care without her consent *unless* her identity is protected. Thus hypotheticals, without names or other identifiers, can be discussed openly so long as the individual patient cannot be identified.

A related question arises when at a teaching hospital a patient's case is presented at rounds. Even though the patient is helped by the presentation, it is not part of the patient's direct care, and the patient's consent must be obtained prior to such "public" disclosures if the patient is identifiable.

Do health professionals have the right to discuss the patient's case with his family without his express consent?

While the AMA has contended that "reporting to one spouse information about the medical condition of the other is not a breach of confidentiality," [27] only two cases have been found that support this proposition, and each is of dubious value. The first is a 1963 Louisiana case that rested on the proposition that the husband had a right to know about his wife's condition because "he is head and master of the family and responsible for its debts." [28] The only other case is a 1966 memorandum opinion of the New York Supreme Court sitting in Nassau County. This case also involved disclosure to a husband, and the court cited the Louisiana case in denying liability. As if unsure of his position, however, Judge Paul J. Widlitz added: "At any rate, a physician who reveals the nature of the condition of the patient to the patient's husband may hardly be charged with reprehensible conduct." [29]

The better rule is that no disclosures to spouses or relatives should be permitted without the patient's express consent.

What recommendations did the Privacy Commission make concerning medical records?

The Privacy Protection Study Commission, set up by Congress in 1974 to study individual privacy rights and record-keeping practices, issued its final report in July, 1977. The Commission based its recommendations on findings that medical records now contain more information and are available to more users than ever before; that the control of health care providers over these records has been greatly diluted; that restoration of this control is not possible; that free patient consent to disclosure is generally illusory; that patients' access to their records is rare; and that there are steps that can be taken to improve the quality of records, enhance patients' awareness of their content, and control their disclosure. Some of the commission's major recommendations are:

1. That each state enact a statute creating individual rights of access to, and correction of, medical records, and an enforceable expectation of confidentiality for medical records.
2. That federal and state penal codes be amended to make it a criminal offense for any individual knowingly to request or obtain medical record information from a medical care provider under false pretenses or through deception.
3. That upon request, an individual who is the subject of a medical record maintained by a medical care provider, or another responsible person designated by the individual, be allowed to have access to that medical record, including the opportunity to see and copy it; and have the opportunity to correct or amend the record.
4. That each medical care provider be required to take affirmative measures to assure that the medical records it maintains are made available only to authorized recipients and on a "need-to-know" basis.
5. That any disclosure of medical record information by a medical care provider be limited only to information necessary to accomplish the purpose for which the disclosure is made.
6. That each medical care provider be required to notify an individual on whom it maintains a medical record of the disclosures that may be made of information in the record without the individual's express authorization.

Can patients be photographed by health care professionals?

Yes, as long as the patient's consent is obtained. While most of the cases regarding photographs of patients involved the publication of the photos in newspapers or magazines, documentaries and television programs have recently begun to use actual films made in hospitals or mental institutions. For example, in the late 1960s, film-maker and lawyer Frederick Wiseman shot eighty thousand feet of film inside a state mental institution in Massachusetts; the result was the documentary *Titicut Follies*. The Supreme Judicial Court of Massachusetts enjoined its showing to public audiences in the state:

> The Commissioner and Superintendent, under reasonable standards of custodial conduct, could hardly permit merely curious members of the public access to Bridgewater to view directly many activities shown on the film. We think it equally inconsistent with their custodial duties to permit the general public (as opposed to members of groups with a legitimate, significant interest) to view films showing inmates naked or exhibiting painful aspects of mental disease.[30]

Elsewhere in the decision, the court used the following words to describe the invasion of privacy: "collective, indecent intrusion"; "massive, unrestrained"; "embarrassing."

The patient's right to privacy is superior to any private and usually superior to any public interest in obtaining information about their medical care. This means that *no* film, not even pictures for the medical record, should be taken of patients without their prior consent. This point was dramatically made in a 1976 case from Maine, which concerned a patient who was dying of cancer of the larynx.[31] Both a laryngectomy and a subsequent radical neck dissection were performed. The surgeon took pictures, solely for use in the medical record and not for publication, of the progress of the disease. On the day before the patient died the physician entered his room, placed some blue toweling under his head for color contrast, and took several photographs. There was evidence from which the jury could have concluded that the patient raised a clenched fist and moved his head in an attempt to get out of the camera's range. His wife had also informed the physician she "didn't think that Henry wanted his picture taken." The trial court granted a motion for a directed verdict for the physician, but the Maine Supreme Court reversed, saying that the physician's actions amounted to a violation of the patient's right to privacy:

> Absent express consent . . . the touching of the patient in the manner described by the evidence in this case would constitute assault and battery if it was part of an undertaking which, in legal effect, was an invasion of plaintiff's "right to be let alone."

> We are urged to declare as a matter of law that it is the physician's right to complete the photographic record by capturing on film B.'s appearance in his final dying hours, even without the patient's consent or over his objections. This we are unwilling to do.

> The facial characteristics or peculiar cast of one's features, whether normal or distorted, belong to the individual and may not be reproduced without his permission.[32]

Do health care professionals have a "right of privacy"?
This question generally arises when a state agency demands certain information from physicians about their patients, and the physicians refuse, arguing that disclosure of the information would be harmful to their patients and disrupt their practicing their profession as they deem appropriate, and therefore violate the physicians' "right of privacy" implicit in the doctor-patient relationship. This is a classic instance where the interests of the physician and patient are identical; neither wants confidential information about the patient disclosed.

This issue was raised, for example, in challenging a New York statute that required that all prescriptions for Schedule II drugs be made out in triplicate and that one copy be forwarded to a state agency for placement on a computer tape.[33] The physicians alleged that the statute impaired their right to practice medicine free of "unwarranted state interference" because it deterred them from writing certain prescriptions for fear their patients' records might become public. The court summarily dismissed this argument, saying that whatever right of privacy physicians had in the doctor-patient relationship was "derivative from, and therefore no stronger than, the patients'." The statute itself was upheld on the basis that it served a rational state purpose (making sure dangerous drugs were used only for legitimate medical purposes), and had sufficient built-in safeguards to protect the patients' right to privacy. Specifically, the forms were received by the state agency, coded, and the information placed on computer tapes. The forms themselves were put in a vault, stored for five years, and then destroyed. The room in which the tapes were kept was surrounded by a locked wire fence and protected by an alarm system. The tapes were kept in a locked cabinet, and when used, the computer was run "off-line," which means that no terminal outside of the computer room could read or record any information. Disclosure of data was prohibited by statute and was a crime punishable by up to a year in prison. Only seventeen state employees and twenty-four investigators were authorized to use the files.

In a related case, the Alaska Supreme Court ruled that, under the state's conflict-of-interest statutes, a physician who is a public official need not divulge the names of his patients who have paid him more than $100. The court indicated, however, that the statute could be amended to provide protections like those in the New York drug statute, and then disclosure would be necessary.[34] The court permitted the physician to argue that such a disclosure would violate the rights of his patients, and noted that generally the fact that a patient has gone to a particular physician is not private. However, the court thought it could be if, for example, the professional was "a psychiatrist, psychologist, or physician who specialized in treating sexual problems or veneral disease."

NOTES

1. Ervin, *Civilized Man's Most Valued Right*, 2 PRISM 15 (June 1974); *cf.* A. WESTIN & M. BAHER, DATA BANKS IN A FREE SOCIETY 17–20 (New York: Quadrangle, 1973); A. MILLER, THE ASSAULT ON PRIVACY 184–220 (New York: New American Library, 1972).
2. Hammonds v. Aetna Cas. & Sur. Co., 243 F. Supp. 793 (N.D. Ohio 1965).
3. In Curry v. Corn (277 N.Y.S.2d 470 [1966]), for example, the physician disclosed information to his patient's husband, who was contemplating a divorce action. In Schaffer v. Spicer (215 N.W.2d 134 [S.D. 1974]), the

wife's psychiatrist disclosed information to the husband's attorney to aid him in a child-custody case. Representative of the insurance cases are Hague v. Williams (181 A.2d 345 [N.J. 1962]), where the pediatrician of an infant informed a life insurance company of a congenital heart defect that he had not informed the child's parents of, and Hammonds v. Aetna (*supra* note 2), where the physician revealed information to an insurance company when the insurance company falsely represented to him that his patient was suing him for malpractice. Cases involving reporting to employers include Beatty v. Baston (13 Ohio L. Abs. 481 [Ohio App. 1932]), where the physician revealed to a patient's employer during a workman's compensation action that the patient had venereal disease; Clark v. Geraci (208 N.Y.S.2d 564 [S. Ct. N.Y. 1960]), where a civilian employee of the Air Force asked his doctor to make an incomplete disclosure to his employer to explain absences, but the doctor made a complete disclosure including the patient's alcoholism; and the recent case of Horne v. Patton (287 So.2d 824 (Ala. 1973]), which involved the disclosure of a longstanding nervous condition.

4. 8 WIGMORE ON EVIDENCE §2380a. Retention of the privilege was also the most controversial item in the new Federal Rules of Evidence. While initial versions eliminated the privilege entirely, the final version provides that the privilege shall "be governed by the principles of the common law as they may be interpreted by the courts of the United States in the light of reason and experience." Where, however, state law governs a case, the privilege shall be "determined in accordance with state law." (Rule 501) There are, however, numerous exceptions to the privilege rule. The most important are:

1. Communications made to a doctor when no doctor-patient relationship exists.
2. Communications made to a doctor that are not for the purposes of diagnosis and treatment or are not necessary to the purposes of diagnosis and treatment (e.g., who inflicted the gunshot wound and why).
3. In actions involving commitment proceedings, issues as to wills, actions on insurance policies.
4. In actions in which the patient brings his physical or

mental condition into question (e.g., personal injury suit for damages, raising an insanity defense, malpractice action against a doctor or hospital).

5. Reports required by state statutes (e.g., gunshot wounds, acute poisoning, child abuse, motor vehicle accidents, and, in some states, venereal disease).

6. Information given to the doctor in the presence of another not related professionally to the doctor or known by the patient.

5. A. WESTIN, PRIVACY AND FREEDOM 7 (New York: Atheneum, 1967).

6. Horne v. Patton, 287 So.2d 824, 830 (Ala. 1973).

7. Miller, *Personal Privacy in the Computer Age,* 67 MICH. L. REV. 1091, 1107 (1968).

8. In 1939, for example, *Time* magazine published a story in its "Medicine" section with a photograph of the patient, a young woman who was receiving treatment for uncontrollable gluttony aparently induced by a condition of the pancreas (Barber v. Time, Inc. 159 S.W.2d 291 [Mo. 1942]). Other cases, like Horne v. Patton (*supra* note 3), however, indicate that publication is not necessary to sustain an invasion-of-privacy action. For example, having unauthorized persons in a delivery room (DeMay v. Roberts, 9 N.W. 146 [Mich. 1881]) or, by analogy, permitting unauthorized persons to view confidential medical records may also be an invasion of privacy.

9. CAL. HEALTH & SAFETY CODE, §2554 (Supp. 1970).

10. Landeros v. Flood, 17 Cal. 3d 399, 131 Cal. Rptr. 69, 551 P.2d 389 (1976).

11. N.Y. PENAL CODE, §265.25 (Supp. 1969). *And see generally* Rose, *Pathology Reports and Autopsy Protocols: Confidentiality, Privilege and Accessibility,* 57 AM. J. CRIM. PROC. 144 (1972), *and* Denver Pub. Co. v. Dreyfus, 520 P.2d 104 (Col. 1974) (autopsy reports open to public under Open Records Act). A physician does not need a statute to release confidential medical information when a danger to the public exists. The leading case enunciating this exception, Simonsen v. Swenson (177 N.W. 831), was decided by the Supreme Court of Nebraska in 1920. In that case a fellow who was visiting a small town was seen by a physician who was also the physician for the hotel in which he was staying. The physician diagnosed syphilis and advised the patient to "get out of town" or he would

tell the hotel. When the patient remained in town the doctor notified the landlady, who disinfected his room and removed his belongings to the hallway. The court decided that the doctor had the right to reveal just as much information concerning a contagious disease as was necessary for others to take proper precautions against becoming infected with it and that his actions under the circumstances were justified.

12. Stone, *The Tarasoff Decisions: Suing Psychotherapists to Safeguard Society,* 90 HARV. L. REV. 358 (1976); *and see* Note, *Where the Public Peril Begins: A Survey of Psychotherapists to Determine the Effects of Tarasoff,* 31 STANFORD L. REV. 165 (1978).

13. Hoffmann v. Blackmon, 241 So.2d 752 (Fla. App. 1970); *and see* Wojcik v. Aluminum Co. of America, 183 N.Y.S. 2d 351, 357–58 (1959).

14. Jones v. Stanko, 118 Ohio St. 147, 160 N.E. 456 (1928).

15. Davis v. Rodman, 147 Ark. 385, 227 S.W. 612 (1921).

16. Skillings v. Allen, 143 Minn. 323, 173 N.W. 663 (1919).

17. Tarasoff v. Regents of U. of California, 131 Cal. Rptr. 14, 551 P.2d 334 (1976).

18. *See* Stone, *supra* note 12.

19. *See* McIntosh v. Milano, 168 N.J. Super. 466 (1979).

20. Under a similar theory, clauses by which the patient has agreed not to sue the hospital for negligence have been ruled invalid because the patient really had no choice but to sign the form (Tunkl v. Regents of Univ. of California, 60 Cal.2d 92, 383 P.2d 441 [1963]). One could argue that it is impossible to give consent for release of medical records before they are in existence (e.g., at the beginning of a hospital stay rather than at the end) since at that time one can have no reasonable idea of what they might contain.

21. Note, *Medical Practice and the Right to Privacy,* 43 MINN. L. REV. 943, 960 (1959).

22. This study, called The Georgia "Free Consent" Experiment, is described in A. WESTIN, COMPUTERS, HEALTH RECORDS, AND CITIZEN RIGHTS, National Bureau of Standards Monograph 157, (Washington, D.C.: U.S. Govt. Printing Office, 1976) at 243–45.

23. *Id.* at 245.

24. PRIVACY PROTECTION STUDY COMMISSION, PERSONAL PRI-

VACY IN AN INFORMATION SOCIETY, (Washington, D.C.: U.S. Govt. Printing Office, 1977) at 314.

25. *Id.* citing AMERICAN PSYCHIATRIC ASSOCIATION, CONFIDENTIALITY AND THIRD PARTIES (Washington, D.C.: APA, 1975) at 13.

26. See material on minors' consent in chapters IV and X.

27. *Disclosure of Confidential Information,* 216 JAMA 385 (1971).

28. Pennison v. Provident Life & Accident Ins. Co., 154 So.2d 617, 618 (La. Ct. App. 1963).

29. Curry v. Corn, 217 N.Y.S.2d 470, 472, 52 Misc. 2d 1035 (1966).

30. Commonwealth v. Wiseman, 356 Mass. 251, 249 N.E.2d 610, 616 (1969).

31. Berthiame v. Pratt, 365 A.2d 792 (Me. 1976).

32. *Id.* at 796–97. *Compare* Knight v. Penobscot Bay Medical Center et al., 420 A.2d 915 (Me. 1980) (affirming a jury verdict for the hospital in which the husband of a staff nurse had viewed a birth and the jury had been instructed to find in favor of the plaintiff only if it found the intrusion was *intentional* and "would be highly offensive to a reasonable person.").

33. Whalen v. Roe, 429 U.S. 589 (1977).

34. Falcon v. Alaska Pub. Offices Comm'n, 570 P.2d 469 (Alaska 1977). *Cf.* Doctors Hospital of Sarasota v. Califano, 455 F. Supp. 476 (M.D. Fla. 1978).

X

Childbirth, Abortion, and Sterilization

In no area of medicine has the effect of legal changes been as far-reaching and dramatic as in the area of abortion. Since criminal laws restricting access to abortions were declared unconstitutional, abortions have become the most frequently performed surgical procedure in the United States—accounting for the termination of one in three pregnancies. Most of the remaining pregnancies, of course, end in a live birth, and both consumers and providers have been demanding changes in the manner and place of birth. Limitations on family size have brought increased concern over the health of the fetus. New methods of prenatal diagnosis of birth defects have therefore become critical to many pregnant patients.

This is the only chapter of the book that deals with specific types of medical intervention. It is here for the reasons stated above, and to serve as a paradigm of how changes in the law can affect medical practice and the rights of both patients and their providers.

The role of the law in childbirth is often obscure and frequently misunderstood. This is because the law plays many roles, and these roles differ considerably depending upon the place of birth. In addition, the law relating to childbirth is changing through legislation, court decisions, opinions of attorneys general, and hospital policies.

The foundations of the current law are based on a long tradition of protecting the public from medical quacks and on a more recent desire to protect children from abuse by their parents. Since both licensure laws and child abuse statutes have ample rationales, independent of childbirth, neither is likely to be easily abandoned. The challenge for those desiring change is to work for modifications within the framework of these laws. In general, the law is very conservative and is likely to reflect standard medical practice; it varies from state to state; and it is outcome-oriented.[1] These characteristics affect the answers to most of the questions in this chapter.

Do physicians and patients have a right to use "alternative" forms of child delivery in hospitals?

This issue has been most directly addressed by "husband in the delivery room" cases. While most hospitals with maternity wards currently permit husband-coached childbirth (e.g., Lamaze or psychoprophylactic), in which the father is with the mother throughout labor and delivery, lawsuits to compel a change in the policies of those institutions that do not allow this procedure have so far all been unsuccessful. This is true whether the hospital is private or public, and whether the plaintiff is a pregnant woman or her obstetrician.

In the first appellate decision on this question, a Montana court reversed a lower court ruling in favor of an obstetrician who had challenged a hospital rule that forbade the presence of fathers in the delivery room.[2] The administrator of the private Catholic hospital contended that the rule was based on a concern for the spread of infection, the chance of an increase in malpractice suits, the possible disturbance of doctors in the doctors' locker room, the increased costs of surgical gowns, the potential for invasion of the privacy of other patients, and was, as well, a measure for the promotion of staff harmony. Without analyzing the merits of these contentions, the court concluded simply that as long as minimal due process was accorded the physician, and the rule adopted was not arbitrary or capricious, the court would not intrude itself "into the administration of the hospital where the hospital had acted in good faith on competent medical advice."[3]

The only other case to reach the appellate level on the merits involved a suit by prospective parents and their physician against a public hospital.[4] They contended that the hospital's policy denying fathers a right to be in the delivery room violated constitutional rights, specifically, the "right of marital privacy" enunciated in the birth-control and abortion decisions. The lower court dismissed their suit, and the appeals court affirmed in a 2–1 decision.[5] The court made a number of comments that highlight the problems future courts will have to overcome before recognizing a constitutional right of a woman to have the father of her child with her during a hospital delivery.

Perhaps the most important stumbling block is that of precedent. The judges were extremely concerned that, if they found a constitutional right for a husband to be present in the delivery room during childbirth, they would "perhaps" be required to allow other persons about to undergo serious medical procedures the right to be accompanied by a person of their choice. We disagree with the court's view that such an outcome is mandated by a decision of this kind. Childbirth can be distinguished in a number of ways from other procedures—e.g., it is a natural process happening to a healthy woman; it is performed in these cases under local or no anesthesia; and it is primarily concerned with reproduction.

It was the court's inability to make such a distinction that reinforced their determination to find against the plaintiffs. In fact, while conceding that "the birth of a child is an event of unequalled importance in the lives of most married couples," the court found the birth procedure itself, "in its medical aspects," to be comparable to other serious hospital procedures, and "extraordinary" in nature. This, of course, rejects the entire rationale of the "natural" childbirth movement, which is that childbirth is normal, not pathological, and that in the vast majority of births little or no medical intervention is either required or desirable.[6]

But where are the physician and hospital-bound couple left until this or a similar approach is adopted by the courts? In general, both the couple and the physician they choose must follow hospital policy in regard to deliveries (including such things as the presence of the father and others, method of delivery, etc.). The woman, however, does have the right to refuse any particular medical procedure or drug offered (e.g., fetal monitor, anesthesia, episiotomy).[7] Control is reactive only, since the patient cannot demand that things happen in a certain way, but can only refuse certain things that are offered. Given the proper hospital environment and supportive health care professionals, this may be entirely satisfactory. If it is not, the only currently viable alternative is for patients to give birth outside of the hospital, either in a birth center or at home.

Who may attend a home birth?

In every state, physicians may attend home births. As for other attendents, such as nurse-midwives and lay-midwives, this question will be governed by the law of the particular state.

Statutes and qualifications vary, but in states that have specific legislation providing for the licensing of midwives, it is likely that courts would find that anyone not a physician or licensed midwife who held himself out as an expert on childbirth and attended a childbirth would be guilty of the crime of practicing either medicine or midwifery without a license (in a number of states one must have been compensated to be prosecuted). The court's reasoning in reaching this conclusion would probably parallel that of a California Supreme Court decision that found that the legislature had an "interest in regulating the qualifications of those who hold themselves out as childbirth attendants . . . for many women must necessarily rely on those with qualifications which they cannot personally verify." [8] The rationale in that the legislature can reasonably find that the only way to protect the health of the public in the matter of childbirth is to insure that those who hold themselves out as experts to the public are required to meet certain standards and be licensed. And once this finding is made by the enactment of a licensing statute, anyone practicing outside of its limitations would be guilty of the crime of practicing without a license.

The parents' primary duty is to the potential child. No state requires women to take any affirmative action to safeguard their fetuses. However, all states have passed child abuse statutes that forbid parents from abusing their children, and, in general, require them to provide their children with necessary medical attention. Parents may in general make a decision to have a home birth with impunity. If they have reason to know that complications are likely to develop that will require hospital care to save the child from death or permanent injury, however, and the child dies or is permanently injured because of the home birth, the parents could be held criminally liable. The charge would be child abuse in both cases, and possibly manslaugher (depending on the cause of death and its predictability) if the child dies.[9] This general rule should dissuade parents from attempting to manage home births by themselves, and encourage them to seek a licensed attendant at the home birth, or to seek hospitalization when it is indicated to protect the health of the child.

Is it malpractice for a physician to participate in a home birth?

No. Physicians' fear of the potential of increased malpractice liability for participation in home births is probably based on ignorance of the law of medical malpractice, combined with the climate of fear that has been created in many states.[10] Indeed, at least one physician—himself a specialist in medical malpractice—has argued in a book on malpractice written for the public that a physician-attended home birth in New York City is de facto evidence of negligence.[11] This is simply wrong. So long as the decision to have a home birth is made by the woman after she has been fully informed of the risks and potential complications, and so long as all generally accepted medical steps have been taken concerning screening the woman and emergency back-up facilities, it is highly unlikely that any malpractice action against a physician would be successful. Indeed, because of the absence of things like general anesthesia and the presence of a well-informed and participating woman, a physician is probably less likely to be sued for malpractice in a home birth setting than in a hospital birth.

In attending childbirth and counseling the pregnant woman, the physician probably has a duty toward the fetus to provide it with adequate medical care both before and during the delivery.[12] This duty will probably not usually prevent a physician from participating in a home delivery, but will require the physician to perform any standard screening tests for high-risk pregnancies, and to attempt to make sure such couples make use of hospital facilities for birth.

What actions might be taken against a physician who takes part in a home birth?

The medical profession's reaction to home birth has not been enthusiastic. In Massachusetts, for example, the Board of Registration in Medicine seriously considered a regulation prohibiting physicians from participating in home births. The regulation was rejected, not because the Board members support home birth as an alternative, but because they decided it was inappropriate to attempt to interfere with the way a physician desired to practice and the way women wanted to have their babies. The Board also recognized that such a regulation would not prevent home births, but would only insure that they would not be attended by physicians. The fact that this issue even reached the Board is ironic, since only about 200 to 500 home births occurred in Massachusetts in 1977 out of about 70,000 total births—about 7 per 1,000 births, using the highest estimates.

Nevertheless, the issue has become highly politicized. One physician, the past president of the Massachusetts section of the American College of Obstetrics and Gynecology, has been quoted as saying home-birthers are "kooks, the lunatic fringe, people who have emotional problems they're acting out." [13] While a law was enacted to permit the licensing of nurse-midwives, it specified that they could practice only in a hospital or clinic, and then only under the supervision of a physician.

Two specific types of doctor-instigated activities merit discussion, as they are likely to have an impact on both in-hospital and out-of-hospital births. The first is the denial of childbirth privileges in the hospital to family practitioners; the second is the attempt to deny staff privileges altogether to physicians participating in home births.

1. Denial of Obstetrical Privileges

Denial of obstetrical privileges to family practitioners could lead them and their patients to seek alternative settings for childbirth. At least one hospital in Massachusetts, for example, has denied obstetrical privileges to a family practitioner. [14] The primary motivation seems to have been economic—not enough births to go around for the obstetricians on the staff. Nevertheless, the rationale set forth publicly was patient safety and the greater training and experience of board certified obstetricians to "manage" childbirth. Whatever one thinks of this rationale, the courts could affirm such a policy decision without looking behind it because they are loath to second-guess hospitals in the area of patient care. In an analogous case, for example, the Illinois Court of Appeals upheld a rule adopted by a hospital board for their obstetrics and gynecology department requiring any surgeon to obtain the consultation of one of its members prior to any major gynecological operation.[15] A board certified surgeon challenged the rule, and lost. The court noted that hospital boards "are responsible for upgrading the standards of health care to be maintained in the hospital . . . and the court is charged with the narrow responsibility of assuring that the qualifications imposed by the Board are reasonably related to the operation of the hospital and fairly administered." [16]

2. *Denial of Privileges for Participating in Home Birth*

In November, 1976, the Obstetrics-Gynecology Department of Yale-New Haven Hospital adopted the following "departmental policy": "Hereafter any physician with OB privileges at YNHH who intentionally participates in a non-emergency 'home delivery' will be viewed as no longer fulfilling the professional expectations of the OB staff of the hospital, and will immediately have OB admitting privileges revoked."

This policy is legally dubious because it has nothing to do with in-hospital care and, therefore, can make no pretext about being for the safety of hospital patients. As to nonhospital patients, the hospital has no legitimate concern with their free exercise of the legal option of home birth. The primary interest they seem to have is economic and, if the attempt is to join in a conspiracy to restrain trade (in home births), the activity might also violate the antitrust laws. Finally, the promulgating authority seems ambiguous in this case, and summary revocation of privileges is inconsistent with the "fair administration" policy.

Do physicians have an obligation to provide genetic counseling to their pregnant patients?

Yes. The legal basis for this obligation is well illustrated in a pair of New York cases decided in late 1978.[17] The first involved Dolores Becker who, in 1974, at the age of thirty-six, became pregnant and was under the exclusive care of her obstetrician from the tenth week of her pregnancy until the child's birth. Her child was born with Down's syndrome. Ms. Becker alleged that she was not advised of the availability of amniocentesis or its ability to detect Down's syndrome *in utero,* and that if she had been so advised she would have had an abortion if the test indicated her fetus was affected.

A companion case, decided at the same time, concerned Hetty and Steven Park, who in 1969 had a child afflicted with polycystic kidney disease that died five hours after birth. Following this tragedy, they asked Ms. Park's obstetricians what the chances were of future children being so affected. The physicians allegedly replied (incorrectly) that the disease was not hereditary and the chances of her having another similarly affected child were "practically nil." Based on this information Mrs. Park became pregnant again, and again gave birth to a child suffering from polycystic kidney disease. Their second child, however, survived for two and a half years before succumbing to the disease.

The court faced two issues: (1) Should a defective child be permitted to sue his physician (or anyone) for "wrongful life" on the theory that he would have been better off if he never existed? and (2) Should the parents of a defective child whose birth would have been prevented but for the negligence of a physician be able to recover the costs of caring for their defective child?

The court refused to permit the child to sue for "wrongful life" because it suffered no "legally cognizable injury." In the court's words: "Whether it is better never to have been born at all than to have been born with even gross deficiencies is a mystery more properly to be left to the philosophers and the theologians." [18]

The actions by both sets of parents, on the other hand, were upheld. Accepting their version of the facts, the court found that they had stated a proper malpractice claim (i.e., that the doctor had breached a duty to the patient that had caused damage) against the physician involved and that the alleged damages—monetary expenses for the care and treatment of the children—could be accurately measured.[19]

The court, however, refused to permit recovery for

emotional or psychological damages because permitting such an action would "inevitably lead to the drawing of artificial and arbitrary boundaries." One such consideration the court mentioned is offsetting the emotional trauma against the parental "love that even an abnormality cannot fully dampen."

More specifically, the court ruled that if the parents could prove all of the allegations in a trial, the Beckers could recover the sums expended for long-term institutional care of their retarded child, and the Parks could recover the sums expended for the care and treatment of their child until her death.

In neither case was any money actually paid to the parents (the Beckers had placed their child for adoption before the court decision, and in April, 1979, a jury decided that the physicians in the Park case did not make the statements attributed to them). But the legal principle remains: physicians must give accurate information to their patients, and cannot withhold material information (such as the existence of a vital diagnostic test) from them. This is consistent with the doctrine of informed consent, good legal principles, and the reasonable expectations of pregnant women under a physician's care. "The physician does not guarantee a healthy child, but the reasonable expectation of the patient is that she will be apprised of any information the physician has that the child might be defective and of the alternative ways to proceed, so that the patient can determine what action to take." [20]

Under what circumstances may a state regulate or prohibit abortions?

Until 1973, states had very broad power to limit and proscribe abortions. In that year the U.S. Supreme Court in *Roe* v. *Wade* held that the constitutional right to privacy permitted a woman and her physician to decide whether or not she would have an abortion.[21] The court held that the right to privacy is a "fundamental right," though not an absolute one. The state may abridge a woman's right to decide to have an abortion if it can demonstrate a "compelling state interest."

During the first trimester, since the fetus is quite undeveloped and the procedure is less risky to the pregnant woman than childbirth, the state has no compelling interests. In the second trimester, the abortion procedure becomes more risky, and the state may regulate the procedure in a manner designed to protect the woman's life and health. For example, the state may require that abortions be performed only in hospitals or clinics. At the point of fetal viability, somewhere near the beginning of the third trimester, the state has a compelling interest in "protecting fetal life" and may, if it chooses, proscribe abortion altogether, unless the abortion is "necessary to preserve the life or health of the mother." [22]

What does "viability" mean?

Because a state may regulate abortion to the greatest extent after viability, defining the term has raised a good deal of controversy. In *Roe*, the Supreme Court defined viability as the point at which the fetus is "potentially able to live outside the mother's womb, albeit with artificial aid." [23] and, later, as when it is capable "of meaningful life outside the mother's womb." [24]

Who has the right to determine when a fetus is viable?

Only a physician can make a determination of viability. A year after *Roe* v. *Wade* was decided, Missouri passed a statute that defined fetal viability as that stage in fetal development when the life of the "unborn child may be continued indefinitely outside womb by natural or artificial life-supportive systems." This definition caused concern, because the term "indefinitely" could mean a very short period of time as well as a long period of time. If the term meant a short period of time, then the point of viability, and therefore the point when abortion could be most strictly regulated, would occur very early in pregnancy. The Supreme Court [25] found that the term "continued indefinitely" might favor the statute's opponents, since that point may well occur later in pregnancy than the point at which the fetus is "potentially able to live outside the mother's womb." The court went on to say that, regardless of the meaning of the term "indefinitely," viability is *essentially* a *medical concept*, and the determination of viability of a *particular fetus* "rests with the physician in the exercise of his professional judgment." [26]

In an even more recent case, the U.S. Supreme Court

emphasized the very limited role of the state in determining viability:

> Viability is reached when, in the judgment of the attending physician on the particular facts of the case before him, there is a reasonable likelihood of the fetus' sustained survival outside the womb, with or without artificial support. Because this point may differ with each pregnancy, neither the legislature nor the courts may proclaim one of the elements entering into the ascertainment of viability—be it weeks of gestation or fetal weight or any other single factor—as the determinant of when the State has a compelling interest in the life or health of the fetus. Viability is the critical point. And we have recognized no attempt to stretch the point of viability one way or the other.[27]

This very powerful language should foreclose any future attempts at limiting the physician's role in the determination of viability.

May a state require a woman to obtain the consent of her husband as a condition to her obtaining an abortion?

No. The Supreme Court has held that since a state does not have veto power over a woman's decision to abort in the early stage of pregnancy, it cannot delegate this power to any other person, even a spouse. The Court decided this issue on rather practical grounds: when the husband and wife disagree over the decision to abort, only one party can prevail. Since the woman is more directly and immediately affected by the pregnancy, the balance weighs in her favor.

May a state require that a minor woman obtain the consent of her parents as a condition to her receiving an abortion?

In a limited set of circumstances. The Supreme Court has held that parents may not be given a veto power over the decision of a "competent" or "mature" minor who desires an abortion.[28] Such a minor would be one who is "sufficiently mature to understand the procedure and to make an intelligent assessment of her circumstances with the advice of her physician." [29]

In an attempt to overcome the prohibition of parental

veto power, Massachusetts passed a statute which contained the following requirements:

1. Minor females must have consent of both parents prior to receiving an abortion.
2. If one or both parents refuse to consent, the minor may apply to a court to receive judicial consent. The judge must consent to the abortion if he finds that the best interests of the minor will be served by an abortion. The judge must disregard all parental objections, and other considerations which are not based exclusively on the best interests standard.
3. Even if the judge finds that the minor is capable of making, and has made, an informed and reasonable decision to have an abortion, he may withhold his consent if he finds that the minor's best interests will not be served by an abortion.
4. A minor who desires an abortion may not obtain judicial consent without first seeking parental consent.[30]

It was argued that this statute did not give parents an absolute veto since it was possible for a minor female to obtain consent from a judge if her parents refused to consent. The U.S. Supreme Court held that the statute was unconstitutional.[31] Eight justices agreed that the statute was unconstitutional because it permits a judge to withhold authorization for an abortion from a mature minor. It seems the Supreme Court will not permit the exercise of a veto over the decision of a mature minor to have an abortion by anyone, whether a parent or the sovereign. Second, these justices agreed that any statute that requires parental involvement in every instance, even if such involvement only amounts to notification or consultation, is unconstitutional.

Four justices discuss the requirements for a statute that they believe would be constitutional. They would uphold a statute that presents a minor female with two options for obtaining an abortion. The first option would enable her to obtain an abortion if she receives the consent of her parents. However, there must be an alternative method to this. This method would involve a procedure whereby the minor could apply to some agent of the state (a judge, administrative agency, or state officer) for permission to undergo an abortion, without first being required to approach her parents. This agent could decide if the minor was sufficiently mature and competent to consent to the abortion. If it is found the minor does meet this standard, then she must be allowed to obtain the abortion. If the minor is immature or not competent, she must be allowed to obtain the abortion without parental involvement if it is found to be in her best interests. The four justices require that these proceedings, and any appeals that may follow, be completed with "anonymity and sufficient expedition to provide an effective opportunity for an abortion to be obtained." [32] Four justices who agreed that the Massachusetts statute was unconstitutional refused to comment on these guidelines, arguing that the Court should not offer advisory opinions on statutes that do not yet exist. Although the substantive right of minors to obtain abortions without parental involvement has been clarified by this decision, the procedural steps a state may require for a minor trying to exercise these rights is still unresolved.

May a state require a physician or health care facility to keep records and make reports to the state concerning abortions they perform?

Yes. "Record keeping and reporting requirements that are reasonably directed to the preservation of maternal health and that properly respect a patient's confidentiality and privacy are permissible." [33] This is so even during the first trimester, since such record keeping and reporting provisions do not have a significant impact on the abortion decision or the physician-patient relationship. Such requirements may not, however, be unduly burdensome.

May a state require a woman to give informed consent prior to abortion?

Yes. This requirement does not single out abortions since informed consent must be given prior to the performance of other surgical procedures, and since it does not unduly burden the decision to abort, the requirement is permissible. In approving an informed consent requirement, the U.S. Supreme Court accepted as the definition of informed consent

The giving of information to the patient as to just what would be done and as to the consequences. To ascribe more meaning than this might well confine the attending physician in an undesired and uncomfortable straitjacket in the practice of his profession.[34]

This standard was set forth by the court in 1976. Nevertheless, in 1978 Louisiana passed a statute requiring a physician to give every patient desiring an abortion eight specific "facts." These include the following:

3. That the unborn child is a human life from the moment of conception and that there has been described in detail the anatomical and physiological characteristics of the particular unborn child at the gestational point of development at which time the abortion is to be performed, including, but not limited to, appearance, mobility, tactile sensitivity, including pain, perception or response, brain and heart function, the presence of internal organs and the presence of external members.

5. That abortion is a major surgical procedure which can result in serious complications, including hemorrhage, perforated uterus, infection, menstrual disturbances, sterility and miscarriages and prematurity in subsequent pregnancies, and that abortion may leave essentially unaffected or may worsen any existing psychological problems she may have, and can result in severe emotional disturbances.[35]

This is not designed to inform the woman as to what will be done and the consequences, but to require a physician to describe to the woman the Louisiana legislature's view of fetal development and abortion. The statute is currently under attack in court and will likely be struck down. A less restrictive informed consent provision was found to be unconstitutional by an Illinois federal district court,[36] and a similar provision in an Akron, Ohio, ordinance has also been struck down.[37]

Are states required to pay for abortions performed on Medicaid recipients?

No. The Supreme Court has decided four cases on this subject, three dealing with "unnecessary" abortions [38] and one dealing with "necessary" or therapeutic abortions.[39] In all the cases the Court held that the states have no constitutional obligation to pay for abortions. In the case concerning necessary abortions, the Court ruled that a statute that permitted payment for abortions that were necessary to preserve the *life* of the mother, but did not permit payment for abortions for any other reasons, was constitutional.

Although this case was decided by a 5–4 vote of the justices, with the four dissenters vehemently disagreeing with the outcome, it is unlikely that this decision will be overruled. Those who support state-funded abortions for poor women must now focus their attention on the state and federal legislatures in order to get them to support such programs.

May a state, city, or town prohibit the establishment of an abortion clinic by adopting discriminatory zoning or licensure laws?

No. In 1975 an abortion clinic entered into a lease in Southborough, Massachusetts, in order to acquire premises in which to operate. After taking the appropriate steps to obtain a certificate of need, the town selectmen voted to amend their zoning by-laws to prohibit all abortion clinics. Every other type of medical facility was permitted to locate in the town, and the only other universally prohibited uses for all districts were "trailer campers," "commercial racetracks," "junk yards," and "piggeries or fur farms." The Massachusetts Supreme Judicial Court held that such action constituted an abridgement of a fundamental right and was therefore invalid.[40] The court also held that even if abortion services were available in adjacent areas, the town could not act as it did, because one town could not deprive a person of a fundamental right on the basis that it was available in another town.

In a similar case, Cleveland, Ohio, prohibited the further issuance of licenses permitting abortion services where there already were other abortion clinics in the same city.[41] Because of the other clinics the court found this ban did not "unduly burden" either the abortion decision or the doctor-patient relationship, and therefore the ordinance was valid.

A locality may not ban the establishment or operation

of *all* abortion clinics through restrictive zoning and licensure ordinances. Unlike the situations in the Medicaid cases discussed earlier, by banning abortion clinics in a particular locale, there exists state action that totally prohibits the obtaining of an abortion. If local governments were permitted to ban abortion facilities, and all local governments in a state exercised this authority, the local governments would have effectively outlawed abortions in the entire state. This was explicitly prohibited in *Roe* v. *Wade*. Zoning laws will not be an effective means of depriving women of their right to receive abortions.

May a state outlaw the advertising of abortion services?
No. Some states have passed laws that make the advertising of abortion services illegal,[42] but the Supreme Court's recent rulings holding that truthful commercial speech is protected by the First Amendment,[43] and its latest ruling striking down a ban on contraceptive advertisements,[44] indicates that such a ban is unconstitutional.[45] For further information, see Chapter XIV on advertising.

May a health care provider be required to participate in the performance of abortions?
A number of states have "conscience clauses" in their statutes which protect health care providers who do not wish to participate in abortions. A Georgia statute states:

A physician, or any other person who is a member of or associated with the staff of a hospital, or any other employee of a hospital in which an abortion has been authorized, who shall state in writing an objection to such abortion on moral or religious grounds, shall not be required to participate in the medical procedures which will result in the abortion, and the refusal of any such person to participate therein shall not form the basis of any claim for damages on account of such refusal or for any disciplinary or recriminatory action against such person.[46]

The U.S. Supreme Court has found that such a statute offers "appropriate protection" to individual health care providers.[47] In states with such statutes, those morally or religiously opposed to abortion are protected from any discrimination based on such beliefs. In states without such statutes, the health care provider who refuses to participate in abortions runs the risk of disciplinary action by the institution.

Must individuals consent before they are sterilized?

Although competent individuals must consent before they are sterilized, a number of states have statutes permitting the sterilization of mentally retarded individuals without their consent. The U.S. Supreme Court in 1927 upheld the constitutionality of such statutes in *Buck* v. *Bell*, a case that has not been overruled.[48] Indeed, in 1976, the North Carolina Supreme Court relied on *Buck* in upholding its state's involuntary sterilization statutes.[49] Although some courts still rely on the state's general *parens patriae* power to order the sterilization of incompetents for their "best interests," the modern trend is that in the absence of a specific statute authorizing a court to order the sterilization of an incompetent person, such sterilization may not be done.[50] Additionally, those states that do have such statutes provide that before an involuntary sterilization can be done, the incompetent person must have a hearing, be represented by counsel, and be accorded other due-process rights. For their own protection, health care providers should not participate in an involuntary sterilization without making sure that such a procedure is authorized.

In some states involuntary sterilizations are absolutely prohibited. The entire Massachusetts involuntary sterilization statute reads as follows:

No physician shall perform, other than in an emergency, an operation which is intended to result in the sterilization of an individual unless he has a knowledgeable consent in writing from such individual. A physician who performs said operation without such consent shall be punished by a fine of not more than ten thousand dollars.[51]

Are there special guidelines for federally funded sterilizations?

Yes. In 1973 the Secretary of Health, Education, and Welfare promulgated regulations that permitted sterilization of incompetent minors and mentally incompetent adults after a review by a review committee and a court review that establish that such sterilization is in the incompetent's "best interest." A federal district court struck down these regulations, finding that Congress only funded family planning services that were dispensed on a voluntary basis.[52] As a result, HHS has promulgated new regulations that provide that federal funds can be used to sterilize only individuals who

1. are twenty-one years old or older;
2. are not mentally incompetent or institutionalized;
3. have voluntarily given their informed consent pursuant to stringent disclosure requirements; and
4. have signed a specified consent form.

After the consent form has been signed, the sterilization procedure may not be performed for thirty days, except in certain specific instances.[53]

May a state require a spouse's consent prior to a sterilization procedure?

As discussed above, a state may not require spousal consent as a condition for a person to receive an abortion. As a result, it would appear that such a requirement is not permissible in regard to sterilization, since it would violate a person's fundamental right to make procreative decisions. Such a statute was struck down by a Georgia federal district court.[54]

NOTES

1. *See* Annas, *Legal Aspects of Homebirths and Other Childbirth Alternatives,* in SAFE ALTERNATIVES IN CHILDBIRTH 161–81 (Stewart & Stewart, eds.; Chapel Hill: NAPSAC, 1976), *and* Annas, *Childbirth and the Law: How to Work Within Old Law, Avoid Malpractice, and Influence New Legislation in Maternity Care,* in 21ST CENTURY OBSTETRICS NOW! vol. II, 557–67 (Stewart & Stewart, eds. Chapel Hill: NAPSAC, 1977).
2. St. Vincent's Hosp. v. Hulit, 520 P.2d 99 (Mont. 1974).
3. It is of interest to note that while the court lifted the

temporary restraining order, the hospital has apparently continued to permit fathers in the delivery room. (Private communication, Peg Beals, Nov. 11, 1975.)

4. Fitzgerald v. Porter Mem. Hosp., 523 F.2d 716 (7th Cir. 1975).

5. An excellent article by attorney John J. McMahon has suggested that another, nonconstitutional, approach to the courts would be more successful. He has argued very eloquently that courts should be pressed to view hospitals as enterprises "affected with a public interest" and as such apply the common law generally applied to such enterprises to hospitals. This would require that hospital policy decisions be both "procedurally fair" and "substantially rational." If this approach is adopted by the state courts (some have already done so), restrictions concerning childbirth practices that could not be proven to be "substantially rational" would be subject to challenge and hospitals would have the burden of proving the soundness of their policies on the basis of expert medical testimony —a burden that is much higher than that which the courts currently require them to meet in this area. McMahon, *Judicial Review of Internal Policy Decisions of Private Nonprofit Hospitals: A Common Law Approach*, 3 AM J. LAW & MED. 149–82 (1977).

6. *See* Chapter IV.

7. Bowland v. Municipal Ct. for Santa Cruz City, 134 Cal. 630, 638 (1976). *And see* Note, *A "Birth Right": Home Births, Midwives, and the Right to Privacy*, 12 Pacific Law J. 97 (July, 1980).

8. Robertson, *Involuntary Enthanasia of Defective Newborns*, 27 STANFORD L. REV. 213 (1975).

9. Annas, Katz, & Trakimas, *Medical Malpractice Litigation Under National Health Insurance: Essential or Expendable?* 1975 DUKE L. J. 1335–73. *And see* discussion in Chapter XII.

10. R. E. GOTS, THE TRUTH ABOUT MEDICAL MALPRACTICE 48 (New York: Stein & Day, 1975).

11. Commonwealth v. Edelin, 359 N.E.2d 4 (Mass. 1976).

12. Dr. Saul Lerner as quoted in Harvey, *Homebirths,* Boston Globe Magazine, New England, Oct. 16, 1977, at 18.

13. American Med. News, Oct. 3, 1977, at 13. On the economic factors involved see *Big Surplus Likely in Surgery,*

OB-GYN, U.S. Panel Predicts, Am. Med. News, Oct. 3, 1980, at 1, 10.

14. Fahey v. Holy Family Hosp., 336 N.E.2d 309 (Ill. App. 1975).

15. Kahn v. Suburban Community Hosp. 340 N.E.2d 398 (Ohio, 1976), *citing* Sosa v. Board of Managers of Val Verde Me. Hosp., 437 F.2d 173 (5th Cir. 1971).

16. Becker v. Schwartz *and* Park v. Chessin, 46 N.Y. 401, 413 N.Y.S.2d 895, 386 N.E.2d 807 (1978), *and see* Annas, *Medical Paternity and Wrongful Life,* 9(3) HASTINGS CENTER RPT. 15 (June, 1979).

17. *Accord,* Gleitman v. Cosgrove, 49 N.J. 22, 227 A.2d 689 (1967).

18. *Accord,* Jacobs v. Theimer, 519 S.W.2d 846 (Tex. 1975).

19. Annas & Coyne, *"Fitness" for Birth and Reproduction: Legal Implications of Genetic Screening,* 9 FAMILY L. Q. 463, 478 (1975). *And see* Capron, *The Continuing Wrong of "Wrongful Life,"* and Shaw, *The Potential Plaintiff: Preconception and Prenatal Torts* in GENETICS AND THE LAW II (A. Milunsky & G. Annas, eds.; New York: Plenum, 1980).

20. 410 U.S. 113 (1973).

21. *Id.* at 164.

22. *Id.* at 160.

23. *Id.* at 163.

24. Planned Parenthood of Cent. Mo. v. Danforth, 428 U.S. 52 (1976).

25. *Id.* at 55.

26. Colauti v. Franklin, 439 U.S. 379 (1979).

27. Planned Parenthood, *supra* note 24, at 72–4.

28. *Id.*

29. MASS. GEN. LAWS, ch. 112 §125; Baird v. Attorney General 360 N.E.2d 288 (Mass. 1977).

30. Bellotti v. Baird, 444 U.S. 622 (1979).

31. *Id.* at 4974.

32. Planned Parenthood, *supra* note 24, at 80.

33. *Id.* at 5201 n.8.

34. LA. REV. STAT. 40:1299.35.6

35. Wynn v. Scott, 449 F. Supp. 1302, 1316 (N.D. Ill. 1978).

36. Akron Center for Reproduction Health v. City of Akron, 479 F. Supp. 1172 (N.D. Ohio, Aug. 22, 1979).

37. Beal v. Doe, 432 U.S. 438 (1977); Maher v. Roe, 432 U.S. 464 (1977); Poelker v. Doe, 432 U.S. 519. *And see*

Annas, *Let Them Eat Cake*, 7(4) Hastings Center Rpt. 8 (Aug. 1977).

38. Harris v. McRae, 100 S. Ct. 2671 (1980). *And see* Annas, *The Supreme Court and Abortion: The Irrelevance of Medical Judgment*, 10(5) Hastings Center Rpt. 23 (Oct. 1980), *Contra.* Moe v. Sec'y, 1981 Mass. Adv. Sh. 464.

39. Framingham Clinic v. Board of Selectman of Southborough, 367 N.E.2d 606 (Mass. 1977); *and see* Planned Parenthood of Minnesota v. Citizens for Community Action, 558 F.2d 861 (8th Cir. 1977).

40. West Side Women's Serv. v. City of Cleveland, 450 F. Supp. 796 (N.D. Ohio, 1978).

41. *See, e.g.,* La. Rev. Stat. 14:88 (absolute ban on placing or carrying advertisements for abortion services; violation punishable by a fine of up to $15,000 and/or up to one year imprisonment with or without hard labor).

42. Virginia State Bd. of Pharmacy v. Virginia Citizens Consumer Council, 425 U.S. 748 (1976).

43. Carey v. Population Services, 431 U.S. 678 (1977).

44. *See also* Preterm, Inc. v. MBTA, Civ. No. 74–159–M (D.C. Mass. 1974), *discussed in* 3 Fam. Planning/Pop. Rptr. 76 (Aug. 1974) (striking down a ban on abortion services advertising adopted by a public transportation authority).

45. Ga. Crim. Code, ch. 26–1202(e).

46. Doe v. Bolten 410 U.S. 179, 198 (1973).

47. 274 U.S. 200 (1927).

48. *In re* Moore, 221 S.E.2d 307 (N.C. 1976).

49. *See, e.g.,* Frazier v. Levi, 440 S.W. 2d 393 (Tex. Ct. Civ. App. 1969). *See generally* Baron, *Voluntary Sterilization of the Mentally Retarded,* in Genetics and the Law 267, 274 (A. Milunsky & G. Annas, eds.; New York: Plenum, 1975).

50. Mass. Gen. Laws ch. 112 §12 W.

51. Relf v. Weinberger, 372 F. Supp. 1196 (D.D.C. 1974), *injunction vacated,* Relf v. Weinberger, C. A. No. 74–1797 (D.C. Cir. 1977).

52. 43 Fed. Reg. 52,146–75 (Nov. 8, 1978).

53. Coe v. Bolton, Civ. Action No. C76–785A (D.C. Ga., Sept. 30, 1976), *summary in* 36 Citation 30 (Nov. 15, 1977); *and see* Murray v. VanDevander, 522 P.2d 302 (Okla. Ct. of App., 1974).

XI

Care of the Dying

Discussion of death has been transformed from taboo to high fashion. Following the publication of Elisabeth Kübler-Ross's *On Death and Dying* in 1969, there has been an avalanche of books, newspaper and magazine articles, journals, and Broadway plays on the subject. Almost two million Americans die annually, and an additional million have a terminal diagnosis at any given time. An estimated 80 percent die in hospitals or nursing homes. Thus, a large number of people are either dying or caring for dying patients in health care institutions. The trend is to treat the dying and their condition more honestly and candidly.

Nurses have much responsibility, and often little direction, in this area. A recent study of Seattle nursing homes, for example, showed that nurses often made the decision of whether or not to treat a high fever, in situations where nontreatment often meant death.[1] And some of the most compelling passages in the 1979 best-seller, *Nurse,* concern nursing decisions and actions with dying patients.[2]

In many ways, increased attention given to the dying is a paradigm for all patients. Dying patients simply present the issues more dramatically, since their condition is often the most desperate and stark.

Some of the needs and concerns of dying patients and their caretakers, however, are unique: definition of death, autopsy, organ donation, and orders not to resuscitate. It is also ironic that the most popularly discussed patient right has been the "right to die"; this is the last thing most patients want, and most people would rank access to health care well ahead of cessation of medical intervention. It is well to keep all of this in mind: open discussion of death is a product of the 1970s, and we are not yet altogether comfortable with it. There are many issues surrounding the dead and dying about which society has not yet developed a coherent policy.

This chapter will focus on issues most pertinent to the dying patient, and on the problems faced by those professionals charged with care of the dying, including determination of when death has taken place and disposition of the body.

Does a terminally ill patient have a right to know that his providers consider his condition terminal?

Yes. There is no logical justification for withholding this information from a patient. Surveys from the 1950s and early 1960s indicated that while 90 percent of all patients wanted to know their diagnosis,[3] even if terminal, between 60 and 90 percent of all physicians preferred to withhold such a diagnosis.[4] A more recent survey revealed a dramatic shift, with 97 percent of physicians now indicating that their general policy is to disclose such a diagnosis.[5] Much of this shift can be attributed to society's changing attitudes and more open discussion of death. It may also reflect a realistic assessment of who is dying, and who has to make plans for death.

Previous arguments that telling the truth may be against the precept "first do no harm"[6] seem to be giving way to the understanding that it is generally deceit and not truth that injures the patient. This also accords with the law: for example, no consent to treatment can be fairly described as informed if the physician believes that no matter what is done, the patient will not recover. Prognosis information is material to any decision the patient might make about treatment, and withholding it from the patient invalidates the consent; such consent is gotten under false pretenses.[7]

The patient has a right to this knowledge; he also has a right to refuse it. Therefore, if a patient indicates that such information is not wanted, health care providers have an obligation not to force this information on the patient. Usually the best strategy is to answer all questions honestly and kindly. This is also the stance the law is most likely to support.

Does a nurse have a right to inform the patient of a terminal diagnosis if the physician orders him not to?

Yes, if the patient indicates a desire for the information. The nurse has an independent obligation to the patient, and physicians have no authority to order nurses either to lie to patients or to withhold critical information from patients who ask to be told. The nurse can, and probably should, carefully discuss the rationale for withholding the information with the physician, but should make it clear that the ultimate decision rests with the patient, not the physician. Again, the best strategy is to always answer questions honestly. This is not only best for the patient, it is also best for health care providers in general. There are times where nurses may be placing their jobs on the line in pursuing such a course—and the law may not recognize their right to be reinstated if they are summarily discharged for fulfilling their professional obligation—but unless professional nurses are willing to take some risks, patients will continue to suffer.[8]

The legacy of deception and withholding information from patients is that many patients no longer believe what health professionals tell them. A number of oncologists have told us, for example, that the hardest task they have is persuading patients that they do *not* have cancer. It is important for all of us that these attitudes, and the practices which breed them, be changed.

Does the health provider have a right not to disclose a patient's diagnosis or prognosis to the family, regardless of their demands, if the patient does not want it disclosed?

Yes. This information, like all other medical information learned about the patient in the context of a doctor-patient relationship, is confidential and cannot be disclosed without the patient's consent. Telling the family instead of the patient is a traditional action in many hospitals, but has no legal basis (other than that it is arguably bestowed by custom), and is directly contradictory to the law relating to confidentiality of medical information.[9]

The practice can lead to a pattern of deception as continuous efforts are made to keep the truth from the patient (who may know anyway) "for her own good." The ones who profit from such deception are not the terminally ill, but their families and health care providers.

The patients are denied the opportunity to discuss their own deaths, and are treated like children. Tolstoy describes the dehumanizing effect in "The Death of Ivan Ilyich":

> What tormented Ivan Ilyich most was the deception, the lie, which for some reason they all accepted, that he was not dying but was simply ill, and that he only need keep quiet and undergo a treatment and then something very good would result. . . . This deception tortured him—their not wishing him to admit what they all knew and what he knew. . . . Those lies—lies enacted over him on the eve of his death and destined to degrade this awful, solemn act to the level of their visiting, their curtains, their sturgeon for dinner—were a terrible agony for Ivan Ilyich.[10]

The "survivor knows best" attitude is illustrated by the words of a woman who described the death of her uncle as beautiful: "John died happy, never even realizing he was seriously ill."

While right implies duty, it also implies option. In the case of a patient who clearly expresses a desire not to be told a terminal diagnosis, it is proper for the physician to ask who the patient would like told her diagnosis, and inform that person instead.

Does a health provider have a right to honor the refusal of treatment by a terminally ill patient?

Yes. A patient does not lose his right to refuse treatment simply because he has been given a prognosis of imminent death. The usual rationale for not honoring the refusal of treatment by the terminally ill is that they are incompetent or do not understand the consequences (usually death) of their refusal. Without discussing all the issues involved in the determination of competency it should be noted that a terminally ill label does not in itself give health care providers any additional rights with regard to treating a patient.[11] Courts have consistently held that adult patients have the right to refuse treatment, including life-saving treatment, in such cases as rejection of surgery or chemotherapy for cancer, blood transfusions, and amputation. It should be emphasized that while adults may refuse treatment for themselves, they do not have a legal right to refuse life-saving treatment for their children, even for religious reasons.[12]

The adult's right to refuse treatment is a constitutional one, and can only be overridden if the state can demonstrate a compelling interest in preserving the life of the patient. While four such interests have been suggested by the courts—preserving the value of life, preventing suicide, protecting innocent third parties, and preserving the integrity of the medical profession—*none* of these reasons can ever be compelling in the case of a terminally ill patient who wants to die.[13] Therefore we would argue that a competent terminally ill patient has an *absolute* constitutional right to refuse treatment.[14] Since the right to refuse treatment in these circumstances is an expression of the sanctity of self-determination, one court has noted that "the value of life as so perceived is lessened not by a decision to refuse treatment, but by the failure to allow a competent human being the right of choice." [15]

Do health providers have a right to follow the wishes of a patient after the patient becomes incompetent?

Courts have held that terminally ill patients do not lose their rights to refuse treatment when they become incompetent.[16] However, since they are incompetent, this right to refuse must be exercised for them by another individual —the next of kin, a guardian, family members, the physician (with or without family members), an ethics committee, or a court of law. These decisions must be made consistent with the "best interests" of the terminally ill patient, although courts have split on whether this test is an objective one (i.e., What do most competent people in this situation do?) or a subjective one (i.e., What do we think this patient would do if he could make the decision himself?).[17] In the absence of an advance declaration of desires by the patient, these two tests are substantially identical, since it is reasonable to assume that people generally act in their own best interests. This seems to make the question a straightforward one; but it is in many cases almost impossible to determine what really is in the patient's best interests, as opposed to the best interests of the family, the hospital, the physician or society.

All seem to agree, however, that there are mentally incompetent patients who are seriously ill who receive too much treatment. Karen Ann Quinlan has become the symbol of this recognition. Most also agree that if they were in a situation like Ms. Quinlan's, they would want all treatment ended. One solution is to devise a mechanism by which individuals can tell their physicians and family what they want done to them in a situation when they are unable to make decisions themselves. The primary mechanism advocated to date is the "living will."

What is a "living will"?

Like China's barefoot doctors, who are neither doctors nor barefoot, a living will is neither alive nor a will. It is

---

To My Family, My Physician, My Lawyer and All Others Whom It May Concern

Death is as much a reality as birth, growth, maturity and old age—it is the one certainty of life. If the time comes when I can no longer take part in decisions for my own future, let this statement stand as an expression of my wishes and directions, while I am still of sound mind.

If at such a time the situation should arise in which there is no reasonable expectation of my recovery from extreme physical or mental disability, I direct that I be allowed to die and not be kept alive by medications, artificial means or "heroic measures." I do, however, ask that medication be mercifully administered to me to alleviate suffering even though this may shorten my remaining life.

This statement is made after careful consideration and is in accordance with my strong convictions and beliefs. I want the wishes and directions here expressed carried out to the extent permitted by law. Insofar as they are not legally enforceable, I hope that those to whom this Will is addressed will regard themselves as morally bound by these provisions.

a declaration of what steps one wants, and more importantly does not want, taken in the situation of a terminal illness. It is termed "living" because it takes effect while one is still alive, albeit incompetent or comatose. It is primarily an attempt to permit currently competent individuals to refuse consent in advance to certain extraordinary or heroic procedures under certain circumstances. The most widely known form of the living will is one prepared and distributed to millions of people by Concern for Dying of New York.[18]

Their latest version also contains suggestions—either to appoint someone to make binding decisions concerning medical care or at least to indicate the names of persons with whom their views have been discussed; to mention specific types of treatments objected to (e.g., resuscitation, nasogastric tube feedings, and mechanical respiration); to indicate a wish to die at home; and to indicate any desire to donate organs.

May health care providers follow the wishes of a patient as expressed in a living will?

Yes, but there are enough problems with them that in the absence of a statute, they do not have to. The most important problem with a living will is that it may not ensure that what the patient wants to happen will actually happen once he is no longer able to express his own desires about treatment. There are a number of reasons for this. First, the physicians caring for the patient may not be aware that he has signed such a document. Unless it somehow gets into the medical record, put there at the patient's request before he becomes incompetent, or by a relative or family physician or attorney thereafter, no one is likely to know about it. Second, even if the medical professionals know about the existence of the document, there may be a dispute about what the terms mean. What is a "reasonable expectation of recovery"? what is "recovery"? what are "heroic measures"? etc. There can be good-faith disagreements about these terms, and they underscore the need to be specific in such documents. Third, the caretakers may believe that the patient was in no position to make such a decision before the fact, and may have changed his mind (had he had the opportunity) when the catastrophic disease that was once only a possibility actually struck. A counterargument is that the person no longer has a "mind" to change, and thus his last declaration on this subject should be taken as superior to anyone else's determination of his best interests. Finally, physicians and nurses may not want to honor a living will if they strongly disagree with it. In this case they not only can use some of the arguments mentioned but can also be relatively content in the knowledge that no legal harm is likely to befall them for refusing to comply with the mandate of a patient's living will.[19]

This is not to say such a document is meaningless; only that there are major practical problems with it. For a patient who has signed such a document, and a physician who wishes to honor it, the document can stand as the best evidence of the patient's actual wishes—and the physician can follow its directives with little fear of adverse legal consequences.[20] Also, if signed by a patient who knows he is terminally ill, the document can act as a binding refusal of consent to the types of treatment specified. It would be a battery (unauthorized offensive touching) for a physician to treat the patient in this case—and a suit for the pain, suffering, and expense of such unauthorized and specifically refused treatment on behalf of the patient would have an excellent chance of success.[21]

Is the living will "legal"?

Yes. In every state a living will is a legal statement of the patient's desires; there is no public policy against a terminally ill patient refusing treatment. On the other hand, only ten states [22] as of this writing actually have statutes designed to make the living will a more effective instrument for patients. Unfortunately, these statutes have often created more problems than they solve—and the quest for a workable living will statute continues.

What statutory steps can be taken to enhance the living will's effectiveness?

There are two major ways to ensure that a patient's autonomy will be respected after he is no longer able to speak for himself: the first is to let the patient appoint a representative to speak for him in such cases; and the second is to make his living will, or directive of nontreatment, binding on his caretakers. The first has an aura of simplicity, and has been endorsed by a variety of ethicists and physicians.[23] It raises the problem of picking a representative for oneself, and permits the representative to ignore the patient's wishes at the crucial time—which she might do, for example, if the physician persuaded her that the case were not really hopeless, there was a new drug, etc. While the problems are worth exploring, the proposal has the great advantage of giving the medical professionals someone to talk to; more importantly, it gives the patient someone to talk, legally and authoritatively, for him. The proposal merits serious consideration.

The second approach, and the one that has most often been tried to date, is to make the declaration of nonconsent binding on the caretakers. Professor Alexander Capron has insightfully pointed out the four characteristics legislation designed for this purpose should possess. It should

1. Set forth the minimal content of binding directions to physicians.
2. Provide a means to ensure that the document accurately expresses the patient's desires (i.e., that the patient was competent when he made the declaration, that it was not made under fraud or duress, and that it has not been revoked).
3. Supply a method of resolving disagreements about interpretation of the declaration, and of deciding what to do in cases not specifically covered by the declaration.
4. Provide punishment for intentional misstatements of, or deviations from, a patient's wishes.[24]

We would add that the document should also be tailor-made for each individual so that it can accurately and adequately reflect his desires.

Statutes enacted to date not only fail to meet these requirements, they actually add confusion to the state of the law as it existed before they were enacted. The most notorious example is the California statute—the first in the nation.[25] While the California legislature deserves much praise for taking on this issue first, the statute has been generally ineffective, because of compromises during the legislative process. Any new legislation in California, or elsewhere, should address the issues outlined above. The original California statute has the following flaws, among others:

1. To be binding on health care providers, the declaration has to be signed fourteen days or more after the patient is diagnosed as having a terminal illness (thus eliminating almost all patients from its protection).
2. The definition of terminal illness requires that death be "imminent" whether or not artificial means are used (thus the only patients who qualify are those who will die anyway no matter what medicine does).
3. The statute has no effective penalty for noncompliance by a physician, it would only be considered unprofessional conduct.
4. Restrictions on who can witness the signing of a living will are so strict that many people would not be able to find a qualified witness.

Nor is California's the worst statute. Others have attempted to undermine rather than promote patient autonomy. For example, the Arkansas statute permits others to execute a directive for an incompetent patient.[26] This is not at all what the living will is aimed at; instead it encourages others whom we have not designated to make nontreatment decisions in which we have no voice. Other legislative proposals have lumped living wills together not only with proxy consents for children and incompetents, but with definitions of death as well.[27] This hodgepodge approach to legislation generally ends in chaos. North Carolina's original statute (which has since been amended) required that *after* the physician had pronounced a patient dead under the state's new brain death criteria, she must then seek the family's permission to remove respiratory support equipment (from the corpse?).[28] Such silliness is likely to be avoided only if the issues involved are dealt with carefully, and one at a time.

Such statutes nonetheless govern the actions of health care providers; and knowledge of the provisions of these statutes in your own state is essential. If the applicable law is not a sensible one, you should join in the effort to get it repealed or amended.

Must nurses follow an oral order not to resuscitate?

Good medical practice requires that all physicians' orders be documented and written in the physician's order sheet, and often in the patient's progress notes as well. This practice can be compromised only in emergency situations. Since there is almost by definition no such thing as an emergency order not to resuscitate, oral orders not to resuscitate are improper and should not be followed by anyone.

It is accepted medical practice to document all such orders carefully, in both the patient's progress notes and in the physician's order sheet, to have the physician sign the order, and to have the order include an explanation of why it is given.[29]

There are many good reasons for such a policy. First, it makes it clear to all that there is no criminal activity going on—what is being done is consistent with accepted medical practice and is accordingly done in a manner consistent with all other legitimate medical orders. Second, it makes the authority and reasons for the order clear to all involved; if there is doubt or dissension, it can be expressed to the person who made the order. Finally, it not only protects the physician, it also protects the nurses who follow such an order. If they are later challenged (in or out of court) by the patient's family or the district attorney as to why they did not attempt to resuscitate the patient, they can show them a documented physician's order. Without this documentation it is their word against the physician's (should the physician who refused to write out the order for fear of "legal consequences" also refuse to acknowledge his oral order), and they could be charged with professional negligence, and possibly manslaughter, for failure to perform their duty to resuscitate.

The hospital and its nursing staff should have a clear, written policy that they will not follow any order not to resuscitate unless it is clearly documented in the chart and signed, with reasons for the order clearly spelled out. Only such a policy can protect both them and their patients.[30]

When is a person dead?

The general rule is that a person is dead when the doctor says he's dead. This rule implies two things: a physician generally determines death (and signs the death certificate); and he must pronounce it based on accepted medical criteria. In the past decade the criteria have expanded from lack of spontaneous respiration and heartbeat to include a definition that encompasses irreversible cessation of brain functions, or "brain death."

This alternative definition was originally proposed as a way to obtain organs from a donor while the donor's heart was still beating, thus optimizing chances for a successful transplant.[31] Since first proposed in 1968, nineteen states have adopted legislation that makes brain death "legal."[32] In August, 1978, the National Conference of Commissioners on Uniform State Laws approved and recommended for enactment in all states the Uniform Death Act:

> For legal and medical purposes, an individual who has sustained irreversible cessation of all functioning of the brain, including the brain stem, is dead. A determination under this section must be made in accordance with reasonable medical standards.

The approved comment to this act notes that it "does not preclude a determination of death under other legal or medical criteria," and that the word *functioning* "expresses the idea of *purposeful* activity." [33]

The absence of a statute, of course, does not mean there is an absence of law on death. Good medical practice in this area will be accepted as good law. For example, the continuance of a heartbeat by medical heroics has been used as a defense in about a dozen murder cases around the country in states in which no statutory definition exists. The argument has been that the patient was "killed" when the ventilator was turned off. In all of these cases courts have found the brain death definition is legally acceptable as long as it has been adopted by the medical profession of the state, and accordingly that death was produced by the action that killed the brain, and not by the later action that terminated the heart beat.

In short, it is safe to conclude that physicians can apply *any* definition of death for both medical and legal purposes, so long as it is a definition that is accepted by the medical profession. This does not mean that consultation should not be required in difficult or debatable cases, or that such cases should not be resolved in favor of continuing medical efforts. It only means that when accepted medical criteria for death are met, the law will support the physician's decision that the patient is in fact dead.[34]

The definition of brain death does *not* include the cases of people like Karen Ann Quinlan, who are in a "persistent vegetative state," or people who are in comas but do not meet other accepted criteria. Some commentators, notably medical ethicist Robert Veatch, have urged that we could take advantage of the statutory activity to redefine death completely, based not on biological activity but on a concept of personhood. He has proposed a definition of death based on "irreversible cessation of spontaneous cerebral functions." [35] While this proposal merits debate and discussion, it is important to note that it is not currently the law anywhere. To date, *predictability* that traditional death criteria (i.e., cessation of spontaneous heartbeat and respiration) will inevitably occur soon, rather than an examination of the quality of life of the patient, has been the major rationale of advocates of new definitions of death.

Must family members be consulted about continued treatment after a patient has been declared dead based on brain death criteria?

No. There is no legal obligation to treat a dead person, and a patient is dead after he has been declared dead under accepted medical criteria. Involving the family in this manner only tends to distort and confuse the issues—which are medical, not issues of consent or proxy consent. The proper procedure is to declare the patient dead, note the time and the reasons for the determination in the chart, turn off all machines, such as ventilators, that are sustaining the patient's bodily functions, and then inform the family that the patient has died. There may be reasons to keep a patient's body on a ventilator after death for a short time, but there is no legal requirement to do so.

Do health care professionals or students have a right to practice their skills on a brain dead patient?

No. This may be done only with the prior written consent of the patient, or with the consent of the next of kin given *after* the patient has been declared dead. Before death, only the patient has the right to consent to nonbeneficial research or training on his body; after death the relatives, who have to bury the body and care for it before burial, have this exclusive right. Any unauthorized use or mutilation of the body after death is both illegal and unethical. We realize that fresh corpses are frequently used to practice such things as vaginal exams and intubations, and agree that it is sometimes better to use dead bodies than live ones for such practice. Nevertheless we believe consent should be obtained in such instances.

When does a health professional have a right to remove organs for transplantation?

Under the Uniform Anatomical Gift Act, which is law in one form or another in all fifty states, any person eighteen years or older and of sound mind may make a gift of all or any part of his body to the following persons for the following purposes:

1. To any hospital, surgeon, or physician, for medical or dental education, research, advancement of medical or dental science, therapy, or transplantation.

UNIFORM DONOR CARD

of _____

Print or type name of donor

In the hope that I may help others, I hereby make this anatomical gift, if medically acceptable, to take effect upon my death. The words and marks below indicate my desires. I give:

(a) _____ any needed organs or parts

(b) _____ only the following organs or parts

_____

Specify the organ(s) or part(s)

for the purposes of transplantation, therapy, medical research or education;

(c) _____ my body for anatomical study if needed.

Limitations or special wishes, if any: _____

---

2. To any accredited medical or dental school, college, or university for education, research, advancement of medical or dental science, or therapy.
3. To any bank or storage facility, for medical or dental education, research, advancement of medical or dental science, therapy, or transplantation.
4. To any specified individual for therapy or transplantation needed by him.

The gift can be made by a provision in a will (the donation provisions take effect immediately upon death, without the necessity of probate) or by signing, in the presence of two witnesses, a card like the sample on page 227.

This card is usually carried by the person who signed it at all times.[36] In most states the gift can be revoked either by destroying the card or by an oral revocation in the presence of two witnesses.

Can an individual place conditions on the organ donation?

Yes. As the above answer indicates, a person can specify which organs are to be donated and the person or institution to whom they are to be donated. A person may also specify how his body is to be buried following its medical use. The donee may accept or reject the gift. If accepted, and if only part of the body is donated, that part must be removed without unnecessary mutilation and the remainder of the body turned over to the surviving spouse or other person responsible for burial.

The next of kin may also consent to organ donation following death.

Can a relative override a person's wishes about donation of her body or organs after a person dies?

This may not be done if the person has followed the provisions of the Uniform Anatomical Gift Act of the state of which she was a resident. The gift legally takes effect immediately upon death and is binding on the relatives. Few hospitals will, however, follow the deceased's wishes over strong objections from the family, because the institutions generally consider it prudent not to insist on the gift.

Must donors be screened before their body parts are used in transplantation?

Donors must be carefully screened to assure that their body parts are suitable for transplantation. Both physicians and the hospital in which the transplant is performed may be held liable for damages if deficient screening results in injury to the donee.

In one case, for example, two different patients received corneal transplants from the same donor. The transplanted corneas infected both eyes, resulting in total blindness. The patients sued. The eyes had been removed by a first-year ophthalmology resident, who had reviewed the incomplete chart of the deceased patient and had secured permission of the deceased's wife for the removal of his eyes. The hospital had no checklist that could be used as a guide, and the resident based his decision solely on what he had learned orally from senior residents.

On review, it was found that published criteria existed, which were fairly uniform around the country. These standards contraindicated use of any cadaver that had a history of certain medical conditions. The donor's record indicated he was a "60 year old white male, heavy alcoholic with cirrhosis of the liver proven at autopsy" and had suffered from several other serious diseases. The court concluded that "whoever may have had the responsibility of determining the suitability of the cornea for transplant would have been required, in the exercise of due care, to review carefully and exhaustively the medical history of the proposed donor." The jury could also have found the hospital itself was negligent "in failing to set up a procedure which would assure that the party responsible for determining the suitability of the cornea for transplant would have access to all of the relevant medical records of the proposed donor.[37]

Recipients of tissue transplants have a right to rely upon those who select the donor to properly screen for certain conditions that would contraindicate use. This principle is applicable to all types of donations, from hearts and kidneys to sperm and bone. Physicians and hospitals engaged in transplantation are well advised to develop and follow strict standards of donor screening.[38]

Who has the legal authority to consent to an autopsy?

Under the statutes of most states, the next of kin (the surviving spouse, if there is one, then other survivors in order of family relationship—usually adult children, parents, siblings) has the right to consent to the autopsy. It has been held by courts on numerous occasions that there can be no property interest in a dead body; the next of kin does, however, have an interest in assuring that the deceased is properly buried.[39] This interest is strong enough to give the next of kin the right to possession of the body in the same condition as it was at the time of death.[40] Only an official autopsy by a coroner or medical examiner can override this interest, and even in this case the coroner or medical examiner must be acting in good faith or the autopsy is illegal.[41]

A hospital can be held liable in a civil suit for refusing to deliver a body and instead inducing a coroner to perform an autopsy.[42] It can also be held liable, of course, for performing an autopsy without permission or for going beyond the scope of the permission.[43] In one case the hospital was held liable for payment of damages for mental suffering in the sum of $1,500 when an autopsy was performed without consent even though the widow did not detect the autopsy at the funeral and found out about it only when she read the death certificate ten days later.[44] The consent form had been signed by the doctor and two nurses as witnesses before being presented to the widow. She refused to sign it, but it was placed in the record anyway, and the doctor who performed the autopsy thought that permission had been granted because of the presence of the form signed by the medical attendants.

The general rule is that the extent of damages awarded for an unauthorized autopsy is not measured primarily by the extent of the mutilation of the body but by the effect of the procedure on the "feelings and emotions of the surviving relatives who have the duty of burial."[45]

Can a patient consent, before his death, to have an autopsy performed on his own body?

Laws in about half of the states specifically give the patient this right. Also, since under the provisions of the Uniform Anatomical Gift Act a person may donate all or part of his body for education, research, and the advancement of medical science, he may give his body to a hospital for the sole purpose of performing an autopsy. He can make this consent binding upon his survivors by executing an instrument under the provisions of the Uniform Anatomical Gift Act explained above. However, few doctors or hospitals would perform the autopsy, even with this authorization, over strong family objection.

Can the hospital retain any portion of the body after autopsy?

No. The hospital cannot retain any tissues or organs without the permission of the person who consented to the autopsy. Standard forms for permission generally include permission to retain samples, and the rule against retention does not cover limited small portions of organs taken for further study. The person consenting to the autopsy, however, has the right to place whatever limitations on the consent he wishes.

The reasonable expectation of the public is that larger portions of the body will not be retained, even for research, without consent. For example, in mid-1979 it was disclosed that an associate medical examiner in Milwaukee had removed and was storing the testicles from about seventy males that she had performed autopsies on over a three-year period. The incident received much publicity. She defended the practice in the name of medical research (although she had not commenced any on the testicles she had collected), saying, "In view of the fact that testicles are removed during an autopsy, I don't see why it is a crime, as has been implied, to put them in a jar instead of back in the body." [46] The answer, of course, is that it is the individual and the next of kin who have the right to decide how the body will be disposed of, not the medical examiner.

Can terminally ill patients be used as subjects of human experimentation?

Yes. The issue of human experimentation in general was dealt with in Chapter VII; the limitations are similar, but special care is necessary to ensure that these patients are not taken advantage of because of their terminal condition. Terminally ill patients have been subjected to many major abuses in the past. The reasons are relatively straightforward. When a physician realizes there is no longer anything she can do for the patient, there may be a tendency to ask what the patient can do for the physician. If the physician is engaged in research, the research project can often assume more importance than a single patient. For example, if a physician believes she is engaged in research that might one day cure cancer, she can probably justify using cancer victims for research, even though she knows her experimental drug will never cure them.

Institutional Review Boards (IRBs) have even approved cancer chemotherapy experiments on dying patients with the proviso that they *not* be told the average survival rate for individuals with their types of cancer. In one case, an average survival rate of fourteen weeks for patients with brain cancer was not told to the cancer victims when they were asked to consent to an experimental drug program. The IRB agreed that the experimental drug could not significantly help them. The rationale for withholding this information was that it would be "cruel" to tell patients this. It was, apparently, not thought to be cruel to use patients as a means of a research without their full knowledge of the situation.

Cancer chemotherapy is not the only area in which physicians may be less than candid with terminally ill research subjects. Many cases of innovative surgery have been performed on terminally ill subjects who received less than full information. Dr. Christiaan Barnard, for example, purposely led Louis Washkansky to believe that the first heart-transplant operation had an 80 percent chance of success—instead of telling him that the 80 percent referred to his coming out of surgery alive, not to getting better as a result of it. Dr. Barnard justifies this deception thus:

He had not asked for odds or any details. . . . He was ready to accept it because he was at the end of the line, waiting for a transfer. What else was there to say? . . . *For a dying man, it is not a difficult decision because he is at the end.* If a lion chases you to the bank of a river filled with crocodiles, you will leap into the water convinced you have a chance to swim to the other side. But you would never accept such odds if there were no lion. (Emphasis supplied) [47]

What Barnard purposely overlooks is that since he misstated the odds his patient did not even have the option to accept or reject them—Barnard had made the decision for him. Similarly, Dr. Denton Cooley, who performed the first artificial heart implantation, was not completely candid with his patient, Haskell Karp. Dr. Cooley describes Mr. Karp in words reminiscent of Dr. Barnard's: "He was a drowning man. A drowning man can't be too particular what he's going to use as a possible life preserver. It was a desperate thing, and he knew it." [48] Similar experiences were involved in the first transplantation of a non-human heart into a human, the first implantation of an artificial heart valve, and the first recipient of human kidneys and monkey kidneys.[49]

In response to experimentation with the left ventricular assist device (LVAD—a partially implanted heart for temporary use following some forms of open heart surgery) the Committee on Ethics of the American Heart Association published experimentation guidelines. Noting the likelihood of a "strong mutual dependency" existing between the surgeon and his patient, the committee suggested that both the patient and his family may have lost their ability to give a meaningful consent, and recommended the routine participation of a third party (an independent individual or a committee) in the consent process "to make the consent more genuine." As to the argument made above by Barnard and Cooley, the committee noted: "It is insufficient to claim in a narrow context of high-risk treatment that the patient would be dead had he not been revived. The joint context of both innovative therapy and of research ought to comprise an ethical sensitivity to outcome that goes beyond the mere completion of the trial." [50]

We agree with the Committee; every effort must be taken to insure that their consent to experimental therapy is fully informed and is their own.

NOTES

1. Brown & Thompson, *Nontreatment of Fever in Extended-Care Facilities,* 300 NEW ENG. J. MED. 1246, 1250 (1979).
2. P. ANDERSON, NURSE (New York: St. Martin's Press, 1978).

3. Friesen & Kelly, *Do Cancer Patients Want to be Told?*, 27 SURGERY 825 (1950); Samp & Currieri, *Questionnaire Survey on Public Cancer Education Obtained from Cancer Patients and Their Families*, 10 CANCER 382 (1957).

4. *See, e.g.*, Fitts & Ravdin, *What Philadelphia Physicians Tell Patients with Cancer*, 153 JAMA 901 (1953); Oken, *What to Tell Cancer Patients*, 175 JAMA 1120 (1961); and Rennick, *What Should Physicians Tell Cancer Patients?* 2 NEW MED. MATERIA 51 (March 1960).

5. Novack *et al.*, *Changes in Physicians' Attitudes Toward Telling the Cancer Patient*, 241 JAMA 897 (1979).

6. *See, e.g.*, Bernard C. Meyer, "Ours is a profession which traditionally has been guided by a precept that transcends the virtue of uttering truth for truth's sake; that is, 'So far as possible, do not harm.'" in *Truth and the Physician* in ETHICAL ISSUES IN MEDICINE 176 (Fuller & Torrey, eds.; Boston: Little, Brown, 1968).

7. *See generally* discussion in Chapter IV. The therapeutic privilege is not applicable in this situation; by the physician's own admission, the proposed treatment will not be effective in preventing death.

8. *See generally* discussion of nurses' employment rights in Chapter XV; *and see* Greenlaw, *Responding to Patients' Requests for Information*, 1(4) NURSING LAW & ETHICS 6 (Apr. 1980).

9. *See* Chapter IX.

10. L. TOLSTOY, THE DEATH OF IVAN ILYCH AND OTHER STORIES (New York: New American Library, 1960) at 137.

11. For a general discussion of the patient's right to refuse treatment *see* Chapter IV.

12. *See* cases and discussion in Chapter IV.

13. *See* Annas, *Reconciling Quinlan and Saikewicz: Decision Making for the Terminally Ill Incompetent*, 4 AM. J. LAW & MEDICINE 367, 373–375 (1979).

14. *Id.*

15. Superintendent of Belchertown v. Saikewicz, 1977 Mass. Adv. Sh. 2461, 2478, 370 N.E.2d 417, 426 (1977).

16. See discussion at Chapter IV; and Annas, *Reconciling*, *supra* note 13, at 375–76.

17. *Id.*

18. Copies can be obtained from Concern for Dying, 250 West 57th St., New York, N.Y. 10019. One of the authors (GJA) is a member of the board of directors.

19. *See, e.g.*, R. VEATCH, DEATH, DYING, AND THE BIOLOGICAL REVOLUTION 180–86 (New Haven: Yale University Press, 1976); *and* G. ANNAS, THE RIGHTS OF HOSPITAL PATIENTS 84 (New York: Avon Books, 1975).

20. *See generally* discussion of refusing treatment at Chapter IV and accompanying notes.

21. *Id.*

22. California, Idaho, Nevada, Texas, Oregon, Arkansas, New Mexico, North Carolina, Washington, Kansas. *See* Raible, *The Right to Refuse Treatment and Natural Death Legislation*, 5(4) MEDICOLEGAL NEWS 6 (Fall, 1977).

23. *See, e.g.*, Bok, *Personal Directions for Care at the End of Life*, 295 NEW ENG. J. MED. 367 (1976), and Relman, *Michigan's Sensible 'Living Will'*, 300 NEW ENG. J. MED. 1270 (1979).

24. Capron, *The Development of Law on Human Death*, in BRAIN DEATH: INTERRELATED MEDICAL AND SOCIAL ISSUES 54 (J. Korein, ed., New York Academy of Sciences, vol. 315, 1978).

25. CAL. HEALTH & SAFETY CODE §7185–95 (West Cum. Supp. 1977).

26. 1977 Ark. Acts 879.

27. *E.g.*, the Massachusetts bill in 1978, filed by the Medical and Hospital Associations in response to the *Saikewicz* case. *See* Carroll, *Who Speaks for Incompetent Patients? The Case of Joseph Saikewicz*, TRUSTEE 19, 24, (Dec. 1978).

28. 1977 N.C. Adv. Legis. Serv. ch. 815, §90–322. *See* Annas, *Death and Dying*, CIV. LIB. REV. 78 (July, 1978) (roundup book review).

29. Rabkin, Gillerman, & Rice, *Orders Not to Resuscitate*, 295 NEW ENG. J. MED. 364 (1976). *Standards for Cardiopulmonary Resuscitation (CPR) and Emergency Cardiac Care (ECC)*, 227 JAMA (Supp.) 833, 864 (1974).

30. Annas, *Reconciling, supra* note 13, at 383, n. 44; *and Cf.* Dunn, *Northwestern Memorial Hospital Policy Regarding Orders Not to Resuscitate* (Oct. 12, 1977) in Critical Issues in Health Care 141–46 (New York Journal Seminars, N.Y., 1978).

31. Ad Hoc Committee of the Harvard Medical School to Examine the Definition of Brain Death, *A Definition of Irreversible Coma*, 206 JAMA 337 (1968).

32. Alaska, California, Georgia, Hawaii, Idaho, Illinois, Iowa,

Kansas, Louisiana, Maryland, Michigan, Montana, New Mexico, North Carolina, Oklahoma, Oregon, Tennessee, Virginia, West Virginia. One state supreme court has adopted the brain-death concept by decision, Commonwealth v. Golston, 366 N.E.2d 744 (Mass. 1977).

Many of the statutes differ, some speaking only in terms of irreversible cessation of brain functioning, others include the traditional irreversible cessation of spontaneous respiratory and circulatory functions. See Capron, *Legal Definitions of Death* in BRAIN DEATH, *supra* note 24, at 349, 354; and Capron & Kass, *A Statutory Definition of the Standards for Determining Brain Death: An Appraisal and a Proposal*, 121 U. PA. L. REV. 87 (1972).

33. The entire definition of "functioning" is: " 'Functioning' is a critical word in the Act. It expresses the idea of *purposeful* activity. In a dead brain, some meaningless cellular processes, detectable by sensitive monitoring equipment, could create legal confusion if the word 'activity' were substituted for 'functioning.' "

34. For a complete discussion of the medical, legal, and ethical issues surrounding brain death see BRAIN DEATH, *supra* note 24.

35. R. VEATCH, DEATH, DYING, AND THE BIOLOGICAL REVOLUTION 76 (New Haven: Yale University Press, 1976).

36. Copies of this form may be obtained from the National Kidney Foundation, 116 East 27th Street, New York, N.Y. 10016.

37. Ravenis v. Detroit Gen. Hosp., 63 Mich. App. 79, 234 N.W.2d 411 (1975); discussed in more detail in Annas, *Screening Donors for Tissue Transplantation,* 6 ORTHOPAEDIC REV. 83 (Jan. 1977).

38. *Cf.* Annas, *Fathers Anonymous: Beyond the Best Interests of the Sperm Donor,* 14 FAMILY L.Q. 1, 6–9 (1980).

39. *See* Leno v. St. Joseph Hosp. 302 N.E.2d 58, 60 (Ill. 1973); Waltz, *Legal Liability for Unauthorized Autopsies and Related Procedures,* 16 J. FOR. SCI. 1 (1971); Note, *The Private Autopsy: Problems of Consent.* 41 DENVER L. J. 239 (1964); Comment, *Property Interest in a Dead Body,* 2 ARK. L. REV. 124 (1947); Comment, *Property Rights in Dead Bodies,* 71 W. VA. L. REV. 377 (1969).

40. Infield v. Cope, 58 N.M. 308, 270 P.2d 716 (1954).

41. Gahn v. Leary, 61 N.E.2d 845 (Mass. 1945).

42. *E.g.*, Darcy v. Presbyterian Hosp., 95 N.E. 695 (N.Y. 1911).

43. Torres v. State, 228 N.Y.S.2d 1005 (Ct. Claims 1962); Gould v. State, 46 N.Y.S.2d 313 (Ct. Claims 1944).

44. French v. Ochsner Clinic, 200 So.2d 371 (La. App. 1967).

45. *Id., and* Sworski v. Simons, 208 Minn. 201, 293 N.W. 309 (1940). *Cf.* Johnson v. Women's Hosp., 527 S.W.2d 133 (Tenn. Ct. App. 1975) discussed in Annas. *The Cases of the Live, Buried Mother and the Dead Unburied Baby: Negligence or Outrageous Conduct?* 5(3) ORTHOPAEDIC REV. 71 (Mar. 1976).

46. Rosenberg, *Examiner Says She Will Stop Stealing Testicles from Dead,* Milwaukee Journal, June 26, 1979, at 1.

47. C. BARNARD, ONE LIFE 348 (New York: Macmillan, 1961).

48. *Quoted in* J. THORWALD, THE PATIENTS 402 (New York: Harcourt Brace Jovanovich, 1971).

49. These and others are discussed in G. ANNAS, L. GLANTZ, & B. KATZ, INFORMED CONSENT TO HUMAN EXPERIMENTATION: THE SUBJECT'S DILEMMA 11–17 (Cambridge, Mass.: Ballinger, 1977).

50. Committee on Ethics of the American Heart Association, *Ethical Consideration of the Left Ventricular Assist Device,* 235 JAMA 823 (1976). *Cf.* Annas & Healey, *The Patient Rights Advocate—Redefining the Doctor-Patient Relationship in the Hospital Context,* 27 VAND. L. REV. 243 (1974). *And see* Schneck, *Doctors Approve Artificial Heart for Human Use,* N. Y. Times, Jan. 28, 1981 at A10.

PART THREE

Rights Regarding Liability and Income

XII

Malpractice Litigation

Litigation over medical malpractice is not new. The first recorded case occurred in England in the thirteenth century, and one of the earliest suits in the United States took place in 1794.[1] By 1945, physicians had indicated their alarm at the increase in such claims.[2] Alternatives to the jury trial, such as having a disinterested physician adjudicate claims by patients, were recommended, mainly by physicians. In 1872, the American Medical Association recommended that, in medical malpractice cases that required expert testimony, physicians be appointed independent arbiters by the judge.[3]

In spite of this traditional concern, there was no medical malpractice "crisis" as we know it until well into the 1970s. Sickness was accepted by most people as a common occurrence. Medicine was a limited science, and adverse results were often regarded as the expected outcome.

Since World War II the number of malpractice suits, in absolute numbers, has increased steadily. Even today, however, though the medical malpractice situation in the United States is generally considered to be a problem, most physicians still go through their entire professional lives without being sued, and those who are sued are rarely sued more than once. Most hospitals, regardless of size, go through an entire year without having a single claim filed against them. Jury trials of these claims are unusual. The majority of cases, whether settled out of court or decided by a jury, are won by the physician-defendant.[4]

In a recent study prepared by the National Association of Insurance Commissioners, the average payout for claims that were upheld was about $13,000, with expenses for the losing defendant totaling about $2,500.[5] Expenses for winning defendants were about $1,000. The report studied about 24,000 claims closed between July 1, 1975, and June 30, 1976, the height of the medical malpractice crisis. About 72 percent of these cases were won by the defendant, whether physician, hospital, or allied health professional. Accordingly, the odds were almost 3 to 1 that the defendant would be successful. Only 4 percent of cases were settled by trial, at which the defendant had a 4 to 1 chance of winning. Before a review panel, the defendant also had a 4 to 1 chance of being found not liable. The lowest awards came about through out-of-court settlements, with awards 20 percent higher after losing a trial, 55 percent higher in official arbitration, 79 percent higher in a review panel, and nearly 4 times as high if settled during a trial.

Another report, recently released by HHS, found that, except for death, the size of the award varied proportionately with the seriousness of the injury.[6] Thus, the average award for insignificant or temporary injuries was about $7,500; for permanent, total disability about $150,000; and for death about $57,600.

The study reported that orthopedic conditions were most likely to be associated with successful claims. Of all surgical procedures, obstetrical ones were most likely to be successful. Of the total number of physicians involved in claims, one-third were surgeons, particularly neurosurgeons, orthopedic surgeons, and plastic surgeons, 20 percent were in general or family practices, and 13 percent practiced obstetrics/gynecology. Those least often sued practiced pediatrics, internal medicine, ophthalmology, and radiology.

The report compared its current data to that available in 1970, and found that there was a large increase, 94 percent, in the size of the average award. However, it also found that the percentage of claims producing awards remained the same, and that there was no particular difference in the distribution of claims by severity of injury or in the distribution in the specialties of doctors for whom payment was made.

The fear of being sued permeates the medical community and affects almost every facet of the system. It affects health care practices and forms of medical treatment, the distribution of health manpower, the modes of processing claims through the legal system, and the attitudes of the public toward the delivery of health care and toward the doctor-patient relationship in particular.

Numerous critics place much of the blame for this situation on the tort liability system.[7] In 1975 and 1976, all fifty states enacted legislation dealing with some aspect of medical malpractice, effecting numerous major changes in tort law and procedure. This chapter will examine the current system of medical malpractice, and discuss several major changes proposed to be made in that system.

What is professional negligence or malpractice?

Malpractice or negligence (the terms can be used interchangeably) is the failure of a health care provider to exercise the reasonable and ordinary care a qualified practitioner would exercise under the same or similar circumstances. The provider is obligated to use the same degree of skill and care in treating the patient as would be exercised by the average reasonable practitioner with the same level of education and training.[8] She generally does not guarantee the outcome, but undertakes to use diligence and ordinary skill in treating the patient. If the patient does not improve or even gets worse, or if an unexpected and untoward result occurs in the course of treatment, no inference of negligence is drawn. Thus, the practitioner holds herself out as qualified to make a careful diagnosis and plan of treatment and to use good judgment in carrying out the treatment. She is not liable solely because her treatment had a poor result.

What are the elements of a malpractice claim?

A valid malpractice claim against a health care provider must have four elements: duty, breach, causation, and damages. *Duty* to a patient is defined by the standard of care. The standard by which a provider's actions are measured is that of the reasonable practitioner under the same or similar circumstances. *Breach* of that duty by specific conduct on the part of the practitioner, by action or inaction, will be measured against the applicable standard of care. *Proximate cause* denotes a causal connection between the provider's conduct and the damages alleged by the patient. The plaintiff cannot recover any money damages for improper conduct on the part of the defendant if the breach of duty itself produced no harm or injury.[9] The final element is the actual injury or *damages* suffered by the patient.

How is "standard practice" or "custom" defined?

Most medical and surgical treatment that is found to be negligent involves either a doctor who did not follow the standard practice in treating the condition, or a doctor who undertook to administer proper treatment, but did so in an inadequate or incorrect manner. A doctor who adopts the standard and accepted procedures will generally not be considered negligent, no matter what the outcome of the case.

However, "standard practice" may be difficult to define in some areas. Usually, medical opinion as to the appropriate treatment of an illness is divided. If the treatment is in accord with a recognized system, it is not negligence simply to use it. If a physician can demonstrate that he used a method that is approved by at least a "respectable minority" of the medical community, the patient would then have to prove that the method was applied in a negligent manner. This is so even if, in retrospect, it is apparent that another method would have produced better results. Health professionals are obligated to keep up with advances in medical and surgical treatment, and the standard of practice changes with new developments.

Thus, with rare exceptions, custom is the controlling factor in determining the standard of care. One famous exception is a case in which ophthalmologists were found liable for failure to test a young patient for glaucoma, even though their actions conformed to the standard of their specialty.[10] This case has not been followed. The general rule is still that, without medical evidence that the standard of practice in a particular field is actually negligent, conformity to the standard is a good defense. Custom is usually set by the medical community itself, by considering what other doctors would do. However, it may also be set by other mechanisms, such as statutes or regulations.

Can a physician be sued for a wrong diagnosis?

The standard of care applicable to diagnosis is the same as that applied to treatment—that is, it requires that the physician use the same degree of skill, care, and knowledge that would be used by the average reasonable physician with his level of training.[11] His diagnosis is not alone sufficient to warrant the imposition of liability. A physician who meets the standard of a reasonably careful physician is not liable even if she makes an error in judgment or a mistake in diagnosis. The issue of liability usually involves whether the physician used the usual and customary inquiries, examinations, and tests in order to determine the nature of the patient's condition. In line with this, the physician has an obligation to keep up with advances in medical science. If she failed to use certain tests or other diagnostic aids in current use when she saw the patient, because she didn't know about them, she would be liable for her failure to use them.

However, if the physician has performed all the accepted tests which a reasonable practitioner would consider appropriate, has taken into consideration all relevant symptoms, and made a careful evaluation of this information in light of the patient's past and present history, she is not negligent simply because she is wrong. Thus, if a number of different diagnoses could provide explanations of a patient's condition, choosing among them is a matter of medical judgment, and if the physician reasonably chooses what turns out to be the wrong one, she is not liable. Additionally, before a physician is liable in damages for misdiagnosis, it must be shown that the misdiagnosis in fact caused damage to the patient. Thus, the patient must establish not only that the misdiagnosis constituted negligence, but also that it resulted in some damage to him.

Do health professionals guarantee a favorable outcome of treatment?

Generally not. Usually the contract between the provider and the patient does not include a guarantee of a good result.[12] However, it is possible for a provider, without his realizing it, to change the terms of the contract and specifically include such a guarantee. In those instances it does not matter whether the provider's actions met the medical community standard, but rather whether he achieved what was promised.

A binding contract requires an offer, acceptance, and

consideration: the provider must specifically offer to accomplish something, the patient must accept that offer, with consideration in the form of the fee for service, either paid or promised. Failure to achieve the promised result makes the provider liable for breach of contract.

For example, in one case the doctor treated a patient for ear trouble, telling him that he should undergo stapes mobilization operations. He allegedly advised the patient that, even though his condition might not be improved by the operations, his hearing would not be worsened as a result. After three operations, the patient's hearing was much worse. The patient based his lawsuit on the breach of an express contract. The trial court held that the facts alleged were sufficient to find that there was an enforceable contract, and the Supreme Court of Kansas, on appeal, agreed.[13]

Are all physicians held to the same standard of care, regardless of where they practice?

Traditionally, the standard of care required of a nonspecialist physician was that commonly possessed and practiced by other physicians in the same or similar communities.[14] Some courts have even restricted the rule to the same community. The reason given for these restrictions had been the opinion that there were significant differences between the facilities, opportunities for consultation, and the extent of medical knowledge of doctors practicing in different places, particularly between those practicing in large cities and those in rural areas. For example, in one older case a Boston surgeon was not permitted to testify as to the standard applicable to a physician who practiced in a small New Hampshire town.[15] In some states this rule is still strictly followed. Thus, in one case, testimony by physicians from Minnesota was not admissible on the standard of practice in a Michigan community,[16] and in another, expert witnesses from New York were not permitted to testify for a patient in a Louisiana malpractice action.[17]

With progress in medical education, exchange of medical knowledge, and availability of medical centers, the reason for the "locality rule" has been reduced. Through the years the rule has been altered; in some states it has been modified, while in others it has been completely abandoned.[18] This is the modern trend. In most jurisdictions, the local standard of practice may be considered by the jury as a factor, but will not be the sole determinant.

What is the standard of care required of a specialist?

The law imposes a higher duty on the specialist than on the general practitioner. By definition, a specialist is a physician who devotes special attention to a particular organ or area of the body, to the treatment of a particular disease, or to a particular category of patients. The specialist is required to possess that degree of knowledge and ability and to exercise that amount of care and skill ordinarily possessed and exercised by physicians practicing in the same specialty. This rule has been adopted by all states and applies to all specialties.[19]

For example, in one case it was alleged that an obstetrics and gynecology resident negligently performed a circumcision.[20] There was evidence that he had previously performed 600 to 800 circumcisions. The court held him to the standard of a specialist, even though he had not completed his formal training. He was, accordingly, expected to have more skill in performing the procedure than a general practitioner. The obvious result is that a specialist may be found liable in a situation in which a general practitioner would not.

Most states no longer apply the locality rule in establishing the standard of care for a specialist, even the states that retain the locality rule for general practitioners. The specialist is increasingly held to a national standard in his particular field. Thus, in a recent case, the only question before the Michigan Supreme Court was whether the trial court in Kalamazoo, Michigan, was in error in not permitting the testimony of the expert, a board certified surgeon practicing in Chicago, who was unfamiliar with the practice of surgery in Kalamazoo or similar communities. The court held that it was a reversible error to exclude the surgeon's testimony, stating that "it does not matter whether the practice in Chicago and in Kalamazoo is similar; the standard for a specialist is a national standard, not a local one." [21] Similarly, the court in another case held that the locality rule should not apply to the standard of care of nationally certified specialists. Since the defendant obstetrician was certified by a national board, the standard of care should be determined by the practice within his profession nationally.[22]

When does a provider have a duty to refer his patient to a specialist or to seek consultation?

If the provider does not possess that degree of competence, knowledge, and skill necessary to diagnose or treat the patient's condition, she has a duty to so inform the patient and refer the patient to another provider or specialist.[23] Thus, in a malpractice case against an orthodontist, a finding of negligence was based on the failure of the practitioner to inform the adolescent patient's mother of his concern about his own ability to properly treat the patient's problem.[24]

A general practitioner is obligated to refer a patient to a specialist when, under the same or similar circumstances, a reasonable physician would have made the referral. If he fails to do so, the general practitioner may be held by the court in a malpractice action to the standard of the specialist to whom the patient should have been referred.

The requirements for referral may be affected by factors like the unavailability of an appropriate consultant or facility and the unavailability of reasonable transportation. Obviously, the law does not require the physician to perform an impossible or useless act.

What are the provider's responsibilities after she has referred the patient to a specialist?

Once a provider has referred a patient to a qualified specialist for care, and has turned over the patient to him, she is relieved from the case and no longer has any duty to the patient. The only exception might be if she learns, *after* the referral, that the specialist is not qualified to treat her patient; she then probably has an obligation to notify her patient of this and recommend a substitute, qualified specialist. Of course there is a duty not to refer to individuals who are known, or should have been known, as incompetents in the first place.

Illustrating the general rule is a case in which a general practitioner referred his patient to a mental health clinic for psychiatric help. The patient visited the clinic twice, but a month after his initial visit with the general practitioner, he committed suicide. In a suit brought by the patient's mother for abandonment, the court held that the doctor was not liable. In the words of the court, "A physician who upon initial examination determines that he is incapable of helping his patient, and who refers a patient to a source of competent medical assistance, should be held liable neither for the actions of subsequent treating professionals nor for his refusal to become further involved in the case." [25]

However, if the patient is referred to a specialist for a particular problem only or for limited care, and returns to his primary care physician, the physician has the duty not only to resume her care, but also to obtain information regarding continued care from the specialist.[26] Similarly, if a doctor is relieved of duty when a patient is transferred to another hospital, her only obligation is to continue treatment when the patient is returned to her care.[27]

What are the responsibilities of a physician called in to consult?

A consultant is a doctor who is called in for a special and specific purpose, usually by the primary care physician, because he has special expertise on a particular matter. The difference between his special employment and the general employment of the primary care physician is mainly one of obligation to continue treatment.[28] A consultant's duty to the patient is a limited one.

A physician who is employed for a specific occasion or service is under no duty to continue his visits or treatment thereafter, and is consequently not liable for abandonment if he ceases treatment of his patient after performing the specific service.[29] In some types of surgery, for example, the doctor's responsibility may extend only to performance of the surgery and not to aftercare.[30]

A consulting physician can be held liable *only* for damages that result from his connection with the case. He will not be liable for previous or subsequent negligent acts of another physician.[31]

When may a provider terminate care of a patient?

The general rule is that once a provider-patient relationship is established, it continues until:

1. It is revoked by consent of both provider and patient.

2. It is revoked by the patient.
3. The provider's services are no longer necessary.
4. The provider withdraws from the case after reasonable notice to the patient.[32]

When the provider-patient relationship is terminated for reasons other than these, by unilateral action of the provider, abandonment has occurred. Other grounds for finding abandonment are premature discharge; failure to instruct on return visits on the use of medication; [33] termination of relationship for nonpayment of bills without adequate notice; [34] failure to provide continuity of care (frequency of visits).[35] A doctor may also be charged with abandonment if he fails to supervise and treat the patient throughout the course of the illness.[36] If the patient suffers injury as a result of the abandonment, the doctor may be successfully sued for damages.

However, there are many circumstances in which a provider may be justified in terminating the provider-patient relationship. These include:

1. *Implied termination by the patient*. This occurs in circumstances where, for example, the patient doesn't return for appointments, or fails to follow clear instructions to call the provider if certain symptoms develop.[37] Under these circumstances the relationship is considered terminated by implied revocation of the patient, and the provider is under no obligation to follow up on patient care, or to give notice to the patient, although it is recommended that notice be given.

2. *Intervening illness or vacation:* If a provider becomes ill or goes on vacation, he can suspend the relationship during that period without the concurrence of his patients. However, he is obligated to refer them to a provider or providers with the same level of skill and competence.[38]

3. *Limit of practice:* A provider has the right to limit his practice to a given geographic area or subject matter. For example, a provider is under no obligation to make house calls when he has limited his practice to his office.[39]

4. *Referral:* If a provider has referred a patient to a specialist for care, he is generally not obligated to continue treatment of that patient and is not liable for abandonment.[40]

5. *Almost any reason* so long as it is done at a point that does not jeopardize the patient's health, and ample time and notice and referral suggestions are given so that the patient can find another qualified provider.

How is it established at trial that a provider failed to meet the recognized standard of medical practice?

Ordinarily, for the patient to prevail, he must present the testimony of an expert medical witness in order to establish that the provider failed to fulfill his duty and that, as a result, the patient was injured. This is so because the standard of care is that of the reasonably prudent provider, so in most cases only another provider can establish that. The expert witness explains what the health care community recognizes as the standard of care in a particular situation, and further gives his opinion as to whether or not the provided-defendant's conduct met that. A jury of laypeople is generally considered incompetent to know independently the standard of care in a health matter, or whether the defendant complied with it, so as a matter of law the plaintiff's care will be dismissed unless he can present the necessary expert testimony. In jurisdictions that still recognize the locality rule, the expert must be able to testify as to the standard in the same or similar community.[41]

Thus, the Florida Supreme Court upheld a summary judgment for a physician who was sued for alleged negligence in performing a hysterectomy.[42] A patient with a prolapsed uterus underwent a vaginal hysterectomy. During the procedure, the surgeon punctured her bladder while attempting to separate it from the uterus. A urologist was consulted, and the surgeon repaired the incision. Ten days following the patient's discharge, the surgeon discovered a vesicovaginal fistula during a postoperative examination. He referred her to a urologist, and a second operation was performed to close the fistula.

In a malpractice suit against the surgeon, the patient claimed he negligently punctured and repaired her bladder. However, she produced no expert testimony to support her allegation. The court stated that a lay jury could only speculate on whether the surgeon proceeded properly, and that in the absence of expert testimony, there was no case for the jury.

When the case involves a specialist, usually the expert witness is from the same specialty. The witness must be familiar with the particular procedure of concern in the lawsuit, but generally does not have to perform it as a common part of his own practice. As long as the subject matter of the case is common to both individuals, a specialist in one area may be permitted to testify against a specialist in another.[43] Similarly, a specialist may testify to the standard of care of a general practitioner as long as he is familiar with the applicable standard of care.[44]

Thus, in a suit claiming that an oral surgeon was negligent in not informing the patient of the risks involved in a procedure to correct a problem of gaps between his teeth, the court ruled that the patient's only expert witness, an ear, nose, and throat specialist, was not qualified to testify as to the appropriate standard of care.[45] Since there was no showing of the required standard of dental care, the claim could not prevail.

Can a provider ever be found negligent without expert testimony?

The general rule that requires expert testimony in malpractice cases does not apply in situations where the negligence is so obvious that lay people can determine it without the help of expert witnesses. This doctrine of *res ipsa loquitur*—"the thing speaks for itself"—is applicable when all three of the following conditions are met:

1. An injury has occurred of a type that does not ordinarily occur in the absence of negligence;
2. The instrumentality or conduct that caused the injury was, at the time of the injury, in the exclusive control of the defendant; and
3. The plaintiff was not guilty of contributory negligence.[46]

For example, a *res ipsa loquitur* instruction was given to the jury in a successful suit against a dentist by a patient who suffered a whiplash injury when a headrest on a dental chair fell back.[47] Negligence is still required, the only change being that the defendant may be required to make some showing that he was not at fault. The extent of this required showing varies with the jurisdiction involved.

Statistics show that it plays a part in fewer than 15 percent of all medical malpractice cases that reach the appellate level.[48] Beyond that, *res ipsa* is not applied in the majority of jurisdictions, and only California has applied it liberally.[49]

The *res ipsa loquitur* doctrine has been held applicable mainly in cases involving foreign objects and slipping instruments in surgical procedures, burns from heating equipment, and injury to part of the patient's body outside the area to be treated. The jury is deemed to be qualified to conclude, without expert advice, that negligence has occurred when a sponge or other object is left in a patient following surgery.[50] For example, in a recent case, the Minnesota Supreme Court ruled that it was appropriate to apply *res ipsa loquitur* in an action involving a surgeon who was in exclusive control of a scalpel that broke during an operation, leaving part of it in the patient.[51] However, the more complicated the treatment or procedure involved, the less likely it is that it will be considered obvious enough for a jury to infer negligence.[52]

A number of states have passed statutes modifying the doctrine in medical malpractice actions.[53] Most restricted its application to enumerated situations, such as foreign objects, explosions, or burns. The Washington statute requires a plaintiff to prove by a preponderance of the evidence that the defendant in a medical malpractice action was negligent.[54] This negates the use of the *res ipsa* doctrine altogether.

When may a lawsuit be barred by the statute of limitations?

Other then proving the absence of negligence, the major defense to malpractice actions is the assertion that the applicable statute of limitations has expired, or "run," thereby barring the initiation of the suit. A statute of limitations sets the time period within which a person must commence a particular type of lawsuit. This is to ensure that adjudication takes place soon after the occurrence of the alleged negligence, so that witnesses and other evidence are more likely to be available, and so that people do not have to go through life with the threat of suits being brought for things done long ago.

Many states have statutes of limitations specifically applicable to medical malpractice actions. If not, usually the statute applicable to tort actions will govern. A lawsuit not started within the specified time period is barred and will be dismissed on a motion by the defendant. State laws differ on the length of time provided for starting an action and on when the time period begins to run.

The time period begins to run when the elements of the cause of action have accrued: when the negligent act allegedly occurred; [55] when the doctor-patient relationship or continuous series of treatments ended; [56] or when the harm to the patient was or reasonably should have been discovered (the discovery rule).

The modern trend is application of the discovery rule.[57] It is a rule of common sense: how could the injured patient be expected to bring a lawsuit when he neither knew nor reasonably could have known that he was injured? Some states limit application of the rule to cases involving allegations of foreign objects being left in patients following surgery. Thus, it was held inapplicable in cases involving misdiagnosis,[58] drug treatment,[59] and the incorrect administration of a blood test.[60] However, other states extend the rule to all cases of medical malpractice.[61]

A statute of limitations may be "tolled," or prevented from running, for a variety of reasons. The most common ones are the fact that the injured patient is a minor,[62] is insane,[63] or is in the armed services, and that the defendant is absent from the state or has fraudulently concealed the basis for the suit.[64] In a Florida case, a patient died of irreversible brain damage allegedly due to the negligence of the defendants.[65] The court stated that the four-year statute of limitations began to run when the plaintiffs became aware of the patient's deteriorated condition. Under Florida law, a physician is under an affirmative duty to disclose the course of the condition. Failure to disclose the facts would extend the limitations period; and termination of the physician-patient relationship did not extinguish the continuing duty to disclose.

About thirty-seven states have taken action to redefine their statutes of limitations in such a way as to restrict the number of lawsuits being brought.[66] Existing statutes specifically applicable to malpractice suits have been shortened; statutes have been enacted in states where none existed; and the application of the discovery rule has been curtailed. They fall into the following categories:

1. A flat statutory limit, with no exceptions.[67]
2. A flat statutory limit, but with an exception for late-discovered injuries.[68]
3. A flat statutory limit, between one and three years, a discovery exception, but an overall cutoff point.[69]
4. An overall cutoff point on all claims except in the foreign object and/or the fraudulent concealment situation.[70]
5. A cutoff of liability at a certain age, usually eight or ten years of age, for suits based on injuries to minors that would otherwise be barred by the general statutory period.[71]

Obviously the trend is to legislate limited statutory time periods for medical malpractice actions and to cut off the "long tails" of potential liability following medical incidents.

What is a contingent fee?

Few lawyers handle medical malpractice cases on any basis other than for a contingent fee. Under this system, a lawyer is paid only for his expenses unless the suit is won, in which case he takes about 30 to 50 percent of the award. This payment system is often cited as contributing to the rise in malpractice claims.[72] It is argued that contingent fees encourage lawyers to pursue claims of doubtful merit, or to require unjustifiably large amounts for legitimate claims, in the hope of achieving recovery through settlement or awards from sympathetic juries.

Legislation has been enacted in many states to regulate plaintiffs' attorneys' fees. These have taken various forms. One course provides that the court review an attorney's proposed fees and approve what it considers to be "reasonable fees."[73] Several set a fixed percentage ceiling for contingent fees in malpractice actions.[74] Others adopt a sliding scale, most often expressed in terms of a percentage of the award.[75] Under this arrangement, as the amount recovered increases, the lawyer's percentage declines.

In attempting to establish reasonable guidelines concerning the amount that a plaintiff's attorney can receive from the injured patient's award, these statutory provisions perform a needed service. However, to the extent that they reduce the number of claims brought by diminishing the willingness of attorneys to handle certain meritorious claims, they are a disservice to those injured patients who cannot otherwise afford counsel.

The contingent fee structure actually compels lawyers to screen out claims that are spurious or for which recovery appears less than probable, as well as to refuse claims for which damages would not amount to a sum sufficient to reimburse their expenses. Since the attorney, rather than the patient, bears the financial risk of losing the suit, she has no incentive to invest any time or money in a claim for which recovery appears doubtful.[76] In addition, with the average unregulated fee rate, approximately one-third of recovery, many lawyers decline malpractice cases which will probably achieve settlements or awards of less than $10,000 because the expected compensation for the amount of time expended is not seen as worthwhile.[77] The threshold value for the acceptance of cases for which recovery is less than probable would, on the average, be higher. Thus, although the vast majority of malpractice claims have been found to have some merit, most are rejected by the lawyers to whom they are brought.[78] This also means that only a small percentage of injured patients who seek legal help actually obtain it.

Of course, when two malpractice claims with similar prospects of recovery compete for an attorney's time, the traditional contingent fee structure, with its flat percentage of reimbursement, may encourage acceptance of the more shocking and sensational case, since it has the greater likelihood of eliciting jury sympathy and, accordingly, a larger recovery. The sliding scale fee structure would eliminate the purely financial inducement to accept claims with potentially large awards.

Considering the patient's choice of possible schemes for payment of counsel fees, patients with large potential recoveries might prefer a *per diem* rate if they were certain of recovery, but most would prefer the lawyer to bear the financial risk of losing a case. In this sense, the contingent fee system encourages the filing of more cases by permitting the poor and lower-middle-class patient to seek legal aid that he would never be able to afford under a *per diem* scheme.

It is instructive to note that the rise in the cost of malpractice suits here is comparable to that in Great Britain, although the contingent fee for attorneys is not employed there.[79]

Is there a ceiling on the amount a patient can recover in a lawsuit?

A ceiling on the amount of total damages that can be awarded in a particular case has been proposed in numerous statutes. Several statutes place a maximum ceiling only on the amount of noneconomic injury that may be compensated for in a medical malpractice suit. This type of provision limits only the amount of damages that may be awarded for "pain and suffering," but does not in any way limit the amount that a plaintiff may recover for lost wages or actual out-of-pocket expenses, including the cost of present or future medical care. Thus, in California and the Virgin Islands, a $250,000 limit was placed on the recovery for noneconomic loss, including pain and suffering, physical impairment, disfigurement, and other nonpecuniary losses.[80] Ohio and South Dakota adopted similar laws, which place a $200,000 and a $500,000 ceiling, respectively, on general damages.[81]

Indiana, Louisiana, Illinois, and Nebraska, for example, placed an absolute limit of $500,000 on recovery for a single injury or death.[82] In Illinois, the provider is liable for all damages up to the limit. In the other four states, a patient compensation fund is responsible for recoveries between $100,000 and $500,000.

In Idaho, a physician complying with financial responsibility requirements is liable to one patient for no more than $150,000, and to two or more patients for no more than $300,000, for conduct relating to a single occurrence or course of treatment.[83] Since no patient compensation fund is provided, the limitations place an effective ceiling on a patient's ability to recover. Another provision states that complying providers shall be liable only for "compensatory damages not previously paid or satisfied by any other person or from any other source," thus repealing the collateral-source rule and eliminating punitive damages in medical malpractice cases. North Dakota adopted a statute similar to Idaho's, except that the liability of a health care provider is limited to $500,000 per patient and $1,000,000 in the aggregate per year.[84]

In Virginia, the legislature imposed an absolute limit of $750,000 on recovery for a single injury or death.[85] The legislature in Oregon provided that a physician's liability is limited to $100,000, $300,000, or $500,000 per claim or in the aggregate, depending on the nature of his practice.[86] A patient-compensation fund assumes liability for every recovery above the physician's liability, but recoveries are prorated to the extent that the fund, which operates on a year-to-year basis, cannot pay all claims in full. In Pennsylvania, the excess fund has a limit on recovery of $1,000,000 per claim and $3,000,000 in the aggregate.[87] Pennsylvania does not limit punitive damages for willful or wanton misconduct, while in Oregon the patient-compensation fund is not liable for punitive damages. In Wisconsin, the patient's recovery is limited to $500,000 per claim when the excess fund falls below specified reserve amounts.[88] Otherwise, there is no limitation on the total amount of damages that may be recovered. Other states with limitations on recovery are New Hampshire and Texas.

Provisions establishing limitations on damages have been subject to constitutional attacks in several state courts. Both the Idaho Supreme Court[89] and the Nebraska Supreme Court[90] found that the limitation-of-recovery provision was constitutional. However, the Illinois Supreme Court held that the ceiling of $500,000 placed only on medical malpractice recoveries and in no other cases was special legislation in violation of the state constitution.[91] The court concluded that this limitation of a plaintiff's recovery without a corresponding expansion of his rights in another area, an absence of a *quid pro quo* exchange, rendered the statute unconstitutional.

Similar provisions in the constitutions of other states will probably form the basis of similar challenges. It is also possible that successful challenges will be made on the basis of the due process and equal protection clauses of the state and federal constitutions. It appears likely that the reasoning of the Illinois court will be followed in other jurisdictions, since the limits have been set in a somewhat arbitrary fashion and deprive an injured individual of a part of his right to an otherwise legally recognized recovery that is in excess of the limit. Such a provision has implications for the underlying rationale of the tort-liability system, which is that the burden for injuries should be placed on the individual responsible for them. With recovery limits, the burden is shifted to the injured party or victim. Thus, a ceiling may help to contain costs, but only at the expense of seriously injured patients. This seems unfair, and undermines a major purpose of the tort-liability system, which is to provide an injured party with an opportunity to be compensated for injury.

What is a pretrial screening panel?

A pretrial screening panel is a mechanism aimed at providing a private, informal procedure under which nonmeritorious claims can be screened out quickly and inexpensively and as many other cases as possible settled amicably. Before 1975, only New Hampshire had provided for pretrial review by statute, and one other state, New Jersey, had established a procedure by court rule. Since then, about twenty-seven legislatures have established statutory plans.[92] Additionally, a small number of voluntary, nonstatutory mediation plans sponsored by state or local medical societies and bar associations are available, such as that operating in Colorado.

With such a large number of statutes, the mechanisms created for the nonbinding pretrial review of medical malpractice claims vary considerably in scope and procedure. However, some generalizations can be made.

The typical pretrial review applies to any malpractice action brought against one or more health care providers, regardless of the size of the claimed damages. The panel may consist of three to seven members, including at least one attorney, one health care provider, and frequently one consumer member who is neither an attorney nor a physician.

The hearing itself is almost always informal. The parties have the choice of accepting the panel's decision, negotiating their own settlement, or rejecting the decision of the panel and proceeding to court. When court action is undertaken, and the panel's decision had been in favor of the patient, the panel is often obligated to help the patient obtain the necessary expert medical testimony for trial. On the other hand, the party that loses before the panel may face various "penalty" provisions for deciding to disregard the panel decision and go to court.

Many of the statutes contain provisions designed to strengthen the impact of the pretrial screening on the ultimate resolution of the case. For example, some states provide that the findings of the panel are admissible at a later trial on the matter.[93] Since a negative panel decision is likely to be somewhat persuasive with the jury and lessen the chances of the losing party's prevailing at trial, the provision tends to deter the losing party from proceeding with his case. Some statutes require the party rejecting the panel decision to post a cost bond with the court, which is payable if the opposing party prevails at trial.[94] Others provide that, if the court decides that a party made a frivolous claim or frivolously denied liability, costs of the panel and/or court are to be borne by that party.[95] Finally, some jurisdictions provide that, after a certain period of time, if neither side has rejected the panel's decision, it becomes final and binding.[96]

The courts have been divided over the constitutionality of statutes setting up mandatory pretrial screening. While in some courts they have withstood constitutional challenge,[97] other courts have had more trouble with them, with several state courts ruling them unconstitutional.[98]

Even some states in which the pretrial process has been ruled constitutional are nevertheless encountering concerns about the system. For example, although New York courts found the screening procedure mandated by state statute to be constitutional,[99] recently a committee of state supreme court judges unanimously recommended abandoning the system because it had not encouraged pretrial settlement, reduced the number of cases, or lowered juries' awards.[100] In general, there is not much available information on the effectiveness of pretrial screening.

Does a provider have the right to require a patient to sign a binding arbitration agreement before treatment?

Generally not. Arbitration is a nongovernmental procedure for settlement of disputes between private parties.

Parties to a dispute submit their differences to the judgment of an impartial party appointed either by mutual consent or by statute or court decision. Both approaches are being used to a small extent to settle malpractice disputes. Imposed arbitration is generally applied to disputes under a certain maximum amount, with the jury trial system preserved for the larger cases.

About eleven states have passed legislation specifically providing for binding arbitration of medical malpractice claims by written agreement of the parties.[101] Otherwise, malpractice claims can be arbitrated in at least thirty states under the general arbitration statute. All of the statutes generally provide that an individual's right to receive medical treatment shall not be prejudiced in any way by his decision whether or not to enter into an arbitration agreement. Most of the statutes that permit the agreement to cover future malpractice claims also provide for a certain period of time, following either execution of the agreement or the provision of services, in which the patient may reject the arbitration agreement. Only one jurisdiction, Puerto Rico, has a law that provides for mandatory binding arbitration of medical malpractice claims.[102] Another means for providing arbitration is to offer it as part of the plan of a group health care organization, such as a health maintenance organization. The agreement to submit malpractice claims to binding arbitration is part of the subscriber's contract. Because an individual is not required to become a member of such a group, the acceptance of the obligation to arbitrate is considered voluntary.

One major concern with arbitration is the potential for a constitutional challenge; it could be argued to be a violation of an individual's right to trial by jury under the state constitution. Because of this possibility, provisions to make the arbitration decision binding may be enacted only along with voluntary agreements to arbitrate so that they entail a knowing waiver of the right to a jury trial.

Thus, agreements to arbitrate will be analyzed by courts to determine whether they were entered into knowingly and voluntarily. This has already been done by courts in California and New York, with the decisions differing depending to a large extent on the facts of the cases that indicate the patient's level of awareness of the waiver.[103]

What is the future of the tort-liability system as a means for resolving medical malpractice claims under national health insurance?

In general, full health care coverage under one of the proposed "comprehensive benefits" national health insurance plans should reduce the number of malpractice suits, although not necessarily with a corresponding reduction in the occurrence of medical negligence. Those persons who suffer minor injuries allegedly due to negligence and who therefore require a small amount of additional medical care will probably not sue their health care provider, since their insurance will cover the cost of the original and any additional medical care. However, eliminating a certain number of private malpractice suits, and therefore some of the "police" function that these actions perform, will put additional strain on either internal or administrative regulatory procedures to check the occurrence of medical negligence. The tort-liability system affects the quality of medical care, compensation provided to injured patients, and the responsiveness of the health care system to the consumer. To the extent that national health insurance will limit recourse to this system, alternative procedures must be designed and implemented to respond to these issues. Medical malpractice litigation will likely remain a key factor in any mechanism developed to meet this need.[104]

NOTES

1. Cross v. Guthrey, 2 Root 90 (Conn. 1794). *See* Gussow, *Answers Can and Must Be Found to the Malpractice Situation,* J. LEGAL MED. (Mar. 1975) at 20.
2. Burns, *Malpractice Suits in American Medicine before the Civil War,* 43 BULL. HIST. MED. 41, 52 (1969). *See* J. ELWELL, A MEDICO-LEGAL TREATISE ON MALPRACTICE AND MEDICAL EVIDENCE, COMPRISING THE ELEMENTS OF MEDICAL JURISPRUDENCE, 82 (1866).
3. D. KONOLD, A HISTORY OF AMERICAN MEDICAL ETHICS: 1847–1912, at 50–51 (1962).
4. *New Study Upsets Old Views of Malpractice Risks,* Med. News, Sept. 19, 1977, at 3. *See,* U.S. Dept. of Health

Education, and Welfare, Report of the Secretary's Commission on Medical Malpractice (1973).

5. National Association of Insurance Commissioners, NAIC Malpractice Claims (Milwaukee, May 1977).

6. Medical Malpractice Claims, HEW/Industry Study of Medical Malpractice Insurance Claims, Public Health Service and Health Care Financing Administration (Oct. 20, 1978).

7. *See* Dornette, *Medical Injury Insurance—A Possible Remedy for the Malpractice Problem*, 78 CASE & COMMENT 25 (Sept.-Oct. 1973); Dornette, *Medical Injury Insurance—Proposed Model Legislation*, J. LEGAL MED., Mar. 1975, at 24; Havighurst & Tancredi *"Medical Adversity Insurance"—A No-Fault Approach to Medical Malpractice and Quality Assurance*, 613 INS. L. J. 69 (1974); Keaton, *Compensation for Medical Accidents*, 121 U. PA. L. REV. 590 (1973); O'Connell, *The Best Way to Adapt No Fault Insurance to Malpractice*, MED. ECON., June 23, 1975, at 106; O'Connell, *Proposed: "No-Fault" Insurance to Stem Malpractice Suits*, PRISM, July 1974, at 12.

8. *E.g.*, Dinner v. Thorp, 54 Wash.2d 90, 338 P.2d 137 (1959); Wilson v. Martin Mem. Hosp., 232 N.C. 362, 61 S.E.2d 102 (1950).

9. *E.g.*, Morse v. Moretti, 403 F.2d 564 (D.C. Cir. 1968); Reder v. Hanson, 338 F.2d 244 (8th Cir. 1964).

10. Helling v. Carey, 519 P.2d 981 (Wash. 1974). *See* Le Beuf v. Atkins, No. 4980–I (Ct. App., Wash., Dec. 29, 1980) (dentist liable for not performing "simple test"); Toth v. Community Hosp. at Glen Cove, 239 N.E.2d 368 (N.Y. 1968).

11. *E.g.*, Lab v. Hall, 200 So.2d 556 (Dist. Ct. App., Fla. 1967).

12. *E.g.*, Hill v. Boughton, 146 Fla. 512, 1 So.2d 610 (1941).

13. Noel v. Proud, 367 P.2d 61 (Kan. 1961).

14. *E.g.*, Williams v. Chamberlain, 316 S.W.2d 505 (Mo. 1958).

15. Michael v. Roberts, 91 N.H. 499, 23 A.2d 361 (1941).

16. Koch v. Gorrilla, 552 F.2d 1170 (6th Cir. 1977).

17. Samuels v. Doctors Hosp., 414 F. Supp. 1124 (D.C. La. 1976).

18. *E.g.*, Brune v. Belinkoff, 235 N.E.2d 793 (Mass. 1968); Murphy v. Little, 145 S.E.2d 760 (Ga. 1965); Douglas

v. Bussabarger, 438 P.2d 829 (Wash. 1968); Blain v. Eblen, 461 S.W.2d 370 (Ky. 1978). *See* Tallbull v. Whitney, 564 P.2d 162 (Mont. 1977).

19. *E.g.*, Barnes v. Bovenmyer, 122 N.W.2d 312 (Iowa 1963); Louis v. Read, 193 A.2d 255 (N.J. 1963); Belk v. Schweizer, 149 S.E.2d 565 (N.C. 1966); Siirila v. Barrios, 228 N.W.2d 801 (Mich. Ct. App. 1975), *aff'd*, Siirila v. Barrios, 248 N.W.2d 171 (Mich. 1976).

20. Valentine v. Kaiser Foundation Hosps., 12 Cal. Rptr. 26 (1961).

21. Francisco v. Parchment Med. Clinic, 407 Mich. 325, 285 N.W.2d 39 (1979). Sup. Ct., Nov. 13, 1979.

22. Robbins v. Footer, 553 F.2d 123 (D.C. Cir. 1977).

23. *E.g.*, Tvedt v. Haugen, 70 N.D. 338, 294 N.W. 183 (1940).

24. Clark v. Laughlin, 137 Cal. Rptr. 354 (Ct. App. 1977).

25. Brandt v. Grubin, 131 N.J. Super. 182, 329 A.2d 82, 89 (1974).

26. Holder, *Duty to Consult*, 266 JAMA 11 (1973); Bruni v. Tatsumi, 46 Ohio St. 2d 127, 364 N.E.2d 673 (1976).

27. Clark v. Wichman, 72 N.J. Super. 486, 179 A.2d 38 (1962) (an orthopedic surgeon does not have to continue care of a patient when that patient is transferred to a psychiatric hospital by court order, until the patient is returned to his care).

28. Annot., 57 A.L.R.2d 463 (1958).

29. *Id.*

30. Sheridan v. Quarrier, 127 Conn. 279, 16 A.2d 479 (1940), *and see* Bruni v. Tatsumi, 46 Ohio St. 2d 127, 346 N.E. 2d 673 (1976).

31. *See supra* note 28.

32. Comment, *The Action of Abandonment in Medical Malpractice Litigation*, 36 TULANE L. REV. 834, 835 (1962).

33. Christy v. Saliterman, 179 N.W.2d 288 (Minn. 1970).

34. Gray v. Davidson, 130 P.2d 341 (Wash. 1941).

35. Holder, *Abandonment*, Part 2, 225 JAMA 1285, 1286 (1973).

36. Capps v. Valk, 189 Kan. 287, 369 P.2d 238 (1962) (doctor failed to check that resident had removed an eight-inch drain from the patient's body). *See* Livingston v. Portland Gen. Hosp., 357 P.2d 543 (Ore. 1960) (abandonment by dentist). *See generally* W. HOWARD &

A. Parks, The Dentist and the Law 94–95 (St. Louis: C. V. Mosby, 1973).

37. Robert v. Woods, 206 F. Supp. 579 (D.C.S.D. Ala. 1962) (doctor has not abandoned patient where patient does not return for weekly checkups following surgery); Nash v. Meyers, 31 P.2d 273 (Idaho 1934) (doctor has not abandoned patient where patient doesn't return to office "if anything goes wrong" and doctor refuses to make house calls).

38. Holder, *Abandonment*, Part 3, 225 JAMA 1429 (1973).

39. Vidrine v. Mayes, 127 So.2d 809 (La. App. 1961) (plaintiff wished a home delivery, which the doctor said he would not perform; at the time of the delivery, complications arose, and the plaintiff's husband requested the doctor to come to the house; the doctor refused and told the husband to bring his wife to the hospital where he would treat her; after a delay of six hours the plaintiff was brought to the hospital, where her child was stillborn; the court held that abandonment had not occurred because a doctor has the right to limit his practice and is not obligated to make house calls and also he is not required to accept employment on terms determined by the patient); Nash v. Meyers, 31 P.2d 273 (Idaho 1934) (a doctor is not obligated to make house calls where he has instructed the patient to come to his office if anything goes wrong [complications from an illegal abortion]).

40. Brandt v. Grubin, 131 N.J. Super. 182, 329 A.2d 82 (1974).

41. *E.g.*, Raitt v. Johns Hopkins Hosp., 336 A.2d 90 (Md. 1975); Mills v. Levy, 537 F.2d 1331 (5th Cir. 1976).

42. Sims v. Helms, 345 So.2d 721 (Fla. 1977). *See, e.g.*, Buckroyd v. Bunten, 237 N.W.2d 808 (Iowa 1976); Marshall v. Tomaselli, 372 A.2d 1280 (R.I. 1977).

43. Radman v. Harold, 367 A.2d 472 (Md. Ct. App. 1977). *But see* Callahan v. William Beaumont Hosp., 254 N.W. 2d 31 (Mich. 1977).

44. Siirila v. Barrios, 248 N.W.2d 171 (Mich. 1976).

45. Llera v. Wisner, 557 P.2d 805 (Mont. 1976).

46. *E.g.*, Mondot v. Vallejo Gen. Hosp., 313 P.2d 78 (Cal. 1957); Irick v. Andrew, 545 S.W.2d 557 (Tex. Ct. Civil App. 1976).

47. Sharp v. Hess, Docket NCC 10639–B (Cal. Super. Ct., Los Angeles Co., Sept. 18, 1975).

48. Dietz, Baird, & Berul, *The Medical Malpractice Legal System.* In U.S. Dep't of Health, Education & Welfare, Report of the Secretary's Commission on Medical Malpractice; Appendix 87, 128 (1973).

49. Roth, *The Medical Malpractice Insurance Crisis: Its Causes, the Effects, and Proposed Solutions,* INS. COUNSEL J., July 1977, at 469, 477–78.

50. *E.g.,* Seneris v. Haas, 291 P.2d 915 (Cal. 1955).

51. Young v. Caspers, 249 N.W.2d 713 (Minn. 1977).

52. Harris v. Cafritz Mem. Hosp., 364 A.2d 135 (D.C. Ct. App. 1976).

53. These include Alaska, Arizona, Delaware, Florida, Idaho, Louisiana, Nevada, North Dakota, Oklahoma, Rhode Island, Tennessee, Vermont, and Washington.

54. Wash. Rev. Code §4.24.290 (Supp. 1975).

55. Tantista v. Szendey, 158 Me. 228, 182 A.2d 660 (1962).

56. Peters v. Golds, 366 F. Supp. 150 (Mich. 1973); Millbaugh v. Gilmore, 30 Ohio 2d 319, 285 N.E.2d 19 (1972).

57. *E.g.,* Waldman v. Rohrbaugh, 241 Md. 137, 215 A.2d 825 (1969); Tramutola v. Bortone, 118 N.J. Super. 503, 288 A.2d 863 (1972), *rev'd in part on other grounds and modified in part on other grounds,* 63 N.J. 9, 304 A.2d 197 (1973); Flanagan v. Mount Eden Gen. Hosp., 24 N.Y.2d 427, 248 N.E.2d 871, 301 N.Y.S.2d 23 (1969). *But see* Owen v. Wilson, 537 S.W.2d 543 (Ark. 1976).

58. Robinson v. Weaver, 350 S.W.2d 18 (Tex. 1977).

59. Proewig v. Zaino, 394 N.Y.S.2d 446 (N.Y. Sup. Ct., App. Div. 1977).

60. Simmons v. Riverside Methodist Hosp., 336 N.E.2d 460 (Ohio Ct. App. 1975).

61. Sanchez v. South Hoover Hosp., 132 Cal. Rptr. 657, 553 P.2d 1129 (1976); Moran v. Napolitano, 363 A.2d 346 (N.J. 1976).

62. Graham v. Sisco, 248 Ark. 6, 449 S.W.2d 949 (1970); Chaffin v. NiCosia, 310 N.E.2d 867 (Ind. 1974).

63. Miller v. Dickert, 190 S.E.2d 459 (S.C. 1972).

64. Swope v. Printz, 468 S.W.2d 34 (Mo. 1971).

65. Nardone v. Reynolds, 538 F.2d 1131 (5th Cir. 1976).

66. Alabama, Arizona, California, Colorado, Delaware, Florida, Georgia, Hawaii, Illinois, Indiana, Iowa, Kansas,

Louisiana, Maryland, Massachusetts, Michigan, Minnesota, Mississippi, Missouri, Nebraska, Nevada, New Hamphire, New Mexico, New York, North Carolina, North Dakota, Ohio, Oklahoma, Oregon, Rhode Island, South Carolina, South Dakota, Tennessee, Texas, Utah, Washington, Wyoming.

67. *E.g.*, Tex. Ins. Code art. 5.82, §2 (two years from tort complained of).

68. *E.g.*, Nev. Rev. Stat. §11.400 (four years, or two years from date of discovery).

69. *E.g.*, La. Rev. Stat. tit. 9, §5628 (Supp. 1979) (one year, one year from discovery, and a three-year outside limit for all claims).

70. *E.g.*, Tenn. Pub. Law 1975 ch. 299, §15ca (exception for foreign object and fraudulent concealment); N.Y. Civ. Prac. Law, §214-a (exception for foreign objects).

71. *E.g.*, Cal. Civ. Proc. Code, §340.5; Nev. Rev. Stat. §11.400.

72. Hirsh, *Malpractice Crisis: Fact or Fiction?* Case & Comm., July–Aug. 1975 at 6; Smith, *Whose Malpractice Crisis?* 127 J. La. St. Med. Soc'y 293 (1975).

73. Arizona, Iowa, Kansas, Maryland, Nebraska, Tennessee, Washington.

74. Idaho, Oregon.

75. California, Delaware, Hawaii, Indiana, Michigan, New Jersey, New York, Ohio, Pennsylvania, Wisconsin.

76. Annas, Katz, & Trakimas, *Medical Malpractice Litigation under National Health Insurance: Essential or Expendable?* 1975 Duke L. J. 1335, 1344.

77. *See* Dietz, Baird, & Beru, *The Medical Malpractice Legal System, in* U.S. Dept. of Health, Education, and Welfare, Report of the Secretary's Commission on Medical Malpractice, Appendix 87, 119 (1973).

78. Malpractice in Focus: The Problem . . . and Some Solutions 2 (AMA source document prepared by editors of Prism, Aug. 1975).

79. Curran, *The British Experience in Medical Malpractice: An Upward Trend*, 288 New Eng. J. Med. 249 (1973). And on the comparative effectiveness of the contingency fee system in aiding victims, *see* The Insight Team of The London Times, Suffer the Children: The Story of the Thalidomide Tragedy (New York: Viking Press, 1979).

80. CAL. CIV. CODE, §3333.2(b); V.I. CODE, §27:166(b).
81. OHIO REV. CODE, §2307.43; S.D. Codified Laws Ann §21–3–11.
82. IND. ANN. STAT. §16–9, 5–2–2(b); LA. REV. STAT. ANN., §40:1299.42(B)(2); ILL. REV. STAT., ch. 70, §101; NEB. REV. STAT., §44–2825.
83. IDAHO CODE §39–4204. §39–4205 contains similar limitations on the liability of hospitals.
84. N.D. CENT. CODE, §26–40–11.
85. VA. CODE, §8–654.8.
86. ORE. LAWS, §2315.
87. 40 PA. CONS. STAT. ANN §1301.701 (Purdon).
88. WIS. STAT. ANN., §655.27(b).
89. Jones v. State Bd. of Med., 555 P.2d 399 (Idaho 1976).
90. Prendergast v. Nelson, 199 Neb. 97, 256 N.W.2d 657 (1977).
91. Wright v. Central DuPage Hosp. Ass'n, 347 N.E.2d 736 (Ill. 1976).
92. Alabama, Alaska, Arkansas, Arizona, Connecticut, Delaware, Florida, Hawaii, Idaho, Indiana, Kansas, Louisiana, Maine, Maryland, Massachusetts, Missouri, Montana, Nebraska, Nevada, New Mexico, New York, North Dakota, Pennsylvania, Rhode Island, Tennessee, Virginia, Wisconsin. See LaCroix v. Caron, No. 2468, Docket # Yor–80–26 (Sup. Jud. co., Maine, Dec. 12, 1980) for an interpretation of the Maine Health Security Act.
93. Alaska, Arizona, Delaware, Florida, Indiana, Louisiana, Maryland, Massachusetts, Nebraska, New York, Ohio, Pennsylvania, Rhode Island, Tennessee, Virginia, Wisconsin.
94. Arizona, Massachusetts.
95. Alaska, Illinois, Rhode Island, Wisconsin.
96. Illinois, Maryland, Pennsylvania, Rhode Island.
97. Prendergast v. Nelson, supra note 90.
98. E.g., Florida. See Wright v. Central DuPage Hosp. Ass'n, 347 N.E.2d 736 (Ill. 1976).
99. Comiskey v. Arlen, 390 N.Y.S.2d 122 (1976); Halpern v. Gozan, 381 N.Y.S.2d 744 (1975).
100. Malpractice Panels Draw New Opposition, Med. World News, April 14, 1980, at 14. See S. LAW & S. POLAN, PAIN AND PROFIT: THE POLITICS OF MALPRACTICE 127 (New York: Harper & Row, 1978).

101. Alabama, Alaska, California, Illinois, Louisiana, Maine, Michigan, Ohio, South Dakota, Vermont, Virginia.

102. U.S. Dept. of Health Education, and Welfare, Public Health Service, Legal Topics Relating to Medical Malpractice 37, Contract #282-76-0321 GS (1977).

103. Dickinson v. Kaiser Found. Hosps., 2d Cir. No. 59308 (Ct. App., Calif., Dec. 4, 1980) (upheld agreement to arbitrate); Madden v. Kaiser Found. Hosps., 17 Cal.2d 699, 131 Cal. Rptr. 882, 552 P.2d 1178 (1976) (upheld agreement to arbitrate); Wheeler v. St. Joseph Hosp., 63 Cal. App.2d 357, 133 Cal. Rptr. 775 (Cal. Ct. App., 4th Div. 1976) (invalidated agreement to arbitrate); Linden v. Baron, N.Y.L.J., July 21, 1977, at 21 (Sup. Ct. Part 1) (invalidated agreement to arbitrate).

104. Annas, Katz, & Trakima, *supra* note 76.

XIII

Malpractice Insurance
and Countersuits

This chapter deals with some of the practical aspects of preparing for and defending a malpractice charge. It begins with a discussion of medical malpractice insurance and what the health care professional can expect from the malpractice insurance company when he is sued. The discussion continues on to topics of liability of professional corporations, the disadvantages of "going bare," and the pros and cons of initiating a countersuit after one has successfully defended a malpractice suit.

What is medical malpractice insurance?

It is a type of liability insurance—an agreement in which the *insurer* promises to assume a loss or liability imposed by law on the *insured,* in exchange for a *premium.* Medical malpractice insurance protects physicians for liability arising from the special risks inherent in medical practice. Similar liability insurance may be purchased by other independent health care practitioners and by hospitals. The insurer also undertakes the actual defense of the insured against any malpractice claims.[1]

The typical malpractice policy is a relatively short instrument, compared with the average automobile liability policy or life insurance contract.[2] Most malpractice policies are fairly uniform in basic content, and are divided into three parts.

The first part, the insuring agreement, sets out the basic promise of the insurer to pay damages, up to the policy limits, arising out of the insured's asserted malpractice, and to provide legal counsel to defend the lawsuit. A standard clause of this type would provide for the defense, upon appropriate notice by the insured, of any "malpractice, error or mistake resulting from the practice of the insured's profession." Litigation by the insured against the insurance company often centers around the definition of the terms "malpractice, error or mistake." For example, do assault and battery, defamation, breach of contract, undue familiarity, or false imprisonment fall within that term? Are injuries that result from equipment failure covered? Beyond that, what acts or omissions may likely be considered outside "the practice of the insured's profession"? Malpractice insurance need not be confined to traditional claims of bodily injury and mental suffering. It may include other causes of action, if they are directly related to the insured's practice of his profession.

The second section encompasses conditions of the contract, including any understandings between the parties that form part of the basis of the contract. For example, if a physician represents that he is a member in good standing of the state medical society, but his membership had lapsed and he was not, the insurer is entitled to cancel. Similarly, in one case, a physician, upon moving from Alabama to Louisiana, made misrepresentations to an insurance company concerning his licensing problems with the first state.[3] The company stated that the policy would not have been renewed if the true circumstances had been known. Because the policy was renewed on the strength of the physician's misrepresentations, the court ruled that it was null and void.

The most commonly specified conditions are those requiring prompt notice by the insured to the insurer of any malpractice claim against him, the obligation on the part of the insured to cooperate with the insurer in the defense of any such claim, and the reservation by the insurer of the right to make settlement agreements. These are discussed in more detail later in this chapter.

The final section deals with exclusionary clauses, or provisions specifying those classes of liability that are not covered by the policy. Insurance provisions limiting the insurer's liability do not violate public policy if the terms are unambiguous.[4] The most common ones are exclusion of liability for the results of criminal acts, acts performed while the physician is under the influence of alcohol or drugs, and failure to achieve a guaranteed result. Some exclusions, such as those limiting the range of specialty practice of the physician, or denying coverage for acts of employees, can be removed by payment of an additional premium.

In general, liability insurance is viewed as a classic example of a contract of adhesion, one in which one party, the insurer, is in a position to dictate to a large extent the terms of the agreement with the other party. Because of this, courts tend to interpret this type of contract in favor of the party in the weaker bargaining position. Thus, courts are likely to interpret the insurance policy in light of the insured's reasonable expectations. If any doubt or ambiguity exists, it will be resolved against the insurance company.[5]

What period of time does a malpractice policy cover?

There are two types of insurance offered: the *occurrence* policy and the *claims-made* policy.

The traditional occurrence policy covers damages resulting from professional services rendered during the period in which the premium was paid. Such a policy covers any claim resulting from an occurrence during the policy period, even if the claim itself is made later.

An occurrence policy is typically worded as follows:

> This policy applies only to acts, errors, or omissions that occur in or are ancillary to the practice of medicine within the State of _____ _____ during the policy period.[6]

The advantage of an occurrence policy is that an insured physician is protected for years after committing the negligent act.[7]

There is a trend towards greater use of the claims-made policy. Such a policy covers the insured only for claims actually asserted against him *during the policy period*, regardless of whether the occurrence took place during that period. Under this form of insurance, once the policy period is ended, the insured is no longer covered.

A claims-made policy is typically worded as follows:

> **(a)** *During the Policy Period*
> The insurance afforded by this policy applies to errors, omissions, or negligent acts that occur during this policy period, if claim therefor is first made against the insured during this policy period.
>
> **(b)** *Prior to the Policy Period*
> The insurance afforded by this policy also applies to errors, omissions, or negligent acts that occur within the United States of America prior to the effective date of this policy, if claim thereon is first made against the insured during this policy period.[8]

The insured is therefore left unprotected against later claims if he allows his policy to lapse. For example, when a physician retires, he would have no coverage for past errors that might form the basis for later claims. With an occurrence policy, he would have been covered after his retirement for any earlier acts of malpractice.

To resolve this problem with the claims-made policy, the insured may obtain a "tail coverage" policy. This may take the form of an endorsement attached to the claims-made policy to permit its continuation after the normal expiration date, to cover later claims arising from the period when the original policy was in effect. Since experience has shown that it takes about three years for the majority of claims related to a particular policy period to be filed,[9] it is essential to arrange for such coverage for at least three years after the original policy expires.

Is the provider responsible for notifying the insurance company of possible malpractice claims?

Yes. Malpractice policies uniformly contain "timely notice" provisions, which require the provider to report "as soon as possible" any "malpractice, error or mistake" or "any threatened claim or suit." Failure to do so is generally considered a material breach of the policy, which thereby relieves the insurance company of liability.[10]

For example, in one action, complications developed after each of two operations performed by a physician. He received a letter from an attorney stating that the patient was asserting a claim against him, but failed to notify his insurance company until five months after receipt of the letter (and five weeks after suit was filed). His policy required notice as soon as practicable after he became aware of the alleged injury. The court found that the physician had failed to comply with this provision, that this failure constituted a material breach of the policy, and that the insurance company was therefore relieved of liability.[11]

In another case, a physician performed an operation to correct an inguinal hernia. A subsequent operation by another surgeon, necessitated by the patient's continuing pain, revealed that a suture had passed through the edge of the femoral nerve. The first physician then admitted he had caused the injury, and canceled his surgery bill. However, he did not notify his insurance company until more than five months later—two days after receiving a letter from the patient's attorney. His policy required that notice be given as soon as practicable after the physician becomes aware of an alleged injury. The court noted that the physician became aware of such an alleged injury following the second operation, and at that point he should have given notice. By not doing so, he breached his policy.[12]

Even if a physician believes she is not liable for a threatened suit, it is advisable for her to notify her insurance company.[13] Nevertheless, some courts hold that reasonable belief of nonliability will excuse a delay in giving this notice. Thus, in a New York decision, the court held that an insurance company may not automatically disclaim liability to an insured because of his failure to give the requisite notice required by the terms of his policy.[14] This was so even though the dentist in question had failed to report both the death of a patient due to a possible allergic reaction to penicillin and a call from the chief medical examiner's office regarding an investigation into the death, but notified the company only when he received a malpractice complaint, more than a year later. The court noted that at the time of the oral surgery the dentist had taken a medical history, including questioning the patient regarding any possible allergy to penicillin, and that a reasonable dentist in his position would have acted similarly. Therefore, the dentist had every reason to believe that he was not liable for the death.

Some courts hold that the physician's failure to give timely notice under the policy releases the insurer from liability only if the insurer is prejudiced by such failure.[15] The policy may also contain a specified time period during which notice must be given. Otherwise, a reasonable time period will be implied.[16] Beyond that, even with what appear to be rigid time periods, courts have generally favored the insured, holding that reasonable notice under the circumstances is adequate. Thus, in a Nebraska case, a court held an insurance company obligated to defend a physician under its policy even though it received late notice of a malpractice suit against the physician.[17] The physician in the matter had originally referred the malpractice complaint to his insurance agent, who relayed it to the wrong insurance company. It wasn't until several years later that the wrong insurance company discovered it was not the physician's insurer at the time of the incident, the agent having switched companies without informing the physician. The proper company, upon notification, refused to defend. The highest court of the state said that the notice given was reasonable under the circumstances. Accordingly, the insurance company was liable under the policy.

Must the provider cooperate with the insurance company in the defense of a malpractice claim?

Yes. Malpractice policies usually require that the insured cooperate with the insurer in the event of a suit. This includes assisting the company in the preparation and defense of the claim. Generally these clauses also obligate the insured not to intentionally take any steps that would materially and substantially have an adverse effect on the defense. Such a provision is necessary since, without the assistance of the insured physician in the preparation of the case, the insurance company would be under an almost insurmountable disadvantage. Just what the insured must do in order to comply with this requirement must be determined on a case-by-case basis. For example, it includes the attendance of the insured physician at the trial when practical.[18] The effect of a failure on the part of the physician to cooperate may be to relieve the company of its obligations under the insurance policy.

What are punitive damages? Would the insurance company pay them?

Punitive damages are those damages awarded by a jury against a defendant that are over and above the damages awarded to cover the actual injuries received by the plaintiff (compensatory damages). Punitive damages are awarded to punish the defendant for actions on his part that involve actual malice or reckless disregard. The purpose of such damages is to serve as a deterrent to such actions in the future. When the action involved in a medical malpractice case is an aggravated disregard of professional duty, punitive damages have been found appropriate.[19] Jurisdictions vary as to whether punitive damages are allowed in medical malpractice actions.

When the wording of a policy covers liability generally, the insurer may be required to pay not only compensatory damages but those assessed as a penalty as well. When the scope of coverage of the policy is limited to actual compensatory damages, the insurer would be liable only for those damages specified in the contract. Many policies limit their coverage in this way.

Do malpractice policies provide coverage for the result of acts that are not considered to be part of medical practice?

This varies, depending on the exact terms of the policy and on the public policy implications of providing coverage. For example, one court has found that an insurance company has a duty to defend a physician in a suit for libel and slander where it could be shown that the statements were not made with actual malice.[20] In this case, an anesthesiologist had sued another physician, alleging that the insured had made numerous remarks impugning his professional reputation.

However, in a recent decision, the court ruled that a psychiatrist's insurer was not obligated to defend a malpractice action based on the psychiatrist's fornication "therapy" with a woman patient.[21] The psychiatrist had earlier been found to have committed malpractice when he "prescribed and personally administered multiple, repetitive doses of *fornicatus Hartogus*" under the guise of treating the patient for lesbianism.[22] The patient was awarded $150,000, and the psychiatrist thereafter sued his insurance company for failing to defend him in the malpractice action.

The court noted that the psychiatrist at all times knew, and had so stated at the previous trial, that what he was doing was not part of the doctor-patient relationship. Since the psychiatrist knew that his actions were for his personal satisfaction and did not constitute medical practice, the court reasoned that they were never intended to be included in the protective coverage of a malpractice policy. Beyond that, the court ruled that, as a matter of public policy, it must find in favor of the insurance company, since to hold otherwise could be to "indemnify immorality and to pay the expenses of prurience." [23]

Does a malpractice insurance policy cover criminal acts?

In general, an insurance contract protects a person from civil liability, but will not pay for the defense of criminal actions or exempt the insured from responsibility for such actions.[24]

For example, in one case, a physician's practice insurance company was held not to be liable for his fraudulent acts.[25] The physician had examined an applicant for life insurance on behalf of an insurance company. Instead of submitting an electrocardiogram of the seventy-two-year-old applicant, the physician certified and submitted an electrocardiogram of the applicant's insurance agent, who was much younger and healthier. The life insurance company issued two polices, the applicant died a short time later, and the company paid off on the policies. Thereafter, it sued the physician and his malpractice insurer.

The court found that the malpractice insurance company had agreed to pay for the physician's obligations for any malpractice, error, or mistake he committed. In a separate trial, the physician had been found guilty of conspiracy to defraud the life insurance company. The court stated that the physician had been found guilty of fraud, not malpractice, and that his liability insurer was not liable for that. Analogously, it has been held that an attorney's malpractice insurance company did not have to indemnify him for liability for the misappropriation and embezzlement of a client's funds by his law partner.[26]

However, in another case, a liability insurer was ordered to defend a policyholder pharmacist against charges that he improperly refilled a patient's prescription without express physician authorization, which violated state law.[27] The insurance company contended that it was not obligated to provide such a defense since policy coverage is forfeited when there has been a willful violation of a penal statute. The court ruled that the complaint contained claims of traditional negligence or malpractice, as well as liability for failure to inform or warn the patient. Accordingly, the provision in the policy that relieved the insurance company of all responsibility for an insured's criminal acts was not available to the carrier.

May an insurance company settle a medical-malpractice claim without the consent of the insured provider?

It depends on the terms of the contract. In most insurance contracts the carrier reserves the right to compromise, or settle, any claims or suit. Settlement problems usually involve the question of the insured's consent.

Many malpractice policies contain a clause that gives the provider the right to reject the insurer's decision to settle the case. An insurance company that settles a malpractice action without the consent of the provider having such a policy would be guilty of a breach of contract and liable for any damages resulting therefrom.[28] However, if the provider unreasonably refuses to settle a claim and the insurance company loses the suit, the company's liability may be limited to the settlement offer.

Conversely, in the absence of such a clause, the insurer has the authority to make the settlement decision, whether or not the provider agrees. The provider may pursue discussions with the insurance company, but the ultimate authority regarding settlement remains with the insurance company.

On the other hand, the refusal of an insurance company to accept a reasonable settlement offer may make the insurer liable for the full judgment, even if it exceeds policy coverage limits.[29] If the company acted in a willful manner and in bad faith, the insured may also be covered for any attorney and other expenses incurred, and even punitive damages or damages for emotional distress.[30] This is also true even if there is a "provider agreement" clause, assuming the provider wants to accept the settlement offer.

In determining whether the insurance company has acted appropriately in rejecting a settlement offer, numerous factors are considered:

1. The insurer must take into account the interests of the insured and give him at least as much consideration as it does its own interests.
2. The insurer must realistically evaluate the case and the potential magnitude of a possible award.
3. The insurance company must properly investigate the circumstances of the claim.
4. The insurer must reasonably consider the seriousness of the injuries involved.

In making its decision, the company cannot totally ignore the desires of the insured, nor can it substitute the judgment of a panel of experts for its own obligation of case evaluation, relying on the panel's determination of non-negligence to justify a refusal to settle.[31] The insurance company has a duty to effect a reasonable settlement based upon probability, and in determining whether the insurer conformed to this standard, the potential of a judgment in excess of the policy limit becomes a primary factor. Courts have held that the insurer must conduct itself as though it alone were liable for the entire amount of the judgment.[32]

In addition, the insurance company cannot wait until just before trial to make an offer for its policy limits.[33] It must give proper consideration within a specified time to demands of claimants offering to accept policy limits. Also, because the insurance company controls the settlement of the claim, it has a duty to initiate and perform its own investigation into the validity and value of the claim. The duty of the insurance company to its insured is fiduciary in nature: the insurer has an affirmative duty to explore settlement possibilities, and must initiate negotiations if settlement for the policy limit is in the best interest of the insured.[34]

Does an insurance company have an obligation to appeal an adverse judgment in a malpractice action?

This depends on the exact terms of the insurance policy. Under the insurance contract, an insurer may be responsible to appeal those adverse malpractice verdicts which are appealable.[35] If it does not do it, this would be a breach of contract, so that the company would be liable for any subsequent damages suffered by the insured. This could also include mental distress caused by the insurer's failure to appeal the judgment.

Should a provider who is sued for malpractice retain her own attorney?

Most insurance contracts specify that the insurer has the right to designate counsel to represent the insured party in the malpractice action. However, there may be circumstances in which it might nevertheless be wise for a provider to hire her own attorney.

The first situation is when the plaintiff's damage request exceeds the physician's insurance policy limits. The provider will be personally liable for any excess judgment. Therefore, it might be advisable to have personal counsel to represent her interests with respect to any possible liability beyond the coverage limits. In particular, the lawyer might be able to protect the provider should the insurance company fail to accept a good faith settlement offer within policy limits.

Another example would be when the insurance company is claiming that, under the terms of the insurance contract, it has no obligation to defend the provider. Here the interests of the provider are in obvious conflict with those of the insurance company. A privately retained lawyer may want to bring suit against the insurer on the issue of coverage.

May an insurance company cancel a policy without good cause?

An insurance policy is a voluntary contract, and the parties may designate any grounds and methods of cancellation they desire. Most cases hold that policy clauses that permit cancellation by either party are enforceable, as long as the terms of cancellation have been met.[36] Malpractice policies usually contain clauses that allow cancellation by the insurance company after ten days' notice.

But there are some limitations on this. For example, the physician in one suit claimed that his insurance had been canceled to punish him for having testified in a malpractice action against another physician and as a way to deter him from testifying should the case come up for retrial, as well as to dissuade other physicians insured by this particular company from testifying in malpractice actions.[37] The court held that using a contractual right of cancellation to intimidate a witness in a lawsuit contravenes public policy and therefore constitutes a breach of contract. The court noted that, if an insurance contract conflicts with public policy, it is illegal and void. Thus, if the physician had been found liable for malpractice after the cancellation but before the term of the policy had run, he would likely be entitled to damages in an amount up to the limit of the policy. In this way, a physician would be protected and would be able to proceed in practice as if the cancellation had never occurred.

In a similar case, a physician claimed that his malpractice insurance had been canceled to coerce other physicians to agree to a 141 percent premium increase.[38] The court said that cancellation of the policy by the insurer violated an implied covenant of good faith and fair dealing. It went on to say that the insurance company did not have an absolute right to cancel its policies, and that it was against public policy to permit conspiracies by insurance companies to avoid contractual liability.

In a malpractice action, must a provider reveal that he has insurance coverage?

In many states, case law and/or statutes require that the defendant in personal injury cases, including medical malpractice actions, reveal the extent of his insurance coverage upon request by the plaintiff.[39] The purpose of this is to enable both parties to make a realistic appraisal of the case and encourage settlement within the policy limits. On the other hand, those states that exclude evidence as to a physician's insurance consider it to be irrelevant to establish either negligence or damages, and that its admission would pose a danger of misuse by the jury.[40]

Can a professional corporation be sued?

Yes. A professional corporation can be sued the same way any other private corporate group can be sued for negligence and the like. Liability of a corporation is generally limited to the corporation's assets, so that the corporate entity would need to purchase insurance to cover this possibility. However, in some states this liability limitation does not apply to professional corporations, such as those composed of physicians, so that the individual physician may be sued personally and may be called upon to meet a damage award beyond the corporate assets. In those jurisdictions, it is prudent for physicians in professional corporations to carry individual malpractice insurance.

Other than a medical malpractice insurance policy, will any other type of insurance policy provide liability coverage?

Probably not, but it would depend on the specific terms of the policy in question. In one case, a physician brought an action against the carrier of his homeowner's insurance policy, claiming that it had an obligation to provide him a defense in a medical malpractice action.[41] The homeowner's policy was primarily designed to provide protection for exposure incidental to home ownership and personal hazards outside of business risks. The contract contained clauses excluding coverage for personal liability and medical payments arising out of the rendering or failure to render professional physician services. The court held that, in light of the exclusionary clause, the insurance company had no duty to defend the physician in the malpractice action.

What does it mean to "go bare"? Is it a viable alternative to having malpractice insurance?

Put very simply, "going bare" or being self-insured means practicing medicine without professional liability insurance. In general, insurance is a program in which risk is shared and transferred. Contributions to the pool are made by premiums, and losses are indemnified from the pool.[42] In such a program, the larger the base, or the number of insured, the larger the reserves and the easier it becomes to meet losses. For the self-insured physician, the base is one, and the reserves limited to the physician's own assets. In deciding whether to become self-insured, consideration should be given to the physician's type of practice and locality of practice, since physicians in certain specialties and areas of the country are sued with greater frequency than others.

A physician is subject to attachment of her assets in order to satisfy a judgment obtained against her, so another aspect of a self-insurance plan is to protect these assets from being reached by future creditors. A first step in legally accomplishing this should probably be seeking the advice of a lawyer who specializes in gift law and bankruptcy law.

In theory, any transfer of assets may be set aside as a "fraud upon creditors," whether the transfer was made before or after knowledge of a malpractice claim. If a physician transfers her assets to her spouse or children after the provision of the medical care that is the basis for the suit, then under the Uniform Fraudulent Conveyances Act, which has been enacted into law in most states, any transfer made without receiving full cash value or fair consideration in return is deemed to be fraudulent. The judgment creditor (the holder of a malpractice judgment) may go against these assets and satisfy his judgment from them.

While the patient may reach these assets, the physician may not be able to.[43] Once personal or real property is divested, it cannot be reclaimed, but becomes the property of the recipient, which is taxable to the recipient if its value exceeds the lifetime gift exclusion. Thus, divesting all personal property to avoid a future judgment is dangerous. The available defenses to a challenge to a transfer as fraudulent depend upon the particular case, such as whether the transfer had another legitimate purpose; whether the physician retained any control or interest in the proceeds; the time of the transfer; and whether any real consideration was given by the party to whom the assets were transferred.

Beyond that, a physician who has no assets is not necessarily judgment-proof. A judgment against a physician stays with him. Not only present possessions, but future inheritance and, in some states, daily earnings could be attached. The physician without insurance or substantial assets who is found liable in a malpractice action may be forced to pay a percentage of his future income to the judgment creditor, or patient, until the debt is satisfied. However, wages are partially protected from attachment in most jurisdictions, as are "fees" and "commissions." States have varying amounts of protection in regard to the limits placed on this exemption. For example, in Colorado, 70 percent of earnings are exempt from execution, while Georgia law protects $50 per week.[44] Other exemptions to attachment in most states, such as the homestead exemption for the family home and the exemption for clothes, vehicles, household goods, and other personal items, offer only nominal protection.

In general, malpractice judgments, including punitive damage awards, are dischargeable in bankruptcy, as are other tort judgments, unless the claim involves fraud, or the tort is willful and malicious. That is, such debts can be canceled if the physician goes through bankruptcy proceedings.

Briefly, the debtor submits a schedule or list of his obligations to the federal bankruptcy court, together with a representation that his assets are inadequate to pay them. A trustee is appointed to act for the debtor as regards her property, who collects her assets and distributes them to the creditors on a *pro rata* basis in a specified order of priority. Finally, the dischargeable debts are declared to be null and void.

All of the nonexempt assets of the debtor are available for distribution to creditors by the trustee, who also has the authority to seek and set aside prior transfers of property that may have been done as a fraud upon creditors. Transfers made within twelve months of the filing of the bankruptcy petition made with the "intent to hinder, delay, or defraud" creditors may be set aside. If a creditor can show reasonable grounds to believe that this occurred, the burden shifts to the petitioner to prove otherwise. Beyond that, transfers could be set aside as fraudulent outside of the framework of bankruptcy at any time within the applicable state statute of limitations for fraud claims, so that the twelve-month period is not an absolute limit. A final limitation is that one may avail himself of bankruptcy proceedings only once every six years.

It should also be remembered that, even if a physician

is judgment-proof, she will still need legal defense if sued, and the fee can be quite large. Some sort of financial assets or contribution by the party to whom assets were previously transferred would be necessary.

Can a health professional sue the patient and his attorney for bringing a frivolous malpractice suit against him?

Yes. There are a number of theories on which suit can be brought, and as recently as 1976 they have been hailed by the American Medical Association as a new weapon that could "discourage the filing of frivolous or nonmeritorious cases. . . ." [45] Suit can be brought on one or more of four grounds: (1) defamation; (2) malicious prosecution; (3) abuse of process; and (4) legal malpractice. The first three can be discussed very briefly because there are few examples and they are almost never successful.

1. *Defamation*

Defamation is almost never available for countersuers because of the *absolute* privilege for judicial proceedings, which shields the judge, jurors, witnesses, and counsel from legal recourse from remarks, utterances, and writings associated with such proceedings. This immunity also includes any proceedings that are "quasi-judicial" in nature, such as an administrative proceeding to revoke a physician's license or to otherwise restrict his medical activities. Therefore, from a practical viewpoint, there is little chance of successful redress by a sued physician on the basis of defamation unless the patient-plaintiff or her attorney have made demonstrably false charges of incompetence and improper professional conduct outside of the courthouse in public gatherings or in the press.[46]

2. *Malicious Prosecution*

In an action for malicious prosecution, the health care professional must prove three things concerning the original malpractice action: (1) that it was terminated in his favor; (2) that it was instituted without probable cause; and (3) that it was motivated by malice of the patient or attorney. The health care professional who settles a malpractice case can never countersue on this basis because settlement, while not an admission of fault, means the case was not terminated in his favor. Thus no settlement can be permitted by the insurer if the health care provider desires to countersue on this basis.[47] Lack of probable cause can be shown only "by prosecuting a claim which a reasonable lawyer would not regard as tenable or by unreasonably neglecting to investigate the facts and the law in making his determination to proceed." [48] Filing a claim just before the statute of limitations runs out, but without adequate investigation, is justified if the case was brought to the lawyer just before the statute was to run out, and the lawyer believed the case meritorious. Malice itself can usually be inferred from the filing of a claim without probable cause.[49]

3. Abuse of Process

The key to this action is a showing that the patient and her lawyer "misused" the legal system in bringing their original malpractice claim. The usual element of proof is that they had an "ulterior purpose or motive," such as coercing a physician to waive his fee, rather than a meritorious case.[50] This action does not require successful termination of the original lawsuit, and is not barred by settlement of the original lawsuit without admission of liability, nor does it require a demonstration that the suit was initiated without probable cause.[51] Nevertheless, such cases are extremely difficult to win. For example, in one case where a physician successfully sued an attorney for abuse of process, the lawyer did not obtain his client's medical records, never conferred with a physician, and, shortly before trial, was willing to settle for $750. The jury found malice on the basis that he was trying coerce a nuisance settlement and returned a verdict of $35,000 and $50,000 punitive damages.[52]

The fourth basis, legal malpractice, is the subject of the next question.

Do lawyers owe health care professionals a duty not to file frivolous suits?

Dr. Leonard Berlin, whose trial-court victory was in a countersuit for legal malpractice was later reversed on appeal, put the rationale for such suits bluntly:

The school bully who harasses innocent children in the playground isn't stopped by reporting to his par-

ents (the bar association or licensing authority)—
he's only stopped by a punch in the face. Lawyers
who abuse the court system similarly can only be
stopped through the same system.[53]

Under a similar rationale, the California Medical Association is currently providing financial and legal research
support in at least 20 countersuit cases in that state.[54]
Nevertheless, as of this writing, there have been *no*
appeals court decisions in favor of countersuers on this
basis, and only two published out of court settlements: A
Boca Raton, Florida, cardiologist collected $15,000 from
two lawyers; and a physician in Montana collected $9,800
—which covered all his expenses of defending the original
malpractice case.[55] In Florida, a $175,000 jury award to
an orthopedic surgeon (reduced to $75,000 by the judge)
is currently on appeal.[56]

The following three cases are representative of the few
that have reached the appeals courts to date, and other
courts are likely to follow their reasoning.

In a Texas case a physician was granted summary judgment in his favor in a suit for failure to properly treat and
diagnose injuries sustained by the plaintiff in an accident.
The physician then sued both the plaintiff and his lawyer,
saying they should have known that the suit was ground-
less and unfounded, and that the allegations made were
untrue. He sought $750,000, alleging mental trauma re-
quiring psychiatric treatment, increases in his malpractice
premiums, public ridicule, and loss of earnings. The lower
court granted summary judgment in favor of the attorney
and his client, and the appeals court affirmed. In a very
brief opinion the court made it clear that under Texas law
attorneys simply could not be sued on the basis of the
facts alleged by the physician, noting that he failed to
properly allege a case for abuse of process, malicious
prosecution, contempt of court, or invasion of privacy—
the only actions the court seemed to consider as plausible
under the circumstances.[57]

A more recent New York case involved a physician who
was sued for negligent treatment of a patient even though
he did not see the patient at all during the course of the
illness in question. The physician sought $200,000 from
the lawyer for (among other things) failing to properly

investigate the case, filing a frivolous lawsuit, and practicing law in "a malicious and unethical fashion with a reckless disregard for the truth or falsity of the allegations." The court quickly disposed of the notion that the attorney had any duty toward the defendant-physician in a malpractice suit:

> The courts of this State have consistently held that an attorney is not liable to third parties for the negligent performance of his obligations to a client, even where such negligence results in damage to third parties . . . for to hold an attorney personally responsible for instituting a frivolous action on behalf of a client would operate to discourage free resort to the courts for the resolution of controversies, contrary to public policy.[58]

The final case involved a surgeon who had performed an emergency hernia repair operation on a three-month-old boy. The parents alleged she had damaged one of the infant's testicles in the operation and filed suit on this basis. At trial all expert witnesses, including the two called by the plaintiff, testified on behalf of the surgeon. All said there was no evidence of damage. The plaintiff's lawyer had not spoken to his witnesses prior to trial about their testimony. The surgeon accordingly sued the lawyer for $6,000, alleging he "owed an affirmative duty to her and to the public at large to refrain from filing groundless litigation," and that he would have known the suit was groundless with a minimum of investigation. The court found that the lawyer's clients could certainly sue the lawyer for "negligence or ineptitude" causing the loss of the case. In examining the canons of legal ethics, however, the court was unable to find a clear duty on the part of lawyers to the defendants in the suits they prosecute. The court noted that the canons *permitted* a lawyer "who discovers his client has no case" to withdraw from the case, but did not require it, if the client was determined to continue. The court concluded its discussion by noting (similar to the New York court) that the courts must be open to all persons for "redress of wrongs," and that permitting such a lawsuit against an attorney would have a "chilling effect . . . on the basic right of a citizen to seek redress in court for what he considers to be a wrong."[59]

What should the health care professional consider before initiating a countersuit?

The primary consideration is the validity of the claim; the second consideration is what the provider wants to get out of it. There are few health care professionals who have the stamina and desire of Dr. Leonard Berlin to devote four years of their lives to litigation, writing, and speaking on the topic of countersuits.[60] Others might believe that meritorious countersuits will discourage future frivolous lawsuits, and it may have this effect on the margin. Still others may gain a psychological revenge on a negligent lawyer.

One should realize, however, that the probability of success is slight, the cost of such litigation high, and continued litigation takes the health care provider away from her work and into a foreign arena that is likely to prove psychologically traumatic.[61] In addition, a frivolous countersuit could itself lead to a "counter-countersuit" and so on indefinitely. The first such counter-counter suit was filed by attorney Harry Burglass against Dr. Rowena Spenser—they are the principals in the last case discussed in the answer to the preceding question—and her attorneys for malicious prosecution, defamation of character, and "experimenting" with a new point of law at the expense of his reputation. He is suing for $902,500.[62] It could also lead to a counterclaim on the original action. For example, in one case a countersuit led to a counterclaim for breach of contract.[63]

NOTES

1. R. Long, The Law of Liability Insurance §1.02, at 1–4; J. Waltz & F. Inbau, Medical Jurisprudence 302 (N.Y.: Macmillan, 1971).

2. Schroeder, *Insurance Protection and Damage Awards in Medical Malpractice*, 25 Ohio St. L.J. 323, 325 (1964).

3. Aetna Cas. & Sur. Co. v. Evers, 590 F.2d 600 (5th Cir. 1979).

4. *E.g.*, Sherwood v. Stein, 261 La. 358, 259 So.2d 876 (1972). *See* Note, *A Study of Medical Malpractice Insur-*

ance: Maintaining Rates and Availability, 9 IND. L. REV. 594, 599 (1976).

5. *E.g.,* Casey v. Transamerica Life Ins. & Annuity Co. 511 F.2d 577 (7th Cir. 1975); Orion Ins. Co. v. Firemen's Ins. Co., 46 Cal. App.3d 374, 120 Cal. Rptr. 222 (1975).

6. See Kroll, *Choosing the Right Legal Liability Insurance,* 22 PRAC. LAWYER 41, 42 (1976).

7. Comment, *The "Claims Made" Dilemma in Professional Liability Insurance,* 22 U.C.L.A.L. REV. 925 (1975).

8. Kroll, *supra* note 6.

9. Martin, *Forming a Mutual Malpractice Insurance Company,* 29 TAX LAWYER 581, 584 (1977).

10. Adametz, *Timely Notice to Liability Insurer,* 209 JAMA 1271 (1969); Hall, *Physician's Obligations to Insurance Company,* 199 JAMA 185 (1967).

11. Bergh v. Canadian Universal Ins. Co., 197 So.2d 847 (Fla. 1967).

12. Sohm v. United States Fid. & Guar. Co., 352 F.2d 65 (6th Cir. 1965).

13. United States Fid. & Guar. Co. v. Ditoro, 206 F. Supp. 528 (M.D. Pa. 1962).

14. Public Serv. Mut. Ins. Co. v. Levy, 395 N.Y.S.2d 1 (N.Y. Sup. Ct., App. Div. 1977).

15. *See, e.g.,* Canadian Universal Ins. Co. v. Northwest Hosp. Inc., 389 F.2d 559 (7th Cir. 1968).

16. D. LOUISELL & H. WILLIAMS, 2 MEDICAL MALPRACTICE ¶20.05, at 593.1 (New York: Matthew Bender, 1973).

17. Zukaitis v. Aetna Cas. & Sur. Co., 236 N.W.2d 819 (Neb. 1975).

18. See Medical Protective Co. v. Light, 48 Ohio App. 508, 194 N.E. 446 (1934).

19. Noe v. Kaiser Foundation Hosps. 435 P.2d 306 (Cal. 1967).

20. 33 CITATION 6 (A.M.A., April 15, 1976).

21. Hartogs v. Employer Mut. Liab. Co., 89 Misc.2d 468, 391 N.Y.S.2d 962 (1977).

22. Roy v. Hartogs, 381 N.Y.S.2d 587 (1976).

23. 391 N.Y.S.2d at 965.

24. A. MORITZ & R. MORRIS, HANDBOOK OF LEGAL MEDICINE 153 (4th ed.; St. Louis: C. V. Mosby, 1975).

25. McFarling v. Azar, 519 F.2d 1075 (5th Cir. 1975).

26. St. Paul Fire & Marine Ins. Co. v. Aragona, 365 A.2d 309 (Md. Ct. of Special App., 1976).

27. Schwamb v. Firemen's Ins. Co., 394 N.Y.S.2d 632, 363 N.E.2d 356 (N.Y. Ct. App. 1977).

28. Rogers v. Robson, Masters, Ryan, Brummond & Belon, 74 Ill. App. 3d 467 (1979), aff'd 81 Ill. 2d 201 (1980). *See* Holloway v. Pacific Indem. Co., 422 F. Supp. 1036 (D.C. Mich. 1976).

29. *See* Canadian Universal Ins. Co. v. Employers Surplus Lines Ins. Co., 325 So.2d 29 (Fla. Dist. Ct. App. 1976); Firemen's Fund Ins. Co. v. Security Ins. Co., 367 A.2d 864 (N.J. 1976).

30. Gruenberg v. Aetna Ins. Co., 9 Cal.3d 566, 510 P.2d 1032, 108 Cal. Rptr. 480 (1973).

31. Garner v. American Mut. Liab. Ins. Co., 31 Cal. App.3d 843, 107 Cal. Rptr. 604 (1973).

32. *E.g.*, Johansen v. California State Auto. Ass'n. Inter-Ins. Bureau, 123 Cal. Rptr. 288, 538 P.2d 744 (1975).

33. Maguire v. Allstate Ins. Co., 341 F. Supp. 866 (D. Del. 1972).

34. Rova Farms Resort, Inc. v. Investors Ins. Co. of America, 65 N.J. 474, 323 A.2d 495 (1974).

35. Palmer v. Pacific Indem. Co., 74 Mich. App. 259, 254 N.W.2d 52 (1977).

36. Note, *Insurance Law—Medical Malpractice Insurance— Cancellation of Policy to Deter Doctors from Providing Expert Testimony*, B.C. INDUS. & COMM. L. REV., March 1970 at 545, 549.

37. L'Orange v. Medical Protective Co., 394 F.2d 57 (6th Cir. 1968).

38. Spindle v. Travelers Ins. Cos., 136 Cal. Rptr. 404 (Cal. Ct. App. 1977).

39. *E.g.*, Folgate v. Brookhaven Mem. Hosp. 381 N.Y.S.2d 384 (N.Y. Sup. Ct. 1976) (referred to a recently enacted state statute).

40. *E.g.*, Poulin v. Zartman, 548 P.2d 1299 (Ala. 1976).

41. Torres v. Sentry Ins., 558 P.2d 400 (Okla. 1976).

42. Takahashi, *Self-Insurance: Can It Be a Viable Alternative in the Crisis?* FAH REV. (Feb. 1977) at 43.

43. Dixon, *"Going Bare" May Be Hazardous to Your Fiscal Health*, J. LEGAL MED. (Nov.–Dec. 1976) at 23.

44. Downey, *Some Rights and Liabilities of "Going Bare,"* J. LEGAL MED. (June 1977) at 13, 14.

45. American Medical News, June 14, 1976 at 1.

46. PROSSER, LAW OF TORTS 777–81 (4th ed. St. Paul: West

Pub. Co., 1971), *See,* e.g., Star v. Simonelli, 428 N.Y.S. 2d 617 (App. Div. 1980).

47. Note, *Malicious Prosecution: An Effective Attack on Spurious Medical Malpractice Claims?* 26 CASE W. RES. L. REV. 653 (1976). *And see* Note, *Physican Countersuits: Malicious Prosecution, Defamation and Abuse of Process as Remedies for Meritless Medical Malpractice Suits,* 45 CIN. L. REV. 604 (1976).

48. Norton v. Hines, 49 Cal. App.3d 917, 123 Cal. Rptr. 237 (1975).

49. *See Malicious Prosecution, supra* note 47 at 660. *And see* Butler v. Morgan, 590 S.W.2d 543 (Tex. Civ. App. 1979).

50. Patete v. Baker, 302 N.E.2d 416, 14 Ill. App.3d 385 (1973), Babb v. Sup. Ct. of Sonoma Co., 3 Cal.3d 841, 497 P.2d 379 (1971).

51. Cassidy v. Cain, 251 N.E.2d 852 (1969).

52. Bull v. McCluskey, 615 P.2d 957 (Nev. 1980). A settlement for $5,000 has also been reported in the press. Lee v. Wright discussed in *Dentist Wins Liability Countersuit,* Am. Med. News, April 20, 1979, at 3.

53. *Dr. Berlin Tells Why He Countersued,* American Medical News, Impact/4, March 28, 1977.

54. Tell, *Doctors Find No Cure in Countersuits,* NATIONAL LAW J. (Feb. 12, 1979) at 1, 8.

55. *Id.*

56. Sullivan v. Terry, No. 75–565–CA (19th Judicial Cir., Fla. Ct. App.).

57. Wolfe v. Arroyo, 543 S.W.2d 11 (Tex. Ct. App. 1976).

58. Drago v. Buonagurio, 89 Misc.2d 171, 391 N.Y.S.2d 61 (Sup. Ct. 1977), *rev'd,* 61 App. Div. 2d 282, 402 N.Y.S. 2d 250 (3rd Dept. 1978), *rev'd,* N.Y.2d 778, 413 N.Y.S. 2d 910, 386 N.E.2d 821 (1978). *And see* Note, *Physician's Cause of Action against Attorneys for Institution of Unjustified Medical Malpractice Actions: The Aftermath of Drago v. Buonagurio,* 44 ALBANY L. REV. 188 (1979).

59. Spencer v. Burglass, 337 So.2d 569 (La. Ct. App. 4th Cir. 1976), *cert. den.* 340 So.2d 990 (La. 1977). *And see* O'Toole v. Franklin 279 Ore. 513, 569 P.2d 561 (1977); Carroll v. Kalar, 112 Ariz. 595, 545 P.2d 411 (1976); Bickel v. Mackie, 447 F. Supp. 1376 (N.D. Iowa 1978); Petrou v. Hale, 260 S.E.2d 130 (N.C. App. 1979). *See*

Birnbaum, *Physicians Counterattack: Liability of Lawyers for Instituting Unjustified Medical Malpractice Actions*, 45 FORDHAM L. REV. 1003 (1977).

60. *See, e.g.*, Berlin, *Make Sure Your Malpractice Defense Attorney Defends You*, Medical Economics, July 11, 1977, at 17.

61. *See generally* Tillotson & Sagall, *Physician Countersuits: More Than Having to Say You're Sorry*, MEDICOLEGAL NEWS (Summer, 1977) at 1.

62. American Medical News, Aug. 1, 1977, at 1. The case is proceeding: Burglass v. Spencer, 370 So.2d 577 (La. 1979).

63. Cooper v. Reaves, 365 So.2d 670 (Ala. 1978).

XIV

Advertising and Compensation

This chapter deals more explicitly than any other with two of the major business aspects of health care: advertising services and getting paid for them. Since it is related to the free-speech issues raised by advertising, the problem of defamation is also included.

Recent years have seen a myriad of lawsuits and regulations designed to increase competition in the health care fields, with emphasis on the right to advertise. Similarly, defamation has taken on new importance to health care professionals with the establishment of professional standards review organizations, utilization review, claims review by insurance companies, and other forms of peer review. Many who serve as reviewers are concerned about their potential liability, as are many who aid licensing boards in disciplinary proceedings. Finally, health professionals deserve to get paid for the services they provide for patients, and many legal issues are raised by the interpretation and enforcement of contracts between providers and patients.

What is the origin of restrictions on advertising by physicians?

The early movement in this area was designed primarily to ban fraudulent advertising by quacks and advertising for fraudulent drug remedies. Just after World War I, organized medicine was particularly interested in discouraging group practices, and used a ban on advertising to this end. There was also the feeling that advertising was an unseemly practice for a learned profession.[1] Whatever the early motives, the medical licensure laws or regulations of licensing boards in two-thirds of the states either restrict or completely prohibit solicitation and advertising.[2] Also, local medical societies have adopted the AMA's ban on "solicitation," resulting in a virtually total lack of advertising by doctors. Dentists, pharmacists, optometrists, and other health care providers have been similarly treated either by state law or by professional ethical codes.

How has the ban on advertising been enforced?

Surprisingly, the ban on advertising has not been enforced by state licensing agencies, but has been enforced by local medical societies. Although these local medical societies do not have the power to revoke a physician's license, they can expel him from the local medical society. Such expulsion may result in the loss of hospital privileges, may require other physicians not to refer patients to a physician so expelled, and may greatly increase the cost of a physician's malpractice insurance.[3] This relatively informal system has been extremely effective.

Is it legal for medical societies to ban advertising by their members?

In recent action, the Federal Trade Commission (FTC) has documented the practices of the AMA and certain local medical societies in enforcing the ban against advertising by physicians.[4] The administrative law judge for the FTC found that the AMA's and local societies' restrictive practices have deprived consumers of information necessary to make an informed choice of health care, and have discouraged, restricted, or eliminated new methods of health care. As a result, the FTC found that the ban on advertising constituted unfair methods of competition and unfair acts, and violated the Federal Trade Commission Act. The FTC ordered the parties to refrain from such acts in the future. Medical societies are free, however, to curb false or deceptive advertising. The U.S. Court of Appeals upheld the F.T.C.'s action.[5]

It is important to note that after the FTC's action was started in 1975, the AMA issued updated guidelines on physicians' advertising. In 1976 the Judicial Council of the AMA stated that the Principles of Medical Ethics

do not proscribe advertising: they proscribe the solicitation of patients. Advertising means the action of making information or intention known to the public. The public is entitled to know the names of physicians, the type of their practices, the locations of their offices, their office hours, and other useful information that will enable people to make a more informed choice of physician.[6]

Although the rest of the statement is somewhat vague, it does permit doctors to advertise through the "accepted local media," and lists office signs, professional cards, telephone-directory listings, and "reputable directories" as "examples" of "acceptable media." The physician, under these guidelines, is entitled to publish information regarding fees, and may also publish other "relevant facts" about himself, as long as they are not false, misleading, or deceptive.

May states outlaw advertising by health care professionals?

Many states have laws or regulations that prohibit such advertising. Early court decisions found such state practices proper. One 1935 Supreme Court case found that a state ban on advertising by dentists did not violate the due-process clause of the Fourteenth Amendment.[7] Other cases upheld restrictions on advertisements for optometrists' services [8] and for eyeglass frames.[9] And in one case the Supreme Court held that "commercial speech" was not protected by the Constitution.[10] Recent cases, however, have reexamined and overruled this position, opening the door for professional advertising.

The more recent cases scrutinize state prohibitions on advertising in terms of the First Amendment's protection of free speech. In 1975, a newspaper in Virginia published an advertisement announcing that abortions were legal in New York, and offered the services of an agency there.[11] The publisher was found guilty of violating a Virginia statute that made the circulation of any publication to encourage or promote the obtaining of an abortion "illegal." The Supreme Court in this case, however, noted that the advertisement did more that simply propose a commercial transaction; it continued "factual matter of clear public interest." [12] Therefore, although there was a strong indication that commercial speech would now be protected by the First Amendment, there was still some slight question.

Is commercial speech (advertising) protected by the First Amendment?

Yes. The case that decided this involved a Virginia statute that prohibited pharmacists from advertising drug prices.[13] The issue was whether the statement, "I will sell you the X prescription at the Y price" is protected by the First Amendment. The answer is an unqualified "Yes." [14]

The state tried to justify its ban by arguing that it was necessary to protect the consumer's health—that advertising will drive down prices, which will force the pharmacist to economize and render an inferior service; or that customers will shop around, which will make individual attention and the practice of monitoring impossible. The Court countered these arguments by pointing out that the high professional standards of pharmacists are guaranteed by the close regulation to which pharmacists in Virginia are subject, and that a pharmacist who is derelict in his duty is subject to license revocation. The court noted that a pharmacist will now be able to advertise his superior product, and contrast it to that of a low-cost, high-volume prescription-drug retailer, and went on to say that the state may set professional standards for pharmacists, or subsidize or protect them in other ways. But the state may not do so by "keeping the public in ignorance of the entirely lawful terms that competing pharmacists are offering." [15]

As a result of this case, a state may not prohibit a truthful advertisement for a *product*. However, the Court reserved the question of advertising for professional *services*.[16]

May a state prohibit the advertising of professional services?

No. The relevant case involved two lawyers who placed an advertisement in a newspaper offering "legal services at very reasonable fees," and listed their fees for certain specific services such as uncontested divorces, personal bankruptcy proceedings, and adoptions.[17] This advertisement violated disciplinary rules of the state bar, and the lawyers were suspended from practice for one week. The U.S. Supreme Court held that the total prohibition of such advertising violates the First Amendment. However, the Court pointed out that its ruling in this case was limited to price advertising, and not to advertising regarding the *quality* of the offered services. Additionally, the court reserved the question of the regulation on in-person solicitation.

In attempting to justify its advertising ban the state made a number of arguments that are analogous to those made to justify bans on advertisements for health care services.

1. It was argued that price advertising would bring about commercialization, which would undermine the attorney's sense of dignity and self-worth. As a corollary, it was argued that such advertising would undermine the client's trust in his attorney once the client perceived that the lawyer is motivated by profit.

The Court responded by pointing out that clients already know that lawyers charge for services, and that bankers and engineers advertise without having their reputations put in question. The Court also noted that the public's inability to locate a competent attorney at a reasonable price caused more public cynicism with regard to the profession than the existence of advertising.

2. The state argued that all lawyers' advertising would be misleading because services are so individualized that the consumer of such services cannot know ahead of time what services he needs, and because advertising would highlight irrelevant factors and fail to show the relevant factor of skill.

The Court responded by pointing out that routine services, such as the ones advertised, could be fairly advertised with a price, that for years lawyers had used minimum fee schedules mandated by their bar associations for a variety of services (a practice found to be illegal [18]), and that lawyers are often retained for a particular purpose by a client, such as an adoption or divorce. In responding to the final point, the Court found it odd that the state would argue that the public is better served by no advertising than by merely incomplete advertising. It was also felt that such an argument underestimated the public's sophistication and its knowledge of the limits of advertising.

3. The state argued that advertising would increase over-

head costs, which would be passed on to clients in the form of higher fees. Additionally, increased costs would create a barrier to young attorneys entering the market.

The Court pointed out that these arguments are not based on anything unique about attorneys, and therefore it could not see why price advertising would not lower costs. It also pointed out that the availability of advertising would make it easier for a new lawyer to enter the marketplace.

4. The state argued that advertising would lead to lower quality service.

The Court responded by saying that those who offer shoddy service in an effort to increase income will do so regardless of advertising.

Although the Supreme Court forcefully struck down prohibitions on price advertising for professional services, it emphasized that false, deceptive or misleading advertising may be prohibited. It also hinted that advertising regarding quality of services (a matter not addressed in this case) is not susceptible to measurement or verification and therefore may be subject to special restriction. Finally, the Court suggested that reasonable restrictions on the time, place, and manner of advertising may be permissible, and that advertising on electronic media may warrant special consideration.

Every point that the Court made in this case is applicable to the health professions.

How have these cases affected the health care professions?

Since these cases were decided, a number of courts and legislatures have acted: a Tennessee court has struck down a prohibition on advertising by optometrists,[19] an Ohio court has struck down a prohibition on dentists' advertising,[20] a federal court in Virginia struck down a state ban on physicians' providing information to a consumer organization so that it could issue a directory,[21] and a New York federal court decided that clinical laboratories can advertise to the general public.[22] On July 28, 1977, the New York Board of Regents voted to permit all professionals under its jurisdiction to advertise.[23]

What limits have been placed on advertising subsequent to these decisions?

A superior court judge in California has upheld certain state-mandated limitations on physician advertisements, including bans on the use of before-and-after photographs, testimonials from satisfied patients, and statements comparing physicians' methods.[24] The U.S. Supreme Court has upheld the Texas Optometry Act, which prohibits the practice of optometry under a trade name, since such a practice could deceive consumers in a number of ways, and does not provide them with any useful information.[25] Additionally, at least seventeen states have barred lawyer billboard advertising by lawyers,[26] which will eventually lead to a test of the Supreme Court's language that seems to permit restriction on time, place, and manner of advertising.

What is the difference between solicitation and advertising?

The line between advertising and solicitation is far from clear, but one can think of advertising as messages directed to the general public, whereas solicitation is an attempt to induce a particular consumer to avail himself of a specific provider's products or services.

Although the AMA's principle of medical ethics prohibits "solicitation," its definition really seems to encompass advertising practices it wishes to discourage. Thus, it defines "solicitation" as the attempt to obtain patients by "persuasion or influence," or by using statements that contain testimonials, that create or are likely to create unjustified expectations of favorable results, that are self-laudatory and imply the physician has skills superior to other physicians in his field, or that contain misrepresentations. Since all these practices may be contained in a newspaper advertisement, it would seem that these are really advertising guidelines, and do not truly describe the problem of solicitation.

The year after the U.S. Supreme Court issued its ruling permitting lawyers to advertise, it upheld disciplinary action against an attorney accused of soliciting clients.[27] In this case a lawyer went to the hospital room of an automobile accident victim and convinced her to employ him as her attorney. He also approached a passenger in the car who was released from the hospital one day prior to his approaching her. The Court held that such in-person solicitation by a lawyer for remunerative employment may exert so much pressure on the potential client, may be so one-sided, and may so discourage the potential client from engaging in a critical comparison of the availability, nature, and prices of legal services, that the practice may be prohibited. The Court was also concerned that, unlike printed advertising, in-person solicitation is not open to public scrutiny.

The Court decided another case the same day that demonstrates the hazy nature of the line between permissible and impermissible conduct. This case involved a lawyer who, at the request of a community organization, gave a lecture on the legal rights of women who had been subject to abusive sterilization practices.[28] The lawyer was also a cooperating attorney for the local branch of the American Civil Liberties Union, which was willing to represent women who were illegally sterilized, free of charge. Some time later, the organizer of the lecture informed the lawyer that one of the women who had attended the lecture wished to file a lawsuit against her doctor. The lawyer wrote this woman a letter informing her that the ACLU would be willing to represent her in this case. As it turned out, this woman later decided not to sue; however, the lawyer involved was disciplined by the bar association for solicitation. The Supreme Court decided that the lawyer's activity was permissible inasmuch as it did not involve in-person solicitation for gain. Neither the lawyer nor the ACLU would be enriched by prosecuting this action, and the woman received the letter after learning about her rights and telling another person that she desired to file a suit. As a result, the letter did not afford any significant opportunity for overreaching or coercion. The Court also pointed out that the lawyer's actions were taken to express political beliefs and to advance the civil-liberties objectives of the ACLU rather than to derive financial gain, and were, therefore, further protected under the First Amendment.

After these cases were decided, lawyers in New York [29] and Minnesota [30] were disciplined for direct-mail solicitation of new clients. In these cases the lawyers made offers to represent people, each in one specific type of case—real-estate transactions in one case, and representation against the manufacturer of the Dalkon Shield IUD in the other. In both cases appeals have been filed.

The area of solicitation is very poorly defined at this point. As a general rule, in-person solicitation for purposes of personal gain may be prohibited because of the potential for coercion and overreaching. This issue of mail solicitation is unresolved.

What is defamation?

Defamation is an "invasion of the interest in reputation and good name," and consists of two separate legal actions: libel, which involves writing, and slander, which involves verbal communications.[31] It involves communications that would "diminish the esteem, respect, goodwill or confidence in which the plaintiff is held, or . . . excite adverse, derogatory or unpleasant feelings or opinions against him."[32] Certain categories of slander and libel enable a plaintiff to successfully bring such a suit without proving actual damages. One of these categories involves the loss of reputation by those engaged in a business or profession.[33]

In order for someone to commit either libel or slander the defamatory statement must be "published," that is, communicated to a third party. Such communication can be made orally, in writing, by pictures, gestures, or otherwise.

Do different standards exist for public and nonpublic figures?

Yes. In the landmark 1964 decision *New York Times* v. *Sullivan,* the Supreme Court drew a distinction between "public officials" and nonpublic persons.[34] In that case the *New York Times* published an advertisement placed by a civil rights group that contained a few insignificant misstatements of fact. The police commissioner of Montgomery, Alabama, sued the *Times* for libel, and received a verdict of $500,000. The Supreme Court overturned the verdict, and expressed fear that such judgments would have a chilling effect on the free press. This was especially true here since the Alabama law, like those of most states at the time, held a publisher of a false and defamatory statement strictly liable, and responsible even for errors committed in good faith. Thus, the court adopted a rule that a public official could not recover damages for a defamatory falsehood relating to his official conduct unless he could prove that the statement was made "with knowledge that it was false or with reckless disregard of whether it was false or not." [35] In later opinions this rule has been extended to cover "public figures," not just "public officials." [36]

A more recent case distinguished between three types of public figure.[37] First, there are those who have general fame and notoriety in the community and are public figures for all purposes. Second, there are those who are "involuntary public figures," for example, someone who has been arrested, or is under investigation by a public official. The third category involves those who voluntarily inject themselves into a public controversy in order to influence the outcome. The second and third categories mean that a person will be a public figure for some purpose and not for others.[38] When a person is a "public figure," it is extremely difficult for him to win a defamation suit. However, after this case, even a nonpublic figure must prove that the defamatory falsehood was the defendant's fault. This will probably involve some sort of negligence standard, although that determination will be initially left up to individual states.[39]

Since it is very difficult for a public figure to win a defamation suit, a good deal of time has been spent by the courts in making this determination. It is an area fraught with confusion. One federal judge has stated that "defining public figures is much like trying to nail a jellyfish to the wall." [40] Recently the courts seem inclined to exclude people from the public-figure category whenever possible. For example, it has recently been held that a wealthy socialite was not a public figure in regard to the details of her divorce; [41] that a well-known civil-liberties lawyer representing a family in a civil suit against a policeman was not a public figure; [42] and that a researcher funded with federal money who was "awarded" the "Golden Fleece Award" by Senator William Proxmire of Wisconsin was not a public figure when he sued the senator.[43]

Although most of these cases involve suits against the media, these principles would also be applicable to private individuals since they, too, are protected by the First Amendment.[44] Therefore, if an individual is sued for defamation, he may argue that the plaintiff is a public figure which, if true, would require the plaintiff to prove his case under the more stringent standard.

What other defenses are available to defendants in defamation cases?

Truth is a defense to both slander and libel, even if the defendant's motives are less than pure.[45]

Additionally, there are individuals who, because of their positions, are absolutely immune from suits imputing slander and libel. These include judges, jurors, witnesses, attorneys, and others involved in a judicial proceedings and quasi-judicial proceedings such as license-revocation proceedings. Individuals involved in legislative proceedings and executive proceedings are also immune from suit. Federal officials acting within their scope of duty are immune from such suits even when their actions approach malice.[46]

Finally, there exists a qualified privilege. This comes about when the publication is "fairly made by a person in the discharge of some public or private duty, whether legal or moral, or in the conduct of his own affairs, in matters where his interest is concerned." [47] This qualified privilege has been invoked to insulate speech designed to protect the safety of another person, or one who acts in the public interest. This would include communications made to those who would be expected to take official action for the protection of the public. In order for the qualified privilege to exist, the person making the communication must act in good faith, and not out of ill will.

How has the law of defamation been applied to the health care field?

Because a health professional's reputation is so important an asset, there are a number of defamation cases involving health professionals.

In one case a nurse asked another nurse to give a patient morphine when magnesium sulfate was ordered by the physician.[48] Although the morphine was not given, the second nurse discussed the incident with a third nurse, and filed a report at the request of the charge nurse. The first nurse sued the second nurse, alleging defamation. The court found that the report and any other actions taken in her professional capacity were privileged and could not form the basis for a suit against her. Remarks made to third persons not within the scope of her duty were not privileged. Although this case involved Veterans' Administration nurses, who have certain immunity as federal officials, this case demonstrates a generally valid point: reports made in an official capacity designed to protect future patients will tend to be privileged, whereas idle gossip will not be so treated.

In another case a physician sued CBS for a broadcast in which he was portrayed as improperly prescribing amphetamines. The court ruled that he was not a public figure, and could therefore prove his case using a relatively low standard of proof.[49] A letter from an insurance company to a patient that states it will not pay a claim for medical treatment because the treatment was not needed was found to be a privileged communication when the physician sued the company.[50] An orderly successfully sued a nurse and hospital for falsely alleging that he stole money from a patient.[51] In another case a chief-of-staff loudly accused a physician of lying and incompetence during an argument in a hallway that was witnessed by several persons. At a dinner with several other physicians the chief-of-staff again made statements about this physician's incompetence, dishonesty, and lack of integrity. The slandered physician received $35,000 for these false indignities.[52]

Is it defamation to report a health professional to a disciplinary board?

As long as such action is taken in good faith and without improper motives, such acts will be covered by a qualified privilege. Additionally, thirty-five states grant some form of specific immunity from civil liability to persons providing information in regard to disciplinary proceedings, and many states give immunity to peer-review committees.[53]

In some states a variety of individuals are *required* to report certain facts concerning physicians. In fourteen states medical societies are required to report disciplinary action they have taken against physicians; hospitals in eighteen states are required to report doctors who have lost their privileges following medical misconduct; clerks of courts in ten states are required to report judgments against physicians in malpractice actions; and in some states physicians are required to report to the disciplinary board information about another physician's misconduct, or any treatment rendered to a physician for alcoholism, drug addiction, and mental disorders.[54] Any report made pursuant to mandated reporting requirements are privileged.

Recently, the State of California has brought disciplinary actions against two surgeons and a nurse for not taking proper action against an anesthesiologist who they allegedly knew was sexually molesting unconscious female patients.[55] Where one is required to report and does not do so, such inaction may support a charge of unprofessional conduct. In this regard it is interesting to note that the AMA Code of Ethics states that physicians "should expose, without hesitation, illegal or unethical conduct of fellow members of the profession." [56]

What can a health professional do to help prevent a successful defamation suit being brought against him?

If a health care professional becomes aware of conduct that he believes should be exposed, certain steps must be followed. Since truth is a defense against charges of defamation, reasonable steps must be taken to assure oneself of the facts. Hearsay and innuendo must be ignored. The report should be made to the proper state or institutional official—and in many states such reports are absolutely privileged. The report should contain objective statements of *fact*, since facts can be verified. The allegation, for example, that someone is a "quack" provides little information and may indicate ill will.[57] One who makes a factual statement in good faith will have little to worry about in terms of defamation suits.

What is a legally enforceable contract?

An analysis of the means by which medical personnel may obtain payment for providing services must discuss the law of contracts. Any service performed by a health care provider for a patient may be construed as a contract, and, as such, entitles him to compensation. However, there may be instances when it will be difficult to prove the existence of a contract.

In general, a legally enforceable contract may be defined as a binding agreement, in a form recognized by law, between two or more competent persons or entities, to do or refrain from doing some lawful act. *Binding*, as used in this context, refers to the presence of legal consideration—any benefit, advantage, labor, price, etc., that is given by one party to the other as an inducement to make the contract.

There are two types of contracts, *express* and *implied*.

An *express* contract arises when its terms, conditions, and consideration are specifically stated and understood by and between the parties. It may be either oral or written.

An *implied* contract is inferred either from the facts or circumstances of the particular situation (*implied in fact*) or from legal considerations (*implied in law*). An implied-in-fact contract will be found to exist if the following four factors are demonstrated:

1. The rendering of a service by one individual for another—for example, a physician for a patient;
2. for which the physician reasonably expected payment;
3. and for which the patient knew or reasonably should have known the physician would expect payments;
4. the patient had an opportunity to reject the physician's services but failed to do so.

Accordingly, if the patient goes to a physician, or calls him, and nothing is specifically said about the fee, the physician is nevertheless entitled to compensation for the services he provided. Thus, while the facts may fail to show that there was a contract formed through mutual assent of the parties, as the process is outlined above, the law will impose a contract upon the parties so that one party will not be unjustly enriched to the other's detriment. Therefore, the party receiving the service will be required to pay for it (and thus will not be unjustly enriched), while the performing party will be entitled to compensation for his performance (and will not therefore suffer a detriment or loss).[58]

What may the physician charge as a fee for his service?

When the contract between the patient and the provider is express, and in the absence of misrepresentation by the provider, the patient who has promised to pay the provider will be bound by that promise to pay the full fee, even though the fee itself may be challenged as excessive or large.[59] However, when the contract is merely implied in fact or in law, the patient will be held responsible to pay the fee only to the extent of its reasonable value.[60] In a court hearing on the matter, the physician will have the burden of proof as to the value of his services.

Just what amount is reasonable depends upon many factors, including:

1. The qualifications of the provider.
2. The amount of time spent in providing the services.
3. The difficulty and/or delicacy of the service provided.
4. The customary fees of other similar providers for like services.
5. The materials used.
6. The patient's ability to pay.[61]

The latter factor is, however, a controversial one. Although many courts allow the consideration of ability to pay in its determination of "reasonableness," there are others that do not consider it appropriate.[62] The AMA's Principles of Ethics do not explicitly mention it, but permit consideration of a patient's ability to pay in determining the physician's fee.[63]

Is a patient obliged to pay for emergency medical care?

When a patient is unconscious and in need of emergency medical care, the law implies a privilege for the physician to render what care is necessary. The patient in such a situation cannot specifically bind himself by an agreement to pay for these services. However, the law will imply a duty to so pay.[64] This implied obligation is to pay a reasonable fee for the emergency medical care rendered. It should be noted that in most jurisdictions, physicians who charge for emergency care are not covered by the state's Good Samaritan statute, even when it would otherwise be applicable.[65]

Does a provider's right to compensation for his services depend on a successful outcome?

Not generally. Thus, in the usual case, a physician who treats a patient will still be entitled to payment if the patient is dissatisfied with the treatment or its results, if the treatment is ineffective, or even if the patient dies.[66] However, in the rare case a provider may contract to cure the patient, and if the provider fails then to do so, the patient would not be liable for any charge. In one case, a physician specifically agreed to cure his patient for a set fee.[67] The patient gave the physician a note in order to secure payment. When this was not paid and the physician sued, the defense was raised that the physician had not succeeded in curing the patient, and therefore was not entitled to payment. The court said a physician may make an express agreement to either cure or not charge, and will therefore be bound by the general rules of contract.

Who pays for services provided a minor?

Minors, like the mentally infirm and intoxicated persons, are treated as a special class by the law, and as such are afforded special privileges with respect to their contracts. Generally, the law provides that the contracts of these persons are not void or totally ineffectual. But their contracts are considered voidable, or cancelable, at the option of the minor, the mentally infirm, or intoxicated individual. Thus, a minor may make a positive statement of disaffirmance and avoid his contract with the provider of the service, but it must be done before reaching the age of majority, or within a reasonable time thereafter. A health care provider must consult the statute in his own state for the legal age at which a minor can no longer disaffirm a contract.

However, the law also imposes an exception to the rule permitting the minor's avoidance. If the minor is "emancipated," as that term is defined by state statute, the minor is solely liable for his medical bills. An emancipated minor is usually defined as one who is married, a parent, in the military, or living away from home while exercising financial independence. However, the minor's agreement is not like that of an adult; upon suit, his liability is not what he originally promised to pay for the services rendered, but for its reasonable value.

Generally, however, a minor will be treated at the request of the parent or guardian. Services rendered in response to a parent's or guardian's request are the financial responsibility of that parent or guardian, and the provider may seek payment from that party.

Beyond that, when a minor contracts for the provision by another of a "necessary," the parent will be financially responsible if the following three conditions apply. The necessary provided—either food, clothing, shelter, or medical care—must be one (1) that has been provided for the personal use of the minor; (2) of which the minor was in need; and (3) for which the minor's parent or guardian refused to provide.[68] This is based on the common law rule that a parent is bound to support his minor child. For example, in one case, a seventeen-year-old girl fractured her leg during a sporting event. Although the foot became badly discolored and difficult to walk on, her parents thought it was merely a sprain and refused to get medical care. Several days later, upon the advice of a friend, she went to the plaintiff for an examination. He took an X-ray, discovered a fracture, and applied a cast. The parents thereupon refused to pay for the physician's services. The physician sued, and although his action was dismissed by the lower courts, the state supreme court reversed and entered judgment for the plaintiff.[69]

Conversely, a parent may contract to pay for the medical care of an adult child, but he is not obligated to do so.[70] And a child is generally not responsible for the medical care provided a parent unless the child specifically assumes that obligation or unless a state statute requires it.[71]

What if a patient wants to pay his fees in installments?

If a patient wants to pay in monthly installments, he may have a financial problem of which the provider should be aware. It is legal to charge the patient a credit or service charge. It should be noted, though, that if the patient is not financially secure, the service charge added to his bill would merely be another burden to bear.

The AMA considers the charging of an interest or penalty on delinquent fee payments to be contrary to the best interest of the public and the profession. However, it is also deemed proper for a physician to charge a service fee to cover the cost of rebilling as long as the patient has been notified in advance of this practice.[72]

The acceptance of installment payments, when interest is charged, subjects the physician to the Federal Truth in Lending Act, which requires, in general, that creditors disclose the finance charges and the annual percentage rate on the credit transaction. Thus, should an interest rate of 2 percent per month be charged, the monthly statement to the patient must show in boldface type, or otherwise conspicuously, the monthly (2 percent) *and* the annual rate (24 percent).

How does one choose a collection agency?

The first rule of choosing a collection agency is to investigate the agency personally. Secure references on the bureau and its manager. Inquire of other professionals as to the agency's reputation in the community. Is the agency well established, or has it only recently begun operations? Who are its customers? Is the agency affiliated with a national or statewide certified association, and, if so, is this agency in good standing with the organization?

Second, one author has stated that you get what you pay for in collection agencies.[73] While only a few will require a contract to be drawn between you and it, most legitimate bureaus work on a contingency basis, charging a percentage of the amount collected. National figures show that an agency's charges of collection run to approximately $0.37 for every $1.00 collected, but bargain rates may be obtained.

According to the AMA's Opinion on Collection Agencies, a physician should consider his ethical responsibilities in referring a delinquent account to a collection agency. Among those considerations, a physician should be concerned with the patient's ability to pay the fee that is due. A physician should not use a collection agency that employs unfair or abusive tactics.[74] Furthermore, a physician must be concerned about maintaining the confidentiality of the doctor-patient relationship. Accordingly, he should ensure that the collection agency is provided only the patient's name and the amount of money owed, and no other information. With certain specialties, such as psychiatry, for which revealing even the name of a patient may be a breach of confidentiality, it may be inappropriate to make use of collection agencies at all.

Should a physician sue a patient for collection of his fees?

It has been suggested that suit would normally be inadvisable when

1. The claim for recovery is small, so that the expenses of litigation and attorney's fees would exceed the claim.
2. The judgment obtained against the debtor-patient would be uncollectable, i.e., the debtor has so bad a credit rating that he could not pay the judgment ordered.
3. The patient-debtor has a defense to the claim.
4. When the patient is so disgruntled with the health care services, treatment, etc., that he claims nothing is owed.[75]

Suit should be seriously considered when no real dispute exists between the physician and the patient, when the only dispute existing is to the amount of the fee due, or when the question exists as to who is responsible for paying the bill.[76] In deciding whether to use legal action in the form of attachment of property, garnishment of wages, or liens, consideration should be given to the effectiveness of the results that could be obtained by suit, the monetary costs of suit, the costs in terms of public relations, and the amount of time involved.

Can a provider collect for an unpaid medical bill against the estate of a deceased patient?

When a patient dies with an outstanding medical bill, state statutes providing for the settlement of estates require that all creditors, including providers, file their claims within a specified period of time. Failure to so file this itemized bill for services rendered will lead to the claim's being barred.[77] The period of time for presenting claims varies with the jurisdiction, but is usually around six months or a year. The statutes also vary as regards the entity to whom the claim must be presented. It may be the probate court or it may be the decedent's personal representative.

Some state laws give a physician a preferred standing concerning payment for services rendered during the decedent's last illness.[78] These statutes generally provide that if someone dies insolvent, the expenses of his funeral and his last illness are to be paid ahead of other claims against his estate. This may mean that the physician who treated the decedent during his last illness will receive full payment, while other creditors will receive only partial satisfaction or none at all.

What should a provider do if a patient sends partial payment for a bill but indicates that it is payment in full?

Should the provider cash the check or should it be returned with a demand for full payment? The answer here depends on the statutes in effect in the state in which a particular physician practices. In some states, the patient's obligation to pay the provider will be fulfilled when he gives, and the provider accepts, something different or less than that to which the provider is entitled. This is the legal theory of "accord and satisfaction."

However, before this doctrine will extinguish the obligation to pay the full bill, the following four elements, or facts, must be present:

1. The debt must be disputed by the patient on good-faith grounds or it must be unliquidated (uncertain in amount).
2. The payment must be accompanied by an express statement that the payment is given in full satisfaction of the debt.
3. Both parties must intend, either expressly or implicitly, to settle the matter.
4. The creditor-provider must cash the check or hold it for an unreasonable amount of time.

If one of these elements is factually lacking, the payment accepted will not release the debtor from his obligation. Thus, if there is no dispute as to the amount due, acceptance of less than total payment will not imply accord and satisfaction.[79]

What defenses may be claimed by a patient to avoid payment of a medical bill?

In addition to accord and satisfaction, discussed above, the patient may raise quite a number of defenses to a collection suit. These include payment, breach of an express contract to cure, malpractice, illegality of the service performed, the fact that the services were rendered gratis or on the credit of another, expiration of the statute of limitations (the period, as defined by state law, within which suit must be brought), and noncompletion of agreed-upon treatment. For example, a Louisiana court found that a patient was obligated to pay a balance due a dentist who acted pursuant to a three-year-old agreement with the patient to fit a prosthetic device.[80] Although begun, the dental treatment was never completed. However, the court determined that the patient had contributed to the impossibility of completion of the dental procedure by, among other things, his failure to return to the dentist's office. The dentist was ordered to deliver the prosthetic devices to the patient, who was free to have them fitted by another dentist or to renegotiate his contract with the first dentist for completion of the dental work.

Another possible defense is to argue that a compromise has been reached in a dispute between the provider and the patient regarding settlement of the account. In such a situation the compromise supersedes any previous claim, and the physician can no longer use the original fee as the basis for a suit.[81] By the same token, the patient can no longer claim that the physician's fee was excessive or that his services were not properly performed.[82]

In another situation, if a provider knowingly makes false representations to his patient, this fraud will give the patient adequate grounds to avoid a claim for payment for services rendered. It can also form the basis for a suit by the patient to recover any fees already paid. For example, in one case the doctor indicated to the patient that medical services were required which the physician knew to be unnecessary.[83] In a similar case, the physician claimed to be able to cure what he knew was an uncurable condition.[84] In both these cases the courts determined that not only could the physicians in question not recover any further compensation, but they had to return those fees already collected.

If the patient is indigent and has no private insurance, are there any government agencies that might pay the provider's fees?

Providers should know the basic eligibility requirements of several of the main medical opportunities for individuals provided by the government.

1. *Medicare*

In general, Medicare is a federal health insurance program for people aged sixty-five or over and for persons who are disabled or who have chronic renal disorders. Its protection includes costs of in-patient hospital care, posthospital extended care, and posthospital home health care under Part A of the coverage. Part B coverage, for which a monthly premium is paid, provides supplemental protection against costs of physicians' services, medical services and supplies, home health care services, out-patient hospital services and therapy, and other services.[85]

2. *Medicaid*

Medicaid is an assistance program funded by federal, state, and local taxes. Although the various states design their own programs within federal guidelines, and each state Medicaid program thus is different, Medicaid is generally for certain specific kinds of needy and low-income persons, such as the aged (sixty-five or older), the blind, the disabled, members of families with dependent children, and other children. Some state programs also include as eligible those persons who are generally categorized as needy and have low incomes. The Medicaid program pays for at least these services: in-patient hospital care, out-patient hospital services, other laboratory and X-ray services, skilled nursing-facility services, and family planning services. Many states also pay for other services, such as dental care, prescription drugs, eyeglasses, etc.

3. *The Veterans' Administration*

This agency provides free medical care to a veteran seeking care for a service-connected disability or for a non-service-connected disability associated with a service-connected disability. If the veteran proves inability to pay for services rendered, the veteran seeking care for a non-service-connected disability will be given free care if (1) the veteran was discharged from the service for line-of-duty disabilities, or (2) the veteran is over sixty-five years of age, or served during wartime, or is eligible for a non-service-connected disability after January 31, 1953.[86]

4. *Other Programs*

Services may be provided without charge by the Federal Public Health Service for merchant seamen, coast guardsmen, and Native Americans. Similarly, many state and county or township governments provide for the medical care of indigent residents. If the patient is suffering from drug abuse or alcoholism, two federal programs assure treatment in private and public hospitals that receive federal funds.[87]

How do insurance plans determine the amount they will pay?

While private insurers are, at an ever-increasing rate, adopting those payment schemes employed by the Medicare program, many still pay claims in a different manner. Generally, the insurance company will establish an "acceptable range" of provider charges for a given service or item in a given locale, based on its claim reviews and consultations with local medical societies. After having chosen a percentile, usually 90 percent, the insurer will pay a claim that is not greater than the charge equaling that 90th percentile. However, provision is also usually made for the payment of fees in excess of the determined level, on justification by the provider.

The key to reimbursement under Medicare is "reasonableness." Under both Parts A and B, payment for a service or item can be made if it is a "reasonable charge," as interpreted to be the lower of the provider's actual charge, the "customary" charge, or the "prevailing" charge. The "actual charge" is what is charged by the provider. The "customary charge" of this provider is the charge normally billed by him to a majority of his patients for the given service as indicated in that provider's fee profile maintained by Medicare. The "prevailing charge," however, is based upon a consideration of what similar providers customarily charged for a similar service in the preceding year.[88] Therefore, the effect of this scheme is to fix the reimbursement level, thereby implicitly setting the provider's fee. Payment under the various Medicaid programs is similar.[89]

Not unlike the Medicare reimbursement system is that currently in effect under many Blue Cross–Blue Shield plans. However, under these, payment is made based on the lower of the "usual" or the "customary" charges. "Usual" is defined as what the provider normally charges for the particular service. "Customary" is a charge falling

below the 90th percentile of charge data collected during
the prior twelve months on other similar providers. Blue
Cross may also consider geographic locality and specialty
designations in its reimbursement determinations.[90]

An important consideration in this area is the extent to
which the physician may bill the beneficiary in excess of
the reasonable charge paid by the program. Under Medicare, the physician has the option of "accepting assignment" on the individual claim. If the physician does so, he
bills Medicare directly and receives direct payment of
80 percent of the reasonable charge. The physician may
then bill the patient for the 20 percent coinsurance plus
any deductible amount that the patient has not yet paid
during that accounting period. The physician may not bill
the patient for any additional amount above the reasonable charge. If the physician refuses assignment, he must
directly bill the patient, who can then receive reimbursement from Medicare for up to 80 percent of the reasonable
charge, exclusive of any deductible payments. Many Medicare beneficiaries now purchase supplemental health insurance to fill in the gaps left by Medicare deductibles,
coinsurance, and noncovered services.

In contrast with Medicare, Medicaid is generally a mandatory assignment program, and physicians can collect no
more for any given service than the maximum payment
allowed by the state Medicaid agency. Those Medicare
beneficiaries who are also Medicaid recipients must be
treated as full assignment patients by participating physicians.

A physician may also become a "participating" provider
under the Blue Cross plan. A "participating" provider is
one who, in effect, is under contract with a Blue Cross–
Blue Shield plan to provide services on items to the plan's
enrollees, and accepts as payment in full the amount paid
by the plan.

**Assuming the patient has some type of insurance cover-
age, how are claims processed?**

Generally, claims processing is similar, regardless of
whether the patient has private insurance like Blue Cross–
Blue Shield, or receives public assistance like Medicaid.
The submitted claim is first examined by a claims reviewer
or adjuster in reference to the insurance contract. Is the

patient insured? Is the service or item provided a covered benefit under the contract? Is the service or item provided at an appropriate charge? These threshold questions are first answered. If there is coverage, the claims reviewer authorizes payment. If some problem is encountered with respect to coverage, the claim will be referred to a claims analyst or to the medical director's office for further examination and decision. Each program also includes a process for disputing a claims decision, such as appeal to higher authorities within the insurance company or by judicial review (see discussion below).

How can a physician establish an efficient claims process?

Because of the intricacies of claims processing by several different groups of insurers—Blue Cross, Medicare, Medicaid, commercial insurers—it may be wise to have one member of the physician's staff deal with the processing of claims. This person should become an insurance specialist and become intimately familiar with the insurance programs and the people administering them. To ensure prompt payment, the physician should in a sense become the patient's advocate in dealing before the insurance companies or programs.

The physician should also learn to handle insurance claim forms efficiently and effectively. When the patient visits the office for an appointment, he should be asked to complete the claim form—i.e., review it for his signature, name, address, and policy number. The date of receipt should be stamped on the form. If the form must be mailed to a party other than the insurance company, the form should be noted as to mailing instructions. Information on and acknowledgment of receipt of the insurance forms should be logged in the patient's record or other record, with a notation as to when the form was mailed to the insurance company or program. An itemized bill for services should always be attached to the completed claims form, unless such information is included on the form itself.[91]

It has also been suggested that claims processing could be facilitated by more fully informing the patient of what is expected of him. Thus, when a new patient comes into a physician's office, he should be given a printed form outlining the doctor's policy on insurance. It should be made clear that the provider will aid in the processing of the claims form, but that the insurance contract is one between the patient and the insurer, and that the contract determines what is and what is not covered.

Mistakes or omissions in a claims form require the insurance company to return it, causing a delay in processing the claim. Examples of mistakes include misspellings, transposed claim numbers, use of nonstandard medical terminology, or the use of an improper service designation. Make sure that the letter suffix is included as the claim number of Medicare beneficiaries. If the service provided was part of a concurrent claim, it should be so indicated, with diagnosis requiring such listed. Furthermore, if the patient encountered complications not apparent from the diagnosis, explain the circumstances to facilitate the claim processing.

Several suggestions regarding the processing of medical claims forms should be noted. It's a good idea to maintain a supply of Medicare forms in the office, in case Medicare patients do not bring their own for completion. Furthermore, the physician should give the patient two copies of his itemized bill, so that one may be attached to the claims form and the other may be kept by the patient for his records. If the patient has a supplemental insurance coverage in addition to Medicare, claims should be sent first to Medicare. When the patient receives the Explanation of Medicare Benefits form and, possibly, payments from Medicare, make a copy of this form, attach it to the supplemental insurance form, and mail both to the supplemental insurance company.

If the provider or insured patient is unsatisfied with the reimbursement determination, is there a right to appeal?

The appellate process for private insurance coverage is usually provided for in the particular insurance contract.

Appeals under Medicare are more complicated. Under Medicare's two coverage plans—Part A, Hospital Insurance, and Part B, Supplemental Medical Insurance (see discussion above), appeals regarding reimbursements may be obtained as follows. Questions concerning the amount of benefits payable under Part A are to be resolved, after administrative review, in an administrative hearing held by the Department of Health and Human Services, which administers Medicare, as set forth in the Social Security Act.[92] However, this hearing is not available to the insured unless the amount in controversy is at least $100. At the quasi-judicial hearing, the insured is offered the opportunity to present his case by introducing evidence and witnesses, and by cross-examining adverse witnesses. A record transcript of the hearing is made for further appeal.[93] An insured may seek judicial review of an unfavorable decision if the amount in controversy is at least $1000. Under 1972 Amendments to the Social Security Act, providers of services under Part A may appeal Medicare cost determinations by filing a claim with a Provider Reimbursement Review Board if the dispute involves at least $10,000 or if the Medicare intermediary delayed more than twelve months in determining the amount of payments to the provider.[94] This board conducts a hearing and considers all evidence before the intermediary which made the initial decision and all other evidence before it. Judicial review of this board's determination may be obtained in a federal district court.

An insured Medicare patient may also appeal questions regarding payments and coverage under Part B.[95] The patient must first request review of the carrier's initial determination within six months of the notification of the decision.[96] However, the process is administrative review only. Thus, the carrier, on receiving a request for review, again looks at the claim. Further administrative review may be had by administrative hearing conducted by Medicare's carrier if the claim involves $100 or more. A hearing officer presides at the hearing and makes the final decision after hearing oral arguments or seeing written documents. No judicial review or further appeal to HHS is afforded.

It is unclear whether or how providers of services may appeal Part B determinations.[97]

How does the federal government protect against abuse by providers under the Medicare and Medicaid programs?

Waste, fraud, and program abuse account for more than $4.5 billion in annual losses in the Medicare and Medicaid programs, according to recent HHS estimates.[98] Public and congressional uproar over these figures has prompted Medicare and Medicaid administrators, in conjunction with the Justice Department, to pursue program offenders more actively. In 1977, the courts handed down 227 convictions for criminal fraud involving federal programs.[99] Thus, a provider who abuses or defrauds the Medicare or Medicaid programs runs a real risk of being discovered and prosecuted.

Two federal statutes have been passed to deal with program fraud and abuse.[100] "Program abuse," although not defined in the statute, includes activities in which providers "operate in a manner 'inconsistent with accepted sound medical or business practices' " and which result in unreasonable costs to the Medicaid or Medicare patient.[101] Examples of possible program abuse include negligent billing practices, the rendering of frequent unnecessary services, or disregard of assignment obligations. The penalties for conviction include suspension of payments, suspension from the program, recoupment of any overpayment, or a combination of these. "Program fraud," again not specifically defined, broadly includes such acts as flagrant breach of the assignment process, the making of false representation regarding conditions of participation in the program, making a false statement or representation of a material fact in connection with receiving benefits, and receiving, paying, soliciting, or offering rebates, kickbacks, bribes, or other remuneration in exchange for doing business under Medicare or Medicaid.[102] The last set of prohibited activities are *per se* violations of the statutes and, thus, the government need not prove specific intent or knowledge on the part of the provider of the unlawfulness of his actions. In addition, as a result of a conviction for fraud or abuse of the programs, a provider may properly be suspended from practicing his profession or have his license revoked.[103]

Similarly, a practitioner may have action taken against his license because of his fraudulent activities in dealing with a private insurance company.[104] For example, a dentist was charged with fraudulently practicing dentistry and unprofessional conduct by the Committee on Professional Conduct of the State Board of Dentistry. He admitted submitting a number of false and fraudulent bills and claims to an insurance company. The board suspended the dentist's license for six months, and a New York court affirmed the decision.

NOTES

1. J. Burrows, A.M.A.: Voice of American Medicine (Baltimore: Johns Hopkins Press, 1963).
2. Canby & Gellhorn, *Physician Advertising: The First Amendment and the Sherman Act,* 19 Duke L. J. 543, 546 (1978).
3. *Id.*
4. *In re* American Medical Association *et al.,* Federal Trade Commission Docket No. 9064 (Initial Decision, Nov. 13, 1978).
5. A.M.A. v. F.T.C., Trade Cas. P63, 569, Oct. 7, 1980 (2d Cir.).
6. 235 JAMA 2328 (1976).
7. Semler v. Oregon Bd. of Dental Examiners, 294 U.S. 608 (1935).
8. Head v. New Mexico Bd., 374 U.S. 424 (1963).
9. Williamson v. Lee Optical, 348 U.S. 483 (1955).
10. Valentine v. Chrestensen, 316 U.S. 52 (1942).
11. Bigelow v. Virginia, 421 U.S. 809 (1975).
12. *Id.* at 822.
13. Va. Code Ann. §54–524.35(3).
14. Virginia State Bd., v. Virginia Citizens Consumer Council, 425 U.S. 748 (1976).
15. *Id.* at 769, 770.
16. *Id.* at 773, n.25.
17. Bates v. State Bar of Ariz., 433 U.S. 350 (1977).
18. Goldfarb v. Virginia State Bar, 421 U.S. 773 (1975).
19. Horner-Rausch Optical Co. v. Ashley, 547 S.W.2d 884 (1976).
20. 46 U.S.L.W. 2414 (Ohio Ct. Common Pleas, Franklin County, Jan. 14, 1978).
21. Health Sys. Agency of No. Va. v. Virginia State Bd. of Med., 45 U.S.L.W. 2253 (Nov. 11, 1976).
22. Metpath, Inc. v. Imperato, 450 F. Supp. 115 (S.D.N.Y. 1978).
23. F. Stock, *Professional Advertising,* 68 Am. J. Pub. Health 1207 (Dec. 1978).
24. *Judge Upholds M.D. Ad Law,* American Medical News, Jan. 11, 1980.
25. Friedman v. Rogers 440 U.S. 1, *reh. denied* 441 U.S. 917 (1979).

26. Aklement, *Lawyers Won't Quit Fight to Advertise on Billboards,* National Law Journal, Nov. 19, 1979, at **6.**
27. Ohralik v. Ohio State Bar, 436 U.S. 447 (1978).
28. *In re* Edna Smith Primus, 436 U.S. 412 (1978).
29. *In re* Koffler, 70 A.D.2d 252, 420 N.Y.S.2d 560 (2d Dept. 1979).
30. *In re* Application for Discipline of Robert J. Appert and Gerald Pyle, Minn. Sup. Ct. File 48803, reported in National Law Journal, April 28, 1980, page 1.
31. PROSSER, LAW OF TORTS, 737 (4th ed., West. 1971).
32. *Id.* at 739.
33. *Id.* at 757.
34. 376 U.S. 254 (1964).
35. *Id.* at 279, 280.
36. Rosenbloom v. Metromedia, Inc., 403 U.S. 29 (1971).
37. Gertz v. Robert Welch, Inc., 418 U.S. 323 (1974).
38. TRIBE, AMERICAN CONSTITUTIONAL LAW 644 (Mineola, N.Y.: Foundation Press, 1978).
39. *Id.* at 645.
40. Rosanova v. Playboy Enterprises, 411 F. Supp. 440, 443 (S.D. Ga. 1976).
41. Time, Inc. v. Firestone, 424 U.S. 448 (1976).
42. *Supra* note 37.
43. Hutchinson v. Proxmire, 443 U.S. 111 (1979); *see* Tybor, *The Libel War Escalates,* National Law Journal, Apr. 21, 1980, at 1.
44. *See* TRIBE, *supra* note 38, at 639, n.6.
45. PROSSER, *supra* note 31, at 797.
46. Barr v. Mateo, 360 U.S. 564 (1959).
47. PROSSER, *supra* note 31, at 786, quoting Toogood v. Spyring 1 C.M. & R.181, 149 Eng. Rep. 1044 (1834); *and see* Mayfield v. Gleichert, 484 S.W.2d 619, 625 (Tex. 1972).
48. Malone v. Longo, 463 F. Supp. 139 (E.D.N.Y. 1979).
49. Greenberg v. C.B.S., 69 A.D.2d 693, N.Y.S.2d 988 (2d Dept. 1979).
50. Turkel v. Aetna Cas. & Sur. Co., 6 Mass. Lawyers Weekly 708 U.S. Dist. Ct. Mass. 1978).
51. Smith v. Dist. of Columbia 399 A.2d 213 (D.C. Ct. of App., Feb. 21, 1979).
52. Bayoud v. Sigler, 555 S.W.2d 913 (Tex. Ct. of Civ. App., Aug. 29, 1977).
53. F. Grad. & N. Marti, Physicians' Licensure and Disci-

pline, 159 (Dobbs Ferry, N.Y.: Oceana Publications, 1980).

54. *Id.* at 138, 139.

55. The Sacramento Bee, B3, Feb. 21, 1980.

56. The American Medical Association Principles of Medical Ethics, §4.

57. *See* McMahon, Letter to the Editor, 302 NEW ENG. J. of MED. 871 (April 10, 1980), discussing the author's experience with the term "quack."

58. Westcott, *Credit, Collections and the Law,* in MEDICAL CREDIT AND COLLECTIONS 110 (Medical Group Management Association, ed.; Denver: 1974).

59. Guild v. Whitlow, 162 Ark. 108, 257 S.W. 383 (1924).

60. *In re* McKeehan's Estate, 358 Pa. 548, 57 A.2d 907 (1948); Poulson v. Foster, 67 S.D. 372, 293 N.W. 361 (1940); Clark v. Diefendorf, 147 A. 33 (Conn. 1929).

61. B. SHARTEL & M. PLANT, THE LAW OF MEDICAL PRACTICE 75, 76 (Springfield, Ill.: Chas. C. Thomas, 1959).

62. *Id.* at 73, 75. *See* A. Moritz & R. Morris, *Compensation for Services,* in DOCTOR AND PATIENT AND THE LAW 53 (5th ed., St. Louis: C. V. Mosby Co., 1971) for cases representative of both sides of the controversy. *See also* Citron v. Fields, 85 P.2d 534 (Calif. 1938); Spencer v. West, 126 So.2d 423 (La. 1960).

63. *Text of AMA's New Principles of Ethics,* American Medical News, Aug. 1/8, 1980, at 9. *See* American Medical Association, Judicial Council Opinions and Reports, Rule 4, 16, at 5, 16 (1977).

64. Schoenberg v. Rose, 145 N.Y.S. 831 (1914).

65. For a further discussion of Good Samaritan statutes, *see* Chapter V.

66. *E.g.,* Mayer v. Piechocinska, 31 N.Y.S.2d 308 (1941); Cotham v. Wisdon, 104 S.W.164 (Ark. 1907); Baird v. Smith, 68 P.2d 979 (Calif. 1937).

67. Helms v. Day, 215 S.W.2d 356 (Tex. 1948).

68. Thompson v. Perr, 238 S.W.2d 22 (Mo. 1951); Osborn v. Weatherford, 170 So. 95 (Ala. 1936). Similarly, *see* Manatee Convalescent Center v. McDonald, No. 80–714 (Dist. Ct. App., Fla., Dec. 31, 1980) for a discussion of a woman's liability for the medical necessaries of her spouse.

69. Greenspan v. Slate, 12 N.J. 426, 97 A.2d 390 (1953).

70. Broadway v. Jeffers, 194 S.E. 642 (S.C. 1938).

71. Lawrence v. Anderson, 184 A. 689 (Vt. 1936).

72. American Medical Association, Judicial Council Opinions and Reports, Rule 4, 31, at 16 (1977). *See* Attorney General Opinion, No. 5809, Michigan, Nov. 3, 1980.

73. Heacox, *How to Choose a Collection Service*, in MEDICAL CREDIT AND COLLECTIONS, *supra* note 58, at 88–89.

74. American Medical Association, Judicial Council Opinions and Reports, Rule 4.03, at 15 (1977).

75. B. SHARTEL & M. PLANT, *supra* note 61, at 80.

76. *See* Porter v. Stormont-Vail Hosp., No. 51, 136 (Sup. Ct. Kan., Dec. 6, 1980). Brown v. Hyslop, 153 Neb. 669, 45 N.W.2d 743 (1951); Cole v. Wagner, 197 N.C. 692, 150 S.E. 339 (1929).

77. Proto v. Chenoweth, 33 Ariz. 261, 263 P. 943 (1928); Barnes v. Baker, 299 S.W. 80 (Mo. App. 1927).

78. Long v. Northrup, 225 Iowa 132, 279 N.W. 104 (1938).

79. Price, *Payment in Full*, in MEDICAL CREDIT AND COLLECTIONS, *supra* note 58, at 106–8.

80. Allen v. Pippin, 327 So.2d 667 (La. Ct. App. 1976).

81. Leff v. Adams, 289 S.W. 102 (Tex. 1926).

82. West v. Wegeforth, 79 Colo. 444, 246 P. 204 (1926).

83. Lake v. Baccus, 59 Ga. App. 656, 2 S.E.2d 121 (1939).

84. Barker v. Weeks, 182 Wash. 384, 47 P.2d 1 (1935).

85. The applicable statutes for Parts A and B are, respectively, 42 U.S.C. §1395(c) and (j), as amended (Supp. 1973).

86. Axlerod, Butler, & Wing, *Representations of Clients in Matters Related to Hospital Bills*, CLEARINGHOUSE REV. (Dec. 1974) at 543–45.

87. *Id.* at 547, 548.

88. *Dealing with Health Insurers*, in ASLM Guide for Internists and Their Staffs, at 3. For the history of federal regulation of fees, *see* Warner, *Trends in the Federal Regulation of Physicians' Fees*, 13 INQUIRY 364 (1976).

89. *Dealing with Health Insurers*, *supra* note 88.

90. *Id.* at 2.

91. *Id.* at 3–5.

92. 42 U.S.C. §1395(ff)(b)(1) and (2), as amended (Supp. 1973).

93. Further details may be found in the Medicare Regulations at 20 C.F.R. §405.701–750 (1978) regarding the conduct of administrative hearings. The reader is also directed to an excellent review of the process in Butler,

Medicare Appeals Procedures: A Constitutional Analysis, 70 Nw. L. Rev. 139 (1975).

94. 42 U.S.C. §1395, as amended (Supp. 1972); 20 C.F.R. §405.1835–1839.

95. 42 U.S.C. §1395(u)(b)(3)(c), as amended (Supp. 1972).

96. 20 C.F.R. §405.807 (1978).

97. Butler, *supra* note 93, at 165–67.

98. American Medical News, April 14, 1978, at 12–13.

99. *Id.*

100. 42 U.S.C. §1395(nn) contains the Medicare anti-fraud and-abuse provisions, and 42 U.S.C. §1396(h) contains the Medicaid counterpart. See Stromberg & Jergesen, *Medicare and Medicaid Anti-Fraud and Abuse Amendments Explained,* HOSPITALS, Aug. 16, 1980, at 64.

101. Epstein & Levy, *The Legal Perspective,* TRUSTEE (Aug. 1978), at 13.

102. *Id.*

103. Carey v. Board of Med. Ex., 136 Cal. Rptr. 91 (1977), has so held. For a more detailed discussion of the issue of loss of license because of conviction for fraud, see Chapter I.

104. Smith v. Nyquist, 383 N.Y.S.2d 443 (N.Y. Sup. Ct., App. Div., 1976).

XV

The Union Movement in Health Care Institutions

Traditionally, the hospital was thought of as a "charity" employer. By hiring the otherwise unemployable, the aged, the handicapped, and the derelicts, hospitals offered them a means for acquiring self-respect, as well as housing, meals, and medical care. Social agencies directed to hospitals people who could not find jobs elsewhere. The New York Commission on Hospital Care described hospitals in the 1850s as "dirty, unventilated, and contaminated with infection. The only lay nurses who could be obtained were women who could get no other employment and were willing to include menial tasks with nursing."[1]

However, hospitals often hired this type of worker in order to keep their costs down by paying less than prevailing wages. This attitude is typified by a comment made by Senator Carl Curtis of Nebraska during a debate over a proposed extension of minimum wage coverage:

My purpose is to exempt from the provisions of this law the voluntary hospitals. These are splendid organizations which provide some employment and some income for people who would otherwise not have any. . . . I think of these charitable, nonprofit hospitals which seek to hold down their labor costs in order that their funds may reach more needy people. . . . many employees serve as a labor of love, as a matter of dedication. . . .[2]

Indeed, many of these workers, a large number of whom belong to minorities, earned so little that they needed supplementary relief from the Welfare Department. Hospital workers in 1959 were paid as little as $26 for a six-day, forty-eight-hour week. Laboratory technicians without PhDs earned $60 a week.

This situation, along with a variety of other reasons, led to attempts to organize hospital workers. The first known attempt to unionize hospital employees took place in San Francisco in the spring of 1919. The issues were shorter hours and improved working conditions. However, it was not until the 1930s that the first large union drive was launched in hospitals. In 1936, the American Federation of Labor organized engine-room, laundry, and dietary employees as well as nurses' aides and orderlies in three San Francisco area hospitals.

In recent years, there has been a marked increase in the organization of health workers at all levels—professional, technical, skilled, and relatively unskilled. This trend towards increased organization for collective activity encompasses the entire health care industry. While the majority of health workers in the United States are still not organized into collective bargaining units—unionization represents about 20 percent of the 2.5 million health workers, compared to about 24 percent of all workers across the country—there is no doubt that the trend will continue and gain momentum.[3] While the goals of health workers in many ways parallel those of workers in other areas, the unique difference in the field of health care delivery is concern for the protection of the interests of a third party, the patient. The balancing of this interest against the protection of the workers' right to organize for their mutual benefit creates the major tension in this area.

May health care workers join labor unions?

Yes. Public Law 93-360, which became effective on August 2, 1974, amended the National Labor Relations Act (NLRA) to include nonprofit hospitals and health care institutions within the jurisdiction of the National Labor Relations Board (NLRB). Before then, union activity was protected at profit-making health care institutions, but nonprofit ones had been excluded. Prior to the 1974 amendments, only twelve states had legislation allowing employees of nonprofit hospitals to unionize; these state statutes have been preempted by inclusion within the federal law.

The original bill, submitted by Congressman Frank Thompson, Jr., of New Jersey was limited to proposing the elimination of the statutory exclusion of hospital employees from the NLRA.[4] However, the amendments as finally passed reflect the Congressional intent to carefully tailor the legislation "to treat the health care industry uniquely." [5] Thus, rather than merely extending NLRA jurisdiction to nonprofit hospitals, Congress included within the bill specific provisions covering the entire health care industry so as to facilitate collective bargaining settlements, while ensuring the continuity of patient care and services.

The policy of the NLRA, as stated in Section 1, is to prevent obstruction of interstate commerce by strikes and labor unrest, to equalize the bargaining power between employees and employers, to assure freedom of association and freedom of contract, and to foster individual peace. Section 7 gives employees the "right to self-organize, right to form, join or assist labor organizations, to bargain collectively through representatives of [their] own choosing, and to engage in other concerted activities for the purpose of collective bargaining or other mutual aid or protection." It also gives them the right to refrain from participating in these activities.

Under NLRA provisions as they apply to non-health care facilities, an employer or labor organization is required, where a collective bargaining agreement is in effect, to provide written notice to the other party at least sixty days prior to the termination or modification of the agreement. There is no notification requirement to any party with regard to initial contract negotiations. In addition, the Federal Mediation and Conciliation Service (FMCS) is required to receive thirty days notice, although there is no obligation on either party to engage in mediation.

These provisions are altered for health care institutions —defined as any hospital, convalescent hospital, health maintenance organization, health clinic, nursing home, extended care facility, or other institution devoted to the care of sick, infirm, or aged persons.[6] The amendment extends the sixty days' notice to ninety days and requires the FMCS to receive sixty days' notice instead of thirty. There is a provision for mandatory mediation by the parties with the

FMCS in the case of collective bargaining, and a requirement of thirty days' notice to FMCS before initial contract dealings.

It should be noted that federal, state, and local governmental hospitals are still excluded from NLRA coverage.

Union activity in federal health care institutions is permitted by separate federal law. An executive order of 1962 clearly outlined for the first time the government's policy regarding collective employee activity. Basically, the order gave all federal employees the right to decide whether or not to join organizations that would represent them in negotiations on terms and conditions of employment. Mechanisms for elections and for selecting the bargaining unit were established as well. A supplementary order was issued in 1963. This defined unfair labor practices similar to those found in the NLRA. However, there were two significant exceptions. Strikes and picketing by government employees were prohibited, and employee organizations were forbidden to discriminate against any individuals on terms and condition of membership because of race, creed, color, or national origin. A new executive order was issued by President Nixon in 1969. This order was meant to strengthen federal labor relations by bringing its provisions more into line with practice in the private sector. The Federal Labor Relations Council was created as a central authority to administer the government's labor program. The Federal Impasse Panel was formed to settle deadlocks in contract negotiations when voluntary efforts fail.

State and municipal hospitals are exempt from the NLRA, since they are also not considered employers for purposes of the legislation.[7] Thus, labor-management relations in such institutions have been generally controlled by the individual states. The right to organize and bargain collectively has been granted to at least some segment of public hospital workers by about thirty-six states.

What are some of the effects of coverage under federal labor laws?

The NLRA prohibits private hospitals from engaging in certain conduct classified as unfair labor practices. Section 8 of the Act prohibits management from:

1. Interfering with, restraining, or coercing employees in the exercise of their rights to organize or bargain collectively.
2. Dominating or interfering with a labor organization with regard to either organization or control.
3. Discriminating against an employee in hiring, terms of employment, or tenure for participating in union activity.
4. Discharging or otherwise discriminating against an employee for filing charges under the NLRA.
5. Refusing to bargain "in good faith."

Thus, firing an employee for holding union membership is not permitted. Beyond that, the employer obviously cannot take direct steps of reprisal against employees active in organizing a union, as this would constitute an unfair labor practice under the NLRA. For example, in one case, a medical assistant had an ongoing dispute over her salary with the business manager of the osteopathic clinic in which she was employed.[8] She enlisted another employee to go with her to talk with the business manager, and she distributed union cards and literature to other employees at the clinic. The following Monday, the employee was fired. A federal appellate court ruled that the discharge constituted an unfair labor practice because it was at least partially based on her unionizing activities, and it ordered the clinic to reinstate the employee.

Similarly, in another case, the court upheld an NLRB order for a hospital to compensate its employees with back pay and interest to the date on which an across-the-board raise had been promised to take effect.[9] The promised raises had been withheld, the court decided, in an effort to discourage the unionization movement that had begun at the hospital in the period between the promise of the raise and its effective date. The withholding of a wage increase can constitute an unfair labor practice in violation of Section 8 of the NLRA if the increase had been promised prior to the union's appearance, if it would have normally been paid as part of a schedule of increases, or if the employer attempts to blame the union for the withholding. However, withholding even under these circumstances becomes illegal only if done to influence employee decisions concerning unionization. Due to statements made by the hospital administrator and the lack of legitimate business purpose, the court determined that the hospital here was improperly motivated in the withholding.

If the employer dominates or controls the employees' union or interferes and supports one of two competing unions, the employer is committing an unfair labor practice. If two unions are competing for members in the hospital and for recognition as the organization to bargain on behalf of the employees, and the hospital permits only one of the unions to use hospital facilities for its organizational activities, it commits an unfair labor practice. Financial assistance to one of the competing unions also constitutes an unfair labor practice.

The NLRA also places duties on labor organizations and prohibits certain employee activities such as mass picketing, assaults on nonstrikers, and following groups of nonstrikers away from the immediate area of the hospital; these constitute coercion and will be ordered stopped by the NLRB. Refusal to bargain in good faith or breach of a collective bargaining contract by the labor union is another example of a union unfair labor practice.

Must an employee be a member of a union to be protected by the NLRA?

No. It is not necessary that a formal organization or union be involved in order for concerted employee actions to be protected by federal labor laws. Any action by two or more employees is generally protected if the act is designed to further the interests of a group of workers, and not merely to benefit a particular individual. Such acts are considered "concerted activities for the purpose of . . . mutual aid or protection" under Section 7 of the act. Thus, employers cannot retaliate against employees for taking such joint action. However, the employer is not under any obligation to bargain with such employees or to act on any presented grievances.

What are the rights of a hospital employee who does not want to join a union?

The 1974 amendments to the NLRA contained a special section intended to protect the rights of persons with religious convictions against unionism.[10] This section provides that employees of health care institutions, who are members of a bona fide religious organization that historically has opposed joining or financially supporting labor unions, cannot be forced to do so as a condition of employment. If the employee works at an institution that has a union contract, he may be required to make contributions to a charitable organization in lieu of paying union dues and initiation fees. This section was apparently added by Congress to ensure job security for the many Seventh Day Adventists employed in the health care industry, but the section is drafted broadly to protect the rights of any employee who objects to unionism on religious grounds.[11]

The rights of health care workers who do no want to join or support unions for personal or political reasons, rather than because of their religious beliefs, vary from state to state. About nineteen states have so-called "right-to-work" laws providing that employees cannot be required to join or contribute to a labor union in that state.[12] State right-to-work laws were validated by Congress in 1947 in a section of the Taft-Hartley Act that expressly authorized states to prohibit employer-union agreements requiring membership in a labor union as a condition of employment.[13] In states without right-to-work legislation, the rights of employees not to join labor unions are governed by federal law.

To understand how federal and state laws operate to protect employees' freedom to choose not to belong to a union, it is helpful to review the traditional types of arrangements designed to assure that all employees in a bargaining unit become union members. "Union security" is a broad term for all forms of compulsory payment of money to a union. Unions typically seek inclusion of some form of union security clause in a collective bargaining agreement to assure bargaining strength, stability, and continued existence of the union in the institution, to discourage "free riders" (employees who refuse to join the union yet enjoy the benefits achieved by the union for all employees in the unit), to prevent "raids" by other unions, and to ensure an adequate financial base for union activities.[14]

There are several types of union security clauses that may be included in a collective bargaining agreement. First the most restrictive is the "closed shop," which requires all employees to be union members before or at the time they are hired. All closed shop agreements are illegal and hence unenforceable under federal law since they interfere with an employer's right to hire employees regardless of union membership.[15] Second is the "union shop," which does not require employees to be union members when hired, but does require them to join the union within a certain period after they are hired. Third is a variant of the union shop, the "agency shop," which does not require employees to become active union members, but requires all employees who are not union members to pay a fee to the union instead of dues for its services as their agent in representing them in collective bargaining negotiations and in administration of the contract.

All states with right-to-work laws prohibit union shop agreements and, by judicial decisions, may prohibit agency shop arrangements as well. Both agreements are permitted under the NLRA, provided that the agreement does not require membership or payment of service fees before thirty days after an employee is hired or the effective date of the contract, whichever is later.[16] The U.S. Supreme Court, however, has limited enforceability of membership provisions of union shop clauses to payment of initiation fees and union dues only.[17] The legal effect of union shop and agency shop clauses is therefore similar. Employees of institutions covered by union shop clauses in reality cannot be forced to join the union or become subject to the union constitution and by-laws, including provisions for compulsory union meeting attendance. Such employees can, however, be forced to pay initiation fees and union dues.

Other types of union security arrangements include the "maintenance-of-membership" clause, which requires only that employees who are already union members when the contract begins retain their membership; the "hiring hall" provision, which provides that applicants for employment are referred to the employer by the union; the "modified union shop," which provides that new employees must join the union after a certain period of time, but current employees who do not wish to join the union need not do so. The "open shop" has a contract with no union-security clauses whatsoever; both old and new employees are free to join or not to join the union as they wish.[18]

It is an unfair labor practice for an employer to discriminate, or for a union to cause an employer to discriminate, against an employee in any aspect of his employment on account of the employee's union affiliation or lack of it.[19] One example was considered in a recent decision.[20] In that case, hospital employees were covered by a union contract with an agency shop provision. Under the clause, union members delinquent in their dues were subject to discharge after ninety days, while nonunion members delinquent in paying their service fee were subject to discharge after only ten days. The court ruled that this provision represented an unfair labor practice by the union, and required that a nonunion employee who had lost her job because of it be reinstated.

Why do employees join unions?

The decision to join a union is generally based upon dissatisfaction with wages and other benefits of employment, and problems with supervisors and the organization of the hospital. An important factor in the health industry is that belonging to a union is not now felt to be as unrespectable or unprofessional as it once was. Money and fringe benefits are not always the only issues to employees. Other issues, such as poor communication, poor supervision, bad working conditions, and inconsistently enforced personnel policies, although less tangible, nevertheless carry considerable weight and may be just as important to employees. One reason for joining a union frequently cited by employees is that they feel that management "does not treat them fairly, decently, or honestly." [21] In some ways the employees feel "meeting employee needs" is not a primary management objective, and view the union as a means for altering that outlook.

What are the rules governing union solicitation in hospitals?

The right of employees to organize and bargain collectively established under the NLRA has traditionally been held to include the right to communicate effectively with one another regarding self-organization at the jobsite.[22] In line with this, the NLRB has established a policy that restrictions on employee solicitation during nonworking time, and on distribution of literature during nonworking time in nonworking areas, are unfair labor practices unless the employer justifies them by a showing of special circumstances that make the restrictions necessary to maintain production or discipline.

In considering application of this policy to health care institutions, the NLRB concluded that the special characteristics of hospitals justify a rule different than that generally applied to order employers. In one case the board found "that the primary function of a hospital is patient care and that a tranquil atmosphere is essential to the carrying out of the function. In order to provide this atmosphere, hospitals may be justified in imposing somewhat more stringent prohibitions than are generally permitted." [23] The board concluded that prohibiting solicitation may be justified in certain situations and required striking the balance against employees' interests in organizational activity. It determined that the balance should be struck by permitting such activity in areas other than immediate patient care areas, such as lounges and cafeterias, unless there could be a showing that disruption to patient care would necessarily result if solicitation and distribution were permitted there.

The board applied its modified presumption in a number of cases involving union organizational activities in hospitals. In important recent reviews of several of these decisions, the U.S. Supreme Court has gone a long way toward delineating the limits of permissible union solicitation in hospitals.[24]

As the rule presently stands, there is a presumption in favor of solicitation away from patient care areas, under a rather narrow definition of "immediate patient care areas" (for example, patients' rooms, operating rooms, and places where patients receive treatment, such as X-ray and therapy areas). The hospital must overcome this presumption by presenting evidence of the negative impact on patient care of allowing such solicitation in any particular area. However, the Supreme Court also questioned whether the board's interpretation adequately considers the practices and methods involved in patient care in a modern hospital:

The Board [bears] a heavy continuing responsibility to review its policies concerning organizational activities in various parts of hospitals. Hospitals carry on a public function of the utmost seriousness and importance. They give rise to unique considerations that do not apply in the industrial settings with which the Board is more familiar. The Board should stand ready to revise its rulings if future experience demonstrates that the well-being of patients is in fact jeopardized.[25]

Thus it may be that the Court will sometime take it upon itself to alter the board's presumption, so that it may become easier for hospitals to prohibit union solicitation in more areas.

It should also be noted that, even if a hospital has a solicitation-and-distribution rule which is legal on its face, it cannot be applied in a discriminatory manner. In one recent case, the NLRB held that the discriminatory application of long-standing dress code rules against wearing buttons or insignia was an unfair labor practice in violation of the NLRA. The employees were allowed to wear buttons for Hospital Week, Doctors' Day, or St. Patrick's Day, but were not allowed to wear union buttons. The board concluded that the dress code was designed more to protect the hospital from union activities than to protect patients.[26] Thus, if a hospital's dress code forbids buttons or insignia, it must strictly and universally enforce that rule. The only exception would seem to be that professional and hospital pins and insignia would be permitted.

Is it necessary to have an election for a union to be recognized by a hospital?

No. The NLRA sets out the procedures by which employees may select a labor organization as their collective bargaining representative. The three major unions in the hospital field are the National Union of Hospital and Health Care Employees (District 1199), headquartered in New York City, and the Service Employees International Union, and the American Federation of State, County, and Municipal Employees, both headquartered in Washington, D.C. (It should be noted that any union may organize in a hospital.)

Some hospitals may be willing to recognize a union quickly and without an election. This may be done by selecting a third party, often an arbitrator, to check the signatures on union authorization cards against those on employer payroll records to determine whether the union actually has a majority. In attempting to organize employees at a hospital, unions solicit applications for membership; a card authorizes the union to act as the collective bargaining agent for the employee in all matters relating to conditions of employment. The impartial third party then determines whether a majority of the employees authorizes the union to act as their exclusive bargaining agent. This procedure satisfies all the requirements of national labor law. Recognition of a union that does not represent a majority of the employees is an unfair labor practice. This rule tends to discourage "sweetheart" contracts that some employers try to make with friendly unions.

How may an NLRB election be obtained?

It is more common for the issue of representation to be determined in an election held under NLRB supervision. The NLRB may conduct such an election when a petition for certification has been filed by an employee, a group of employees, an individual, a labor union acting on the employees' behalf, or an employer. The NLRB must then investigate and must direct an election if it has reasonable cause to believe a question of representation exists. The NLRB requires a "showing of interest"; the union must produce signed cards for at least 30 percent of the employees in the bargaining unit stating that the employees wish the union to represent them. It should be noted that an employee who signs an authorization card is not obligated to vote in favor of the union during the election.

Can the employer campaign before the election?

If an election is necessary, the board will set a date for it. The NLRA provides that, during the pre-election campaigning period "the expressing of any views, arguments, or opinions or the dissemination thereof, whether in written, printed, graphic, or visual form, shall not constitute or be evidence of the unfair labor practice under any provisions of this act if such expression contains no threat of reprisal or force or promise of benefit." [27] An employer may lawfully express his personal opinions and arguments as to the desirability of union representation of employees. However, this expression must be limited to a statement of facts, opinions, and arguments, and must be free of promised benefits or threatened reprisals, either in words or circumstances.

In one case,[28] a hospital was found to have violated the NLRB by restraining employees in the exercise of their rights to self-organization. The hospital took disciplinary action against two nurses who were leading a unionization campaign. Following an appearance by both nurses on a television news broadcast to discuss conditions at the hospital and the reasons for supporting unionization, one received a warning and the other's hours and conditions of employment were restricted. It was found that the nurses' appearance on the broadcast was activity protected by the NLRB, since the statements they made were not only true, but were also directly related to the protected concerted activities then in progress.

What is the voting procedure in an NLRB election?

Elections are usually held on the employer's premises, but under strict supervision of an agent of the NLRB. The hours the election will be held are decided by mutual agreement, or if such is not possible, by a decision of the board. Voting can take place intermittently during the day in order to provide opportunity for all shifts to participate in the election.

A ballot generally offers at least two choices: union or no union. At the voting, a list of employees in the bargaining unit, submitted by the employer, is available. The agent of the NLRB, an employer representative, and a union representative are present at the voting area. Each employee wishing to vote must be identified. Each representative has the right to challenge any vote. The voting is by secret ballot.

In order to be certified, the union must obtain a majority of the valid ballots that are cast. It should be noted that a union will be certified if it receives a majority of the votes. This may not be a majority of the bargaining unit, since not all employees vote in a union election. In the event of a tie vote, the union loses.

If a union has won a majority of the votes cast in the election, it becomes the exclusive bargaining agent, and the board will issue a certification. This certification remains in effect for one year and continues thereafter until it can be shown that the certified representative does not represent a majority of the employees within a bargaining unit. During that year, the certified union has the right to bargain collectively with the employer. If the employees themselves have second thoughts about the desirability of retaining a certain union, they can, after a one-year period, petition the NLRB for a decertification election. They need to show that 30 percent of the membership is dissatisfied with the union in order for the board to order an election. A majority vote for no union in this election would rescind the union's status as the bargaining agent.

What is an "appropriate bargaining unit"?

Determination of what group of employees within a hospital or health care institute constitutes an appropriate unit for purposes of collective bargaining is the first and most important decision that must be made before a representation election can be held.[29] A bargaining unit consists of a group of jobs or job classifications that are entitled to vote in the election and that will be represented by the union in collective bargaining if the union secures a majority vote. If the union and employer don't agree as to what constitutes an appropriate unit, the NLRB is empowered to make unit determinations.[30] The primary criterion used by the NLRB is that of the group in question having a community of interest.[31] Unions as a practical matter consider other factors as well. Too large a unit encompassing employees with conflicts of interest may impede the union's organizational efforts and hinder communications in contract negotiation and administration. On the other hand, too small a unit may curtail the union's bargaining strength and cause division and infighting among institutional employees.[32] A series of fragmented units at one institution may involve increased administration costs to the employer. Unions generally favor relatively small units, since they are easier to organize. Indeed, the smaller and more cohesive the group of employees comprising the unit, the more likely it will be that unit members are effectively represented.[33]

In enacting the 1974 health care amendments to the NLRA, Congress admonished the NLRB to prevent undue proliferation of bargaining units in the health care industry.[34] Unit determination has been the most controversial area of hospital labor relations since 1974, with hospital representatives typically pressing for larger "functionally integrated" units.[35] In May 1975, the NLRB issued eight major decisions establishing initial guidelines for hospital bargaining units.[36] The board specifically rejected proposals to subdivide hospital employees for purposes of unit determination into those directly involved with patient care (professional and nonprofessionals).[37] Instead, it has ruled that the following groups of hospital employees constitute appropriate units:

1. Employee physicians
2. Registered nurses
3. All other professional employees
4. Technical employees
5. Service and maintenance employees
6. Office and clerical employees

In holding that registered nurses may comprise an independent bargaining unit distinct from other professional employees, such as physical therapists and dieticians, the NLRB cited the "peculiar role and responsibilities of registered nurses in the health care industry," and "an impressive history of exclusive representation and collective bargaining." [38] The board classified licensed practical nurses as technical employees [39] and subsequently refused to permit LPNs to join registered nurses in a bargaining unit even when the registered nurses' association desired it.[40]

One issue that frequently arises in defining bargaining units of registered nurses or other professional employees is whether or not a particular employee is a "supervisor." The NLRB expressly exempts from its coverage "any individual employed as a supervisor," [41] and defines the term to include:

any individual having authority, in the interest of the employer, to hire, transfer, suspend, lay off, recall, promote, discharge, assign, reward, or discipline other employees, or responsible to direct them, or to adjust their grievances, or effectively to recommend such action; if in connection with the foregoing the exercise of such authority is not of a merely routine or clerical nature, but requires the use of independent judgment.[42]

Congress's intent in excluding supervisors was twofold: first to assure that rank-and-file employees would be free from undue influence or coercion by supervisors who were members of the same unit; and, second, to prevent supervisors from being placed in a position of divided loyalty and conflict of interest with their employers.[43] In passing the 1974 amendments to the NLRB, Congress recognized that in the health care setting, many employees responsibly direct other employees in patient care, yet lack hiring and firing authority and hence are not "supervisors" acting in the interest of the employer.[44] Hence, the NLRB has held that teaching nurses, charge nurses, and head nurses who direct patient care activities in exercise of their professional skills are not to be classified as supervisors.[45] On the other hand, nursing coordinators or shift supervisors whose jobs are characterized by "such indicia of supervision as authorizing overtime, calling in off-duty employees, revising schedules, making assignments, transfers, and evaluations, and effectively recommending action with respect to hiring" must be excluded from the bargaining unit.[46] Thus, excluded supervisors are those who exercise independent judgment on behalf of the employer, and whose duties are not merely routine or clerical in nature.

The NLRB's criteria for establishment of a separate unit of technical employees—such as LPNs, X-ray technicians, respiratory technicians, laboratory technicians, psychiatric technicians, and operating room technicians—are "specialized training, skills, education, and job requirements," usually evidenced by requirements for certification, registration, or licensing, that distinguish the technicians from other service and maintenance employees.[47] A group of employees may qualify for inclusion in the technical unit, however, even if they are not certified, registered, or licensed.[48] And under special circumstances, LPNs may be certified as a separate unit independent of other technical employees.[49]

The service and maintenance units first certified by the NLRB in 1975 typically included nurses' aides and orderlies, cafeteria workers, dietary and housekeeping employees, technicians not assigned to the technical unit, storeroom and boiler-room employees.[50] The board has since ruled, however, that maintenance employees and skilled craft workers may be placed in a unit separate from other service employees.[51] Federal appeals courts, in reviewing NLRB unit determinations, have cautioned the board against overfragmentation of bargaining units among service and maintenance workers.[52]

In its initial determinations on hospital bargaining units the NLRB carried forward a distinction drawn in other industries between clerical employees in the business office and those whose duties are more closely related to service and maintenance.[53] The office and clerical group may include switchboard operators, admitting clerks, billing, credit, and bookkeeping clerks, cashiers, and data-processers.[54] In subsequent decisions, the board has placed medical records employees and admitting employees in the service and maintenance unit if their job functions are more closely related to direct patient care.[55] In addition, in response to a court directive, the NLRB accepted the stipulation of the hospital-employer and a union that a unit encompassing all clerical employees, including those in the business office, was appropriate for collective bargaining. Significantly, this indicates that the NLRB will now consider bargaining units defined by standards other than the traditional community-of-interest doctrine.[56]

What is "collective bargaining"?

Once a union is organized under the NLRA, the employer is obligated to "bargain in good faith" with its duly designated representative. When there is no collective-bargaining relationship, management has the absolute right to set wages, hours, and working conditions, and to promote, reward, and discipline at will, subject only to certain basic federal or state laws and regulations that pertain to all employees. Once there is an obligation to bargain with employee representatives, there are limits to how management may exercise these rights.

Although the act compels the parties to enter into collective bargaining, it contains no directive for the parties involved to make concessions to one another, or to reach an agreement. Theoretically, an agreement between the parties may never be reached. While a contract generally is successfully negotiated, it may take a few days or a few years. First contracts usually take between six months and a year to agree upon.

There may also be very wide differences in what the different parties want to bargain about. Under the NLRA, possible subjects for collective bargaining are divided into prohibited subjects, mandatory subjects, and voluntary or "permissive" subjects.

Prohibited subjects are subjects already regulated by federal or state law. For example, regardless of the wishes of either or both of the bargaining parties, it is illegal under the NLRA to make a contract requiring workers to become members of a labor organization before they have been employed for 30 days.

Mandatory subjects of bargaining are the common ones such as wages, hours, and terms and conditions of employment. This covers such items as promotions, holidays, vacations, health and disability insurance, sick leave, pension plans, grievance procedures, etc. Employers and employees are required to bargain on this category of subjects. This means that they must meet, discuss, furnish information, try to reach an agreement, and if possible put the agreement into a written contract. To refuse to bargain, or not to bargain in good faith, on these matters is an unfair labor practice that is subject to enforcement of the NLRB and the courts. The phrase "terms and conditions of employment" is generally interpreted very broadly. Although either side can waive or trade its right to bargain about a certain mandatory subject, it cannot be forced to do so by the other party.

"Permissive" subjects include all of the other possible subjects of collective bargaining. Employers and employees can, if they both so desire, bargain about almost anything. However, neither party can insist on bargaining on subjects in this voluntary area or make the reaching of agreement on other matters conditional on concession outside of the mandatory subject areas.

Do health care workers have the right to strike?

Yes. However, in order to protect the public interest by insuring the continuity of health care to the community, the 1974 health care institutions amendment to the NLRA provides for advance notice of any anticipated strike or picketing. Section 8(g) was added to the act, generally prohibiting a labor organization from striking or picketing a health care institution without first giving ten days' notice. Violation of this provision constitutes an unfair labor practice. The ten-day notice is intended to give health care institutions sufficient advance notice of a strike or picketing to permit them to make arrangements for the continuity of patient care. It also gives the NLRB the opportunity, when charges are filed, to make a determination as to the legality of any strike or picketing before it occurs. It should be noted that this notice provision applies to lockouts by the hospital as well as to strikes.

Although it is not intended to require a labor organization to begin a strike or picketing at the precise time specified in the notice, it would be inconsistent with the provision's intent if a union did not act within a reasonable time after that specified in the notice. A strike or picketing commenced within 72 hours after the precise time in the notice would probably be reasonable. Beyond that, if a labor organization did not strike at the specific time noted, at least twelve hours' additional notice should be given of the new time set for the action.[57]

Repeatedly serving ten-day notices on an employer would constitute evidence of a refusal on the part of the union to bargain in good faith. However, a labor organization would not be required to serve a ten-day notice or to wait until the expiration of the ten-day notice when the employer had committed an unfair labor practice.

During the ten-day notice period, the employer would remain free to take any necessary action in order to maintain health care, but would not be permitted to do anything that would undermine the bargaining relationship that would otherwise exist, such as bringing in large numbers of supervisory and other personnel from other facilities to replace strikers. Although not a literal violation of the act, violation of these principles would most likely release the union from its obligation not to engage in economic (that is, an action over economic issues, not over recognition or representation) action during the course of the notice period.

It should be noted that the right to strike may be bargained away by the union. If this is done, mandatory grievance and arbitration procedures are generally substituted.

In the absence of any agreement to the contrary, employees returning to work following an economic strike are entitled to continue in their old positions. In one case, striking nurses originally employed by the hospital to staff doctors' offices in the clinic were returned to duty as floor nurses in the hospital, a less desirable position. The change in work assignment was held to constitute an unfair labor practice.[58]

How are patients affected by the right of health care workers to strike?

Hospitals should not experience any serious disruption of patient care or of the hospital's ability to provide services because of a feared increase in the number of strikes. The notion that unionized employees are more likely to strike is not justified in this field. Traditionally, the underlying reasons for strikes have been union recognition, organizational jurisdiction, worker grievances, and issues pertaining to wages, hours, and working conditions. Prior to the 1974 health care institutions amendment, 95 percent of the strikes in the hospital industry were for union recognition, and not over the various terms of employment once recognition had been achieved. Requiring compliance with NLRA guidelines, which mandate that employers must recognize and bargain with the chosen representative of their employees, has done much to reduce this particular form of labor strife. Further, the major unions in the field have often followed a policy of accepting arbitration in cases when a strike would disrupt essential health services.

Provisions in the 1974 amendment show Congress's wish that every possible approach to a peaceful settlement be fully explored before a strike is called in a hospital. Section 213 of the amendment provides that the director of the Federal Mediation and Conciliation Service may call for an impartial Board of Inquiry, within the negotiation periods, if he determines that a labor dispute threatens to interrupt the delivery of health care. The board, within fifteen days, investigates the labor dispute and makes findings of fact and recommendations for settlement, which it reports not only to the director of the FMCS, but to the parties as well. The status quo is maintained for an additional fifteen days, during which it is hoped that issuance of the board's recommendations, combined with public pressure and good bargaining strategy, will effectively force the parties to reach an agreement. However, experience with Boards of Inquiry has been less than completely successful. Most importantly, if there is a strike, the ten-day prestrike notice requirement allows the hospital to transfer patients and otherwise insure that community health is not affected.

Finally, the continuity of patient care may be affected by the long waits and delays often accompanying consideration of a labor dispute by the NLRB. Accordingly, the NLRB has attempted to give special attention and priority to all charges of unfair labor practices involving health care institutions.

May interns and residents join unions?

In the 1976 *Cedars-Sinai* decision, the NLRB ruled that interns, residents, and clinical fellows at hospitals are students, and not "employees" within the meaning of the National Labor Relations Act.[59] The NLRB reasoned that interns and residents participate in hospital training programs primarily to complete their graduate medical education, rather than to earn a living. The effect of the NRLB's decision is that efforts of interns and residents to organize and achieve recognition are not protected by the NLRA, and that interns and residents can join unions and engage in collective bargaining only if a hospital voluntarily recognizes the house-staff union, or where protected by state labor laws. Although recently challenged in litigation, the Court of Appeals for the District of Columbia held that the NLRB's determination that interns and residents are not employees within the NLRA is not subject to judicial review.[60] At present it is estimated that about 9,000 interns and residents are covered by union contracts negotiated without NLRB protection.[61]

The status of protection of house staff by state labor legislation is not clear after the *Cedars-Sinai* decision, and will vary from state to state. Shortly after its initial decision in *Cedars-Sinai*, the NLRB reaffirmed its conclusion that interns and residents were not "employees" and further declared that its decision was intended to preempt all state labor laws to the contrary.[62] Subsequently, a federal court of appeals ruled that the NLRB had not, by its *Cedars-Sinai* decision, ceded jurisdiction to state labor boards and refused to allow the New York State Labor Relations Board to supervise an election for interns and residents.[63] The Nebraska Supreme Court, however, refused to follow *Cedars-Sinai,* and held that interns and residents are employees within the Nebraska labor laws, and hence that their organizational activities were protected.[64]

However, legislation is annually filed in Congress to amend the NLRA specifically to include house staff. The AMA supports the inclusion of intern's and residents within the NLRA.[65] Proponents of the legislation argue that 84 percent of the house staff's time is spent in patient care, the house staff members are analogous to other types of apprentices protected by federal labor laws, and that permitting house staff to engage in collective bargaining about the employment aspect of their program is not incompatible with its educational component. However, it is not expected that this legislation will be enacted in the near future.

May physicians join unions?

When discussing the issue of physicians' unions, it is necessary to distinguish among those physicians who are bona fide salaried employees of a health care institution, those who have staff privileges at a particular hospital, and those who are solely independent, private practitioners.

The first group are employees like any others, and as such may organize into unions under the protection of the NLRA.

However, the term *employee* is defined in the NLRA to exclude "any individual having the status of an independent contractor." [66] The NLRB applies the common-law definition of independent contractor, which is a person who, unlike an employee, works in his own way, and under no one else's direction as to the details of the work. Thus, the employer has no control or right of control over the way the work is done. Members of a hospital's medical staff, it would appear, are independent contractors and not employees of the particular hospital, although this conclusion may be altered in the future as such physicians have increased responsibilities and duties to perform for the hospital, and as the hospital exercises greater review and control over the medical care offered within its walls.

It is also unlikely that a court would consider the relationship a physician has with an insurance carrier, whether private or governmental, to be one of employment, rather than one of independent contractor. While the insurance carrier may have a direct impact upon the remuneration received by the physician, it has no real control over his working conditions, nor generally does it control in advance the work undertaken by the doctor. Thus, physicians in these categories receive none of the benefits of the NLRA.

Of course, nonemployees may form unions even without the protection afforded by the NLRA. However, nonemployee unions may come into conflict with antitrust laws. The relevant portion of the federal Sherman Antitrust Act proscribes "Every contract, combination . . . or conspiracy, in restraint of trade or commerce among the several states, or with foreign nations." [67] If a physician acts alone, such as in dealings with an insurance carrier regarding reimbursement rates, he is protected from antitrust liability. However, an organization of physicians would have to refrain from any activity aimed at a price-fixing arrangement among its members alone or involving other entities. A price-establishing agreement negotiated between a physicians' union and an institution that pays doctors for their services would violate antitrust laws, in the absence of an applicable exemption. Furthermore, if a physicians' organization, in an effort to enhance its negotiating position, resorts to a work stoppage or strike, it could be considered a boycott or concerted refusal to deal, which would be proscribed by the antitrust laws.

Despite the problems presented by labor and antitrust laws, several physicians' unions have been organized in recent years. These include the Union of American Physicians, the American Federation of Physicians and Dentists, the American Physicians' Guild, the American Physicians' Union, and the National Conference of Physicians' Unions. In response to this, traditional physicians' organizations, such as the American Medical Association, have become increasingly militant in representing the needs and desires of their members, particularly in financial matters. The

AMA has created a "department of negotiations" to encourage collective bargaining by state and local medical societies. Thus, effective utilization of existing medical organizations, such as the AMA and county and state medical societies, is a possible alternative to outright physician unionization.

What are some of the national trends?

The effect of union activity on hospitals since passage of the 1974 amendments has been significant and, it can be assumed, will continue to be. Although efforts to organize have been made for over sixty years, concerted union activity in the health services industry began only about ten years ago. With the protection of the NLRA, unions are expanding in the industry.

In the first year after the amendments, the NLRB conducted 423 representative elections in the health care sector, including 200 in hospitals. Unions won 60 percent of the elections—a percentage considerably higher than the national average.

About one out of every four hospitals has unions, and about one of every five hospital workers is a member. In 1976, new labor contracts increased 30 percent, while the NLRB reported an increase of 25 percent in hospital-related unfair labor relations cases and a 25 percent increase in representative elections.[68]

Unionization is a significant determinant of the wages of nonprofessional hospital employees. However, the effect of unions, while statistically significant, is not high in dollar terms. While 70 percent of the average hospital's budget is allocated for payroll and associated expenses,[69] the union impact on hospital costs appears to be in the range of 1 to 2 percent.[70] Thus, unionization does not appear to be a major contribution to the inflation in hospital costs.

However, recently the rate of growth in the number of new collective bargaining contracts has diminished. After the intense activity of the first few years under the NLRA, the new trend seems to be that union activity among health care workers has settled down to become similar to that in other industries.[71] Yet the pressures of inflation and efforts to contain hospital costs will keep many hospital employees concerned about wage and benefit levels, making union membership more attractive. There is a noticeable division between the more unionized hospitals of metropolitan areas, the Northeast, and the West Coast, and the less unionized hospitals of other areas, which could become even more pronounced in the future. Unionization within individual hospitals will probably also continue to increase.[72] Thus, the pattern of unionization in hospitals increasingly resembles that in many other industries: work units that are large, or located in major cities or more highly unionized regions, are most likely to have unionized employees. Beyond that, the growing desire of many health care professionals, particularly nurses, interns, and residents, for a larger role in the organization of medical care within the hospital will contribute to the continued spread of union activity.

What other work-related rights of health care employees are guaranteed by federal law?

Apart from the NLRA, there are several other major pieces of federal legislation that affect the work-related rights of hospital and other health care employees. Of primary importance is Title VII of the Civil Rights Act of 1964 as amended by the Equal Employment Opportunity Act of 1972, which prohibits employment discrimination on the basis of race, color, religion, sex, or national origin.[73] Title VII recognizes narrow exceptions where sex, religion, or national origin is a bona fide occupational qualification, and for bona fide seniority systems. By virtue of the 1972 amendments, state and local governmental institutions as well as private employers having fifteen or more employees are subject to the act. Title VII also proscribes discrimination by labor unions. The Equal Employment Opportunity Commission (EEOC) is the federal agency established by Title VII to investigate and conciliate complaints, and to bring suits on behalf of aggrieved employees against private employers.

Other important federal nondiscrimination laws include the Age Discrimination in Employment Act of 1967,[74] recently amended to prohibit discrimination on the basis of age against persons between forty and seventy years old, and the Rehabilitation Act of 1973,[75] which prohibits employment discrimination against qualified handicapped persons.

The Fair Labor Standards Act (FLSA) prescribes minimum wages and rates of overtime pay for employees of institutions engaged in interstate commerce, specifically including hospitals and other institutions that care for the sick, aged, or mentally ill.[76] An important component of the FLSA is the Equal Pay Act of 1963, which prohibits sex discrimination in rates of pay for jobs of equal skill, effort, and responsibility, performed under similar conditions.[77] The Equal Pay Act has been held applicable to state and local governmental institutions as well as private employers,[78] but other wage and hour provisions of the FLSA are not binding on state and local governments.[79] Whether or not two jobs are equivalent for purposes of the Equal Pay Act is a factual question, and in the hospital context courts have divided on the issue whether male orderlies are the equivalent of female nurses' aides.[80] One court has ruled that female maid and male janitor positions were equivalent and therefore subject to equal pay provisions.[81]

The Occupational Safety and Health Act (OSHA), passed in 1970, has as its purpose "to provide for the general welfare, to assure so far as possible every working man and woman in the Nation safe and healthful working conditions and to preserve our human resources."[82] In general the act permits the Secretary of Labor to promulgate occupational safety and health standards. He or his authorized representative may, "without delay," enter the premises of any employer who is covered by the act, which includes virtually every private-sector employer. Thereafter, a citation is issued for any violation by the employer, either of a specific standard or of his general obligation to provide a place of employment "free from recognized hazards that are causing or are likely to cause death or serious physical harm." In addition to the citation, the secretary may assess penalties, which the employer may appeal to the independent Occupational Safety and Health Review Commission (OSHRC). Finally, a National Institute for Occupational Safety and Health (NIOSH) was created by the statute and placed within the Department of Health and Human Services with research and educational functions.

All hospitals are either covered by OSHA or by a plan

developed by their own state. OSHA itself applies to all nongovernment employers, and includes all employees, even professionals, of nonprofit and charitable organizations.[83] Federal employees are protected by a provision which requires all federal agencies to establish and maintain an effective and comprehensive safety and health program. Other public employees are covered by approved individual state programs, each of which must provide "and maintain an effective and comprehensive occupational safety and health program applicable to all employees of public agencies of the state and its political subdivisions." Thus, hospitals have a legal obligation, enforceable through action by various parties, including aggrieved employees, to provide safe and healthful working conditions for their employees. One NIOSH report concluded that "the safety record of hospitals is inferior to that of many industries that send accident victims to these facilities." [84] However, safety and health problems in hospitals are getting increased attention. OSHA has helped underscore the importance of this area, and has prompted hospital administrators to improve their hospitals' compliance with current standards of health and safety, by means of accident prevention, environmental control, and prevention of infection and illness.

NOTES

1. *Working in Hospitals: Then and Now,* 1199 News (Sept. 1976) at 9.

2. *Id.* at 33–34.

3. ORGANIZATION OF HEALTH WORKERS AND LABOR CONFLICT, chs. 3–5 (S. Wolfe, ed.; Farmingdale, N.Y.: Baywood Publishing, 1978).

4. Shepard, *Health Care Institution Amendments to the National Labor Relations Act: An Analysis,* 1 AM. J. LAW & MED. 41, 43 (1975).

5. BNA Daily Labor Report No. 146, July 29, 1974, at A-1.

6. 29 U.S.C. §152.

7. *See* Camden-Clark Mem. Hosp., 91 L.R.R.M. 1024 (Dec.

1975); Grey Nuns v. Alaska Nurses' Ass'n, 91 L.R.R.M. 1099 (Dec. 1975).

8. NLRB v. Brown, 546 F.2d 690 (6th Cir. 1976).
9. NLRB v. Otis Hosp. 545 F.2d 252 (1st Cir. 1976).
10. 29 U.S.C. §169 (1976).
11. R. GORMAN, BASIC TEXT ON LABOR LAW, UNIONIZATION AND COLLECTIVE BARGAINING 660 (St. Paul: West Publishing, 1976).
12. Alabama, Arizona, Arkansas, Florida, Georgia, Iowa, Kansas, Mississippi, Nebraska, Nevada, North Carolina, North Dakota, South Carolina, South Dakota, Tennessee, Texas, Utah, Virginia, Wyoming.
13. 29 U.S.C. §164(b) (1976). See Retail Clerks Local 1625 v. Shermerhorn, 373 U.S. 746 (1963).
14. See GORMAN, supra note 11, at 639; N. METZGER & D. POINTER, LABOR-MANAGEMENT RELATIONS IN THE HEALTH SERVICES INDUSTRY 163 (Washington, D.C.: Science & Health Publications, 1972).
15. 29 U.S.C. §158(a)(3) (1976).
16. Id.
17. NLRB v. General Motors Corp., 373 U.S. 734 (1963).
18. For statistics on which provisions are most common in the health care industry, see Juris, Rosmann, Maxey, & Bentivegna, Nationwide Survey Shows Growth in Union Contracts, Hospitals, (March 16, 1977) at 122, 128.
19. 29 U.S.C. §158(a)(3), 158(b)(3) (1976).
20. NLRB v. Hospital and Nursing Home Employees Union Local 113, 567 F.2d 831 (8th Cir. 1977).
21. Joiner & Morris, Management's Response to the Union Phenomenon, HOSPITAL PROGRESS 59, 60–61 (May 1978).
22. Republic Aviation Corp. v. NLRB, 324 U.S. 793 (1945).
23. St. John's Hosp. and School of Nursing, 222 NLRB 1150 (1976).
24. Beth Israel Hosp. v. NLRB, 437 U.S. 483 (1978); NLRB v. Baylor Univ. Med. Center, 439 U.S. 9 (1978); NLRB v. Baptist Hosp. 442 U.S. 773 (1979).
25. Beth Israel Hosp. v. NLRB, 437 U.S. 483, 508 (1978).
26. St. Joseph's Hosp., 225 NLRB 28 (1976).
27. 29 U.S.C. §8C.
28. Community Hosp. v. NLRB, 538 F.2d 607 (4th Cir. 1976).
29. The term "appropriate bargaining unit" derives from the language of Section 9(a) of the NLRA, which sets forth the principle of exclusive representation:

Representatives designated or selected for the purposes of collective bargaining by the majority of the employees in a unit appropriate for such purposes shall be the exclusive representatives of all the employees in such unit for the purposes of collective bargaining. . . . 29 U.S.C. §159(a) (1976).

30. 29 U.S.C. §159(b) (1976). *See generally* GORMAN, *supra* note 11, at 66–76.

31. Historically, in industries outside of health care, the NLRB has approached the question of whether a group of employees in certain job classifications constituted an appropriate unit separate from all plant workers by considering the following factors: (1) whether the proposed unit is a "distinct and homogenous group of skilled craftsmen" or a "functionally distinct department"; (2) the history of collective bargaining at the plant and whether unit fragmentation would be disruptive; (3) whether the group has established and maintained a separate identity; (4) the history of collective bargaining in the industry; (5) the extent of integration of the plant's production process and interdependence of the work done by members of the proposed group with that of other employees; (6) the qualifications of the union seeking to represent the group in question. Mallinckrodt Chem. Workers, 162 NLRB 387 (1976); GORMAN, *supra* note 11, at 84–85.

32. GORMAN, *supra* note 11, at 66–69.

33. *Id.*

34. S. Rep. No. 93–766, 93d Cong. 2d Sess. (1974) at 5, reprinted in [1974] U.S.C.C.A.N., Legislative History, at 3946.

35. *See* Pepe, *Appropriate Health Care Bargaining Units: An Unsettled Question,* 58 HOSPITAL PROGRESS 54 (1977).

36. Mercy Hosps. of Sacramento, Inc., 217 NLRB 131, 89 L.R.R.M. 1097 (1975); Barnert Mem. Hosp. Ass'n, 217 NLRB 132., 89 L.R.R.M. 1083 (1975); St. Catherine's Hosp. of Dominican Sisters of Kinosha, Wisc., 217 NLRB 133, 89 L.R.R.M. 1070 (1975); Newington Children's Hosp., 217 NLRB 134, 89 L.R.R.M. 1108 (1975); Sisters of St. Joseph of Peace, 217 NLRB 135, 89 L.R.R.M. 1082 (1975); Duke University, 217 NLRB 136, 89 L.R.R.M. 1065 (1975); Mount Airy Psychiatric Center, 217 NLRB 137, 89 L.R.R.M. 1067 (1975); Shriners Hosp.

for Crippled Children, 217 NLRB 138, 89 L.R.R.M. 1076 (1975).

37. Mount Airy Psychiatric Center, 217 NLRB 137, 89 L.R.R.M. 1067 (1975).

38. Mercy Hosps. of Sacramento, 217 NLRB 131, 89 L.R.R.M. 1097 (1975). *But see* NLRB v. St. Francis Hosp. of Lynwood, 601 F.2d 404 (9th Cir. 1979).

39. Barnert Mem. Hosp. Ass'n, 217 NLRB 132, 89 L.R.R.M. 1053 (1975); St. Catherine's Hosp. of Dominican Sisters of Kenosha, Wisc., 217 NLRB 133, 89 L.R.R.M. 1070 (1975).

40. Presbyterian Med. Center, 218 NLRB 1266 (1975).

41. 29 U.S.C. §152(3) (1976).

42. 29 U.S.C. §152(11) (1976).

43. *See* the legislative history of the Taft-Hartley Act of 1947.

44. S. Rep. No. 93–766, 2d Sess. (1974), *reprinted in* 1974 U.S.C.C.A.N.

45. Wing Mem. Hosp. Ass'n, 217 NLRB 172 (1975).

46. *Id.* at 1016. *See also* Grey Nuns, 91 L.R.R.M. 1099 (1975).

47. NLRB v. Sweetwater Hosp. Ass'n 604 F.2d 454 (6th Cir. 1978).

48. Barnert Mem. Hosp. Ass'n, 217 NLRB 132, 89 L.R.R.M. 1083 (1975).

49. Bay Med. Center v. NLRB, 588 F.2d 474 (6th Cir. 1978).

50. Barnert Mem. Hosp. Ass'n, 217 NLRB 132, 89 L.R.R.M. 1083 (1975).

51. *See, e.g.,* St. Vincent's Hosp. 223 NLRB 638, 91 L.R.R.M. 1513 (1976).

52. *But see* Jewish Hosp. of Cincinnati, 223 NLRB 91 (1976).

53. Mercy Hosps. of Sacramento, 217 NLRB 131, 89 L.R.R.M. 1082 (1975); Sisters of St. Joseph of Peace, 217 NLRB 135, 89 L.R.R.M. 1082 (1975).

54. *See* Sisters of St. Joseph of Peace, 217 NLRB 135, 89 L.R.R.M. 1082 (1975).

55. *E.g.,* William W. Backus Hosp. 220 NLRB 414, 90 L.R.R.M. 1696 (1975); Heights Hosp., 221 NLRB 563, 90 L.R.R.M. 1675 (1975).

56. Mercy Hosps. of Sacramento, 217 NLRB 765 (1975); NLRB v. Mercy Hosps., 589 F.2d (9th Cir. 1979); Mercy Hosps. of Sacramento, 244 NLRB 34 (1979).

57. 120 Cong. Rec. 6931 (1974).

58. Clinch Valley Clinic Hosp. v. NLRB, 516 F.2d 996 (4th Cir. 1975).

59. Cedars-Sinai Med. Center, 223 NLRB, 57, 91 L.R.R.M. 1398 (1976).

60. Physicians House Staff Ass'n v. Fanning, 104 L.R.R.M. 2940 (1980).

61. *House Staffs Win Legal Protection for Unionizing*, Medical World News, April 30, 1979, at 27.

62. Kansas City Gen. Hosp., 225 NLRB 14A, 93 L.R.R.M. 1362 (1976) ("Kansas City II").

63. NLRB v. Committee of Interns & Residents, 566 F.2d 810 (2d Cir. 1977), *cert. denied* 98 S. Ct. 1449 (1978).

64. House Officers Ass'n v. University of Neb. Med. Center, 255 N.W.2d 258 (Neb. 1977).

65. For example, H. Rep. No. 95–980, 95th Congress, 2d Session (Mar. 16, 1978).

66. 29 U.S.C. §152(3).

67. 15 U.S.C. §1.

68. Keating, *Health Care Labor Relations Literature*, HOSPITAL PROGRESS, July 1977, at 12.

69. Metzger, *The Long Arm of Employee Collective Activity*, TRUSTEE, May 1978, at 48.

70. Fottler, *The Union Impact on Hospital Wages*, 30 INDUSTRY & LAB. REL. REV. 342, 354 (1977).

71. Bentivegna, *Labor Relations: Union Activity Increases among Professionals*, HOSPITAL, Apr. 1, 1979, at 131.

72. Frenzen, *Survey Updates Unionization Activities*, HOSPITAL, Aug. 1, 1978, at 93, 104.

73. 42 U.S.C. §2000(e) *et seq.* (1976).

74. 29 U.S.C. §621 *et seq.* (1976).

75. 29 U.S.C. §793–93 (1976).

76. 29 U.S.C. §201 *et seq.* (1976).

77. 29 U.S.C. §206(d) (1976).

78. Usery v. Allegheny County Inst. Dist., 544 F.2d (3d Cir. 1976).

79. National League of Cities v. Usery, 426 U.S. 833 (1976).

80. *Compare* Brennan v. South Davis Community Hosp., 538 F.2d 859 (10th Cir. 1976) *with* Brennan v. Inglewood, Inc., 412 F. Supp. 362 (D. Miss. 1975). *See also* Eakin v. Ascension Parish Police Jury, 294 So.2d 527 (La. 1974).

81. Brennan v. South Davis Community Hosp., 538 F.2d 859 (10th Cir. 1976).

82. 29 U.S.C. §651–78.
83. 29 C.F.R. §197s.4(b)(1), (4).
84. Hospital Occupational Health Services Study: I: Environmental Health and Safety Control HEW Publication No. (NIOSH) 75–101 (1974).

Appendix A

A Model Patients'
Bill of Rights

Patients have rights, too. Their rights, like those of providers, are articulated in legislation, regulation, case law, and hospital policies. The following bill of rights was developed for and published in *The Rights of Hospital Patients* (New York: Avon, 1975). In it, the term "legal right" is used to refer to a right well recognized by statutory or case law; the term "right" refers to one that would probably be recognized by a court if the proper case was brought to enforce it; and the phrase "we recognize the right" is a statement of what we believe "ought to be."

Once these rights are articulated and recognized, some enforcement mechanism is required. We suggest the employment of a "patients' rights advocate" whose sole job is to aid patients in the enforcement of their rights.

The model bill is set out as it would apply to a patient in chronological order of the patient's relationship with a hospital: sections 1–4 for a person not hospitalized but a potential patient; 5 for emergency admission; 6–15 for in-patients; 16–22 for discharge and after; and 23 relates to all of the 22 preceding rights.

A MODEL PATIENTS' BILL OF RIGHTS

Preamble: As you enter this health care facility, it is our duty to remind you that your health care is a cooperative effort between you as a patient and the doctors and hospital staff. During your stay a patients' rights advocate will be available to you. The duty of the advocate is to assist you in all the decisions you must make and in all situations in which your health and welfare are at stake. The advocate's first responsibility is to help you understand the role of all who will be working with you, and to help you understand what your rights as a patient are. Your advocate can be reached at any time of the day by dialing _____. The following is a list of your rights as a patient. Your advocate's duty is to see to it that you are afforded these rights. You should call your advocate whenever you have any questions or concerns about any of these rights.

1. The patient has a legal right to informed participation in all decisions involving his/her health care program.
2. We recognize the right of all potential patients to know what research and experimental protocols are being used in our facility and what alternatives are available in the community.
3. The patient has a legal right to privacy regarding the source of payment for treatment and care. This right includes access to the highest degree of care without regard to the source of payment for that treatment and care.
4. We recognize the right of a potential patient to complete and accurate information concerning medical care and procedures.
5. The patient has a legal right to prompt attention, especially in an emergency situation.
6. The patient has a legal right to a clear, concise explanation in layperson's terms of all proposed procedures, including the possibilities of any risk of mortality or serious side effects, problems related to recuperation, and probability of success,

and will not be subjected to any procedure without his/her voluntary, competent and understanding consent. The specifics of such consent shall be set out in a written consent form, signed by the patient.

7. The patient has a legal right to a clear, complete, and accurate evaluation of his/her condition and prognosis without treatment before being asked to consent to any test or procedure.

8. We recognize the right of the patient to know the identity and professional status of all those providing service. All personnel have been instructed to introduce themselves, state their status, and explain their role in the health care of the patient. Part of this right is the right of the patient to know the identity of the physician responsible for his/her care.

9. We recognize the right of any patient who does not speak English to have access to an interpreter.

10. The patient has a right to all the information contained in his/her medical record while in the health care facility, and to examine the record on request.

11. We recognize the right of a patient to discuss his/her condition with a consultant specialist, at the patient's request and expense.

12. The patient has a legal right not to have any test or procedure, designed for educational purposes rather than his/her direct personal benefit, performed on him/her.

13. The patient has a legal right to refuse any particular drug, test, procedure, or treatment.

14. The patient has a legal right to privacy of both person and information with respect to: the hospital staff, other doctors, residents, interns and medical students, researchers, nurses, other hospital personnel, and other patients.

15. We recognize the patient's right of access to people outside the health care facility by means of visitors and the telephone. Parents may stay with their children and relatives with terminally ill patients 24 hours a day.

16. The patient has a legal right to leave the health care facility regardless of his/her physical condition or financial status, although the patient may be requested to sign a release stating that he/she is leaving against the medical judgment of his/her doctor or the hospital.

17. The patient has a right not to be transferred to another facility unless he/she has received a complete explanation of the desirability and need for the transfer, the other facility has accepted the patient for transfer, and the patient has agreed to transfer. If the patient does not agree to transfer, the patient has the right to a consultant's opinion on the desirability of transfer.

18. A patient has a right to be notified of his/her impending discharge at least one day before it is accomplished, to insist on a consultation by an expert on the desirability of discharge, and to have a person of the patient's choice notified in advance.

19. The patient has a right, regardless of the source of payment, to examine and receive an itemized and detailed explanation of the total bill for services rendered in the facility.

20. The patient has a right to competent counseling from the hospital staff to help in obtaining financial assistance from public or private sources to meet the expense of services received in the institution.

21. The patient has a right to timely prior notice of the termination of his/her eligibility for reimbursement by any third-party payor for the expense of hospital care.

22. At the termination of his/her stay at the health care facility we recognize the right of a patient to a complete copy of the information contained in his/her medical record.

23. We recognize the right of all patients to have 24-hour-a-day access to a patient's rights advocate who may act on behalf of the patient to assert or protect the rights set out in this document.

Appendix B

How to Use the Law Library

The purpose of this appendix is not to teach you how to use the law library to perform legal research (something very few lawyers know how to do efficiently), but to give you enough information so that you can locate legal materials when necessary. To locate most references cited in this book you will have to use a law library. The first rule of research in any unfamiliar library, of course, is to ask the reference librarian for assistance.

All law schools have substantial libraries, as do many local bar associations. To obtain admission to the law library of your local law school, you may need special permission from the school or the assistance of a law student. Once inside, you will discover the principal problem with writing about "the law" in the United States: each of the fifty states has its own court system and legislature and, therefore, each has its own set of statutes and case reporters. Superimposed on this structure is a system of federal district courts and federal appeals courts. Over them all is the U.S. Supreme Court. In addition, there are not only the statutes of the United States (which are in a set of books called *U.S. Code Annotated,* abbreviated U.S.C. in footnotes), but also the regulations adopted under federal statutes by the executive branch of government such as the FDA, HHS (formerly HEW), and the Department

363

of Agriculture (set forth in another set of books called the *Code of Federal Regulations* (C.F.R.).

The legal literature you are most likely to be interested in locating is *statutes, court decisions* (case law), *regulations, legal periodicals,* and *legal encyclopedias.* Each of these will be discussed briefly.

STATUTES

Statutes are arranged by state, each having its own set of books (usually 50-100 volumes). These statutes are usually arranged by subject matter, and each provision of the statute has a number. If you know the number, the task of locating the statute is not difficult. If you do not, look up the subject matter in the index to the set. Note that since new statutes are passed each year, these volumes have "pocket parts" at the back in which current material is kept.

COURT DECISIONS

If you are looking for a particular case, you probably have the case name and citation. For example, the famous *Darling* case is properly cited as

Darling v. Charleston Community Memorial Hospital, 33 Ill. 2d 326, 211 N.E.2d 253 (1965), *cert. denied,* 383 U.S. 946 (1966).

To locate this case in the library, either find the set of books for the state of Illinois or the set labeled *Northeastern Reporters* (abbreviated N.E.). In the Illinois (Ill.) set, locate the second series (2d.) (Most states begin renumbering their reports after volume 200 or 300, but some do not.) Within that set, find volume 33. The *Darling* case begins in volume 33 at page 326 (or in the N.E. 2d series in volume 211 at page 253). The final part of the citation refers to the fact that the U.S. Supreme Court refused to hear an appeal. This refusal can be found in the *United States Supreme Court Reports* (U.S.) volume 383, at page

946. The year in parenthesis following the case is the year it was decided.

REGULATIONS

Regulations are promulgated under statutory authority. Federal regulations are collected in the Code of Federal Regulations, parts of which are changed almost daily. These changes are reported in the *Federal Register* (Fed. Reg.). State regulations are found in various, nonuniform state publications. In most states, locating regulations will be very difficult.

LEGAL ENCYCLOPEDIAS

Corpus Juris Secundum (C.G.S., the one Perry Mason used) and *American Jurisprudence* (AM. JUR.) are usually located side by side in a conspicuous part of the library. They are legal encyclopedias, general works on various aspects of the law, arranged alphabetically by subject matter.

LEGAL PERIODICALS

The other type of legal material cited in many of the footnotes in this book is legal periodicals. These are usually published at individual law schools and are named after these law schools. For example, 54 B.U.L. REV. is the fifty-fourth volume of the set of *Boston University's Law Reviews*. As with case citations, the volume number appears *before* the name of the journal, the page number immediately after the journal's name. There is a rather unsophisticated and spotty index to these periodicals called the *Guide to Legal Periodicals* that is arranged by subject matter and author's last name.

Anyone desiring detailed information on legal research should refer to one or both of the following excellent volumes: M. Price & H. Bitner, *Effective Legal Research* (4th ed.) (Boston: Little, Brown, 1979); J. Jacobstein & R. Mersky, *Pollock's Fundamentals of Legal Research* (4th ed.) (Brooklyn, N.Y.: Foundation Press, 1973). Those interested in a more detailed treatment of the various aspects of law-making should see R. Covington *et al., Cases and Materials for a Course on Legal Methods* (Mineola, N.Y.: Foundation Press, 1969).

Appendix C

Glossary of Common
Legal Terms

action—The formal legal demand of one's rights from another person brought in court; a lawsuit.

acquittal—The verdict in a criminal trial in which the defendant is found not guilty.

adhesion contract—A contract so heavily restrictive of one party, while so nonrestrictive of another, that doubts arise as to its being a voluntary and uncoerced agreement; implies a grave inequality of bargaining power—e.g., standard-form printed contract prepared by one party and submitted to the other on a "take-it-or-leave-it" basis.

affidavit—A written statement of facts sworn to by the maker and taken before a person officially permitted by law to administer oaths.

agency—A legal relationship in which one person's actions are also considered the actions of another person.

answer—The pleading filed by the defendant in response to plaintiff's complaint.

appeal—The process by which a decision of lower court is brought for review before a court of higher jurisdiction. The party bringing the appeal is the appellant. The party against which the appeal is taken is the appellee.

assault—An unlawful, intentional act done to a person which produces reasonable apprehension of harm.

367

attachment—A proceeding in a law by which one's property is seized; a proceeding to take a defendant's property into legal custody to satisfy plaintiff's demand.

battery—An offensive, intentional, unconsented-to touching of a person.

borrowed-servant rule—A doctrine through which the negligent behavior of one person, who is the servant of another, is imputed to a person who controlled the negligent actor's behavior for a period of time—e.g., a physician in the operating room may be held liable for the negligence of a circulating nurse, even though the nurse is employed by the hospital.

captain-of-the-ship doctrine—A rule that imputes the negligence of one person who was "in charge" generally. Most often applied in the operating room, this doctrine is slowly disappearing from U.S. jurisprudence.

case law—See "common law."

circumstantial evidence—Indirect evidence; secondary facts by which a principal fact may be rationally inferred.

claim—The assertion of a right, as to money or property; the accumulation of facts that give rise to right enforceable in court.

class action—A lawsuit brought by a representative party on behalf of a group, all of whose members have the same or a similar grievance against the defendant.

common law—The part of Anglo-American law that is derived from court decisions (rather than from a statutes and regulations). Also called "case law."

complaint—The plaintiff's initial pleading containing a short and plain statement of the claim upon which relief is sought, an indication of the type of relief requested, and an indication that the court has jurisdiction to hear the case.

consideration—Something to be done or abstained from, by one party to a contract in order to induce another party to enter into a contract.

contract—A legally enforceable agreement between two parties in which each agrees to do something.

corporate negligence—A legal theory which imposes a direct responsibility upon a hospital to take certain actions to safeguard patients and provide quality care.

crime—An act forbidden by statute and punishable by a fine or imprisonment.

damages—Monetary compensation awarded by a court for an injury caused by the act of another. Damages may be actual or compensatory (equal to the amount of loss shown), exemplary or punitive (in excess of the actual loss, and assessed to punish the person for the malicious conduct which caused the injury), or nominal (less than the actual loss—often a trivial amount, which is given because the injury is slight or because the exact amount of injury has not been determined satisfactorily).

defendant—The person against whom a civil or criminal action is brought.

deposition—Pretrial statement of a witness under oath, taken in question-and-answer form as it would be in court, with opportunity given to the adversary to be present and cross-examine.

directed verdict—A verdict returned by the jury at the direction of the trial judge, by whose instruction the jury is bound. In civil proceedings either party may receive a directed verdict in its favor if the opposing party fails to present a *prima facie* case, or fails to present a necessary defense.

due care—The legal duty one owes to another according to the circumstances of a particular case. It is that care which an ordinarily prudent person would have exercised in the given situation; the absence of negligence.

ethics—A system of moral principles; rules of conduct.

evidence—All the means by which any alleged matter of fact, the truth of which is submitted to investigation at trial, is established or disproved. Evidence includes the testimony of witnesses, introduction of records, documents, exhibits, objects or any other probative matter offered for the purpose of inducing belief in the party's contention by the judge or jury.

ex parte—(Latin) In behalf of, on the application of, one party; by or for one party. An *ex parte* judicial proceeding is one brought for the benefit of one party only without notice to or challenge by an adverse party.

expert witness—A witness having special knowledge of the subject about which he is to testify. The knowledge must generally be such as is not normally possessed by the average person.

fiduciary relationship—A relationship of trust and confidence requiring the exercise of fairness and good faith.

fraud—Intentional deception resulting in injury to another. Elements of fraud are: a false and material misrepresentation made by one who either knows its falsity or is ignorant of its truth; the maker's intent that the representation be relied on by the person and in a manner reasonably contemplated; the person's ignorance of the falsity of the representation; the person's rightful or justified reliance; and proximate injury to the person.

good faith—A total absence of any intention to seek an unfair advantage or to defraud another party; an honest and sincere intention to fulfill one's obligations.

guardian ad litem—(Latin) A guardian appointed for the purposes of representing a person believed to be legally incompetent by virtue of age or mental status, in one particular case only. For example, a guardian ad litem might be appointed to represent a child who is proposed as a kidney or bone marrow donor.

hearsay—Evidence which does not proceed from the personal knowledge of the witness, but is a repetition of an out-of-court statement and is offered to prove the truth of the matter asserted. The general rule, subject to various exceptions, is that such statements are inadmissible because they rely on the truth and veracity of outside persons not present for cross-examination.

in loco parentis—(Latin) Doctrine which permits a court to appoint a person to stand in the place of parents and assume all of their legal rights, duties, and obligations with respect to a child.

incompetent—A legal determination, which may only be made through a judicial proceeding, that a person is incapable of managing his own affairs, or making specific types of decisions. Different standards may be applied depending upon the issue involved, i.e., competency to make a will, or competency to consent to or refuse treatment.

indemnity—A contractual arrangement whereby one party agrees to reimburse another for losses of a particular type.

independent contractor—A person who, in the course of his work, is independent of his employer, and whose negligence cannot therefore be imputed to the employer.

informed consent—A doctrine that states that before a patient is asked to consent to a risky or invasive diagnostic or treatment procedure he is entitled to receive certain *information*: (a) a description of the procedure; (b) any alternatives to it and their risks; (c) the risks of death or serious bodily disability from the procedure; (d) the probable results of the procedure, including any problems of recuperation and time of recuperation anticipated; and (e) anything else that is generally disclosed to patients asked to consent to the procedure. It should be noted that the requirement is a *disclosure* one only—similar to a bank disclosure or a *Miranda* warning—and in the therapeutic setting at least, most courts do not require a showing that the patient actually understood the disclosures, only that they were made at a time and in a manner in which he could have understood them, e.g., he was not under the influence of drugs and the disclosures were in lay terms.

informed consent form—Used by health care providers to provide documentary evidence that informed consent was actually obtained from the patient. The form is *evidence* that consent was obtained, and should not be confused with the *process* of actually obtaining it.

jurisdiction—The power given to a court by a constitution or a legislative body to make legally binding decisions over certain persons or property.

liability—The condition of being responsible either for damages resulting from an injurious act or for discharging an obligation or debt.

malpractice—Professional negligence; failure to meet a professional standard of care resulting in harm to another, e.g., failure to provide "good and accepted medical care."

minor—A person under the age of legal competence. In virtually all states a person becomes an adult on his eighteenth birthday.

motion—A formal request made to a judge pertaining to any issue arising during the pendency of a lawsuit.

negligence—Failure to act as an ordinary reasonable person would act under the same circumstances. To prove a *negligence case* the plaintiff must demonstrate: duty, breach of duty, damages, and causation—i.e., the defendant owed him a duty, did not fulfill it, and this "breach of duty" caused the plaintiff "damages" (such as physical injury).

plaintiff—The person who brings a lawsuit against another.

pleadings—The technical means by which parties to a dispute frame the issue for the court. The plaintiff's complaint or declaration is followed by the defendant's answer; subsequent papers are filed as needed.

police power—The constitutional power of the state to protect the health, safety, morals, and general welfare of the public. This power resides in the individual states.

precedent—Term used to describe the situation where a previous case having the same or similar facts as a case presently being decided, has been decided in a particular jurisdiction. The previous case should act as a guide in deciding the present one.

regulations—Rules promulgated by an administrative agency, following specified procedures (e.g., public notice and public hearings), under the authority of a statute. For example, rules governing the practice of medicine promulgated by a Board of Registration of Medicine.

remand—To send back for further proceedings, as when a higher court sends a case back to a lower court.

res ipsa loquitur—(Latin) "The thing speaks for itself." A rebuttable presumption that the defendant was negligent, which arises upon proof that the instrumentality causing the injury was in the defendant's exclusive control, and that the accident was one which ordinarily does not happen in the absence of negligence.

respondeat superior—(Latin) "Let the master answer." Legal doctrine that imposes liability upon the employer for the results of negligent acts of employees acting within the scope of their employment. *Note:* The employee is also liable for his own actions.

sources of law—The law can generally be divided by sources, which indicate both the jurisdiction of the law and how it can be challenged or changed: constitutional, statutory, regulations, case law (or common law), and "private" law.

statute of limitations—The period of time beyond which a plaintiff may not bring a civil suit; the limit varies depending upon the type of suit, and is set by the various state legislatures. For medical malpractice it is generally two to three years, for contracts, six to eight.

statute—A law passed by the legislature and signed by the

governor at the state level and president at the federal level.

subpoena—A court order compelling a witness to appear and testify in a certain proceeding.

summary judgment—Preverdict judgment rendered by the court in response to a motion by a plaintiff or defendant, who claims that the absence of factual dispute on one or more issues eliminates the need to send those issues to the jury.

summons—A notice delivered by a sheriff or other authorized person informing a person that he is the defendant in a civil action and telling him when and where to appear in court to present his side.

tort—A wrong against another person or his property, which is not a crime, and for which the law provides a remedy.

wrongful death—A type of lawsuit brought on behalf of a deceased person's beneficiaries that alleges that death was attributable to the willful or negligent act of another.

Appendix D

Major Health Law Periodicals

1. Published by the
   American Society of Law & Medicine, Inc.
   520 Commonwealth Avenue
   Boston, Mass. 02215
   (a) *Medicolegal News,* a 36-page bimonthly publication with short articles, updates on legal literature, case summaries, and book reviews.
   (b) *The American Journal of Law & Medicine,* a quarterly law review put out in cooperation with Boston University School of Law.
   (c) *Nursing Law & Ethics,* an 8-page monthly newsletter for nurses covering legal and ethical practice issues, published with
   Law–Medicine, Inc.
   14 Beacon St.
   Boston, Mass. 02108
2. Published by the Hastings Center
   360 Broadway
   Hastings-on-Hudson, N.Y. 10706
   (a) *The Hastings Center Report,* a bimonthly collection of articles on the ethical aspects of health care.
   (b) *IRB,* a monthly newsletter designed for members of Institutional Review Boards.

3. Published by the American Medical Association
535 N. Dearborn Street
Chicago, Ill. 60610

The Citation, a biweekly digest of judicial opinions involving medical practice.

4. Published by the National Health Lawyers Association
Suite 708
522 21st Street, N.W.
Washington, D.C. 20006

Health Law Digest, a monthly summary of current court decisions in health law for members.

5. Published by the
American Society of Hospital Attorneys
American Hospital Association
840 N. Lake Shore Drive
Chicago, Ill. 60611

Hospital Law, a monthly summary of legal developments for members of the American Society of Hospital Attorneys.

6. Published by the Bureau of National Affairs, Inc.
1231 25th Street, N.W.
Washington, D.C. 20037

Specialty Law Digest: Health Care, a monthly publication with articles, case summaries, and legislative updates.

7. Published by the American College of Legal Medicine
Suite 1201
1320 N. Astor Street
Chicago, Ill. 60610

American College of Legal Medicine Newsletter, a monthly newsletter for members.

8. Published by GMT Medical Information Systems, Inc.
777 Third Avenue
New York, N.Y. 10017

Legal Aspects of Medical Practice, a monthly periodical including newsbriefs, reviews, and short articles.

Index

376